DUELING ISMS
Soviet and Regional Identity in Central Asia

DUELING ISMS

Soviet and Regional Identity in Central Asia

Nandini Bhattacharya

SHIPRA

The publication of the book is financially supported by ICSSR and the responsibility for the facts stated, opinions expressed or conclusion reached, is entirely that of that author and the ICSSR accepts no responsibility for them

ICSSR Consultant
Prof. Zafar Imam

ISBN: 978-81-7541-370-2

First Published in India in 2008

Dueling Isms: Soviet and Regional Identity in Central Asia

Published by :
SHIPRA PUBLICATIONS
115-A, Vikas Marg, Shakarpur, Delhi-110092 (India)
Tel. : 91-11-65277210, 22500954, Fax : 91-11-22458662
Email : info@shiprapublications.com
www.shiprapublications.com

Foreword

Soviet Union provides an interesting case study of co-existence of nations in a multi-ethnic state. It was a unique experiment in transcending national identity not in the model of "melting pot" variant (a *la* US model), but by fusing the two processes of strengthening national identity structurally and simultaneous strengthening of a supra-national identity — the Soviet identity. The convergence of ethno-national group boundary with the republican boundary and its socio-economic structures shaped social values. Though existing boundaries were regarded by the Soviet leadership as transitory and it was presumed that modernisation — increasing industrialisation, urbanisation, personal mobility, mass communication and socialisation of the population in communist values etc. — would make national identity irrelevant, various nationalities, including those in Central Asia, experienced greater consolidation of their identities.

Soviet modernisation involved both the creation of group (national) boundaries and extensive population mobility that threatened to break down those boundaries. The consolidation of ethno-national identity and the territory that the Soviets assigned to the members of each nationality created strong propensity towards the formation of nation-states in the post-Soviet period, whereas during the years under Soviet rule the republics had become multi-national. Central Asian societies are characterised by diversity and heterogeneity. Accordingly, the independent states need to be multi-ethnic and inclusive.

The states in Central Asia have been caught in a dilemma as to how to carry the process of national consolidation forward that is essential to overcome internal divisions, while creating an inclusive state that has equal space for the ethnic minorities. Within each nationality, there are strong internal differences — clan, tribal and regional — that are on occasions could take very divisive forms. Such a fault-line pushed Tajikistan nearly on the verge of disintegration when a five-year long Civil War (1992-97) pitted Tajiks against Tajiks.

Tajikistan is one of the few states in CIS where the Russian language and culture enjoyed a much higher status. It has very close external ties with the Russian Federation and strongly favours CIS integration. Yet, paradoxically, the republic has witnessed most of its ethnic Russian population migrate out of the republic.

Dr. Nandini Bhattachary has attempted to deal with these issues in her book *Dueling Isms: Soviet and Regional Identity in Central Asia.* She focuses on issues of identity in its various manifestations and Soviet policies towards nationalities in general and Central Asian in particular. Considering many of the stereotypes that exist with regard to Soviet experiment in Central Asia, the author's attempt to revisit those from a non-Western perspective is commendable. These stereotypes include, Russification, colonization, cultural assimilation and so on.

The book begins with a theoretical account of Soviet nationalities policy under the influence of Marxism-Leninism, as well as its articulation in different phases under different leadership. Through a comprehensive account of evolution of Soviet nationalities policy, the author concludes that the policy moved from "Right to national self-determination" of Lenin's times to integration under the "Soviet identity" in the Stalin period and later. The post-Lenin period had witnessed both coercive and non-coercive methods being employed to achieve integration.

Nevertheless, Bhattacharya concludes, "throughout the Soviet history, Central Asian popular attitude showed a sincere attempt to maintain their indigenous identities, which always did not go in tune with the prescribed Soviet model. But at the same time, the Soviet system along with an imposed identity brought a number of material changes, which a substantial number of Central Asians did internalise. Therefore, the general attitude towards the Soviet rule was not one of outright rejection".

I have argued elsewhere that throughout the Soviet period, the Central Asians maintained their local identities in terms of indigenous culture, tradition, language and religion. The attempt to create a supra-national Soviet identity did not negate the different national identities. On the contrary, the idea was to base the Soviet identity on the edifice of equal and flourishing identities of different nationalities living in the Soviet Union. This is the reason why in many non-Russian regions there was a positive attitude to Soviet nationality and regional policy, especially since the 1960s.

Bhattacharya's book brings out this point clearly by stating, "Yet, at the same time, the attitude of these people towards 'Soviet' identity was not one of complete rejection. At least, in the later part of the Soviet rule, a kind of understanding developed where mostly the moderately educated citizens of the republics accepted the practical necessities of the Soviet attachments, the need of bilingualism etc. Thus, though imposed from above, the 'Soviet' identity did percolate down to the popular mind with the passage of time and when it was once again withdrawn from above, republics had a mixed reaction. They could not rejoice in their unexpected independence."

It has been pointed out by many, including myself, that since the 1970s political-administrative cadre were mostly from indigenous nationalities and Russians were dominant mostly in economic-managerial and technocratic positions. There was a lot of space for the regional leadership leading to what the Bhattacharya describes as "a kind of partnership between the local power base and central authority in Moscow". But more than elite cooperation, local culture, language and identity had a larger space during this period. The author has also highlighted various debates regarding economic development in Central Asia as well as regional dimensions of urbanisation and industrialization in Tajikistan, which had a bearing on antagonistic regional identities and alliances in the republic.

Different Central Asian republics embraced Islam at different periods of time and the influence of orthodox Islam was more pronounced in settled Ferghana valley region. The nomadic peoples continued with their pre-Islamic practices even after becoming Muslims. The formation of national republics and development of national identities came in the way of growth of Pan-Islamic identity. Islam survived in a variety of ways – as part of tradition, as underground Sufi sects etc. However, it has not been in all cases the determinant element of identity. Then of course, there was secular education, creation of a Russified indigenous elite and presence of non-Central Asian minorities, which dented the religious dimension of identity of Central Asians. The determining role of religion in Central Asian identity has been taken up very skilfully by the author. Many interesting observations have been made regarding Soviet state's attitude towards Islam in various periods, the revival of religion due to internal and external reasons and so on. The sources cited are also extensive.

So far as Tajikistan is concerned, the role of national as well as sub-regional identities has proved to be quite strong. Subsequent experience after Soviet disintegration also proves this point. For example, during the Tajik civil war (1992-97), entire regions of the country were siding with either the Communist forces or with the Islamic opposition, because of regional loyalties. At the same time, after the victory of the Taliban in Afghanistan in 1996, the Afghan-Tajiks under pressure from Pushtun-led Taliban sought support from their co-ethnics in Tajikistan and the former foes of the civil war come together to form the Northern Alliance, supported by the Tajik government.

Thus, one could see from the whole experience of the Tajik and the Afghan civil wars that ethno-national aspect of the identity remains stronger and religion failed to cement differences and antagonisms based on ethnic identity. This was also evident from the violent incidents that rocked Central Asia in the last years of the Soviet Union. Bhattacharya draws attention to the inter-ethnic riots in the late 1980s and early 1990s in Central Asia, which involved the Muslim nationalities of the USSR – Uzbeks & Meskhetian Turks, Uzbeks & Tajiks, Uzbeks & Kyrgyz, Turkmen & Caucasians etc. The book also brings out very clearly the failure of political Islam to occupy centre stage in Central Asia, particularly Tajikistan, though some eminent experts talked of such possibilities.

The chapter on language and identity is another well-researched one. Bhattacharya does well to highlight the language policy of the Soviet State that strived simultaneously to promote local language and Russian language, as a result of which bilingualism in Central Asia expanded. The chapter also highlights the difference between Central Asia and many other regions of the former Soviet Union. In Central Asia, use of titular language as mother tongue was strongly retained – more so in case of rural population and women. In case of Tajikistan, especially, Soviet experience succeeded in preventing Turkicization of this Persian-speaking group. Enough data has been used to augment the arguments.

The chapter on "Role of Ethnic Factors in the Development of Multilayer Identities in Central Asia" has covered a whole range of issues like Soviet policy, demography, family, marriage, regional identity etc. It discuses various scholarly opinions on these issues and analyses well the materials available on these themes. While nationality relations in Central Asia have been well documented, some space has also been devoted to regional identity in Tajikistan.

The impact of perestroika has been discussed in the chapter, "Perestroika, Glasnost and the Change in Central Asia". Bhattacharya has done a very good analysis of the impact of Gorbachev's reforms in Central Asia. She rightly concludes, "… regional discrimination became even more glaring with the perestroika reforms and this economic discrimination along with the retrenchment of officers on the charge of corruption affected the popular nationalist sentiments bitterly, and the Central Asian response began to surface in a hostile manner".

With all its anti-corruption drives and freedom of expression of opinion, Central Asia did not witness the scale of popular national mobilization like that witnessed in the Baltic republics. Central Asian republics voted overwhelmingly in favour of retaining the USSR in the March 1991 referendum. Though the Central Asian republics had every reason for discontent and resentment toward the Soviet system, and though with glasnost much of their bitterness had began to surface, probably these republics were the most unprepared ones in the USSR to accept such an abrupt demise of the Soviet state, the author points out. Probably the strongest manifestation of assertion of national identity was the adoption of new language laws that elevated the status to that of state language. Another important conclusion is, "Being freed from the Soviet yoke, indigenous self–seeking movements began to develop towards national consciousness. In this process Islam played a major role". However, the author underlines that revival of Islam should not be equated with radical or political Islam.

On the whole, Nandini Bhattacharya should be complemented for the quality of her research on the theme and the region. Some of her conclusions have bearing on the events of post-Soviet Central Asia and on the inter-ethnic relations in the Eurasian region, where initially after the Soviet disintegration there was a nationalising impulse that threatened the internal harmony of the multi-ethnic societies. She rightly observes that the presence of several parallel identities is common to any given human community and Central Asia was no exception in Soviet times. Thus, 'Soviet' identity also accommodated different communities under its "common umbrella without displacing the rest". Soviet system tried to accommodate national, ethnic, linguistic and regional identities as long as they did not clash with Soviet identity. The Soviet system even encouraged some of these identities such as the linguistic identity of the Tajiks", though she underlines that these identities had their relative spheres of influences and were subservient to the larger Soviet identity.

Having gone through the manuscript, it is reasonable to assume that post-Soviet states would do well to draw upon the Soviet legacy and allow minority cultures to flourish while the nation-building efforts are based on the identity and culture of the core titular nation. The author draws attention to the difficulties involved in consolidating national identities in the post-Soviet period. If it was thought that the Soviets were an obstacle to that process and once the Soviet Union goes the process would be smooth, Nandini Bhattacharya's conclusions are otherwise. "The extent of each and every identity ought to be carefully measured before blending them to compose a 'national' identity. At a time of excitement and chaos in Central Asia, an overdose of each element created imbalance in the composition of national identities. But, very interestingly, the revival of national identities did not imply any outright rejection of the Soviet identity. Rather, the mixed experience of the last seventy years under the Soviet rule was accepted as a fait accompli".

This book is an important addition to scholarly writings in India on Central Asia. The quality of research and the lucidity of narration make it an interesting reading. For researchers working on Central Asia, this is an essential book for understanding in a historical perspective the developments in Central Asia in general and Tajikistan in particular.

Dr. Ajay Patnaik
Professor,
Centre for Russian and Central Asian Studies,
School of International Studies,
JNU

Preface

Writing a book on Central Asia in Calcutta, based on an adaptation of my doctoral thesis, is unusual to say the least. I could still take up the challenge primarily due to three related reasons. First, being a student of Russian history, the amazing contrast in virtually every dimension of life between the Tsarist and the Soviet period had always intrigued me. My vexation was further reinforced by the antipodal positions held by experts and commentators of the subject, who either dismissed the Soviet experience as totalitarian or celebrated it as the highest embodiment of human civilisation. Secondly, the end of the Cold War and the most unexpected disintegration of Soviet Union in the wake of Gorbachev's glasnost and perestroika experiments, paved the way for a much needed opening up of a large number of themes hitherto dexterously concealed under the polemical debris of the bipolar confrontation. The Central Asian theatre seemed such an exciting laboratory for new research that its lure was too much to be avoided. Finally, my own interest in the phenomena of nationalism, ethnicity and religion in an unparalleled dialectical relationship with Soviet Marxism, could hardly have found a more appropriate theatre. Little did I know then of the practical difficulties of undertaking research on a subject like this. And yet, after years of grim battle on several fronts, my own experience has been most rewarding and satisfactory for the sheer magnitude of challenge involved in the project more than anything else.

In the course of my work, lack of uniformity in spellings of various Russian and English terms have posed a real problem. In order to avoid confusion, I have standardised spellings and the use of upper and lower cases for formal nouns to the best of my ability. I have used the upper case for Soviet throughout all the Chapters, and lower case for perestroika and glasnost, unless upper case has been used within quotation marks. I have also used new spellings of the names of the Central Asian republics unless otherwise required.

The book owes innumerable debts to several individuals and

institutions. First and foremost, my sincere gratitude and thanks go to my esteemed supervisor, Professor Kunal Chattopadhyay of the Department of History of Jadavpur University, for not only carefully and patiently guiding me over these years, but even more for understanding and sharing my predicaments and allowing me to sustain my own thoughts. Without Professor Chattopadhyay's immense contribution this work would never have seen the light of the day.

Several institutions have extended great support towards the completion of my work. Of these, the National Library, Calcutta, the Central Library of Jawaharlal Nehru University (JNU), New Delhi, the Library of the Institute for Defence Studies and Analysis (IDSA), New Delhi, the Library of Maulana Abul Kalam Azad Institute for Asian Studies, Calcutta, and the Library of the Centre for Studies in Social Sciences, Calcutta, deserve very special mention. Without the untiring contribution of their staff, it would have been impossible to complete the necessary research work for the thesis. I am also grateful to the members of staff of the Central Library, Jadavpur University, the Departmental Library of International Relations, Jadavpur University, the United States Information Centre Library, Calcutta, and the Gorky Sadan Library, Calcutta for their excellent support.

During the years that the book has been in gestation, I have had the good fortune of discussing many of its ideas with several outstanding scholars and experts of Central Asia (and Russia) from India and abroad and benefiting enormously from their esteemed suggestions, comments and healthy criticisms. Of them I am particularly grateful to Professor Ajay Patnaik who not ony assessed the work first hand but was aso extremely generous with his comments and suggestions that immensely improved the quality of the work. I am aso extremely grateful to Professor Purabi Ray, Department of International Relations, Jadavpur University, Professor Hari Vasudevan, Department of History, Calcutta University, Professor Muriel Atkin of George Washington University, USA, Professor Said Amir Arjomand of the State University of New York, USA, Professor Azad N. Shamotav, Head of South Asian Language Department, Tashkent State Institute of Oriental Studies, and Professor Goga Abzakovich Khidayatov of Tashkent for their manifold contributions which are simply too numerous to specify.

I must record my highest appreciation for the care and support of my friend Dr. Sipra Mukherjee, Reader in English, Bhairab Ganguly College, who took the enormous trouble of editing and proof-reading of the entire manuscript.

My sincere thanks and gratitude also extend to Ms. Susmita Bhattacharya, Research Fellow, Maulana Abul Kalam Azad Institute for Asian Studies, Calcutta, for her contribution in helping to translate several Russian primary documents and texts. Dr. Tridib Chakraborti, Faculty with the Department of International Relations, also helped me with research materials and has been a good source of encouragement. Professor Anuradha Chanda of the Department of History of Jadavpur University, has been a constant source of inspiration during these difficult and busy days of research. I must also express my deepest appreciation for the assistance provided by Mr. Mehmudul Hassan, Assistant Librarian, National Library, Calcutta, for his assistance. My sincerest thanks also go to my uncle Professor R.N. Bhattacharya, Professor of Mathematics, Indiana State University, USA, who took the unenviable trouble of collecting primary material on an alien subject and sending them to me. Without these documents, the book would not have been completed. My sincere thanks also extend to Dr. Indivar Kamtekar, Associate Professor of History, JNU, for his excellent gesture in sending several important photocopies at my request.

I am also grateful to the authorities of the Calcutta Girls' College, Calcutta, for granting a very crucial two months leave without which it would have been difficult to complete the work. I am most grateful towards all my colleagues at Calcutta Girls' College for their continuous and unbelievable support during these years. Very special thanks must go to Mr. Ranjan Roy and Mr. Sudhanya Banerjee who took the enormous trouble of typing the manuscript.

Finally, a work that was stretched for nearly seven years, has claimed at least something from all members of my family. Without their support, tolerance, cooperation and affection, I would have perhaps given up the job by now. Although a formal appreciation of their total commitment towards this work is hardly warranted, I recognise the academic suggestions and assistance provided by my father, Mr. Kiran Sankar Bhattacharya and my husband, Mr. Shibashis Chatterjee, with whom, needless to say, I have disagreed on several points.

Above all, I thank the Indian Council of Social Science Research for providing the necessary financial assistance for the publication of my book.

Although this work reflects opinions and suggestions of several scholars, I remain exclusively responsible for all mistakes of both omission and commission.

Contents

Foreword v

Preface xi

1. Introduction 1
2. Socialism and Nationalism 17
3. Political Evolution and Economic Experience: Central Asia under the Soviet Rule 72
4. Religion: The Determining Factor in Central Asian Identity 103
5. Role of Language in the Identity: Formation of Central Asia 131
6. Role of Ethnic Factors in the Development of Multi-Layered Identities in Central Asia 159
7. Perestroika, Glasnost and the Change in Central Asia 216
8. Quest for Identity Continues—Conclusion 244

Bibliography 250

Endnotes 266

Index 287

One

Introduction

Identity is central to the aspiration of a people. Identities are usually the conscious bi-products of long held beliefs, culture, ethnic roots, language, religion and ideology. Identities usually emerge from within, although, in certain outstanding cases, alien identities can be externally imposed. An imposed identity, nevertheless, is never static, for it interacts with the dormant and older identity, either consciously or otherwise. Identities assume stability as they are socialised into the very existence of the people.

The shaping of 'identity', therefore can be far more complex than is usually supposed. The presence of national identities became a regular feature throughout the 19th and 20th centuries as the concept of 'nation-state' emerged as the most popular and accepted form of political organisation. The concept of 'nation' is an imagination based on certain elements of culture (religion and language), memories of history and political experiences of a particular community. In Benedict Anderson's words "... it is an imagined political community—and imagined as both inherently limited and sovereign."[1] He also explained how nations carried within them the past experiences and belongingness to religious and linguistic commonness. In his words: "It would be short sighted, however, to think of the imagined communities of nations as simply growing out of and replacing religious communities and dynastic realms. Beneath the decline of sacred communities, languages and lineages, a fundamental change was taking place in modes of apprehending the world, which, more than anything else, made it possible to 'think' the nation".[2] As long as the notion of one-nation one-state was in vogue, nationalism was explained in terms of one goal—attainment of sovereignty. However, with the emergence and acceptance of multi-national states, the scope and limits of nationalism became more complex and indeterminate.

The 'Soviet-multi-national' experiment, therefore, engendered a different dialogue between the national identities of each member states and the 'supra-national' 'Soviet' identity. There were uneasiness, tensions and clashes over identities within the 'Soviet Socialist' framework, because of its multi-national character on the one hand and the Marxist-socialist goal on the other. These two parameters had conditioned the development of nationalism of different republican communities participating in the Union of Soviet Socialist Republics. After the demise of the USSR, the fifteen successor states, had to undergo the process of redefining their identities and establish themselves as nation-states. Soviet Central Asian republics showed extreme tension, confusion and complexities with the claims and counter-claims of parallel and rival identities to redefine their 'national' identity at this hour of transition.

To go back to the past, the creation of the multi-national Soviet Union along Marxist Socialist principles had posed a serious question about the status of the national republics and the nationalities who joined this system. The target of the USSR was to transcend the bounds of the 'nation state;' and establish a greater community of the 'Soviet people'. The dilemma was aggravated by the two contradictory principles that governed the creation of the USSR: the acceptance of national autonomy for each republic with ethnic-national delimitation in theory and the overbearing omnipresence of the supra-national 'Soviet' authority, mostly represented by the 'Russian' big brothers. This tension between the 'core' and the 'borders' or 'centre' and 'periphery' or 'Russian' and 'non-Russian' people over the rights, independence, autonomy and identity consciousness continued at different levels throughout the Soviet history. In fact, the formative phase of the Soviet rule experienced several types of tensions and complexities over different identities.

The Stalinist era depicted the highest tension concerning the forcible imposition of Soviet ıdentity over the national, regional or other indigenous identities of the non-Russian Soviet people. This period also received the highest attention from a very large number of sociologists who wanted to expose the coercion and dogmatism imposed in the name of Marxist-Leninist principles however. The focus of the present research strictly the post-Stalin era—an era of stability according to Soviet view and the era of stagnation in the eyes of the critiques. This focus was despite the fact that this period, especially from the time of Brezhnev, depicted neither any major change in the official position regarding the nationality issue or national republics, nor did it experience any major upheaval. Interest in this period arose from the many interesting shifts and changes that took place in a silent and insidious manner in the sphere of identities within the USSR in these decades, ... A thorough study of this uneventful period shows how these years of economic stagnation, corruption and ideological errosion generated a feeling of complete disillusionment among the people of the USSR in general and Central Asian republics in particular. Yet, ironically enough, the Central Asian republics had never desired to come out of the USSR and, even after their forcibly bestowed independence as a bi-product of Perestroika, none of these five republics, namely Uzbekistan, Tajikistan, Turkmenistan, Kirgizhia and Kazakhstan, severed their terms once and for all with Russia. They all became members of the newly created CIS (Commonwealth of Independent States) union. This was not a hangover of prolonged dependence, but a practical necessity of utmost seriousness for these republics, whose economy, polity and strategy had become intertwined with white Russia since the Tsarist period. The Soviet era brought a very mixed experience of realisation and maturity of self-consciousness of the people of these republics in the interactions of their many-fold indigenous identities vis-à-vis the prescribed 'Soviet' identity. The last phase of Soviet rule put its silent imprints on the complex development of the identity consciousness of non-Russian people (narodnert). These identities slowly surfaced amidst particular issues and often became angular when regional or national interests were hurt by the all pervasive 'Soviet entity'.

In fact, the issue of Soviet nationalities problem was almost dropped officially when Brezhnev in 1973 announced the birth of a 'new historic community of Soviet people'—who were supposedly united by similar socialist values that held all the diverse nationalities together in harmony and peace. This claim of having found an apparent solution to the nationality problem was one of the major points of debate between the Soviet and Western scholars. Scholars of the Soviet side claimed that the Soviet system was the first in the world to resolve tensions over the nationality issue, without destroying the national identities of the various peoples residing within the USSR. In sharp contrast, the Western and American scholars of the Cold War period wanted to highlight the lack of independence of the non-Russian nationalities, and the discrimination and domination by the 'Russian big-brotherhood' over the backward provinces like Central Asia under the Soviet experience. Both these groups of scholars, involved in an ideological polemic, always furnished partial evidences to substantiate their respective theories. Treated together, writings of both these schools appear to be deliberately biased and misleading and unable to bring out the real picture. A very interesting development among the Soviet intelligentsia during the 70s was to counter-argue the Western critique of the Soviet system in order to reassert the success of the Soviet state. A remarkable work of this category was by an Uzbek scholar R. Tuzumuhamedov who, being a native of Central Asia, viewed the issue from a regional perspective. The very title of the book indicated the firm position taken against the Western critique by the author —*How the National Question was solved in Soviet Central Asia (A Reply to Falsifiers)*.[3] Tuzumuhamedov enlisted the common allegations by the Western critiques, which were as follows:

1. Accusation of Russification or Sovietisation.
2. Misrepresentation of the generous role of the Russian people as colonisers.
3. Lamentation over the lack of freedom to worship Islam and other restrictions on Islamic Practices.
4. To defame the role of the CPSU and its branches in the Union Republic, etc.
5. To accuse the Soviet system as Soviet colonialism.
6. To allege that Central Asian republics had no right of self-determination and the right to secession was not genuine.[4]

However, while refuting these allegations, Tuzumuhamedov stressed the background and intention of the critiques instead of going into a meticulous examination of each point raised. Rather, looking into the indigenous situation, he highlighted the material developments and upliftment in the standard of civilisation achieved through Sovietisation in the entire zone compared to the Tsarist time. Some poems of the Tsarist period were quoted to show the amount of pain endured by these people in the pre-Soviet era. The initial period of Soviet rule was described as 'The programme for overcoming Backwardness'[5], and the period of stability from mid-sixties was marked as 'A leap into socialism'.[6] In the final analysis, the author made two very pointed comments in connection with the 'anti-Soviet slander'. First, he argued that the meaning of national self-determination was not confined to the demonstration of the right to secession.[7] This, however, implied that the Soviet state was not so willing to allow the practice of this particular right. More importantly, he openly declared that, "...being true Marxists and genuine internationalists the Communists do not regard any general democratic principle, including the right to self-determination, as an absolute, but as a means of achieving and defending democracy and the class interests of the working people. Otherwise, any such principle, if considered without regard for its aims, may become an instrument of reaction as history knows very well".[8] Thus, from the perspective of the natives of Soviet Central Asia, he clearly prioritised the need to maintain the Soviet system as a collective of nations and argued that national interests could be served to the extent that this served the Communist Party and its policies.

The subordination or subservience of the national or regional identity to the supra-national commitment to the Communist Party was apparently a position formally represented by the official Soviet speeches and writings. Yet, in reality, the 70s saw the Party coming to a kind of understanding of the limitation of the Soviet Nationalities Policy and its future. This was, of course, not openly admitted by the authorities but could be surmised from the softer tone employed by the leadership on this issue. Most interestingly, the proud announcement of Brezhnev on the successful solution of the nationality problem was nothing but an excuse to avoid discussion of this exceedingly complicated issue. The Soviet regime, from this time onwards, did not want to experiment again on this issue.

The famous three stage formula of Soviet nationalities policy, was: *rastvest* or flowering of nations, followed by *Sbtizhenie* or drawing together of nations culminating in *Slianie* or fusion of nations into the great melting pot of 'Soviet nation'. This final stage, which was a creation of early Soviet era, was silently dropped in all official discussions from the seventies. This implied that the earlier expectation of the fusion or merger of nations had reduced in course of time and, experience had driven home the point that the national identities were much too deep rooted and tough to be removed by any other artificially imposed identity, however great the promise of that new identity might seem. Therefore, in the same speech where Brezhnev spoke of the historic community of the Soviet people, he quite openly sanctioned a place for permanent national distinctions within the Soviet framework. He stated, "...speaking about the new historical community of people, we absolutely do not have in mind that national differences have already vanished, or more so that the fusion of nationalities has already occurred. All nations and nationalities that live in the Soviet Union preserve their national peculiarities, traits of national character, language and their best traditions. They have available all the necessities to achieve still greater flourishing of their national culture".[9] The difference between national and Soviet identities was marked in the cultural level, historic fates and common ideology irrespective of the national affiliation. Brezhnev wrote: "Our people have, independent of their national affiliations, many common traits which unite them in one monolithic whole. This is a community of socio-economic life of basic interests and goals. This is the developing community of Soviet socialist-culture, which subsumes all that is truly valuable from each national culture".[10] Thus, along with the admission of the presence of national identities with their own national culture, the central Soviet leadership duly harped on its subordinate position to the Soviet identity.

Professor Madhavan K. Palat in an interesting study of the Soviet nationalities policy pointed out this disparity between the fixed socialist goal and the subsequent policies drawn for its attainment at different stages of history. In Palat's own expression, "While the goal of communism has remained as permanent and unchanging as the pole star, the socialist means or transition has been subject to periodic revision".[11] This characteristic duality of an unchanging goal and an ever-changing path of its attainment were equally discernible in the sphere of economic-political planning as well as the national issue. More interestingly, this change of course usually took place along with the change of leadership. The era of Brezhnev, thus reflected a period of caution and retreat in many spheres compared to his predecessors, namely, Stalin and Khrushchev. But the retreat was covered up by some false claims like the attainment of "developed socialism" or giving birth to a "new historic community". The characteristic caution of the Brezhnevite era was reflected in the abandonment of the concept of *slianie*. About the impractical concept of *slianic* Palat commented, "The fusion of nations into a single socialist culture and society was an early expectation that rapidly became a reverie, then a fantasy and finally propaganda. We need not dwell on it too long."[12]

The concept of *sblizhenie*, however, had an elaborate scheme which developed step by step in different stages, with the use of various instruments of interactions between the nationalities. The most important instrument of 'drawing together' of nations was the Communist Party which through its Central Committee and regional branches coordinated the representatives of different nationalities. Within this forum national distinctions were not allowed in principle. Again, in reality the domination of the ethnic Russians within party hierarchy was very evident in reality. In contrast, the thin representation of the Central Asian members in the Central Party organ was noteworthy till the end of the Soviet regime. Among the Central Asians, the Uzbek nations were the most influential within the CPSU and its local branches. At times, there were some leaders who, by their sheer personalities, became prominent within the party despite lacking a substantial national background, like Bobojan Gapurov of Tajikistan.[13] Apparently the most impartial instrument of the Soviet system, the Party, was not entirely devoid of national distinctions in practice. Here, the conclusion reached by M.K. Palat is instructive, "to re-iterate, the only point, and a very important one, where all differences are dissolved necessarily, is within the ruling caste, the Party, and in particular, its nomanclatura"[14] This, however, is somewhat questionable when analysed from a practical standpoint.

However, this process of drawing together continued with industrialisation, urbanisation and other forms of modernisation at a rapid scale in the USSR. This phase of *sbilizhenie* continued mainly during the Stalinist and the post-Stalinist eras, from 30s to 60s. The changes most of the societies had to undergo because of this rapid economic growth were justified in terms of socialist development. The Soviet authorities emphasised the combination of national and socialist characters with a famous phrase, "national in form and socialist in content". Bruno Coppieters explained: "This (national in form, socialist in content) meant that the new political community should build socialism with due regard to national differences but that the final aim—the aim inherent in the development of the socialist content according to that particular view of history — was to overcome these differences by a merging of all nationalities in a common Soviet and socialist identity".[15] However, this form and content paradigm did not work according to the expectations of its authors. M.K. Palat ridiculed this concept and its brutal implementation under Stalin thus, "The thirties to the sixties were the decades of coordination or of "drawing together", when the nation was only the form, the skin of the slaughtered beast into which was stuffed the socialist content".[16] Bruno Coppieters concluded that, "However, this aim of unifying content and form, contained in Soviet nationality policy, failed, together with the idea of a common Soviet people and the idea of a homeland for all national communities".[17]

These national forms sanctioned by the Soviet authorities were usually nothing more than symbolic, like the preservation of national flag, emblem and anthem for each national republic. A slim guidebook on Tajikistan claimed, "The symbols of the national sovereignty of the Tajik SSR are its national emblem, flag and anthem". Interestingly enough, the author took the trouble of describing the visual get up of both the emblem and the flag in minute details but remained silent about the anthem.[18] Probably this silence was consciously maintained to avoid criticism from the external world for these anthems of the republics, especially in Central Asia, were nothing but a saga of Russian benevolence. For instance, the Ujbek anthem started with 'Salam Russian brothers'.[19]

This kind of symbolism also marked Great Russian chauvinism in a glaring manner. The national forms of civilisation usually tolerated and encouraged by the Soviet authorities were usually some cultural expressions which did not in any way contradict the Soviet value, or guidelines. For example, another book on Tajikistan, described the capital of Dushanbe as a place of 'Oriental fairly tale' implying that it acted as a centre of traditional culture. "Among the trolley bus passengers clad in European clothes you can see a dignified grey-bearded old man—an aksakal—in a colourful robe belted with a bright kerchief. In a book shop your attention will be caught by girls wearing gay coloured national costumes and gold embriodered skull caps".[20] This kind of description on the part of the Soviet sponsored Russian author show that these conscious converts to Soviet socialist principles too, at least in their subconscious, admitted a sense of alienation towards the oriental appearance of these non-Russian, especially Asian and Muslim, republics of Central Asia. Still, in the sphere of culture, dress and food habits the autonomy was accepted—but demands of strong political entity and share in power distribution or overwhelming attachment to religion (namely Islam) which posed any potential threat to the maintenance of the Soviet system were never encouraged as part of national aspiration or regional autonomy.

Thus, the claim of national unification made by the Soviet propaganda machine appears quite untenable. But at the same time, the story of the regional nationalities was not of outright suppression and domination as claimed by the earlier mentioned Western critiques mentioned earlier. The nationalities, within the given constraint of the Soviet framework, maintained and developed their originality, uniqueness and also interacted with the Russian and other Soviet nationalities. The later part of the Soviet system, namely the post-Stalin era, allowed, though not in theory, but in practice, many important concessions to the nationalities towards autonomy. Many intellectual debates, arising during the 70s, implied the silent acceptance of the 'nation' as a concrete and more lasting phenomenon. Academicians like Yu.V. Bromlei, M.I. Kulichenko, V.I. Kozlov and others began to formulate their own positions on the issue of national self-awareness and its scope within the Soviet multi-national state. While Bromlei stressed "ethnos' as a substitute for the concept of national identity'.[21] Kulichenko argued, "It would even be politically loose not to take advantage of the growth of a people's self-consciousness, not to shape this growth, since it is directly dependent upon a people's recognition of belonging not only to their nation, but also to the new historical entity of the Soviet people".[22] Thus, both these scholars wanted to divert the national loyalty to some other, safer force—either changing the name or linking national feeling with the proposed Soviet internationalism. It thus becomes clear that though the more sensible Soviet scholars at this stage accepted the presence of national self-awareness as a material reality, they could not get over the uneasiness in accepting this reality for its difficult relation with the Soviet model.

However, in order to understand the actual position of the nationalities within the Soviet system, the political power distribution and nature of economic developments within the republics needs to be studied. The Central Asian republics showed a dependency syndrome from the very outset in this sphere because of their backwardness in terms of industries, education and urbanity. The Russian 'big-brotherhood' was manifested in the initial part of Soviet rule through political control and economic monitoring of the zone. But with time, there also developed a formidable group of native elite, trained in the Soviet model, who began to replace the Russian and other Slavic leaders in the highest political and administrative positions. The Brezhnev era saw the culmination of this process when the native leaders held their posts for about two decades or more. This was a part of the general trend during the Brezhnev era which pushed the entire regime towards the practice of gerontocracy. However, other than within the nomenclatura, the relation between the natives of the titular nationalities remained quite distant. The Western scholars blamed this upon the overbearing presence of Russian leadership as a colonial practice. According to this view, this was nothing but a continuation of the old Russian Empire in the new garb of the 'Soviet' system. But, scholars who tried to assess the whole issue from outside the Cold-War polemic, could not be satisfied with such an oversimplistic theory. To them, the Soviet system developed a very complex relation with the Central Asian nationalities in practice which partly resulted from the confined theoretical understanding of the whole issue and partly because of the growing multi-dimensional tensions either arising from within or induced by the outside world. Alexander Motyl clearly stated, "The straightforward imperialist paradigm does injustice to the complex, integrated nature of Soviet state and society by reducing them to "Russia and her colonies".[23] That the Soviet system was not a continuation of old Russian imperialism is proved from the dissatisfaction of a substantial category of ethnic Russians within this system. The 'impersonal' approach and 'artificiality' of the Soviet life brought boredom and suffocation especially to the intellectuals, artists and others who wanted to pursue independence of thought and faith. A kind of similarity could be drawn between the dissatisfied Russian segment and the discontented lot in the Central Asian Republics, from this perspective. A similar kind of discontent shown by both the groups (supposedly the ruler and the ruled) furnished the strongest evidence against the 'colonial' character of this system. However, the negation of 'colonial' character, of course, did not disregard the presence of a distinct hierarchy between the Russian and the non-Russian nationals. Here the Central Asians belonged to a relatively lower grade in the sharing of power, position and economic benefits. There undoubtedly remained a marked difference between the promise and practice of this Marxist-Leninist regime. But the Brezhnev era, with all its limitations, provided a unique combination of coercion and concession to this particular region which kept its impact in the evolution of indigenous identity politics of its people central and alive for a long time to come.

Central Asia, with its centuries old history and rich oriental cultural heritage, had some very strong and distinct identities of her own. The major elements, which helped in the formulation of the indigenous identities, were religion (mainly Islam), language and ethnic attachments. Of these three, the Soviet authority was most uneasy with the Islamic influences; the other two elements received a comparatively better treatment. In fact, language and ethno-cultural entities received conscious encouragement throughout the Soviet period in different degrees. The amount of encouragement shown by the Soviet system to develop indigenous languages in this region was marked by the establishment of vernacular schools, publication of books in local languages and so on. At the same time, the learning of the Russian language became quite an imperative for the natives in order to attain a successful career. This kind of dichotomies on part of the Soviet authorities created tension between local and Soviet identities as the Soviet identity was generally manifested as the Russian identity. However, compared to other non-Russian republics, Central Asians seemed more committed to their mother tongue or *'rodnoi yazik'* as they seldom accepted Russian as their mother-tongue, and even refused to give it the status of the 'second mother-tongue', but preferred to call it just the 'second language'. Even the lure of higher social status and political opportunities could not induce them to shift their allegiance from their national language. This strong pull of indigenous roots was seen to be re-attested again in the case of ethnic identities. There had been indirect encouragement by the Soviet system to strengthen the ethnic roots. The rich and diverse ethnic character of Central Asian republics came into the limelight not only as part of academic research, but was also got encouraged by some of the state policies. The ethno-national identities became quite a recognised issue in the Soviet system, from the time when the mention of nationalities became compulsory in passports. The Soviet citizens were not free to decide their nationalities on their own—it had to be fixed on the basis of their parental origin. Only in the cases of mixed marriages the siblings used to get a choice between the two. There was a tendency among non-Russian nationalities to avail the opportunity of embracing 'Russian' identities, but the Central Asians again, proved a deeper commitment to their ethnic sentiments as they did not show much hankering for becoming a 'Russian national'. Thus, Central Asia, as a distinct culture-zone, could keep her people closely attached to her unique identities. The lure of material opportunities and social status could not shift her peoples' common allegiance. However, the identity or attachment of which the general Central Asian people were most sensitive was their religion—Islam. The equation between the Soviet authorities (both local and Central) and the indigenous population of the region regarding this religious attachment was one of extreme unease. The Soviet system, following Marxist principles, was generally committed to an atheistic position and, as part of Party activity continued atheistic propaganda throughout the USSR. In Central Asia, these propaganda activities were naturally hurled against Islam as a religion and Islam as an institution. Though constitutionally, the Soviet citizens were allowed to follow or not to follow any religion and some of the state sanctioned mosques were allowed to function, there was definite suppression of religious fervour which was generally quite high in these territories. Islam in Central Asia was not only a religious anchor. It was a way of life, and it was a common bond between different ethno-lingual categories. In this sense, Islam, had a supra-national character and was taken to be the toughest contender of the Soviet identity. The Western critiques had shown much sympathy for these "Soviet Muslims' during the Cold War period for their lack of freedom in pursuing Islam and its various tenets within the Soviet framework. Some extended the views of this school further and claimed that the Central Asians with their similar religion and culture were originally a homogenous whole, whom the Soviet authorities had consciously sealed into distinct ethno-linguistic compartments in order to pursue the policy of 'divide and rule'. This approach was, however, revised by other comparatively neutral scholars who, without disregarding the strong presence of Islam and the excesses committed by the Soviet authorities to suppress it, admitted the limitation of Islam in bringing unity to the entire zone. Islam was not monolithic in this region and could provide only one element in the development of local identities. Over-emphasis on Islamic identities often distorted the consciousness of these people. But, when used in power politics, the role of Islam was very prominent as a mobilising factor. Therefore, once the domination of the Soviet system retreated under the spell of perestroika, Islam began to serve as the most powerful element in the identity politics of the Central Asians. But even then, it was proved that 'Islam' was not enough to bring all these people into a united whole.

In fact, when with perestroika from above these republics were forced to obtain independence, a definite power vacuum and ideological flux was precipitated in these republics. At this stage, the forces of Islamic attachments were used to fill in the ideological gap. Islam with its deep-set sentimental bond also worked as a successful mobilising factor in different nationalist movements during perestroika and post-perestroika periods. However, none of the Soviet Central Asian states depicted any outright shift from Soviet socialism to Islamic fundamentalism. Helene' Carriere D'encausse's formula of replacing 'homo-Sovieticus' by 'homo-Islamicus'[24] has proved quite untenable even when the zone was left with its own choice.

Moreover, the experience of perestroika, leading to the demise of the USSR, did not bring much joy to the people of Central Asia, though it brought them freedom. The economic dependence of these territories forced them to cling to the Russian camp even after the end of the Soviet rule. The need for economic viability and strategic security and their political immaturity to act independently impelled all the five republics to join the CIS union. Thus, another 'revolution from above' after seventy years of the Soviet Revolution had once more left these states without sufficient practical choice. The subsequent period of turmoil and transition only revealed the different shades of socio-political, ethno-cultural, religious and ideological forces at work. This hour of crisis sharpened the different elements constitutive of the region's self-consciousness, threatening to cause major disruptions in this trouble-torn land.

Among all these five Central Asian republics, Tajikistan's quest for identity throughout the Soviet period, and especially after it, furnishes perhaps the most interesting case study. Actually, Tajikistan had a very unique combination of many extreme natural traits and diverse ethnic, religious and cultural characteristics among her people. These together turned the development of her self-awareness (*samo-soozhnanie*) as a nation into a very intense yet complex process. Tajikistan as a separate state did not exist before the Soviet occupation of this area. The Soviet authorities had distinguished this category of non-Turkic people and bestowed statehood on them on the basis of national delimitation along ethnic lines. However, this separate ethno-linguistic identity of the Tajiks remained confusing because of their constant interaction with the neighbouring Uzbeks—the leading Turkic people of the region. The Ujbeks, the other non-Turkic people, speaking various dialects of Persian, were clubbed together under Tajik identity which failed to overcome these major differences within the newly created national block. For example, the passivity of the hill areas originated from a completely different ethno-cultural roots—even their religious practices were different as they followed the Ismaili sect while the Sunni creed was generally followed throughout Central Asia including the Tajiks. Along with these inherent complexities within the population, there were some very acute material problems in this state. For Tajikistan was the smallest of the Central Asian republics with the highest density of population and poorest in economic standard.[25] Moreover, geographical proximity to Afghanistan raised the question of security and Islamic fundamentalism in this dissatisfied and complex blend of people, which made the situation most acute for this small republic.

The post-perestroika phase saw riots and turmoil on different grounds almost in all republics—but in Tajikistan the polarity between the two strands was so sharp that this took the shape of a protracted civil war. The two major groups at war against each other were the extremist Islamic party named Islamic Renaissance Party or IRP and the other was the old guards of the Communist nomanklatura. Interestingly, the support base of each extreme force had its distinctive regional character. For example, the Dushanbe-Khojent-Quliab zone, which always received attention under the Soviet rule and could enjoy the benefits of the regime still supported the Communist Party, while Qurgan Tyube, a relatively disturbed and ethnographically complex zone had turned into the seat of the Islamic Renaissance Party (IRP). The backward Badakhshan-Pamir zones created their own Islamic Party *Lal-I-Badakhshani* with their priorities, but could combine with the IRP. There was also a moderate Democratic Party with a milder Islamic intonation, which vacillated between the Communist Party and the fundamentalist Islamic Party.

This struggle for power showed the existence of several strands of identities, overlapping, cutting across and confronting one another in various degrees at this difficult hour. The Tajik people's divided allegiance to this wide variety of regional identities depicted not only some incompatible ideological or emotional attachments but also signified the bifurcation of allegiance for material benefits and political advantages.

Thus, the identity politics of Central Asia, after the Soviet period unleashed the indigenous forces in their full form to interact with each other. The withdrawal of the Soviet system did not at once remove all the seventy years habits and practices under the regime. But, for the Central Asians who were always conscious of their regional, ethnic, linguistic heritage, the imposed Soviet identity was never an alternative to national self-consciousness. Rather, in her given circumstances, full of complexities and constraints, the 'Soviet' identity was somewhat a practical phenomenon which they often welcomed as a blessing (especially in the initial days of rapid growth), often accepted as a *fait accompli* (for example Russian domination in the workplace), and again, often digested as a practical necessity (the acceptance of Russian as the second language).

However, the post-perestroika conflicts were more prominent within or between different ethno-religious groups of different titular republics than between the Russian diaspora and the natives of the republics. This implied that the problem of Russian big-brotherhood was not as acute as projected during the Cold War phase. Rather, once left independent, the task of redefining the national identities of these republics by balancing all these divergent elements together seemed to be a greater challenge.

In the present book, chapter two, entitled, "Socialism and Nationalism", will investigate the theoretical approach towards nation, national identity and nationalism within the Marxist-Leninist framework. An attempt will also be made to trace the evolution of the concept of nation-nationalities and national self-consciousness along the changing leadership of the Party and the State from Lenin to Gorbachev.

The third chapter, titled, "Sovietisation? Russification? Or Empire Building? The Political Evolution and Economic Experience of Central Asia Under Soviet Rule", will be dealing with the political and economic aspects of the Soviet state of post-Stalin era. Here some attempt will be made to investigate the tenability of the allegation of Russification or Soviet empire building put forth by the Western and American scholars involved in Cold War polemics. It will also be investigated here as to how far in reality the Soviet federal structure and socialist economy were practiced in favour of the republics.

The fourth chapter, entitled "Religion as a Determining Factor in Central Asian Identity", will discuss in detail about the uneasy equation between the Soviet authorities (both local and central) and the indigenous population of the region in general over religious attachments. The clash of Soviet atheistic propaganda with overwhelming influence of Islam in Central Asian way of life, will be studied with its multi-dimensional consequences. Attempt will be made to highlight the changing postulates of Soviet authorities towards Islam according to the demand of changing circumstances during the 70s.

In chapter five, entitled "Role of Language in the Identity Formation of Central Asia", the development of the local languages of the titular nationalities of the Central Asian republics as an active component of national identity will be traced. The issue of bilingualism, that is, the simultaneous development of local languages and the spread of the Russian language as the *lingua franca* will be discussed in detail along with the resulting complexities engendered by such a sensitive issue.

In chapter six, entitled "Role of Ethnic Factors in the Development of Multilayer Identities in Central Asia", the ethnic attachments of the people of the zone and its impact on the development of self-consciousness in the regional, national and sub-national levels will be discussed in detail.

In the seventh chapter, entitled "Perestroika, Glasnost and the Change in Central Asia", the effects of perestroika leading to the unexpected independence of the republics will be discussed with a special emphasis on the fate of Tajikistan. The book has tried to find answers to the following questions:

How far was the imposition of Soviet identity aimed at replacing all other components of local identities including Islam in Central Asia? Did the encouragement provided by the Soviet authorities to consolidate modern Tajik identity further complicate the identity politics of Tajikistan?

How far did perestroika promote the quest for identities in a new direction in the Central Asian republics?

Lastly, why did the Tajik identity, instead of consolidating on the basis of indigenous attachments, get fragmented into several sub-national and regional categories which led to a prolonged and bitter civil strife in the post-Soviet Tajik republic?

Consequently, the research will attempt to address these questions and seek to find answers to them.

Two

Socialism and Nationalism

Socialism and nationalism have always been bound together in a complex relationship. Socialists, especially Marxists, call for class unity and a proletarian prospect, so that a new world civilisation could be built. Since the Russian revolution was led by the committed Marxists of the Bolshevik Party or RSDRP, nation formation and national identity in revolutionary Russia had to contend with Marxist principles. At the same time, Marxists were supporters of national equality and the emancipation of oppressed nations. Given the multinational character of Tsarist Russia and the nationalist ferment among non-Russian peoples, Lenin, the most important Bolshevik leader, had to pay thoughtful attention to the problems born out of nationalist discontent. When the Bolshevik regime included vast portions of Central Asia, they promised the same gospel of universal evolution of socialism to communism in these underdeveloped and economically exploited people. Side by side, under Lenin's leadership, the Bolshevik government had also taken up the complex issue of redressal of the grievances of the oppressed nationalities in this region. Thus, from the very inception, there was a pressing need to accommodate nationalism in the Soviet Socialist parameter. But theoretically, this made the task of Soviet socialism quite difficult and complex. Under the banner of socialism, nationalism can be promoted only to a limited extent. In fact, given the chance of unhindered development, they tend to become each-other's impediment. In Marxist analysis, 'nationalism' is actually a manifestation of bourgeois democratic aspiration—therefore, a phenomenon representing a particular ideology and class. So far as the Russian revolution was anti-feudal, the bourgeois-democratic radicalism of oppressed nations was considered progressive. But if nationalism was made the final goal it came into conflict with the goal of cross-nation class-unity and the construction of a classless society (communism). Therefore, nation, nationality, nationalism and nation state never received conceptual priority under Marxist socialism. The Bolsheviks, like the proponents of other revolutionary Marxist currents, were internationalists. At the same time, they, notably Lenin, had come to develop a stand concerning the right of oppressed nations to self-determination. This meant a partial reassessment of the positions of Marx and Engel's. Nonetheless, their internationalism could cause a confrontation with nationalist aspirations in different parts of the USSR. Central Asia, with its mosaic of peoples, felt this conflict keenly.

Nation and Class in Marx and Engels

To begin with, in the writings of Marx and Engels 'nationalism' always received a secondary status as their aim was to attain a classless society where all types of discriminations would disappear from human race.

However, accommodating the phenomenon, their experience from reality taught them the necessity of recognising that nationalism was a thriving force of mid 19th century, and beginning their propaganda literature in 1848, they could not completely ignore the pressure of nationalism as a strong ideology.[1] From the very outset, they were conscious about aggressive nationalism and highlighted the fact that the concepts of empire and colony were born out of this extreme form of nationalism. But at the same time, enough space was provided for suppressed nationalism—especially in the colonial context where the colonised nation was taken with due sympathy (e.g. the case of India).[2]

Marx and Engels were committed to a proletarian world revolution, which would abolish all types of exploitation and oppression, and begin the process of construction of a classless society. This meant a dualistic attitude to nation and nationality. On one hand, they saw nations as ultimately transient identities, to give way to some form of universal association of producers. On the other hand, in 19th Century Europe, they saw a historically progressive role for nationalism. So they could neither ignore the promise of nationalism as a strong political movement, nor take a uniform stand about all forms of nationalism. Thus, they were not only to take a clear stand in support of colonial struggles (in Latin America, in India, etc.), but they were also to support those European national struggles which they felt were contributing to anti-feudal, bourgeois-democratic causes.

It must be stressed that Marx and Engels, unlike most of their contemporary socialists, began as revolutionary democrats. Marx and

Engels argued that the fight for social justice could not be successfully pursued unless it was linked to the struggle for democratic rights. Their idea, that "working men have no country", in fact, extended their commitment to democracy.

However, Marx and Engels had logically accepted the existence of 'nationalism' as a necessary feature of a 'historic phase'—the phase which the contemporary human society was experiencing. Extending the same logical coherence, they believed that nationalism as a phenomenon was the product of a particular phase of human civilisation, attached to a particular social milieu and political ethos—various forms of bourgeois order. It would gradually lose its importance and the bourgeois leadership would be replaced by the dictatorship of the proletariat. As the 'proletariat of all countries' had one and a single goal according to them, the ideological back-up by nationalism becomes irrelevant in their struggle. The Communist Manifesto states, "National differences and antagonism between peoples are daily more and more vanishing, owing to the development of the bourgeoisie, to freedom of commerce, to the world market, to uniformity in the mode of production and in the conditions of life corresponding thereto."[3]

However, from the very inception of the writings of Marx and Engels one can see that they were sympathetic to the nationalist movements leading to a unification, such as the German, Italian, Polish and Hungarian nationalism. But their demand for national unity was supported because of their long cultural heritage and their previous attempts of unity recorded in history. Thus, a concrete past, in favour of national union, made them appear as 'historic' nations—as had been depicted by Hegel and accepted by Marx and Engels.[4] But, the smaller nationalities, with obscure past heritage, and especially those who were a national minority with political views opposed to the mainstream national movements were disregarded as 'non-historic' nations—especially by Engels at one point. As Engels pointed out, "Such in Scotland are the Gaels, the supporters of Stuarts, from 1640 to 1715. Such in France, are the Bretons, the supporters of the Bourbons from 1792 to 1800. Such in Spain, are the Basques, the supporters of Don Carlos. Such, in Australia, are the pan-Slavist Southern Slavs who are nothing but the residual fragment of peoples ...."[5]

These Southern Slavs—the Serbs, the Croats, the Czechs and the Slovaks were in Engels' version, "peoples which have never had a history of their own...are not viable and will never be able to achieve any kind of independence."[6]

Thus, apparently it seemed that Engels grossly disregarded the rational aspirations of certain communities and their future as non-historic. This Hegelian distinction between 'historic' and 'non-historic' was not used by Marx. He visualised the two different types into 'revolutionary' and 'non-revolutionary' nations.[7] Ronaldo Munk, in his book commented, "Essentially, these categories reflect a form of Social Darwinism—a survival of the fittest peoples with the losers being condemned to oblivion."[8]

However, a recent article in Science and Society by E. Haberkern drew attention to the 'non-historic' nation concept of Engels and brought evidence to show that Engels was not irrationally consistent on the point. Rather he had formulated the idea on a particular historic context and his other writings before or after showed his support for the Croats, Magyars, Jewish nationalities thriving for independence.[9]

However, it was found from the practical events that both Marx and Engels preferred to support only those nationalist movements, which, they thought, would be promoting democracy and thereby act as a progressive event in the context of German civilisation. In Marxian analysis, as long as a national government ensures economic progress, it provides some positive impact to the society. To speak of the bourgeois regime, it was approved as long as it promoted the economic development that touched the industrial proletariat as well. About the class struggle in France, Marx stated, "In general, the development of the industrial proletariat is conditioned by the development of the industrial bourgeoisie. Only under the rule of the bourgeoisie does it begin to exist on a broad national basis, which elevates the revolution to a national one...."[10] Another progressive aspect of bourgeois regime was their promotion of international commerce leading to an international society as had been described in the Manifesto—"National differences and antagonism between peoples are daily more and more vanishing, owing to the development of the bourgeoisie, to freedom of commerce to the world market, to uniformity in the mode of production and in the conditions of life corresponding thereto."[11]

But at one point Marx and Engels had a strong and consistent position—that all nationalist movements could not be progressive. Some would be reactionary. Therefore, their support to national movements would never be unconditional.

Actually, the focus of Marx and Engels was always directed at internationalism—transcending the national level of unity. In the

'Communist Manifesto' the national strategies of the proletariat had been described as follows, "The working men have no country. We cannot take from them what they have not got. Since the proletariat must first of all acquire political supremacy, must rise to be the leading class of the nation, must constitute itself the nation, it is, so far, itself national, though not in the bourgeois sense of the word."[12] In another place of the Manifesto, they stated, "Though not in substance, yet in form, the struggle of the proletariat with the bourgeoisie is at first a national struggle. The proletariat of each country must, of course, first of all settle matters, with its own bourgeoisie."[13] Thus, while working out strategies, they could envisage the working class coming to power in each of their respective countries and thus becoming the representatives of the respective nationalities thereby changing the connotation of nationalism. For, in a bourgeois democratic set up, the bourgeois nationalism with its own dynamics kept the workers as outcastes in the national representation. So, whether by internationalism they meant the disappearance of nations altogether is not clear. In Solomon Bloom's analysis, "What the authors [of the Manifesto] foresaw was not the complete disappearance of all national distinctions whatever but specifically the abolition of sharp economic and social differences, economic isolation, invidious distinctions, political rivalries, wars and exploitation of one nation by another."[14] As it was stated in the Manifesto as well, "In proportion as the exploitation of one individual by another is put an end to, the exploitation of one nation by another will also be put an end to. In proportion as the antagonism between classes within the nation vanishes, the hostility of one nation to another will come to an end."[15]

With this legacy V.I. Lenin took up the issue of nation, nationalities and nationalism and tried to accommodate his elaborate thesis of national self-determination without disrupting the Marxist connotation of the idea. Much before coming to power, he kept on developing his thesis in this regard because he could visualise the necessity of paying due attention to these factors which were relevant to their soil. That is why, he continued a simultaneous preparation for the national issues along with the ground work for the revolution.

Lenin and the Nationality Question

Lenin's ideas on nations and national-self-determination were developed in two stages. In the first stage, these ideas were developed as part of his strategy for a democratic revolution in Russia. The second stage saw Lenin developing the strategy of the Russian revolution as a part of the world socialist revolution, and locating the national question as a component of the socialist revolution.

He understood better than his contemporary Marxists the dialectical relationship between internationalism and the right of national self-determination. He felt that only the freedom to secede makes possible free and voluntary union, association, cooperation and in the long run, fusion between nations. On this ground he championed the notion of national self-determination as against imperialist chauvinism. He also realised that the need for self-determination ought to be recognised by the workers movements in the oppressor nation which in turn would eliminate the hostility and suspicion of the oppressed nations. This would help unite the proletariat of both nations, oppressor and oppressed for the international struggle against the imperialist bourgeoisie. Lenin logically showed again and again the viability of his own theory and maintained a consistent approach towards the oppressed nations and colonies, throughout his writings; but he never accepted this political right to be an absolute one, and regarded it as just a passing phase of democracy till socialism and internationalism is reached.

In Lenin's revolutionary strategy, the tsarist state was the main and immediate enemy. And the theory of revolution was formulated in the proper sense in the 2nd Congress of the Party in 1905. The Second Congress also provided the occasion for taking a stand on the national question. The programme stated that while the goal of social democracy was the same all over the world, in Russia the goal assumed a more concrete form. This was because the main obstacle to the socialist programme was the autocratic Tsarist state. Here Lenin sought to find out real enemies of Tsarism—who could be made faithful allies of the proletariat. Here he found the peasantry as allies and the second probable allies were the oppressed nations under the Tsarist rule. As the Russian empire was a multi-national state with an ideology of great Russian supremacy, there were many extra oppressions in practice on the non-Russian subjects, such as the Jews, Poles, Finns, etc. Central Asia or Inner Asia was brought under Russian rule in the course of 19th century, in the name of promoting culture and civilisation. Russian culture was sought to be imposed on these regions. So, Lenin argued, that the people of these oppressed nations were opposed to the Tsarist imperialism and thereby have a common ground of interest with the Russian working class to fight against the Tsarist regime.[16]

Beginning with this specific issue, Lenin could create a general theory of National Self-Determination along the Marxist line—within a socialist framework. In Lenin's own language "...by examining the historic-economic conditions of the national movements, we must inevitably reach the conclusion that the self-determination of nations means the political separation of these nations from alien national bodies, and the formation of an independent national state."[17] According to the London Resolution of 1896, the self-determination implied only the right to secede. Lenin accepted that it is a bourgeois-democratic tendency, yet he accepted that to be an essential principle of socialism during the time of struggle against imperialism. To him this principle would surely help bringing the proletariat of the oppressed nation near the proletariat of the oppressor nation who could then launch their joint campaign against their common enemy, imperialism—"the highest stage in the development of capitalism" in Lenin's own language.[18] Thus, in Lenin's view the right to self-determination, though in origin a bourgeois-democratic principle, would assist the socialist revolution under changed conditions.

Lenin's thesis on national self-determination faced a stiff challenge from Rosa Luxemburg and her party SDKPiL and also from some other Russian socialists. They argued that by supporting natural secession, Lenin was indirectly supporting bourgeois nationalism and delaying the proletarian revolution. And secondly, "the right of self-determination is not applicable to a socialist society"[19] because socialism would naturally abolish every kind of national oppression since it would abolish the class interests that lead to it. They believed that the problem of national oppression would disappear in course of time, with the establishment of socialism. And, national oppression would not fully disappear till a classless society could be established. Therefore, in a capitalist framework, the support to the national independence for all oppressed nations would only help the bourgeois section of the oppressed nations, not the proletariat.

Lenin, now responded that "Our very first thesis said that the liberation of oppressed nations implies a dual transformation in the political sphere: (1) the full equality of nations, (2) freedom of political separation. This refers to the demarcation of state frontier."[20] He distinguished economic oppressions from political oppression and said as the national self-determination was solely a political demand, one should not get disappointed with the fact that it was unable to do away with economic oppression. Regarding the bourgeois nature of the national independence movement, Lenin opined that the proletariat should give the bourgeoisie "only conditional support." But, nevertheless, the proletarian support for national independence would never coincide with the bourgeois policy. Lenin said, "The bourgeoisie always places its national demands in the forefront, and does so in categorical fashion. With the proletariat, however, these demands are subordinated to the interests of the class-struggle. Theoretically, you cannot say in advance whether the bourgeois democratic revolution will end in a given nation seceding from another nation, or in its equality with the latter; in either case, the important thing for the proletariat is to ensure the development of its class."[21]

So, both for Lenin and Luxemburg, the ultimate goal was the same. Only, Luxemburg felt that the national movements at that period of time would divert and delay the proletarian revolution while Lenin realised the necessity of national independence of oppressed nations for the worldwide development of socialism and wanted to utilise some aspects of national movement for proletarian class-struggle, being fully aware of the bourgeois intention active in such cases. Nation—in Lenin's thought was a political entity, rather an economic or cultural organ. Michael Lowy in his article *'Marxists and the National Question,'* stated "On the national question, while most other Marxist writers saw only the economic, cultural or psychological dimension of the problem, Lenin stated clearly that the question of self-determination 'belongs wholly and exclusively to the sphere of political democracy, i.e. to the realm of the right of political secession and the establishment of an independent nation state."[22]

Luxemburg and the SDKPiL members believed in the cultural autonomy of different nationalities. But Lenin opposed this standpoint for two reasons. Firstly, he was perfectly conscious that an 'autonomous' nation could not enjoy rights equal to those of a 'sovereign' nation. So there would remain a discrepancy in political status of a sovereign and an autonomous nation. Secondly, Lenin was opposed to the promotion of national culture as a general principle. In his essay *National Culture* under the compilation *Critical Remarks on the National Question*, he stated that, "The slogan of national culture is a bourgeois fraud. Our slogan is the international culture of democracy and of the world working-class movement".[23] While answering the Bundist argument he explained that international culture did not mean non-national culture in content. The elements of democratic and socialist culture were found, may be in rudimentary form, in every national culture, since in every nation there was the presence of toiling and exploited masses, whose material conditions automatically could give rise to the ideology of democracy and socialism. But, at the same time, every nation also possessed a bourgeois culture in the form, which usually was the hegemonic culture. Therefore, the general "national culture" was the culture of the landlords, the clergy and the bourgeoisie. In advancing the slogan of "the international culture of democracy and of the world working class movement," Lenin stated, "we take from each national culture only its democratic and socialist elements." Here he clearly stated, "We take them only and absolutely in opposition to the bourgeois culture and the bourgeois nationalism of each nation."[24] Bourgeois nationalism and proletarian internationalism were two irreconcilably hostile slogans, with two class camps and two world outlooks on the national question. The advocates of national cultural autonomy would fall prey to the bourgeois nationalist framework as the national culture would always highlight the bourgeois culture.

Then Lenin went on tracing examples from the positions of Marx and Engels regarding national independence in the case of Ireland. In his essay *Proletariat and Right to self-determination* he made this analysis, "Marx demanded the separation of Ireland from Britain although after the separation there may come federation".[25] This demand was placed not from the standpoint of the petty-bourgeois utopia of a peaceful capitalism but from the standpoint of the interests of the revolutionary struggle of the proletariat of the oppressor, i.e., British nation against capitalism. The British proletariat's internationalism would remain a hypocritical phrase if they did not demand the separation of Ireland. In an earlier writing titled *The Utopian Karl Marx and the Practical Luxemburg*, Lenin wrote about the expected position of the proletariat of the oppressor nation towards the movements for self-determination like Ireland, "The policy of Marx and Engels on the Irish question serves as a splendid example of the attitude the proletariat of the oppressor nations should adopt towards national movements, an example which has lost none of its immense practical importance."[26] Thus Lenin had cited cases from history to substantiate his own theory and showed how his attitude resembled that of Marx and Engels in this regard.

Criticising Luxemburg Lenin further said that carried away by the struggle against Polish nationalism Rosa Luxemburg had forgotten the nationalism of the Great Russians. Lenin analysed the Great Russian nationalism as being more feudal in character and content than bourgeois. By Great Russian nationalism he meant the nationalist position of the contemporary ruling classes of Russia. The ruling class of Russia, the feudal landlords and bureaucracy, according to Lenin were completely opposed to the ideas of national equality and self-determination of oppressed nations. At that stage the Russian empire was holding a host of nations and nationalities under control—none of whose autonomy or independent status could be accepted under the traditional imperialist framework. Against this great Russian nationalism, manifested in her imperialist design, Lenin's war of self-determination was waged. Thus, the proletariat, for the historical necessity of the period were bound to support the national self-determination of all suppressed nations under Tsarist imperialism. This was, of course, a passing phase in proletariat movement towards democracy—which in the process would ultimately lead to the establishment of socialism. To quote Lenin, "In the same way as mankind can arrive at the abolition of classes only through a transition period of the dictatorship of the oppressed class, it can arrive at the inevitable integration of nations only through a transition period of the complete emancipation of all oppressed nations, i.e. their freedom to secede."[27]

Favouring national self-determination Lenin was a obviously against any kind of colonial expansion that was manifestation of imperialism. In his compilation *The Socialist Revolution and the Right of Nations to Self-Determination* reformulating socialist strategy during World War I, Lenin wrote *Imperialism, Socialism and the Liberation of Oppressed Nations*[28], where he made imperialism responsible for the growth of militarism, more frequent wars, more powerful reaction, the intensification and expansion of national oppression and colonial plunder. And he clearly stated, "Socialist parties which did not show by all their activity, both now, during the revolution and after its victory, that they would liberate the enslaved nations and build up relations with them on the basis of a free union—and free union is a false phrase without the right to secede—these parties would be betraying socialism."[29] Here, Lenin showed as to how coherence between the proletariat of the oppressor nation and the proletariat of the colonised nation could be made. For the proletarians of the colonizer nation should demand the independence of the colonies. Otherwise, they would not be able to gain the confidence of the colonies' working class. On the other hand, the socialists of the oppressed nations must defend and implement the full and unconditional unity of the workers of oppressed and oppressor nations together. And they should be aware of the threat of bourgeois utilisation of the nationalist movements for their own. The chances of usurpation of national aspirations by the bourgeois class should not, however, prevent the move for material self-determination. Just as "the bourgeois utilisation of republican slogans for the purpose of political deception and financial plunder are unlikely to make the Social-Democrats reject their republicanism."[30]

Regarding the 'defence of father land' concept Lenin believed that genuine national wars alone could be regarded as the 'defence of fatherland' but no war, which would break out with imperialist design, could be defended using this slogan. Writing an essay during the 1st World War, Lenin says, "The present imperialist war stems from the general conditions of the imperialist era ..."[31] Talk of defence of fatherland (on the part of France, England, Belgium) was therefore, a deception of the people, for this was not a national war. Lenin believed that a war was always a continuation of policy. Consequently, one must examine the policy that led to and brought about the war. If the substance of the war was to overthrow alien oppression, then such war would be progressive for the involved oppressed nation. If, however, the 'substance' of a war was redivision of colonies, division of booty, plunder of foreign lands (and such as the war of 1914-16) then all talk of defending the fatherland was "sheer deception of the people."[32]

Lenin, then studied the variety of nationalisms existing in the contemporary world and divided them into three distinct categories. First were the advanced capitalist countries of Western Europe and the United States where progressive bourgeois national movement came to an end long ago. Secondly, Eastern Europe, Austria, the Balkans and particularly Russia, where the bourgeois-democratic national movements had begun to develop only in the late 19th and early 20th century, intensified national struggle. Thirdly, the semi-colonial countries, such as China, Persia and Turkey, and all the colonies which had a combined population of 1,000 million. In these countries, in Lenin's view, "bourgeois democratic movements either have hardly begun, or have still a long way to go."[33] Lenin, from the socialist perspective, refused to realised as valid the nationalist claims of the first category. As the English, French, German or Italians were defending their rights as slave-holders, their colonies, their foreign sphere of influence in the name of 'defence of fatherland'—their imperialist designs should not be accepted under the banner of 'national self-determination'. The second category of 'defence of fatherland' was still somewhat a defence of democracy, native language and political liberty against medievalism. Therefore, Lenin felt that the socialists could lend their moral support to those countries. And for the third category, he proposed unconditional support till their independence from foreign oppression or colonial domination.

From the same socialist perspective Lenin had shown his disapproval to the concept of annexation. He said in his essay "What is Annexation" that "...annexation is violation of the self-determination of a nation, it is the establishment of state frontiers contrary to the will of the population."[34] Lenin's strong support for national self-determination and secession from oppressor state should not mislead anyone into believing that he supported fragmentation of states and formation of small states. In one of his essays entitled *'The Significance of the Right of Self-Determination and its Relation to Federation'*[35] he stated that the right of nations to self-determination implied exclusively the right to independence in the political sense but he carefully distinguished the right to self-determination from the demands for separation, fragmentation and the formation of small states. Here he stressed the element of democracy in order to prevent secessionist move. In his analysis, the closer a democratic state system would be to complete freedom to secede, the less frequent and less ardent would the desire for separation be in practice, because big states would afford indisputable advantages, both from the standpoint of economic progress and from that of the interests of the masses which kept on growing along with the growth of capitalism. "The aim of socialism" said Lenin, "is not only to end the division of mankind into tiny states...."[36] Rather the aim would be to bring the nations closer together and ultimately integrate them with the mission of internationalism.

Lenin's thesis on nations and nationalities also included the national minorities, especially keeping in mind different nationalities who lived in pre-revolution Russian empire. In May, 1914, he made the draft entitled *'Bill on the Equality of Nations and the Safeguarding of the Rights of National Minorities'*[37], which carried his thought on practical policy making in this complex issue. Here it was stated that "All nations in the state are absolutely equal, and all privileges enjoyed by any one nation or any one language are held to be inadmissible and anti-constitutional."[38] Moreover, "In territorial units with a mixed population the number of members on the boards of education shall not be less than 20. ...Areas shall be considered as having a mixed population where a national minority constitutes up to five per cent of the population."[39] "The proportional share of the funds expended on the cultural and educational needs of the national minorities in a given area shall not be less than the proportional share of the national minorities in the whole population of the given area."[40] Thus, he planned to accommodate all the nationalities of Russia within a socialist framework. This accommodation of so many nationalities into one single socialist framework, apparently, did not negate his theory of self-determination and right to secede for, in the ideal socialist situation, enough care was taken by Lenin to depict a situation free from exploitation and domination by the major nationality.

Thus, although Lenin championed the self-determination of oppressed nations and regarded it as the necessary condition for political democracy, yet he did not consider this to be an absolute and unconditional right of the nationalities. L. Kolakowsky in his book *'Main Currents of Marxism'* criticised Lenin's position on national self-determination thus: "He (Lenin) was a convinced opponent of national oppression and proclaimed the right of self-determination, but always with the reservation that it was only in exceptional circumstances that social democracy could support political separatism....This reservation in effect nullified the right of self-determination and turned it into a purely tactical weapon. The party would always try to utilise national aspirations in the struggle for national power, but the 'interests of the proletariat' could never be subordinated to the desire of a whole people."[41]

This was, however, natural for a proletarian leader aspiring for socialism and internationalism—but it was Lenin's open frame of mind that encouraged him to think in terms of political democracy and national independence as a precondition for a socialist society. But one should not try to find a nationalist in Lenin, although Lenin was probably the foremost positive thinker and activist in Marxist socialist trend who gave a serious thought to the nationality question and its various perspectives. National independence was regarded as a preliminary condition for the ensuing revolution. But, as Lenin's vision was primarily fixed on internationalism and socialist revolution, nation, nationality and national independence were treated as a secondary issue. The ultimate goal of Lenin was not to end at the national independence but at the convergence of all nations into the international egalitarian society—transcending all national boundaries. The direction of history over the last century could prove that the nationality question was a more complex, more enduring and more difficult issue which demanded more caution and concentrated attention by the theorists and strategists. But, from Lenin's given time frame, keeping his socialist perspective as a precondition, he showed a remarkably democratic bent of mind on the nationality question.

Stalin's Ideas Towards Nation—Nationalities and Nationalism

The October Revolution saw Joseph Stalin being made the Commission for Nationalities. Later on, he became the leader of the bureaucratic conservative trend which seized power, as well as one of the main architects of Soviet nationalities policy, both in the early, radical era, and in the later, conservative one. His writings on the nationality question are voluminous. The compilation entitled *Marxism and Nationalism*[42] contained as many as thirty articles, on various aspects of the issue dealt with at different times. The approximate time span of these writings extended from 1913 to 1930. The articles in their characteristic specificity can be divided into two broad types, the pre-revolution and post-revolution writings. Mostly, the pre-revolution writings of Stalin on this particular issue were quite optimistic which might have provided positive encouragement to the non-Russian population in the peripheral zone. But at the same time Stalin was probably the first to define nationalism with specific quantification that brought a limit to the aspirations of the oppressed nationalities. Another feature of his writings in this stage was to disqualify the thesis of the Austro-Marxists about nation and nationalities and to uphold Lenin's thesis as the future guideline of the Bolsheviks in Russia. In the post-revolution writings, which are more in number, there may be made two quite obvious divisions. The first is the group of writings published during the Leninist era and the other group written in the post-revolution phase which showed his distinct disapproval towards secessionist tendencies among the nationalities, although he did not negate the theory of national self-determination formulated by Lenin and approved by himself earlier. One can find a steady increase in his skepticism towards secessionist nationalities and attempted justification of his ideas in favour of national autonomy approved within the Soviet framework, in the post-Lenin era.

Stalin's pre-revolution writings on this aspect consist of two major essays, namely, *Marxism and the National Question* and Report on the National Question. The former one was a substantive work done in 1913, which attempted to clear out the doubts about the scope of nationalism within the framework of internationalism envisaged by the SD party of Russia at that time. For, by then the Jewish Bund and the Caucasian Social-Democrats had began to put many specific national demands which the central leadership of the party found it difficult to accommodate in their scope. So there arose a practical need to redefine nation, nationality and nationalism and how far was it safe to sanction these tendencies in a forum aiming at socialist revolution and internationalism. Stalin initially provided a clear definition of a nation which included all the characteristics he approved as necessary features of a nation. Thus, to quote Stalin, "A nation is a historically evolved, stable community of language, territory, economic life and psychological make-up manifested in a community of culture."[43] Here there was special stress on historical evolution—for he primarily made this statement, that, "Thus a nation is not a racial or tribal, but a historically constituted community of people."[44] Did this connote that tribes or races had no history of their own to share? Or did it simply imply that no obscure communities which so long remained unable to appear to the limelight and make their presence felt in the mainstream historical eventualities would remain ineligible to become a nation? The vagueness of the term 'historically evolved' limited the scope of Stalin's definition of nation to a marked level. Infact, this connotation does not fulfil the expectation of Russian nationalism either, for great Russian nation also included several groups with different strands of history. Stalin here appears less realistic and more dogmatic than his predecessor, Lenin. On the other hand he was strongly against the view of Otto Bauer and other Austro-Marxists who stressed the common cultural heritage to Jewish nationalism—which at that historical stage did not have a common land to share.[45]

National movements developed, in Stalin's view, as an answer to national oppression by greater nations. Thus he cited the cases of Czechs, Croats, Hungarians, Ukrainians, Georgians, Armenians etc, all situated in East Europe. He wrote, "In the West, Ireland responded to its exceptional position by a national movement. In the East the awakened nations were bound to respond in the same fashion.

Thus arose the circumstances which impelled the young nation of Eastern Europe into the path of struggle."[46]

But he, following the Marxist direction of thought, believed that the national struggle was not between the nations as a whole—but between the ruling classes of the dominant and the rising classes of upper bourgeoisie of the oppressed nation. Thus, the issue of nationalism, following the old Marxist line of thought was a class issue, rather a general bourgeois aspiration was naturally involved in enhancing their respective national profile—here the bourgeoisie of oppressed nations took up the cause of national liberation, where they were usually successful in placating popular support—but their movements for secession usually had bourgeois strategies. Here the Russian SD party had their moral duty to warn the toiling masses against their class enemies within their own respective nationalities. The nature of the national movement would of course be different in different circumstances. For example, for the Czechs and Germans the struggles were conducted by the urban petty bourgeoisie of the oppressed nation against the big bourgeoisie of the dominant nation, in cases of Ukrainians in Poland, the struggle was between the rural bourgeoisie of the oppressed nation against the landlords of the dominant nation; again in cases of Poland, Lithuania and the Ukraine in Russia the whole 'national' bourgeoisie of the oppressed nations was against the ruling nobility of the dominant nation. However, the bourgeoisie always appeals to its "native folk"..... "Claiming that its own cause is the cause of the nation as a whole."[47] The 'folk' also usually responded to such appeals, because, they all remained primarily victims of national oppression of the dominant nation. To intersect, the 'folk', the peasantry always participated in such national movements of their "land" if the land was affected. The proletariat rallied to the banner of bourgeois nationalism if the class-contradiction and degree of their organisation remained dilute and ill-formed. According to Stalin, "A class-conscious proletariat has its own tried banner and it does not need to march under the banner of the bourgeoisie."[48] In the same essay Stalin clearly stated, "And that is why the class-conscious proletariat cannot rally under the "national flag" of the bourgeoisie."[49] Thus, along with his tacit support for national self-determination, he also made his point clear that the proletariat had nothing substantial to gain from national liberation. Therefore, the path of national autonomy did not seem suitable for a party aiming at socialism and internationalism. Here Stalin's position seemed markedly different from that of Lenin's. In Lenin's view national self-determination always received a priority as that implied some kind of progress. Though Lenin always believed that national autonomy was a transitional phase in human civilisation, he never disregarded its importance for, to Lenin this implied a basic human right of a people which should not be negated by any authority from outside.

Stalin proceeded to provide a positive solution of the 'national problem.' The issues of nation, nationality and nationalism now thus boiled down only into a 'problem' to be solved. Somehow, the stress on right began to fade away in the face of a suitable party strategy for a successful revolution. Stalin now divided the oppressed nations into two categories—the one who would like to secede should be allowed to do so according to the principle of self-determination. And the rest who would somehow prefer to remain within the general framework would be regarded as national minorities. In order to solve their national problem, Stalin provided some practical solutions like, the essentiality of regional autonomy, national equality in all forms such as language, schools, etc. and the promotion of international solidarity of the working class. While granting several kinds of autonomies, Stalin's view resembled his greatest adversaries—the Austro-Marxists. They too stressed on these kinds of lesser autonomies as an alternative to national independence. But their stress was on more cultural autonomy. May be that was why Stalin consciously refrained from keeping the clause of national culture. To him, national culture would not reflect the culture of a nation in general but the culture of the ruling class of that nation and the traditional culture often would carry many oppressive and unscientific qualities which might not suit the scheme of scientific socialism.

In his *Report on the National Question*, delivered at the 7th All Russian Conference of the RSDLP, April 29, 1917, Stalin came up with his reservations against the right of self-determination leading to secession.[50] Rather, he now provided specific conditions before secession—because at this stage, the Russian context in particular came into focus and Stalin believed that secession in most cases would lead to bourgeois domination over the disunited proletariat of the respective nations. He stated, "When we recognise the right of oppressed peoples to secede the right to determine their political destiny, we do not thereby settle the question of whether particular nations should secede from the Russian state at the given moment. I may recognise the right of a nation to secede, but that does not mean that I compel it to secede. A people has a right to secede, but it may or may not exercise that right, according to circumstances. Thus, we are at liberty to agitate for or against secession according to the interests of the proletariat, of the proletarian revolution."[51] However, here the very thought of compelling or refraining from compelling another nation to secede implied a kind of great Russian chauvinism lurking behind the attitude. The use of 'I' to decide or not to decide such issues gave concessions only to Great Russian Chauvinism. Though in theory, Stalin made the options open for both ends—to support or oppose the case of national self-determination leading to secession but even then, he had to admit, that a region determined to move out should not be prevented even though that secession might be detrimental to its people. At the end of the speech, Stalin made four propositions indicating future directions of the party to solve national problems:

1. Recognition of the right of peoples to secession.
2. Regional autonomy for nations remaining within the given state.
3. Special legislation guaranteeing freedom of development for national minorities.
4. A single, individual proletarian body, a single party for the proletarians of all nationalities in the given state.

There were some debates on the issue of secession where some of the party members like Pyatakov demanded a 'straight revolution, "One thing or the other: either we deny the relations the right of secession, in which case it must be stated explicitly, or we do not deny the right."[52] Stalin, however, answered curtly, "...... to limit ourselves to a statement of rights is impossible."[53] Then Stalin cited the cases of Irish movement against British imperialism and movement of Finland for national freedom against the Provisional government. In both cases Stalin preferred to support the movements for they were waged against imperialism. But there might be cases where the proletarian socialist party was active and national self-determination led by the bourgeoisie or even the nobility might lead to unwanted factionalism where the SD party should not take the side of the nationalists. Thus, Stalin, unlike Pyatakov and Zherzhinsky who believed that "every national movement is a reactionary movement"[54], preferred that the issue be decided on the basis of its context and character.

With the October Revolution, the Bolshevik Party came to power and a Soviet system was introduced in Russia and the non-Russian regions which remained within her new framework. As soon as 1918, Stalin wrote, "*The October Revolution and the National Question*"[55], where he tried to reassess the issue from the changed perspective of the contemporary scenario. He used the term 'border regions' to define these non-Russian territories which simultaneously fought Russian imperialism along with the SD party and later on the Bolshevik party. The national movements in these regions up to the February Revolution went along the path of bourgeois revolution in Russia. Everywhere the national movements were headed by the bourgeois-democratic intelligentsia. "'National Councils in Latvia, the Estonian region, Lithuania, Georgia, Armenia, Azerbaijan, the Caucasus, Kirgiztan and the Middle Volga Region; the Rada in the Ukraine and in Belorussia and the "Sfatul Tsarii" in Bessarabia; the "Kurutai" in Crimea and Bashkiria; the "Autonomous Government" in Turkestan, such were the "all-national" institutions around which the national bourgeoisie rallied its forces."[56] Stalin claimed that so far these national organisations were so dominated by the bourgeois class that "The right of nations to self-determination was interpreted to mean the right of the national bourgeoisie in the border regions to take power into its own hand and to take advantage of the February Revolution in order to form its "own" national state.[57] But this development did not bring any improvement in the status of the working class of these nationalities. Therefore, the main cause of Revolution remained unfulfilled. The discontents of the workers and peasants remained the same after the change of February Revolution. Therefore, the major task remained yet to be done.

The October Revolution took up that mission as the primary goal. Once the October Revolution took place, according to Stalin, there appeared a qualitative change in the whole system—the Soviet system aimed at establishing a classless society—which in a broader sense, would remove all kinds of class tensions in the society. Tension amongst nationalities was also expected to be removed in the process. But, national movements in the border regions still continued with the same fervour. This, Stalin could not approve of. Now, the same tendency of national self-determination seemed to be detrimental to the workers' interests. For the Soviet government would remain in favour of the proletariat, whereas the national emancipation would lead the respective nationalities towards the establishment of bourgeois-national governments—which would be detrimental to the interests of the working class. He wrote, "Thus the old bourgeois conception of the principle of self-determination, with its slogan", was exposed and cast aside by the very course of the revolution. The socialist conception of self-determination, with its slogan "All power to the toiling masses of the oppressed nationalities,"[58] entered into its own and obtained the opportunity of being applied in practice.

In another writing titled The National Question in Russia[59] written in 1920, Stalin clearly stated his objects in the constitution of national movements often leading to the demand of secession, which according to him would become detrimental to the interests of workers and peasants. He wrote, "The demand for the secession of the border regions from Russia as the form that should be given to the relations between the centre and border regions must be rejected not only because it is contrary to the very basis of establishing an alliance between the centre and the border region."[60] He showed another risk factor in this secession, "Apart from the fact that the secession of the border regions would undermine the revolutionary might of Central Russia, which is stimulating the movement for the emancipation of the West and the East, the seceded border regions themselves would inevitably fall into bondage to international imperialism."[61] Therefore, he felt that the immediate task of the Russian Communist leaders would be to try their heart and soul to remove the mistrust of the people of border regions and emancipate them from the survivals of the "feudal patriarchal yoke;"[62] He further stated, "In brief, we must prove to the masses that Central, proletarian

Russia is defending their interests, and their interests alone; and this must be proved not only by repressive measures against the ealizedi and the bourgeois nationalists, measures that are frequently incomprehensive to the masses, but primarily by a consistent and well-conceived economic policy."[63] The need to keep the border regions for the security of Mainland Russia became quite apparent from Stalin's attitude from this time onwards. Though he wanted to make the issue appear just the other way round—stressing the disadvantages of the border republics if they left USSR. But the actual fear was of Russian security. Therefore the need to convince these national provinces of their advantages within USSR was harped upon.

For practical policy building in this region, regional autonomy was planned—which in Stalin's version was the "most real and concrete way of uniting the border regions to Central Russia."[64] This regional autonomy had a larger scope than cultural autonomy proposed by the Austro-Marxists. The Soviet autonomy implied the development of cultural and material prosperity of the masses of the regions concerned which would include the foundation of their native schools, courts, administration and government bodies recruited principally from local people. This process of Soviet autonomy would ultimately lead to the goal of "Sovietisation"[65] bore a tacit implication of centralisation or enforced change in a specific direction. And this change under the guidance of Central Russian authority—even though under socialist banner—created a possibility of 'Russification' with a changed new garb of 'Sovietisation.'

To deal with further practical problems regarding the practice of Soviet autonomy, Stalin stated, "One serious obstacle to the realisation of Soviet autonomy is the acute shortage of intellectual forces of local origin in the border regions, the shortage of instructors in every branch of Soviet and party work without exception."[66] Here Stalin openly admitted the fact that to bring this ealizediv of Soviet autonomy the regional intellectuals' involvement was extremely needed—but, mostly that were not very strong—for they were few in number and most of them was non-communists. Thus the Soviet system was trying to convert a vast region of varied nationalities of whom the masses were still unaware, and the intellectuals non-believers in Communism. Still, attempts continued on part of the Soviet government to motivate the masses of the border regions towards a higher degree of proletarian material and spiritual culture without going into clashes with their national features and social practices.

The multi-national states under bourgeois domination could not overcome the evils of national oppression in the sphere of economic exploitation—inspite of state protection for national minorities implying preservation of private property and class inequality, the process ended in different layers of complexities. In contrast to that, the Soviet system was aiming at collective property. Stalin, therefore, felt that the capitalist system, because of private property and capital, disunites people, inflames national enmity and national oppression. Whereas, the collective property and labour under the Soviet system would draw people closer and remove national oppression and national rivalries. So he wrote, "Here, the triumph of the Soviet, and the establishment of the dictatorship of the proletariat is a basic condition for the abolition of oppression, the institution of national equality and the guarantee of the rights of national minorities."[67] But in the same essay, Stalin warned about the possibility of an unconscious tendency of growth of Great Russian Chauvinism or deviation towards dominant-nation spirit. According to him, the Russian communists, who never faced national oppression, might not be genuinely concerned about the national sentiments of the border regions and might unconsciously overpower the party policies. On the contrary, Stalin also warned that the communists of the oppressed nationalities might as well exaggerate the importance of national identities in Party Work putting the interests of the toiling masses into the background. As a result, "This circumstance in its turn leads to a deviation from communism towards bourgeois-democratic nationalism, which at times assumes the forms of Pan-Islamism and Pan-Turkism (in the East)."[68] Both these deviations were harmful for the development of immature Soviet Socialism—the Great Russian chauvinism would lead to a colonising tendency, whereas, over-concern for national identity by the intellectuals of the border regions might undermine the urge of proletarian unity and lead to the reappearance of bourgeois domination in these regions. Therefore, Stalin warned his party about the possible entry of petty bourgeois intellectuals. Thus, so far Stalin's attitude was not completely one-sided, there was the presence of some self-criticism regarding Soviet policy making and practice. But in his *report on the Immediate Tasks of the Party in Connection with the National Problem*[69], delivered at the 10th Congress of the Russian Communist Party, March 10, 1921, he made a specific periodisation in the national problem—when Soviet phase appeared as the era of optimism and the only possible phase of national emancipation and proletarian victory together with this showed a new kind of self-confidence and self-appraisal—was now found in his writings. Another noteworthy development was that so long the national issues were regarded as a national question, but now he blatantly depicted it as a 'problem'. The three stages of the development of nations and nationalities were as follows:

1. The first period—marked by the appearance of nationalities with the rise of capitalism in Western Europe and their domination over the multi-national states of the East—leading to national oppression in the form of imperialism and colonialism.
2. The second phase started with the awakening of the oppressed nations against their national oppressors. This period saw a lot of clashes throughout the world between the oppressors and the oppressed nations and creation of many new nation-states.

3. The third period began with the Soviet experiments—which started by the destruction of capitalism and the abolition of national oppression as prerequisites. But at the same time, Stalin admitted that the inequality between the Russian and non-Russian nationalities which was inherited as a result of different historical experience for years would remain for the time being and could not be removed at once.

In fact, Stalin's attitude from this phase was not accepted uncritically within the CPSU itself. In fact the years from 1921 to 1924, the last 3 years of Lenin showed a severe tension between these two leaders over several issues—where the nationality question was one of the most latent. Problems surfaced in Georgia and Ukraine during this time where taking advantage of Lenin's ill health Stalin moved forward to suppress all nationalist aspirations of these republics and cornered Trotsky who wanted to provide a more democratic alternative to the republics.[70] From this time onwards Stalin began to develop a distinct policy of his own where the maintenance of the Union became the only aim and the later writings of Stalin kept on harping the points of advantages for the nationalities if they remain within the USSR. His great Russian chauvinism, became prominent from this stage.

In his writings Stalin now claimed, "History shows that the only way to abolish national inequality, the only way to establish a regime of fraternal collaboration among the toiling masses of the oppressed and unoppressed peoples is to abolish capitalism and establish a Soviet system."[71] But he did not provide a proper guideline as to how to recover the inequalities between the centre and the border zones already inherited from the feudal and capitalist past experiences.

Although, he generally spoke about the obligation to put an end to that backwardness (economic, political and cultural) bringing equality, this aspect never received priority in the Soviet system. Stalin himself admitted that this kind of backwardness led to the development of dominant nation chauvinism on the part of Russian leaders at times. But he stressed more on the chances of 'deviation' on part of the native communists of the border regions who often confused their class interests with national interests and had expression in some movements of 'Pan-Turkism', 'Pan-Islamism' in the East. Thus, it was evident, that Stalin had been well aware of the forces of nationalism in these regions and also knew their causes of discontent and even the evil impact of Great Russian chauvinism—yet he found the Soviet system to be the best of all experiments to remove all such tensions between centre and the border, in an unprecedented way. The complexities resultant were always underestimated in spite of the awareness of their presence—this naturally intensified the feeling of alienation, rather than drawing the different people closer to the Russians.

In the same essay, he even more forecefully stated, "Obviously, the only regime capable of solving the national problem, that is, of creating conditions which make possible the peaceful coexistence and fraternal collaboration of various peoples and tribes, is the regime of the Soviet government, the regime of the dictatorship of the proletariat."[72]

In 1922, Stalin wrote a very important report on *The Amalgamation of the Soviet Republics*.[73] By the process of amalgamation, the temporary contractual relations between RSFSR, and the border regions were made permanent. "The initiative was taken by the Azerbaidjanian, Armenian and Georgian Republics, which were later joined by Ukrainian and Byelorussian Republics."[74] This was a move towards a closer union, a single federal body with a Central Executive Committee was made up of four republics, namely, the RSFSR, as an integral federal unit, the Transcaucasian Republics, and also Byelorussia. Two independent Soviet republics, Khorezm and Bokhara, which were still not socialist republics, but people's Soviet republics, for the time being remained outside the union for they were not 'socialist'—according to Stalin. Stalin also hoped that, "...these republics, as they internally developed towards socialism, will also come to form part of the federal state which is now being constituted."[75]

The reasons behind such urges for closer union were mainly practical difficulties. The legacy of the Tsarist economy and communication indirectly had put a pressure on the border zones to come closer for their own interests—it was impossible to become economically independent. For example, the south and eastern zone supplied the raw materials like cotton, etc. and north supplied the finished textile products to these areas—this kind of economic distribution could not be changed and made self-sufficient in each zone—for practical constraints. The republics, also wanted to come closer to get the effect of combined financial strength. Again, there remained the fear of external attack from the capitalist world. To combat that external menace, the united strong front was needed. But once they joined the new union, the Republics had become much more dependent on the Central Executive Committee of the USSR—controlled from RSFSR. The classes which finalised this new arrangement of amalgamation implied obvious reduction in the practice of autonomy in the regional sphere.

In April, 1923, Stalin delivered a speech on the National factors in party and state development where he intended to show the change of perspective in this sphere which occurred as a natural result of the New Economic Policy. The NEP, because it encouraged some kind of autonomy, encouraged some kind of self-assertion in the internal life of Russia as well as that of the border regions. Stalin claimed that as a result of this, Great Russian Chauvinism developed and penetrated the party, the administration and the other parts of the federation. Resultantly, that induced the development of local varieties of Chauvinism—in Georgia, Azerbaidjan, Bokhara and Turkestan, etc. The successful way to curb the regional Chauvinism was to establish a relation of faith between the proletariat of the leading nation (Russia) and the backward peasantry of the border nations—who shared a long experience of being the oppressor and the oppressed nations, respectively, during the tsarist regime.

He wrote, "And in order that the Soviet government should become dear also to the peasantry of other nationalities, it must be comprehensible to this peasantry, it must function in their own language; the schools and government bodies must be recruited from among the local people acquainted with the language manners, customs and traditions."[76] Thus, the extinction of all national chauvinism and all kinds of national alienations laid in a very practical solution of providing equal opportunities to all—especially involving the native peoples in the regional Soviets in economic, military and political spheres. Although, Stalin openly admitted that there were factors forwarding and hindering this process of amalgamation the favourable factors according to him were the new Soviet economy, which intended an all-round development instead of lopsided growth of the previous era. The hindering factors were Great Russian Chauvinism. The second important factor was the inequity between nationalities and regions which was inherited by the USSR from the previous system. The third hindrance were the national chauvinism of the non-Russian republics. Although, Stalin admitted that the chauvinism of the latter type mostly resulted as a reaction to Great Russian Chauvinism but feared their potential to convert themselves into aggressive nationalism—where the question of cooperation and amalgamation would become impossible. Both Chauvinisms should be combated as "two aspects of one phenomenon"[77] according to Stalin. Another important point which Stalin raised here was about the amount of independence left to the regions after a successful amalgamation. He openly accepted that some of the independence would have to be sacrificed in the process but all the regions would have the right to become independent by coming out of the amalgamation which he thought to be the ultimate of independence, provided by a federal system to its republics. But that independence was an ultimate and negative kind of a right which would usually seem difficult, often impossible for republics to use. To put it in a different way, this might imply a threat, that too much claim of independence would lead to a break off from the union which might be detrimental to the practical interests of regions who had just started their development in socio-economic sphere under the banner of socialism.

In June 1923, Stalin made a very crucial speech,[78] whereby, he wanted to specify the clear-cut division of 'left' and 'rights' in the republics and showed his disapproval to a particular leader's activity as deviationist from the principle of Marxist socialism. The leader was Sultan Galiev of Central Asia whom Stalin purged from the party for deviationist tendency and collaboration with the right wing nationalists. Stalin explained in the initial part of his speech as to why he suddenly turned his back towards Galiev, whom he used to defend earlier as a potential leader to develop Soviet socialist platform in his native land. Several recent letters of Galiev had been found just before this meeting, which showed his inclination to join the *Basmachi* movement rising in Central Asia at that time.[79] Stalin openly stated his mistrust with Galiev when he said, "As far back as the beginning of 1919 the "Left" comrades reproached me with supporting Sultan Galiev, with trying to save him for the party, with sparing him in the hope that he would cease to be nationalist and become a Marxist[80]. This speech is actually a typical device of Stalin. He now portrays Sultan Galiev as a deviationist. The benign Stalin had "Spared" Lenin in the hope "that he would cease to be nationalist" at the last few years of Lenin, taking advantage of Lenin's illness. This statement made it clear that Galiev was never a convinced Marxist, rather nationalist whom the Bolshevik party cadets were trying to convert into a Marxist. The reason for such attempt was also explained by Stalin as quite self-realised. "There are so few intellectuals, so few thinking people, even so few literate people generally in the Eastern republics and regions that one can count them on one's fingers...It would be criminal not to value every measure to save from corruption people of the East whom we need and to preserve them for the party."[81] Thus, Stalin, who theoretically fought so strongly against Great Russian Chauvinism silently became a prey of it himself. He never recognised the fact that this over-concerned guardianship on part of the Central Party authorities was nothing but imposition of Great Russian Chauvinism on provinces where people were rather more concerned about their national goal than socialist goal. Initially, men like Galiev joined the Bolshevik movement to overthrow the Tsarist yoke from their native land. But after independence, they found it uneasy to carry on under the same banner for Bolshevik party ceased to give equal emphasis on the national question any longer. Thus, the incompatibility of their native interests and the interests of the Bolshevik party and the Soviet system became clear to these leaders like Sultan Galiev. And Galiev began to turn towards the leaders of the internal nationalist movements which the Soviet leaders called secessionist movements like *Basmachi*. Once exposed, Stalin decided to breach all terms with him. "But there is a limit to everything. And the limit in this case was reached when Sultan-Galiev passed from the camp of the Communists to the Party.[82]

Then he also countered the positions taken by Khodzhamov and Ikramov both of whom said that there was no difference between the Tsarist Turkestan and the Soviet Turkestan other than the change of the banner. In answer Stalin stated, "If Turkestan is really a colony, as it was under Tsarism, then the *Basmachi* are right, and it is not we who should be trying Sultan Galiev, but Sultan-Galiev who should be trying us for tolerating the existence of a colony under the Soviet government. But he also accepted the fact that, "...We were not always attentive and did not always succeed in raising in time the practical questions dictated by conditions in the Eastern republics and regions."[83] But he was not at all repentant in his attitude for this inattentiveness on part of the Central Committee. Rather a tone of fait accompli emerged from the same paragraph. An honest confession of the impossibility of raising the standard of culture of these backward zones within a short time was made. Thereby, Stalin was falling prey to a kind of orientalist and colonial discourse. The irreconcilable distance between West and the East was surfacing with a strong sense of arrogance on behalf of the western civilisation. He made a distorted citation of Lenin to justify his position as Stalin stated "Lenin is always crying that we have no culture yet, that there is no possibility of raising Russian culture appreciably in two or three, or even ten years."[84] And then he further proceeded to add, "And if it is impossible to raise Russian culture in two or three, or even ten years, how can we demand a rapid rise in culture in the non-Russian, backward, semi-literate region?"[85] But Lenin actually spoke of a culture acceptable to socialist paradigm, which he thought was yet to be found even in Russian culture.

Thus, most of the drawbacks were cited in the circumstances and the responsibilities on the part of the party and the Soviet government was subtly avoided. Rather the main problem was cited in the ideological incompatibility of Marxism and nationalism. Moreover, the nationalism of border lands became a topic of worry. But the use of the term border region itself indicated a normative judgement. The use of the term 'border' implied that Russia was the core. However, any kind of nationalism seemed unimportant from this time onwards. The need for ealizedive two incompatible ideologies come to an end as the Soviet authorities could firmly establish their stronghold over these vast non-Russian territories. Now nationalism, the most thriving issue for the natives of these regions was to be disregarded for the fear of deviation. Stalin was quite open in his statement about this, "It should be borne in mind that our Communist organisations in the border districts, in the republics and regions, can develop and firmly establish themselves, can become genuine internationalists, Marxist cadres, only if they get rid of their nationalism. Nationalism is the chief ideological obstacle to the training of Marxist cadres, of a Marxist vanguard in the border regions and republics."[86] Thus, once imperialism was won over, now nationalism became the foremost ideological hindrance to Marxism. This showed an ideological shift of position of Stalin himself, as well as the party for nowhere before any of the Bolshevik leaders spoke in such blatant terms against nationalism as an ideology. Actually, this was the time when Lenin had fallen ill and the real power everywhere was being taken over by Stalin. Although he still kept on quoting Lenin, yet the intonation began to change drastically—a distinct growth of Great Russian Chauvinism could be sensed in his writings on nationalities.

Writings in 1924, April, Stalin tried to sum up Lenin's view on nationalities issue, where he tried to show how far Lenin allowed the growth of nationalism and in which context, and also highlighted from which point it became difficult to accommodate nationalism within the framework of Marxism. There the task of educating the workers in the spirit of internationalism came up. For internationalism, Lenin stressed both on the people of greater nations and smaller nations to come out of their nationalist parochialism and move towards socialism. Subordination of particular interest for the greater goal of amalgamation of all nations was prescribed by Lenin which was highlighted by Stalin in his writings.

In a completely different kind of address in 1925 Stalin came up with some more interesting thoughts in this regard. It was his speech delivered at a meeting of students of the University of the East—the speech entitled *The Tasks of the University of the People of The East.*[87] Here the task of the university students to train themselves up as successful communist cadres was stated at the very beginning. Then he ealizedi because of his seldom visit to the region although admitting the fact that these were the regions which needed more visits. Thus, he now showed serious interest in inculcating socialist, internationalist thinking among the students of various regions with different nationalities staying and studying together in one ealizediv.

Stalin stated, "This university embraces representatives of not less than fifty nationalities and ethnic groups of the East...The point is that among the students of the university there are two main groups representing two series of absolutely distinct conditions of developments. The first group is composed of people who came to us from the Soviet East, from lands where the rule of the bourgeoisie no longer exists, where the yoke of imperialism has been overthrown and where the workers are in power. The second group of students is composed of people who have come to us from colonial and dependent countries from countries, where the oppression of imperialism has preserved all its severity, and where independence has still to be won by driving out the imperialists."[88] He further continued as to why this university had one foot in Soviet soil and the other on the colonies and dependent countries. Hence the task of the university became two fold, one was to train the cadres in the Soviet East to carry on their needs, the other was to train cadres to fight imperialism in the colonies in revolutionary spirit. The process of improving the conditions of the people of the Soviet East was provided in a list which consisted of attempts to create more centres of interactions between the workers and peasants, to improve agriculture faster, to improve and advance cooperative organisations to bring the Soviets into closer touch with the masses and to develop national culture. But by national culture, Stalin permitted only that culture, which would not become incompatible with the proletarian culture ascribed by Lenin (in Stalin's opinion) and followed by the Soviet system. Stalin explained, "But it is also true that proletarian culture, which is socialist in context, assumes different forms and modes of expression among the various peoples that have been drawn into the work of socialist construction, depending on differences of language, customs and so forth. Proletarian in content and national in form—such is the universal human culture towards which socialism is marching. National culture, on the other hand, does not cancel proletarian culture, but lends it form. The demand for national culture was a bourgeois demand as long as the bourgeoisie was in power and the consolidation of nations proceeded under the aegis of the bourgeois system. The demand for national culture became a proletarian demand when the proletariat came into power and the consolidation of nations began to proceed under the aegis of Soviet govt."[89] So, the national culture, which did not go against the interests of the proletariat was approved as true national culture, namely, increased attention to the growth of various national languages, highlighting of some obscure nationalities, unknown and not recognised so long. But at the same time, Stalin warned the students of the East of possible deviations. One was the tendency of over-simplification whereby there might be wrong attempts of transplanting the same method of economic development which were successful in the centre of Soviet Union but which would be absolutely inapplicable to the border regions. The situations in these two areas being different, they demanded different treatment—one model could not be applicable to the other because of contextual variation.

The other deviation was excessive stress on local peculiarities. Here he mentioned two types of dangers in this kind of tendency—one was that the aspect of concrete material development which would become secondary for the primacy of national independence. Secondly, this kind of national design might be self-defeating for these border regions for this tendency might lead up to the desire of territorial expansion hampering each other's borderlands. The result would be favourable only for the bourgeois nationalists—opposed to the interests of the innocent toiling mass of the region.

Thus, the issue of national culture ought to be handled carefully—as long as it served socialism, it was welcome, but the moment it crossed that limit, it was despised as a vice or deviation.

Then came up an essay entitled *Deviation on the National Question*[90] in 1930 which was a criticism of both the Great Russian Chauvinism and the local national chauvinism. The former was trying to expand full scale throughout USSR at the cost of the removal of other national cultures and in the name of socialism. One national culture and one national language began to be highlighted and obviously that fortunate language and culture was Russian. Local nationalists, on the other hand began to show tendencies to isolate themselves in order to resist Great-Russian Chauvinism. Thus they began to distance themselves from the process of general socialist developments. The gravest danger in local nationalism in Stalin's eye, was the possible growth of bourgeois nationalism in border regions. Thus he was aware of the dangers in both ways. But from these rising questions one thing became very evident, that the national question, which they thought to be a phenomenon of a passing phase, was not that easy to be resolved. People in general are proved to be more touchy and more involved in the issues of national identities which complicated the political scenario. In fact, Stalin repeatedly spoke of two types of deviations. One could see that for the deviation in border level there were serious threats, and even punishments (Sultan Galiev's case) for becoming enemies of socialism. But although he criticised Great-Russian Chauvinism openly there were no clear-cut indication as to how to control this attitude. In fact, with time, condemnation of Great Russian chauvinism was even reduced. And also, it was never mentioned that the Great Russian Chauvinism might lead up to a qualitative deviation where Soviet system would become a new form of colonisation under the Russians. In another writing on the same theme *Deviations Towards Nationalism*,[91] written in January, 1934, Stalin came up with an even sharper opinion against any kind of national chauvinism. In fact, the novelty of this essay was that here he openly regarded the over emphasis on nationalism to be a move for capitalist design. As he wrote, "It should be observed that the survivals for capitalism in people's minds are much more tenacious in the sphere of the national problem than in any other sphere. They are more tenacious because they are able to disguise themselves well in national costume."[92] Thus when it was found that nationalism was still quite a powerful phenomenon in human minds, even after their experience under Socialist experiment for quite a few years," (In fact, bureaucratic dictatorship inevitably sharpened nationalism) nationalism as an independent ideology did not receive a careful rethinking. Rather, it was still taken to be a manifestation of capitalist trend, sublime in human mind. This, not only implied a kind of inflexibility in Stalin's thought, but also an indirect design to denounce and suppress the national demand as capitalist deviations. Any opposition was denounced as capitalist restoration or conspiracy, therefore punishable even by execution. The instance of Ukraine as a deviationist region had been highlighted by Stalin. But he wrote that Ukraine's case was not the only one in the contemporary USSR. "The fall of Skrypnik and his group in the Ukraine is not an exception. Similar "dislocations" are observed among certain comrades in other national republics as well."[93] The greatest danger in such deviations were not the deviation itself, but attitude of the Soviet authority to let it grow. He wrote, "In the Ukraine, only very recently, the deviation towards Ukrainian nationalism did not represent the major danger; but when we ceased to fight it and allow it to grow to such an extent that it merged with the internationalists, this deviation became the major danger."[94] In the same article, to answer the controversy as to which deviation represented a major danger: the Great-Russian Chauvinism or local nationalism, Stalin carefully stated, "It would be absurd to attempt to give ready made recipes suitable for all times and for all conditions as the major danger is the deviation against which we have ceased fight thereby allowing it to grow into a danger to the state."[95] But from a general understanding it became obvious that as Great Russian Chauvinism would not have a secessionist tendency, the danger in its practice would never be as dangerous as the cases of desperate local nationalism—therefore, indirectly the danger was located in the local national chauvinism. Stalin carefully made it clear that the policy of toleration in such cases would be ended and any such demand ought to be crushed by force. So by the 1930s, forced unity became the clear-cut policy to attain the goal of socialism. Thus, there was only lip service against Great Russian Chauvinism throughout Stalin's writings to bring an apparent look of impartiality. But his opinion against local deviation grew steadily harder until he could justify the use of state force against such developments.

In a different kind of address in the same year Stalin stressed on the mutual friendship among the peoples of the USSR. It was his speech delivered at a conference of Foremost Collective Farmers of

Tajikistan and Turkmenistan in December, 1935. Of course, the speech started with a wish that the farmers would be successful in their cotton yield. He commented, "Consequently, you will make a success of cotton, and a prosperous life is opening up."[96] Thus, the condition of their own improvement would be the direct result of their own toil.

But then he switched on to the broader perspective of friendship among the peoples of the State, "The present conference, your speeches, your actions, go to show that the friendship among the peoples of our great country is growing stronger. That is a very important and noteworthy fact, comrades."[97] And then, in a too simplistic way he stated that days of inequity and oppression were buried with the end of Tsarism and the beginning of Soviet rule. The new 'Bolshevik policy' claimed friendship and brotherhood throughout the country. He also stated with confidence. "The present conference is a vivid proof of the fact that the former mistrust among the peoples of the USSR has long ago been laid to rest, that mistrust has been replaced by complete and mutual trust, that the friendship among the peoples of the USSR is growing and gaining strength. That, comrades, is the most precious thing that the Bolshevik national policy has given us."[98] Here, interestingly, no mention of deviation is found. That implies, all discussions regarding these complexities and problems used to be discussed only at the party level—not to the general mass—specially to a people to whom that could have been a touchy issue.

In a speech at the Extraordinary 8th Congress of the Soviets of the USSR, in November, 1936, Stalin applauded the success of the Soviet constitution for maintaining successfully the multi-national state of a new model, Stalin with extreme confidence stated that the constitution adopted in 1924, had run for a period ".... Long enough to test the experiment"[99] and then added, "This period has shown beyond a doubt that the experiment of forming a multinational state based on socialism has been completely successful."[100] Thus in spite of the presence of serious problems in local level and also in the attitude of the Russian chauvinists, over all national policy of the Bolshevik government was considered successful. And whoever in whatever form wanted to counter this, used to be suppressed as deviationist and an agent of capitalism—thus the enemy of the state.

Thus, under Stalin, nationalism received such a narrow theoretical treatment, that the Leninist ideal of national self-determination simply withered away. Although Stalin provided regular reference to Lenin while writing on nationalism, he never used this aspect anymore after the Leninist era—neither the right of the border nations to leave the federation was highlighted in his later writings. Rather a negation of all strong nationalist demands as deviations and survivals of capitalist designs could be repeatedly found. Their suppression was taken to be a foremost duty to the State. Given this solution, the national question in general seemed to be resolved by the Soviet policy. Therefore, the self-rightous claim of Stalin "As a result we now have a fully formed multi-national socialist state, which has stood all tests, and where stability might well be envied by any national state in any part of the world[101] did not apparently seem self-contradictory.

Nikita S. Khrushchev and the Soviet Nationalities Policy

With Khrushchev, started the 'post-Stalin era in the Soviet history and there were important changes in the policy-making of the Communist Party of the Soviet Union (CPSU). De-Stalinization was started as a conscious process to safeguard the Soviet system and a new tendency to open up towards outer world began. Therefore, Khrushchev was rather preoccupied with explanation of Soviet Foreign Policies on different occasions. Internally, his speeches concentrated on production, inner-party democracy, ideology and so on. Nationalities question inside the USSR, somehow, did not receive his serious attention. But, interestingly, while deciding the position of USSR in world politics, he vehemently opposed colonialism and imperialism. He openly announced his support to nat:onalities who were still fighting against colonial oppression. There were a host of writings on this theme, for example: "They Are Using Force To Keep Countries In Bondage", "Every Assistance To The Struggle For National Independence," "The "Civilisation of Robbers", "The USSR—A Dependable Shield For The Newly Free Peoples", "The Alternative Confronting The Newly Free Peoples", "Socialism and Capitalism"[102] and so on. All these implied Khrushchev's support for nationalities still suffering under colonial yoke. For those who could come out of it or were strugglIng to come out received Soviet support, not only lip service—but also some material aids. Along with this support was related the indirect propaganda of the Soviet socialist system as a model for those newly independent countries.

In this context, Khrushchev stated, "A man longing for freedom and independence, and especially a nation's longing, cannot be killed ... It is not only in words, but in deeds as well, that we side with those who fight for their independence."[103] Again, in another speech, he called the liberation movements against colonialism a 'revolutionary' war. "There will be liberation wars as long as imperialism exists, as long as colonialists exist. Wars of this kind are revolutionary wars. Such wars are not only admissible, but inevitable, for the colonialists do not freely bestow independence on the peoples."[104] Thus, he showed full sympathy to the national aspirations in the pre-independence stage—following the Marxist-Leninist principles. Thus, again, Khrushchev attempted to create a space for socialism in international politics. He made the Soviet power appear as part of a broader movement for peace and progress as he stated, "Marxist-Leninists are striving to unite and consolidate the unity of all the forces opposed to imperialism: the world socialist system, the international working class, the national liberation movement and the broad democratic movement of the masses for peace and progress."[105] But, strangely enough, Khrushchev never even put the example of Soviet experiment of nationality policy as an attempted success. Rather, while dealing with the ideological activities of the party, to strengthen the system he made a passing reference to Great Russian Chauvinism and local nationalities as two hard obstacles yet to be removed from the road to success. Of course, these two evils, according to him were nothing but remnants of capitalism, overburdening the socialist developments. He stated, "At the present stage of communist construction a still more vigorous struggle must be waged against such survivals of capitalism as indolence, parasitism, drunkenness and rowdyism, swindling and money-grabbing, against recurrences of dominant—nation chauvinism and local nationalism, against bureaucratic methods, a wrong attitude towards women, etc. These were needs that should have no place in our fields."[106]

Thus, the problems of Great Russian Chauvinism or local nationalism had come to the category of such evils like drunkenness, indolence, rowdyism, etc. This implied that the role of an ideology, however disapprovable that might be, was completely ignored in Khrushchev's thought. The relative importance of the issue thus suffered under the new leadership.

L.I. Brezhnev and the Soviet Policy on Nationalism

From the Stalinist era the nationality question and the demands of autonomy had begun to be suppressed by subverting the theory of national self-determination of Lenin, although, a formal recognition of the Leninist theory could be seen in Stalin's writings. But, till then, it was a serious issue for which Stalin devoted a number of writings and engaged himself in quite a few political debates in the party level.

Coming to the Brezhnev era, one can feel a marked difference in the attitude. Stalin was at least worried about the nationality question and wanted to resolve them in any possible means. Brezhnev era, on the contrary, showed a sigh of relief as if the problems regarding this complex issue had come to an end. And that also happened not by any conscious policy, but by the natural development of socialism to a higher stage. Therefore, in all the writings and speeches of Brezhnev, nation-nationality and nationalism occurred as an issue which had long been settled and could, therefore, be regarded as one of the greatest achievements of the Soviet socialism. There were occasions where Brezhnev mentioned the nationalities of the non-Russian provinces, as an integral part of the Soviet system. In Brezhnev's observation, the Soviet socialism had by then reached a level where there were complete equality and fraternity amongst the Soviet people and the regional variations and national identities got subsided in the greater identity of 'Soviet people'. This attitude of Brezhnev era implied two things, one was that the complexities and telling demands of economy and foreign policy forced the Soviet government to ignore such issues as nationalities which for the time being did not pose any immediate threat to the system. Another was that, once the focus was shifted from an issue with pretence that it was no more an issue, that implied that the authority from this time onwards, consciously ignored the expectations, demands and sentiments of a huge number of non-Russian population and took them for granted. This attitude was most prominent in Brezhnev's speeches and writings.

"A new historical community, the Soviet people, has taken shape in our country"[107] stated Brezhnev. He also stated the process as to how this community could emerge—"New realised relations, relations of friendship and cooperation, have taken shape between classes and social groups, nations and nationalities, during the years of socialist construction, in joint labour, in the struggle for socialism, and in the battle fought in its defence. All the nations of the Soviet Union demonstrate this monolithic unity by their labour and by their approval of the policy of the Communist Party of the Soviet Union."[108] In the same context, Brezhnev stressed the fact of voluntary drawing together leading to the closer contacts of nationalities without dissolving their national distinctions. L.I. Brezhnev explained, "The Soviet people's social and political unity does not at all imply the disappearance of national distinctions. Thanks to the consistent pursuance of the Leninist nationalities policy, we have, simultaneously with the construction of socialism, successfully solved the nationalities question, for the first time in history. The friendship of the Soviet peoples is indissoluble, and in the process of building communism they are steadily drawing ever closer together and are being mutually enriched in their spiritual life. But, we would be taking a dangerous path if we were artificially to step up this objective process of national integration."[109]

In this way, providing due lip service to Lenin and his ideals, Brezhnev wanted to keep an image of continuity in the Soviet nationality policy. Moreover, although stressing the ever-growing proximity of nationalities, he accepted the presence of national distinctions without hampering the process of integration. Taken verbally, this implied an ideal situation. But, from critical stand point, this statement showed a kind of reluctance to drag the issue any farther. Rather, he preferred to remain satisfied with what had been achieved in the normal course of development and leave the rest to the unknown future. The picture of harmony and friendship was depicted more as a propaganda than a real statement—for had such a solidarity been really achieved, it would not have got dissolved within two decades. By this time, maintenance of one's national distinction, actually meant the maintenance of national languages, traditions and cultures and develop them further. However, the question of parity in economy and political affairs never appeared in the context of nationalities. The question of political and economic equality with mainland Russia was never mentioned while discussing the national issue, for there still remained huge disparity in economic output and development as well as in political participation between the republics of the USSR.

Therefore, the satisfaction of equality and development of the nationalities should be drawn from their development in languages and cultural distinctions—rather than from the experience of equality in real life. That is why whenever there were references to the backward provinces and their relative development under the Soviet system, the stress was always on, how far they could progress from the pre-Soviet stage. It was never mentioned openly still how much these regions lagged behind the standard of mainland Russia. As he said, "Let us recall for a moment the state of the outlying national areas of the country at the time of the Revolution. In economic development, Central Asia and Kazakhstan were at a level quite usual for colonial countries. Poverty, disease and ignorance were the lot of the bulk of the population. Suffice it to say that even in the early 1920s from 90 to 96 per cent of the people in the Central Asian Republics and 82 per cent in Kazakhstan could neither read nor write. The social structure of society was essentially a feudal one."[110] In the same speech, he also stated, "Look at Central Asia and Kazakhstan today! You will find not only first-class cotton fields in Uzbekistan and Turkmenia, the once fallow lands of Kazakhs under crop, flowering orchards and new cattle-breeding farms in Kirghizia and Tajikistan. Today, these Republics are formed of a host of big, modern, beautiful cities, like Tashkent, Alma-Ata, Dushanbe, Frunze and Ashkabad." He also added, "Since the formation of the Union, Kazakhstan's industrial output has increased 600-fold, Tajikistan's over 500-fold, Kirgizia's over 400-fold, Uzbekistan's about 240-fold and Turkmenia's over 130-fold."[111] Regarding cultural affairs, he stated, "The results of cultural development in Kazakhstan and the Central Asian Republics are equally striking. They have achieved virtually 100 per cent literacy. Almost one-half the population in each Republic are men and women with a higher or secondary (complete or incomplete) education. In Uzbekistan alone, there are now more specialists with a higher or secondary special education than the Soviet Union had working in its economy in the late 1920s. Modern science has been firmly established in these Republics: in their national academics there are thousands of scientists engaged in fruitful research."[112]

Brezhnev thus kept on giving accounts as to how and how much these provinces could progress and how such progress could resolve the "nationality question" through the Soviet experiment. And everywhere, the progress was measured in terms of their backward, underdeveloped past—the comparison was never between the Russian Federation, especially European Russia and the Central Asia or Transcaucasian Republics.

Another very interesting attitudinal development can be observed in Brezhnev's speeches, that was to highlight the role of Russian people in the development of non-Russian regions. As the non-Russian regions mostly were much backward, in comparison to Russia in the pre-Soviet period, for the development of the former in the socialist direction special assistance to the latter was needed. Here, Brezhnev stated, "Such assistance and readiness to put in a great effort and even, let us plainly say, to make sacrifices so as to overcome the backwardness of the national outskirts and help them to develop at an accelerated pace was bequeathed by Lenin to the proletariat of Russia as a prime internationalist duty. The Russian working class, the Russian working people have fulfilled this duty with honour. This was in effect a great achievement by a whole class, a whole people, performed in the name of internationalism. The heroic exploit will never be forgotten by the peoples of our country."[113]

Here two very interesting attitudinal development can be observed. Firstly, Brezhnev was quite explicit in saying that it was the Russian comrades who took the initiative of improving the standard of non-Russian backward provinces—an attitude that definitely had a kind of big brotherhood feeling in it. The second had percolated from the first, that for bringing betterment to these regions, the peoples of Russia made "sacrifices". If such feelings existed in the mind of the leader himself, it goes without saying that the same attitude of difference and inequity existed in general minds. This claim of conscious contribution to these regions to develop and cope up with a socialist order implied the acceptance of Great Russian Chauvinism in a very simple, matter-of-fact notion in the official level. In fact, it was taken for granted that the contribution of the Russian people in the making of the Soviet system was the most important element to make the experiment a success. As Brezhnev openly stated, "All the nations and nationalities of our country, above all the Great Russian people, played their role in the formation, consolidation and development of this mighty union of equal nations that have taken the road to socialism. The revolutionary energy, dedication, diligence and profound internationalism of the Russian people have quite legitimately won them the sincere respect of all the other peoples of our socialist motherland."[114] This kind of tacit chauvinism, ingrained in the writings of the leadership, probably could highlight the general attitude of the Russian people towards those non-Russian regions whom, Brezhnev thought, the Russians had uplifted with their sacrifice and international feelings. The political hierarchy of the Russian and non-Russian citizens became evident from such speeches which definitely implied a clear deviation from Leninist ideals. But still, the authority continued to provide due lip service to Lenin and his nationality policy and claimed an unbreakable continuity in the policy regarding the issue.

As Brezhnev stated in the same speech, "The party will continue to strengthen the Union of Soviet Socialist Republics, consistently pursuing the Leninist line of promoting the florescence of the socialist nations and securing their gradual drawing together. The Party will continue to educate all the working people in the spirit of socialist internationalism, intolerance of nationalism, chauvinism, national narrowness and conceit in any form, in a spirit of profound respect for all nations and nationalities."[115]

However, at the end of the same speech, he admitted, "...we have successfully dealt with those aspects of the national problem that we inherited from the pre-Revolutionary past. But in a mature socialist society, national relations continue to be a constantly developing reality, which keeps putting forward fresh tasks and problems."[116] Then he continued, in explanation, that national sentiments would be stronger with "politically immature" people and often nationalistic tendencies would become a part of "parochial tendencies" which Brezhnev could not properly approve of. He plainly stated that this kind of attitude might survive without any objective reasons. "These prejudices survive even when the objective premises for any antagonisms in relations between nations have long since ceased to exist."[117] Thus, Brezhnev was no more interested in finding out the real causes behind such local national sensitivity, rather accepted them as a normal attitude of "politically immature" people—whereby the responsibility of the Soviet system could be avoided. Some of the responsibilities for this were located in the foreign encouragement by politicians and propagandists of the "bourgeois world" to create disunity in the Soviet society.[118] But ultimately, Brezhnev did accept that it was not an easy task to find out the most correct way of developing the individual nations and nationalities and the common interests of the Soviet people as a whole. Thus, it was revealed that although, apparently, Brezhnev had claimed that a successful resolution of the nationality question could be achieved under socialist experiment, nevertheless problems still remained which often seemed inexplicable which was explained in terms of immaturity of political consciousness. He also indirectly admitted that it was not objectively easy to serve all the nations' individual interests in the same common tune of Soviet interests. Thus, inadequacies became evident on both sides, on part of the Soviet government. To serve the national interests, as well as on part of the nationalities to forego their local sentiments in the interests of the greater whole.

But, the most interesting attitude noticeable in Brezhnev was his complacency towards such developments. In spite of knowing the presence of these problems, he only preferred to believe, "The further drawing together of the nations and nationalities of our country is an objective process. The party is against pushing the process, there is no need for that, for it is determined by the entire course of our Soviet life."[119]

In 1973, in a speech in Uzbekhistan, Brezhnev stated that the spectacular achievements in Central Asia used to appear like a miracle to the outsiders who had known the region prior to the Bolshevik Revolution. Then he went on to summarise the amount of achievements in each and every field of development. He said, "In the years of socialist construction, the all-round progress of Central Asia became the common concern of the entire Soviet state. The first all-Union projects—Turksib, the great Ferghana Canal, the Tashkent Textile Mills and many others—were built then. Big financial allocations, machines and equipment in short supply, and whole enterprises were shipped to Central Asia from the centre."[120] Thus, once again the same tune of 'sacrifice' on part of the centre for the well-being of the 'borders' could be found. In the same speech he mentioned as to how much Uzbekistan could achieve in education, agriculture, industry, science, emancipation of women and so on. But behind this overall assessment came out sublime intention to increase the amount of cotton output and stress on work discipline. Thus covered by the gesture of generosity was the instruction for the workforce to be more alert and conscious about their output with which the Soviet system was ultimately concerned.

In a report in 1976 on *The Party's work in the field of ideological education*,[121] Brezhnev mentioned various issues where ideological education was needed and was to be continued. Most astonishingly, the aspects of nationalities and that of secularism were not even mentioned in the list. This implied, as to how the Soviet system lost interest in these issues and ignored them in the mainstream propaganda.

Brezhnev's speeches from 1977 onwards were overtly concerned with the new constitution, its various new facets and the explanation for its introduction. In answering, "Why has it become necessary to draw up a new constitution?"[122] Brezhnev stated that there were huge changes in the Soviet economy, society and general life of the country which demanded a thorough revision of the 1936 constitution. In this context he stated, "Underlying all these changes is the growing social homogeneity of Soviet society. The firm alliance of the working class, the collective farmers and people's intelligentsia has become still stronger. Distinctions between the main social groups are being gradually erased. The very onward march of life brings all nations and national groups of this country even closer together. A new historical community, that of the Soviet people, has emerged."[123] In spite of this verbal declaration about the rise of a new historical community drawn out of different nationalities, he did not support the move for doing away with the federal system by a unicameral Supreme Soviet. This implied a kind of ealizedi in any further attempt of increasing central authority over the autonomous republics. However, Brezhnev had formulated his arguments in this issue as: "A new historical community—the Soviet people—has, as we know, taken shape in the USSR. Some comrades—it is true, they are not many—have drawn incorrect conclusions from this. They propose introducing in the constitution, the concept of an integral Soviet nation, eliminating the Union and Autonomous Republics or drastically curtailing the sovereignty of the Union Republics, depriving them of the right to secede from the USSR and of the right to maintain external relations. The proposal to do away with the Soviet Nationalities and to set up a unicameral Supreme Soviet is along the same lines. I think that the erroneousness of the proposals is quite clear. The Soviet people's social and political unity does not at all imply the disappearance of national distinctions. Thanks to the consistent pursuance of the Leninist nationalities policy, we have, simultaneously with the building of socialism, successfully solved the nationalities question, for the first time in history. The friendship of the Soviet peoples is indissoluble, and in the process of building communism they are steadily drawing ever closer together and their spiritual life is being mutually enriched. But we would be taking a dangerous path if we were artificially to step up this objective process of national integration. That is something Lenin persistently warned against, and we shall not depart from his precepts."[124]

Brezhnev was not in support of further centralisation although he admitted the end of national differences in terms of equality. But national inequalities remained very much which the Brezhnev administration disregarded. Brezhnev, apparently preferred the maintenance of autonomy in the non-Russian republics. Again, elsewhere, he openly stated, "The formation of a historically new social and international community—the Soviet people—has become an important symbol of developed socialism in our country, an indicator of the growing homogeneity of Soviet society, the triumph of the nationalities policy of the CPSU. This means that the common features of Soviet people's behaviour, character and world-view, which do not depend on social and national distinctions, are gradually assuming importance in our country."[125] These two statements seem grossly self-contradictory if both are taken in face value. This kind of contradiction of statements actually indicated a kind of confusion regarding the evolution and status of those non-Russian nationalities in the USSR after more than 50 years. Probably, Brezhnev did not pay much attention to the once serious nationalities question any more. The Brezhnev period is considered the period of bureaucratic stabilization. It is not just a question of Brezhnev not paying attention—rather this was a period when the ruling bureaucracy had "solved" the national question within the bureaucratic framework by promoting a layer of non-Russia bureaucrats, assisted by the Russians. At the same time, it was hoped that economic/material benefits would keep the masses silent. This policy was bound to collapse once the economic stagnation became apparent. For the sake of avoiding the issue, the best possible peaceful means was to state that the issue got resolved in course of socialist developments. But any kind of experimental step which might seriously affect the existing system was consciously avoided in the name of providing autonomy to the regions.

M.A. Suslov: An Ideologue of Brezhnev Era

Suslov's Treatment of Nationality Question

During the time of Brezhnev, one person became quite prominent as a theorist and a protagonist of Russian nationalism in the Communist Party who could not ultimately come to power because of his unexpected death in 1982. He was M.A. Suslov, whose death helped Iurii Andropov to reach the ultimate power. The later part of the Brezhnev era saw a marked rise in the phenomenon of Russian nationalism and its practical development through the Russian party. The initial movement of this nationalist party began with the literacy movements by village prose writers or *derevenshchiki*. And most dangerously, a powerful branch of these Russian Nationalists became National Bolsheviks thereby compromising the so-called principles of socialism and communism. And Mikhail Suslov, who was taken to be one of the very orthodox protagonist of socialist ideology, at his later days supported these Nationalist Bolsheviks. As Suslov was quite powerful as a leader, his support to such development realised a great change in the formal position of the Bolshevik party. That the backward nationalities could develop only with the sympathy, support and sacrifice of the Russian people was evident in Suslov's writings as early as in 1967. In a speech on the Great 50th Anniversary of the USSR he wrote, "We know what a low level of economic and cultural development, what poverty and oppression prevailed among the overwhelming majority of the population, for example, in a vast eastern national outskirts of Tsarist Russia, where feudal relations predominated. There was practically no machine industry in these parts at all. Many nationalities, about 25 million people, did not even have their own written language. In the 50 years of Soviet power the formerly backward nations have traversed a path which it would have taken them whole centuries to cover under capitalism. With the brotherly assistance of the Russian and other peoples of the USSR, they have made the leap from medievalism to the present day in an amazingly short time."[126]

The steady growth of this Russian Party implied a change in the attitude of Russian people reflected in these developments. There were definite and energetic responses towards these Russian nationalist themes and sentiments. Suslov probably sensed this growing tendency for he directed such departments in the party as, ideology, agitation and propaganda, science, secondary and tertiary education and foreign sections.[127]

Thus, the growth of Russian Party must be the manifestation of Great Russian Chauvinism in one form. And the popular support for such revival of nationalistic sentiments showed that the nationality question was not resolved in the course of socialist development. And if the feeling of national attachment and revival was so strong in one faction of the Russians, the most developed and the most prominent ethnic nation inside the USSR—then it becomes evident that the local nationalism would be equally or more sensitive by this time.

Interestingly, this Russian Party was very close to Christian sentiments as well.[128] This Russian party as such was numerically not a very strong group—but its composition was remarkable as it contained mainly dissatisfied intellectuals, writers, artists, painters, etc. These people, with their power of independent thought began to realise the artificiality of the Soviet values. They, through a cultural movement, began to show a nostalgia for the pre-Soviet Russian society. Attachment to rural life, Christian faith and old morals became a natural part of their demonstrations. This attitude was not confined to only within the Russian intellectuals—they had their counterparts from among the republics as well. This movement as part of literary movement will be discussed in details in the chapter on language (Chapter 4). For the time being, it is obvious that if the Great Russian people with all available advantages in their favour felt dissatisfied with the Soviet system, their counterparts in the republics must have experienced a similar feeling of dissatisfaction under the given system—in greater magnitude.

Yurii Andropov and an About-Turn in the Nationalities Policy

Yurii Andropov came to power in 1982 after the death of Brezhnev following a brief interregnum of succession struggle in which he was assisted by the unexpected death of M.A. Suslov. However, Andropov, from his very inception was opposed to this rising trend of Russian nationalism. John B. Dunlop, in his book *The New Russian Nationalism*, stated, "From the beginning Andropov showed himself to be a determined enemy of the Russian nationalists. Standing with him were Soviet technocrats and Marxist-Leninist purists."[129] Infact, much earlier, in 1972, when L.I. Brezhnev was in power, Andropov, in a speech titled, *A Triumph for the Leninist Nationalities Policy* on the occasion of the 50th anniversary of the USSR, stated, "Socialism still encounters such a survival of the past as nationalistic prejudices. They stem basically from the burden of the past, the political immaturity of some people, their allegiance to obsolete traditions and their inability to make out correctly the essentials of social phenomena. Nor should one ignore the fact that our class enemies are also making marked efforts to revive nationalistic prejudices in the minds and behaviour of people. They regard nationalism as the most effective weapon in the ideological struggle. Imperialism relies on it in its attempts to cause "erosion" of the socialist system."[130] Andropov, markedly showed no special position of the Russians in the development of the multi-national federation.

Andropov admitted that there had been discrepancies amongst the different nationalities prior to the birth of the USSR. Although, many of them could be removed, yet some of the differences continued to persist till then. But, whatever was achieved, claimed Andropov, was the achievement of the Leninist policy of the Soviet Union as a whole—"The continued all-round development of each of the Soviet sister Republics, the gradual consolidation of the unity of nations and national minorities, are a component part of the programme of communist construction outlined in the decisions of the 24th CPSU Congress. .... The Soviet government has done much for the development of the nations and national minorities which were backward in the past, for leveling up their economic and cultural standard. However, there are a number of objective circumstances by virtue of which the distinction in this field still persists in one form or another."[131]

Thus, one can see that at least theoretically, the Great Russian Chauvinism did not even tacitly influence Andropov; he was equally opposed to all kinds of nationalistic aspirations and called them deviations from the Marxist-Leninist principles.

When in power, this attitude of Andropov was even more explicit, because by that time he had the experience of suppressing the Russian nationalists who had under Suslov's auspices grown very powerful. J.B. Dunlop stated, "In December 1982, Andropov made his first major speech after becoming general secretary. The statement was devoted to the sixtieth anniversary of the formation of the USSR, and Andropov notably and noticeably downplayed the role of ethnic Russians in the Soviet federation."[132] At the same time Andropov, unlike his predecessors at least verbally admitted that each and every republic had equally important contribution to the successful development of socialism. "Each of the Union Republics—the Russian Federation, the Ukraine and Byelorussia, Uzbekistan and Kazakhstan, Georgia and Azerbaijan, Lithunania and Moldavia, Latvia and Kirghizia, Tajikstan and Armenia, Turkmenia and Estonia—each, I repeat, of Union Republics is making an invaluable contribution to the over-all growth of the economy and culture of the Soviet Union."[133] Regarding the special position held and enjoyed by the Russians, he stated, "The people of our country address special word of gratitude to the Russian people. In none of the republics would present achievements have been conceivable without their disinterested fraternal assistance. The Russian Language which has become a natural part of the life of millions of people of every nationality, is a factor of exceptional importance in the country's economic, political and cultural life in the drawing together of all its nations and nationalities, in making the riches of world civilisation accessible to them."[134]

Thus, Andropov did not disregard the common belief about the Russian contribution in the growth of Soviet system—rather, his target was to establish internationalism—the concept of *sliienie*. The controversial merger theory was thus brought back by Andropov which had been carefully avoided by Brezhnev. And Andropov, though he admitted that the exploitative character of any other multi-national system, "...has been settled successfully finally and irreversibly," by the Soviet authorities, yet he openly declared, "The successes in settling the nationalists question by no means signify that all problems generated by the very fact of the life and work of numerous nations and nationalities in a single state have vanished. This is hardly possible as long as nations exist, as long as there are national distinctions. And these will exist for a long time to come, much longer than class distinctions."[135]

Andropov, after many decades of Soviet leadership, gave a serious thought to the nationalities question and openly admitted that the state needed a newly evolved policy to deal with the existing national question. He also repeatedly harped on the spirit of mutual respect for all nations and nationalities and encouraged internationalism as a force to unite the workers and the youth together. He also spoke about the need of increasing involvement of "people of all nationalities in the management of social and state affairs."[136] However, scholars often misread the enthusiasm of Andropov as he spoke of *slianie* or fusion of nations in his speech on the 60th Anniversary of the USSR in 1982. Martha Brill Olcott analysed that "The emphasis of Andropov's remarks is not on the fusion of nations, but on the continued existence of national differences. ...... Thus while Andropov remains committed to a process of cultural ealizedive, he seems to display a greater awareness of the complexity of the national problem than his predecessor."[137]

Ultimately he confidently assured his countrymen, "Comrades, all this means that problems of relations among nations are still on the agenda in the society of mature socialism. They call for particular care and constant attention on the part of the Communist Party. The Party should delve into them deeply and chart the ways of solving them, enriching the Leninist principles of the nationalities policy with the experience of developed socialism."[138]

After the apparent complacency of the Brezhnev era regarding the nationality question, the serious concern of Andropov on that issue was a sharp turning point in the Soviet main stream policy-making.

Konstantin U. Chernenko and the Complex Turn in the Nationalities Policies

Following the death of Yurii Andropov in 1984, K.U. Chernenko became the general secretary. His regime was even more short-lived for he died in March, 1985. Apparently, Chernenko, followed a very neutral attitude regarding nationalities, keeping semblance with Andropov's policy. He tried to highlight the achievements of socialism to give birth to a new category of peoples, and in his initial speeches there was stress on amalgamation and no preference for Russian nationalists whatsoever. None of his speech, published in 1977, entitled *One Hundred Nations and Nationalities—One People*[139] he repeatedly tried to stress the ealizedive components in Soviet system and nowhere else did he highlight the special contribution of Russians in this development. Of course, he repeatedly boasted on the fact that it was the Soviet socialist regime that made it possible for many backward communities to achieve progress in an unimaginable, pace and conscious concern from the government saved many endangered communities from extinction. This was a characteristic feature of all Soviet mainstream official writings. But what was noteworthy about Chernenko was his stress on all nationalities when speaking of this collective achievement. He firmly stated, "Every one of the nations or ethnic groups in the USSR is an organic part of the Soviet people, and every person belonging to one of these nations or ethnic groups is a Soviet man."[140] But he had also carefully admitted the fact that internationalism as a goal could not be achieved without any obstruction. "Internationalism, then as now, was the cementing material in the building of socialist social relations. True, it would be wrong to think that life of the multinational community was or is free of such phenomena as parochialism or national egoism and narrow-mindedness. There are different traditions. Some of them serve as bridges which carry needless, outdated customs from the past to the present. The wheat of the past is not always, or not immediately sifted from the chaff. The state sees to it that the sifting is done thoroughly, ensuring the unconditional and full equality of all the Soviet nations and ethnic groups (which number more than 100)."[141] In his initial months in power, he, more or less, followed this ideal of a 'uniform communist society' where no special position for the Russian nationalists was granted.

Interestingly enough, within this very small span of time, Chernenko regime saw an about turn towards the Russian nationalists which got manifested in the awarding of Russian nationalist writers by the state by summer, 1984. J.B. Dunlop recorded, "In June 1984, Soloukhin was awarded the prestigious Order of the Red Banner of Labour by the Supreme Soviet of the USSR for "his services in the development of Soviet literature and in connection with his 60th birthday. Only a year previously Soloukhin had been harshly criticised on the pages of Kommunist. At if this was not enough, other Russian Party writers who had been out of favour under Andropov were likewise singled out for awards: Viktor Astaf'ev, Iurii Bondarev, Lenoid Leonev, Nationalist writer Mikhail Aleskseev's important anticollectivisation novel *Drachuny* (Pugnacious Fellows, 1981) was permitted to be nominated for the Lenin Prize, though it did not in fact receive the award. Obviously a major comeback had been achieved by the nationalists."[142]

This return of the nationalist writers back to prominence implied some very big change in Chernenko's policy from this time onwards. In an address in 1984 September, this voice of retreat was clearer as there was tacit encouragement towards the National Bolsheviks and his usual antinationalist and antireligious sentiments were absent.[143] Dunlop conjectured that this retreat of Chernenko resulted from the pressure of the Russian nationalist lobby. He stated, "Both Andropov and Chernenko regimes did choose to return to a policy of strict Leninism on the nationalities issue. Indeed, they went further than Stalin in his last years: the "Russian flavour" (with the exception of the Russian language, which had to serve as the *lingua franca* of the Soviet state) of the "magma of Sovietism" appeared to be a matter of indifference to them.... By heavy-handedly opting for a policy of strict Leninism on the nationalities issue, the Andropov and Chernenko leaderships galvanised and radicalised nationally minded ethnic Russians. The hasty retreat by the Chernenko leadership in mid 1984, may presage other concessions to the Russian nationalists in the near future."[144]

Once again, there was another line of conjecture that Chernenko's sharp shift in nationalities issue, especially regarding the Russian nationalists "coincided with Gorbachev's occupying the post of party secretary for ideology". But as to how far this young ideologue could influence Chernenko and in what direction remains still in the dark.[145]

However, the small phases of Andropov and Chernenko remained very crucial on deciding the future course of USSR's nationalities policy, for both of them had some well-defined course of action on the issue, markedly different from their predecessors. More interestingly, Chernenko's retreat remained as an unresolved riddle of history. At the same time it became evident that their effort to turn the wheel back in order to begin again with purely Leninist ideals proved to be impossible in a soil where the people had already drifted to the point of no return.

Whether these feeble attempts by Andropov and Chernenko to return to Leninist nationalities policy was an innocent attempt of ideological recovery from deviation or was geared by some other self-interests remained unknown. Zhores Medvedev, the brother of Roy Medvedev, a prominent Russian nationalist writer, indicated the possibility of non-Russian origin of Andropov and Chernenko as a plausible cause behind this shift of policy. Zhores wrote,

"There were rumours about Andropov's possible non-Russian origin. His mother's maiden name sounds Jewish and it is possible that Andropov is at least one-quarter Jewish. His surname is not a very common Russian and because he was born in the North Caucasus some rumours suggested that his original name had been Andropian, i.e. Armenian. His late wife was also said to have been Jewish. Russian nationalism constitutes a very strong undercurrent in some official circles, and these rumours were attempted to discredit Andropov." Regarding Chernenko, Zhores Medvedev states, "At the same time Chernenko's supporters firmly maintained that despite his Ukrainian surname he was pure Russian."[146] But howfar these conjectures on personal level carried authenticity to be historically acceptable facts remained indecisive. Nevertheless, this kind of information might act as supporting factors to develop a hypothesis.

Mikhail Gorbachev: The Turn of the Wheel and Reorientation of the Nationalities Policy

M. Gorbachev's tenure was almost synonymous with perestroika, the elaborate reform programme initiated by him as soon as he came to power. He tried to open up a new course in the socialist experiments and replaced dogmatism by liberalism. Gorbachev himself was aware of this sea change ushered in by him as he gave a speech in 1987 to the Young Communist League Congress titled *A New Revolution*. Again in his book perestroika, Chapter I, he analysed the "Revolutionary character of perestroika."[147] Thus, perestroika along with it brought a revolutionary change in the seventy years old regime. It was a change, which the regime could not sustain and ultimately gave way to complete liberalisation removing the socialist appearance. The multinational USSR ultimately broke into the national units and amidst indecision and chaos they began to find their own course—different from Soviet Socialism.

However, the logic behind Gorbachev's perestroika was to combat an all-round economic stagnation and a gradual erosion of the ideological and moral values. The task of an immediate reinvigoration was felt by Gorbachev who, therefore, decided to take up an all-round reform programme and also provided the rationale behind this move. He wrote, "Perestroika is an urgent necessity arising from the profound processes of development in our socialist society. This society is ripe for change. It has long been yearning for it. Any delay in beginning perestroika could have led to an exacerbated internal situation in the near future, which, to put it bluntly, would have been fought with serious social, economic and political crises."[148]

Although he did not belittle the earlier achievements of the USSR as he proudly stated, "However, the Soviet Union is a young state without analogues in history or in the modern world. Over the past seven decades—a short span in the history of human civilisation—our country has travelled a path equal to centuries." He also admitted that, the achievement of Soviet Union was, "...the visible product of the work of several generations of our people. And it is equally clear that my country's progress became possible only thanks to the Revolution."[149]

Then he went on to criticise the economic policy—which was leading towards stagnation and showed his eagerness to come out from such dangerous possibilities by immediate, all-round reform programme.

Apart from this material crisis he also located deviation in the ideological perspective of this socialist state. He openly admitted, "A gradual erosion of the ideological and moral values of our people began .... Propaganda of success—real or imagined—was gaining the upper hand."[150]

In fact, nationalities issue was not in the agenda of Gorbachev in the initial days of perestroika. It was during the implementation of economic changes and combating corruption within the administrative apparati in the republics that he realised the need of revision in the nationalities affairs at the republican level. This will be dealt with in detail in the chapter on perestroika later (Chapter 6). But, for the time being it was evident that even Gorbachev with his unconventional eyes could not and did not see the problems of the non-Russian, especially non-Slav republics from their own perspective. An overwhelming European identity still overshadowed the perestroika scheme. For that matter, Gorbachev's claim of 'our common European homeland' grossly neglected the Asian SSRs from his vision. But as Gorbachev took up the nationality issue, just to keep a logical coherence with perestroika and glasnost and also to be cautious of reactions from the national republics, he had to formulate a critical attitude to the past work done on the nationalities affairs. Gorbachev made a study of the nationality question as part of the allround erosion and decadence of the revolutionary harmony and cooperation of different nationalities in the development of Soviet society—"All the nations and nationalities who inhabit our country made a contribution to the formation and development of our socialist homeland."[151] But he also unhesitatingly admitted, "Regrettably we used to stress our really considerable achievements in the solution of the nationality problem and assessed the situation in high-flown terms."[152] He accepted that along with modernisation of economy, rise of intelligentsia and national self-consciousness, parochial nationalism and national rivalry had emerged as a natural by-product of the entire process.

Moreover, like in all other matters, in nationality affairs, the upcoming generation needed to know the past and "should learn to live in a multi-ethnic state." He said about the new generation, "Nobody has told them of how internationalism has been working to their benefit, and for how many years."[153] Thus, question remained unresolved and chances of mishandling was created by ignoring it through the years.

While describing the earlier achievements he, nevertheless, mentioned the special contribution of the Russians in it. "The Russian nation played an outstanding role in the solution of the nationality question."[154] In another place, in the same essay, he stated, "But at the same time, in our vast multi-ethnic country we cannot do without a common means of communication. The Russian language has naturally come to fulfil this role. Everybody needs this language, and history itself has determined that the objective process of communication develops on the basis of the language of the biggest nation. .... Apparently this was a natural choice."[155] Thus dependence on Russian language and Russian people, however, was taken for granted even by the protagonist of perestroika in most of his ideas and theory of implementing them.

Anyway, he was different from his predecessors in his way of accepting the need to take up the nationality issue as serious, unresolved problem and was ready to show more attention to the non-Russian nationalities' sentiments. He repeatedly stressed the need of cooperation, rapprochement and cohesion.[156] He cited the case of Northern Caucasus where he saw more than seven nationalities residing in peace and harmony and the reason of this success was, "The cultures of all nationalities are being preserved and developed within this small autonomous region."[157] But no promise to increase national autonomy was uttered.

He repeatedly stressed that, "National feelings of people should be respected and cannot be ignored. But speculating on them amounts to political irresponsibility, if not crime."[158] Interestingly, he never mentioned 'nationalism' as a manifestation of bourgeois capitalist society and therefore anti-socialist phenomenon. Here he was definitely a path-breaker in Marxist Leninist thinking. Nevertheless, he did not highlight this difference as such—rather exhibited his formal respect for Lenin and his ideals, "Lenin taught us to display extreme caution and tact in the nationality issue. There cannot and should not be any stereotyped pattern here. One thing is clear, when the fundamental interests of nations converge, when the principle of equality in everything forms the backbone of relations between people—and this is exactly how it is in Soviet society—then any emerging problems and misunderstandings can be settled, even in difficult situations."[159] He, also, for the first time in Soviet history, so openly admitted that if there were problems arising in the nationalities issue that was caused by some administrative mishandling. "I'd like to say once again that if negative phenomena emerge in this highly sensitive sphere of human relations, they emerge not just by themselves, but as a consequence of red tape, and lack of attention to people's lawful rights."[160] Here Gorbachev is really unparalleled in his honest confession and genuine desire of recovery.

He, at the same time, did not lose faith in the principle of socialism and Soviet path. His confidence and hope is revealed in his faith in the possible recovery from any kind of deviation or complication in ethno-national issues, by implementing a democratic and international process. He frankly stated, "We are not going to shun this or other problems which may crop up. We shall tackle them in the framework of the democratic process, consolidating our internationalist community of nations."[161] But of course, he still being committed to the internationalist ideal of the Soviet State, believed that the people of the Soviet Union still thought themselves as part of a 'big international family.' Therefore, Gorbachev believed that on the basis of this strong internationalism existing on the Soviet soil which gave birth to 'Soviet' patriotism, it would not be a difficult task to get over the complications that existed in the sphere of nationality politics. Although, time could prove that the task which Gorbachev found not so difficult was not only difficult but was impossible and irresoluble in the given context of the USSR. Perestroika, therefore, ultimately led to the dissolution of the entire Soviet system along with all her unique characteristics.

However, after a detailed study of the Soviet nationalities policy from Lenin to Gorbachev one might locate a very interesting process of evolution at work. The time of Lenin was full of promises for the nationalities with a single clause of internationalism remaining as a controlling factor. National self-determination at that stage served as a very powerful principle to mobilise this multi-national, multi-ethnic people towards revolution. After the revolution, Lenin, however, could not remain long to experiment his theory in practice. The moment the power of newly settled revolutionary machinery went into the hands of J. Stalin, the promises of Lenin received serious set back and 'national self-determination' as a matter of principle began to get qualified in order to maintain forcible integrity. Moreover, it was the Stalinist era which, although in a very incipid manner, saw the revival of Great Russian Chauvinism. Local national chauvinisms were, however, very strictly curbed under Stalin's hand. Coming to the post-Stalin era, it marked a new phase in the Soviet history in every respect—and the nationality issue was no exception. From this time on, the subject was grossly ignored in the mainstream Soviet polity. Both Khruschev and Brezhnev were to be blamed for their complacency on such a sensitive issue. Khrushcev never even bothered to speak on the nationalities issue of his own state—although he gave firy speeches on the injustice of colonial and imperial forces to exploit and oppress other weaker nationalities. From Brezhnev era one could find a completely self-satisfactory attitude being posed towards the issue of nationality politics of the USSR. The Soviet government under Brezhnev's guidance began to claim that the issue was virtually resolved in the process of socialist developments. Moreover, another dangerous tendency began to creep in. That was the official claim of Russian supremacy in the revolutionary success. And it was during the Brezhnev era that the Russian nationalism began to grow to a high scale. The chief ideologue of this period, M.I. Suslov's tacit encouragement to such developments were to be found. Thus, the Brezhnev era, with its apparent non-committance to the issue, turned the situation even more complicated and ugly. The two short interregnums of Andropov and Chernenko showed attempts to remove the highhandedness of Russian nationalists—but whether these were honest attempts to purify the state policy towards the nationalities or were born out of revenge psyche of the leaders as both of them had a non-Russian origin, could not be decided. Finally, Gorbachev's elaborate reform programme opened the floodgate of long sustained tensions which in their own dynamics led to the ultimate demise of the multi-national state of the USSR. Interestingly, in spite of the variety and attitudinal differences all the leaders, starting from Stalin to Gorbachev had given conscious lip-service to Lenin and his ideals in this regard. This, probably implied that, none of them wanted to be identified as deviationists. Reference to Lenin supposedly provided them the apparent authenticity in the field of application.

Three

Political Evolution and Economic Experience: Central Asia under the Soviet Rule

The institutional structure of the USSR was somewhat confusing as it officially claimed to be a conglomeration of a number of sovereign republics into a federal system based on socialist principle, though, in reality, the overwhelming presence of the centre hardly left much scope for independent decision-making by the republics. The five Central Asian republics were thus, members of the USSR who had entered the system voluntarily and could leave the union if they wished (according to the constitution of the USSR). The case of Tajikistan was slightly different, in the sense, that it initially joined the USSR as part of the Uzbek SSR, but in 1929 was made a separate republic and joined afresh. But the long experience of Soviet rule for them was not one where they could function on their own and develop spontaneously. It was the all pervasive presence of the Communist Party along with its supposedly socialist ideology and egalitarian doctrines that overshadowed all scope and provisions provided according to the constitution and made the republics follow the party dictat. And the Central Asian republics being comparatively backward in the economic sphere and weak in political tradition took time to cope up with the radical change that came with the Soviet regime. Tajikistan being a politically weak and economically barren region, had been one of the most obscure lands in the USSR. In fact, Central Asia always had a marginal presence in the major political processes of the USSR and had to accommodate herself according to the evolution and changes that the Soviet system had undergone.

From the constitutional point there were many dichotomies present in the Soviet state's theory and practice. The most important right mentioned in the constitution which apparently made the republics appear sovereign was the 'right to secede'.[1] But interestingly, the demand for secession needed to be placed through official channel—which should be the regional party organisation, by definition, subordinate to the will of the CPSU or the Central Party Organisation regulated from Moscow.[2] Any move in favour of secession bypassing the Party was regarded as criminal activity or counter-revolutionary propaganda. Again, the right of the Republics to have independence in the field of Foreign Affairs also seemed to be only a verbal commitment. For no practical move could be seen on part of any union republics, not to speak of the Central Asian ones, in this regard throughout the Soviet regime. The stringency of the Stalin era or the relaxation of the Brezhnev era made no difference to the republics to realise the extent of their real power. This huge gap between promise and practice might be explained in two ways. From the structural perspective, the Soviet Union embarked upon a federal system, while the functioning of the government was organised on the basis of party regulation which was highly centralised and hierarchical in its composition. Therefore, the scope for breathing space, provided in the constitution, got negated in the process of one party rule. From a theoretical point of view, neither Marx nor Lenin said Dictatorship of the Proletariat meant one party rule. This was purely Stalinist construct.

But, in practice, the domination of the Party implied the overbearing presence of the Russian leadership over the rest of the vast non-Russian, often non-Slavic (like the Central Asian) populations—in the name of Marxist Communist doctrine. Thus from the very outset, there was a marked disparity between the constitutional position and party politics. Moreover, the party which was in operation was drastically different from the party ideally envisaged at the outset of the revolutionary regime.

In fact, the Soviet Socialist regime always had shown a tendency of leader-oriented policy making and functioning. Thus, the Stalin era, post-Stalin Khrushcev era, Brezhnev era—all signified distinctive phases in the political evolution of the socialist state. Each era had its specific impact on the political development and repercussions on the economic processes of the Central Asian republics as part of the USSR. As in this research the period concerned began with the Brezhnev era, one needs to consider the general political tendency under Brezhnev and the scope and prospect of centre-periphery relation during this time. The position of Central Asia, her history of economic underdevelopment and political dissatisfaction has to be studied from this perspective.

In terms of duration, the period of Brezhnev's leadership was second only to the Stalin era in Soviet history. In view of contemporary Soviet analysts and also Brezhnev himself, the Brezhnev era signified stability and progress in a peaceful and harmonious process.[3] Whereas, in the eyes of the Western critics, the period symbolised stagnation, deterioration in the economic standard as a whole and corruption at the official levels so much so that the situation turned irretrievable after Brezhnev and rapidly moved towards the collapse.[4] Although apparently non-innovative and non-dynamic, the Brezhnev era marked some specific changes in its policy patterns, from its predecessors—Stalin and Khrushchev. The Khrushchev era began with the open announcement of de-Stalinization but Brezhnev's shifts were much more subtle and silent, yet the impact was not very negligible. The evolution of the Soviet political system could be traced from the Stalinist era of personal dictatorship to confrontational leadership of Khruschev to a relatively peaceful corporate leadership under Brezhnev. The role of the political elites became quite important at this stage. According to Seweryn Bialer, "The top leadership that developed in the Brezhnev era was to a large degree collective, almost all of the major bureaucratic interests were represented. No single bureaucratic group or personal machine dominated. Although the role of the party general secretary and his supporters within the Politburo clearly increased from 1972 onward, the latitude the leader enjoyed was still more limited than in the past."[5] Thus, the party organisation was made somewhat broad-based. But, one should not misread a truly democratic advance in this regard. Rather, taking advantage of the weakness of the top leadership, the role of the bureaucracy became all pervasive, there came up the pulls of different interest groups and corruption became rampant. Bialer preferred to call the leadership under Brezhnev as a "table oligarchy'.[6]

The secret of apparent stability under Brezhnev was the lack of any structural change in the political system or major reforms in economic activities. All his plannings were cautious and moderate in nature. The centralised role of the party was highlighted and the dynamics of state polity at both union and republican levels had overwhelming party orientation. Under Brezhnev, the Party became the chief agency of appointment to leadership positions in all bureaucracies, it also functioned as the coordinator and arbitrator of the activities of state institutions at the regional, republican and central levels, on all levels it was in charge of agenda setting which was a key element towards policy making. Earlier, the primary task of the Party apparatus was propaganda and monitoring the loyalty of the bureaucracy. But in Brezhnev era the main role of Party became the coordination of major activities of state initiatives at the central, republican and regional levels.

Ideologically, the Brezhnev era took up the issue of socialism, as an already established fact and harped on the spread of Soviet patriotism which brought the ethnic-national republics closer together following the process of *sblizheniye*. But these claims were far from reality as nothing but ritual lip service was provided to the ideology of socialism as envisaged by Lenin. Rather, given the fact that socialism was already established in the Soviet land, many manifestations of Russian domination came to be portrayed as distinctive 'Soviet' features. Instances included the Soviet patriotism or Soviet nationalism, Soviet culture, etc. which had overwhelming Russian character. In this way, there was imposition of Russian domination over the non-Russian and non-Slavic members of the USSR on the one hand, and on the other, the Soviet identity portrayed in different perspectives carried a universal mission whereby the Soviet state opted for an alternative model to the third world against the US power and the phenomenon of a bipolar world got strengthened. In fact, the Brezhnev era gave much more importance to foreign policy and external glamour of the 'Soviet' myth, suppressing the real pressing domestic issues like economic growth, education or disparities among nationalities.

Moreover, the Soviet leadership of the Brezhnev era had based their rule on the precondition of "mature socialism" whereby the earlier methods of trial and error or experimentation became a closed chapter. Thus, no ideological target was ever to be reached, rather the main task of the party leadership, as well as government administration at all levels seemed to preserve the *status quo*. Bialer observed, "The basic theme of the Brezhnev era was ideological retrenchment and partial retreat. The materials used in mass and party indoctrinations had a dogmatic, uncritical, monotonous tone. Most importantly, there was no serious effort to go beyond the routine slogans and precepts in the attempt to propagate the doctrine to non-believers or doubters. Instead, the emphasis was placed on resistance to and defense against alien ideas."[7] Another task of party philosophers at this stage was to justify and accommodate science with the socialist doctrine. The role of science was encouraged in order to 'get good returns in atheistic propaganda, etc. but this also had another, more practical perspective, that was to justify the overwhelming stress on technology and industrialisation as an essential component of social culture. This introduced artificiality into the Soviet way of life.

Instead of progress, in reality, the sustenance of existing system became the aim of the Brezhnev government and ideology was pushed back to the level of utopia and was used just as a matter of fact or in order to justify the role of the party or any questionable gesture in the foreign policy (eg. intervention in Czechoslovakia, Afghanistan, etc.)

In the day to day functioning of the state popular allegiance and discipline were maintained by the extremely bureaucratic and highly coercive institutions like KGB, and the army. Another remarkable characteristic of Brezhnev's policy was changelessness in the nomanklatura, bureaucracy and Party membership in important positions. During his (1966-82) regime, the average age of the Central Committee members rose from 56 to 63, in the Council of Ministers from 58 to 65; for the Politburo the figures were 55 to 68.[8] Thus, along with stability, Brezhnev sustained the older generation in power along with him. This gerontocracy accelerated the process of stagnation towards collapse.

In general, the long stretched tenure of Brezhnev signified an era of peace and changelessness, when the leader and his people in general prefered to think that the Soviet system was moving at its best, socialism was achieved and reached its mature phase and therefore, society could enjoy the much desired stability. The problems of shortages, individual abuses or corruptions which began to surface, were not seen as a failure of the system, rather were ignored as aberrations. The existing order was accepted by the general people as a fact of life, as it still "provided them with steady employment and a measure of social security in exchange for a modest work load and civic obligations that could in practice often be evaded. Rulers and ruled were bound by an unwritten social compact that encouraged them to leave things as they were."[9] At the same time, "The leadership and elite retain(ed) a fundamental belief in the idea of progress."[10]

The system was being fed an illusion by a leadership that was at least partly cynical. The decline in the productive sphere was knowingly suppressed in order to cover-up the failure of the system.

In fact, the Brezhnev era saw the maturity of the post-revolution generation of the Soviet people. The generation which had experienced the revolution, or even for that matter the havoc of the World War II, had became old. Therefore, the society he faced did not or could not any more envisage the dream of V.I. Lenin with the same enthusiasm as before. Rather, majority of them, whether as ruler or as subjects, preferred to enjoy the existing stability without much questioning its credibility or durability. Thus the Brezhnev era acted only as a lull before an unavoidable chaos, which none of his immediate successors, Andropov or Chernenko, within their limited tanure and old age could handle. And thus, Brezhnev's leadership, in the ultimate analysis, acted as the "Harbinger of Collapse" in Dmitri Volkogonov's expression.[11]

The political condition and developments in Central Asia have to be studied in the light of the general situation under Brezhnev rule. The central motto of the regime was to attain loyalty from the republics without imparting much terror or coercion. Therefore, the policy of involving more native population was consciously planned during this phase. From the point of view of the natives of Central Asia, this era, therefore, signified a development towards political participation both at the party level and in administration.

Central Asia being one of the non-Slavic vast regions under the USSR, required special attention and specific policy determination to maintain itself under the Soviet system. For, Ideological teaching and propaganda were not enough for that—rather effective strategy formulation and their regular implementation became necessary. The objective reality showed the kind of evolution that the system had undergone during the post-Stalin, or post-Khrushchev era upto Gorbachev in political adjustment. In apparent policy determination this era was not very significant, for the trend of changelessness in the name of stability continued everywhere including Central Asia. But the dynamics of changelessness or stable political leadership from amongst the native Central Asians helped maturing a community of politically conscious elites who became the spokesmen of the Soviet ideology. In most of the writings in the Russian newspapers published from the local press there were reflections of the belief of this community in the development and growth of the republics. Whether such writings were genuine reflections of what they believed, or were empty utterances to keep their people unaware of the reality, or were taken to be as strategic postures needed for the upliftment of their individual political career under the regime, remains inexplicable. Some of the reports and articles which came up just at the threshold of perestroika still showed faith in the Soviet system and stressed the fact of enormous economic benefit which Central Asia could make by remaining within the Soviet socialist regime. The centre-page article of *Kommunist Tajikistana* of 4th January 1983, made a detailed assessment of the role of Party, Soviets and collectives in the development of the Tajik SSR and which considered the entire development of the republic to be an achievement of the socialist system.[12] Again, in another article, in Kommunist Tajikistana, the role of socialism in the development of the collectives were assessed in the perspective of fifty years of Soviet experience.[13] Another article entitled 'Vernost Leninizmu' implying 'Faith in Leninism' discussed the success of the Leninist path and the bright future of socialism and world revolution.[14] There had also been articles published in favour of atheism and the success of atheistic propaganda[15] which all implied at least the official stand in the republics in favour of the Soviet regime and preference for the values set by the scientific socialism. This kind of commitment to the socialist principles, though verbal, was probably indication enough that the official stand of the Central Asian party leadership was in favour of the regime and that implied the effectiveness of the apparently peaceful era of Brezhnev and after. The overwhelming presence of Russian party cadres and officials in the bureaucracy was a standard picture of Central Asia from its very inception. In the initial days of Soviet rule, the pro-Soviet sources explained this trend as a benevolent assistance to the backward Central Asia to help her process of socialist development so that she could keep her pace with the rest of USSR. But as the authority had to maintain an apparently federal structure, they needed the inclusion of native cadres and administrative personnel in important posts as well. Here an interesting characteristic could be consistently found in the appointment of Party Secretaries in Central Asia which continued more or less unchanged from the Stalin era that remained unchanged during the post-Stalin period. The post of First Secretaries of the republics were held by the native members whereas the next important post of Second Secretaries were given to the Russian cadres. John H. Miller in his article *Cadre Policy in Nationality Areas* extensively studied the nature and significance of the recruitment of First and Second Secretaries in the non Russian republics in the USSR. According to his observations, "foremost among the centrally appointed administrators in the Soviet system, including its ethnic minority areas, are the party secretaries, and it has been remarked several times, that in non-Russian areas the chief party secretary is conventionally from the titular nationality and his deputy an ethnic Russian."[16] By the time of Brezhnev, the need of philanthropy to promote the co-partisans no more remained a convincing logic. Instead, the inclusion of ethnic population in the functioning of the states began increasingly to be stressed. In such a situation, a system of checks and balances was followed as a matter of policy, where the presence of Russian Second Secretaries symbolised the control of the centre over the republics. In his report to the 24th Congress of the CPSU in 1971, L.I. Brezhnev stated "Many new comrades with good political and specialist qualifications have been promoted to the leadership of local party and Soviet organs, including the post of First Secretary of republican, *kari* and *oblast* party committees. Moreover, the Central Committee has pursued a consistent policy of promoting local personnel; people have been promoted to these posts from the centre only in exceptional circumstances."[17] This kind of overemphasis on the recruitment of local personnel indicated a policy decision on part of the regime to systematically bring the local representation within the Soviet party operation. But, what remained unuttered was the tacit system of remote control by the persistent presence of the Russian Second Secretaries. However, this system of checks and balances would naturally arouse the question on the kind of responsibilities usually shared by these two positions. The task of the First Secretary was very prominent as he had the general power of leadership, supervision and coordination in his region and used to enjoy substantial amount of publicity, so much so, that all First Secretaries used to have a published biography by the government. But there remained some kind of vagueness in the nature of duties of the Second Secretaries. There was less publicity for them, they appeared seldom in public speeches and that led to the assumption that the functions with which these cadres were associated were least publicised. The apparently visible areas of his responsibilities were agriculture, organisation, etc. where, more often than not, the First Secretaries had greater control. The significance of the post of Second Secretary, therefore, was laid elsewhere. And the recruitment of the Second Secretaries from within the Russian nationalities consistently indicated the purpose quite distinctly. In an interview conducted by Mervyn Mathews, it came out that the Second Secretary with this portfolio can presumably veto any suggestion on personnel that the First Secretary might put forward, and thus prevent him from assembling any faction or entourage about himself. He would have considerable influence over the non-Russian cadres pool from which future local leaders (including First Secretaries) would be drawn. It was also claimed that a Second Secretary could recommend the dismissal of a First Secretary, but not vice-versa.[18] John H. Miller analysed, "All this makes the second secretary something rather more than a mere deputy to the first secretary; whether he is one of a partner, or watchdog, or fellow-casual, he functions as an institutionalised check on the first secretary."[19] The recruitment of Russian Second Secretaries in the nationality areas was a conscious policy taken up in the pre-Brezhnev era, presumably in the Khrushchev period, probably with the notion of institutional checks. But ironically, in two cases of corruption involving party leaders, it was found that the Russian Second Secretaries worked hand in hand with the First Secretary and the other local leaders and had been dismissed along with the local leadership. One such event took place in Tajik SSR in 1961 when the First Secretary, the Chairman and the Council of Ministers were sacked along with a number of Tajik officials for falsification of the cotton crop returns. The Russian Second Secretary, P.S Obnosov was also penalised but the charge on him was not as of direct corruption but of 'lack of political principle.' One might recall a similar incident in Uzbekistan during the Stalin era in 1938, when the Uzbek First Secretary Akhmal Khojaev and his associate Faizulla Khojaev were tried for their role in 'undermining the fulfillment of cotton production targets 'and envisaging an independent Uzbek economy.[20] However, the difference between the crimes committed in 1938 in Uzbekistan and in 1961 in Tajikistan were characteristically different, the former was rather a clash of principle and ideology whereas the latter was a case of sheer corruption. And Brezhnev was successor to a legacy where very little of the principles were left with. In a system which has itself lost much real faith in ideology and thrived on certain ritualistic lip service, what kind of a role was expected out of the Russian Second Secretaries was difficult to determine. But it certainly was not of an watchdog of the Soviet socialist ideology. And at least in the Tajik case it was found that even in day-to-day economic and political affairs the Second Secretary was not found effective enough to control regional indiscipline. In an era of corruption and decadence, no policy could remain fool-proof. Other than being the watchdog of ideology and principles, the Second Secretaries probably had some more practical and social tasks to perform in the nationality areas. For, the ethnic compositions in such areas were seldom homogenous and, moreover, in places like Central Asia, there were a good number of Russian residents with white collar jobs. Protection of their interests and the interests of the national minorities in these ethno-culturally sensitive zones were tasks which needed neutral supervision. The Russian Secretary was expected to have the necessary communication link with the non-Russian major nationalities in order to maintain the necessary cohesion. However, as Miller concluded, "The bargaining and diplomatic skills suggested by the above discussion might well be too many to expect in one man. Arguably, what is required is a judicious combination of Russians and non-Russians acting as a check on each other, and a judicious combination of personnel with local ties and knowledge and personnel imported from outside."[21]

Thus, the remote control by the centre through Russian representatives did not seem fool proof in order to maintain authority and domination. Here the Brezhnev era preferred rather to increase its dependency on the local officials and party representatives. Brezhnev's report to the XXIV Congress in 1971 had openly announced this increasing dependency and that it was not an empty utterance could be realised from the study of the positions of local party leadership and ministers during the 60s and 70s. That the increasing dependency or reliance on the regional level leadership could be surmised from the tenure of each posts of First Secretaries in the Central Asian provinces. The Tajik First Secretary Jabar Rasulov came to his office in 1964 and continued to hold it till the onset of perestroika. There were other similar lengthy tenures found with the Uzbek First Secretary Sharaf Rashidov (1959-1983), Turdiakun Usubaliev of Kirgizstan and so on. Such lengthy tenure of office was not any exceptional measure with Central Asia, rather this was one of the outcomes of Brezhnev's general policy of changelessness. The resulting factor was definitely increasing domination of these leaderships in the republican affairs and, more importantly, their relation with the centre. In fact, this overwhelming partnership with Moscow's leadership brought at least one section of the native population (the most fortunate ones) to the limelight. These elements were considered as the new political elites of the regions by Sovietlogists.[22] This was found with the Tashkent-Ferghana based elites, with their pro-Moscow leader in Uzbekistan Sharaf Rashidov being a key promoter of the alliance with Russia along with the import of Russian language and culture. A similar picture could be found with the Leninabad (Quliab) region of Tajikistan which reflected the concentration of pro-Moscow elites. Thus, the local or regional allegience in favour of the centre and its policy-making helped the Brezhnev regime to achieve its target of stability. So, this was a system of partnership which grew along with an interdependent conditioning between the leadership of the centre and those of the regions. Joel C. Moses observed, "Even on the less tangible but symbolic level of leadership style, the Brezhnev era also seemed conspicuous for its encouragement of regionalism as a form of regional identification and enduring sense of in-group solidarity among former provincial party-state cohorts."[23] Moves had also emphasised the role of these regional leaders over economic plannings during the Brezhnev period and in some cases regional pressure on centre over policy decisions through representations. This was definitely, a system of bargain for both the parties, yet in most cases the Central Asian leadership could not utilise this bargain uniformly in favour of their respective republics. Therefore, one might find the growing disparity between the natives who could climb the political ladder successfully and became closer to the centre and the unfortunate rest who remained away from the political influences and, therefore, were alien from the entire Soviet system. Here again, thee were regions which by the dynamism of their leadership could reach much closer to the Moscow leadership and thereby enjoyed more prestige within Central Asia. Such was the republic of Uzbekistan which gained a marked prestige and position during the70s and 80s in the central and regional leadership and her proximity to central leadership made her appear more powerful and influential within the Central Asian region. However, in spite of the shift in policy, the representation of non-Russians in the central party organisation remained scarce. Martha O. Olcott observed, "At the time of Brezhnev's death four non-Russian republic party leaders were members of the politburo: Sk. Rashidov of Uzbekistan and G. Aliev of Azerbaidzhan were candidate members, and D. Kunaev of Kazakhstan and V. Schcherbitsky of the Ukraine were full members of that organisation."[24] Thus, the presence of three representatives from Central Asia and Kazakhstan might indicate a marked upward mobility in the standard, position and power of the local elite leaders. But, these leaders being selfish and corrupt, could do little benefit to their respective republics. Corruption was not a special feature of the Central Asian leadership. At the time of Brezhnev's death, corruption had become systemic, at all levels of the Party and local government, everywhere in the Soviet Union. Martha B. Olcott remarked in the context of the four union level politbureau representatives, "All four men had succeeded in creating powerful networks of personal control in their home republics, and all four could justly be called corrupt, given the manner in which they rewarded the retinues of followers who helped them keep their republic economies functioning. She also added, "At the time of Brezhnev's death, most of the union republics (the Baltic republics excepted) were ruled by local communist overlords."[25] A similar comment was found in the analysis of John Anderson, "Increasingly, however, it appeared that for all the formal structures of control, these elites were treating their territories as feudal fiefs and that by the Brezhnev era even the loyalty of local Russians could not be taken for granted, as such people could be coopted, bribed or intimidated into supporting traditional modes of rule.[26] Actually, an open admittance of Brezhnev period slogans in political sphere implied the withering away of the ideology yet the vaccuum remained covered by some hollow slogans and the leadership preferred to provide only lip service. But for practical purposes—the notion of '*Delovitost*' or 'business like behaviour' became more popular and more appealing. ["The *Delovitost* of the top leaders signifies an overriding concern with the rationalisation of an uncritically accepted system, and above all with enforcing their own power."][27] The same attitudinal approach on the part of the local political elites must have promoted in them unabated power mongering and indiscriminate economic exploits and corruption, thereby jeopardising the whatever limited scope and viability entire system had. Dmitri Volkogonov wrote, "It has long been clear that the communist ship of state was becalmed, its sails sagging, party rule in the centre and the periphery was characterised by the outward appearance of activity concealing internal passivity. Public apathy grew, corruption flourished at every level, the higher, the worse. Deceit, lies and mendacious information became the rule.[28]

However, in spite of the main feature of Brezhnev rule being stagnation, there had been a major step taken technically by the new and extensive constitutional reforms of 1977. The reforms which took place under the new constitution were mainly on economic right, right to education, changes in the election process, strengthening law and order. But all the reforms in these spheres did not prescribe any drastic change. But two special chapters were added to the constitution concerning foreign policy and defence of the socialist motherland which implied the outwardly outlook of the Brezhnev era—the regime's concern about her role in the international arena and the projection of the Soviet image as a successful, mature socialist country. In fact, in the speech at the plenary meeting of the Central Committee on the draft of the constitution Brezhnev provided a set of reasons behind the task undertaken. L.I. Brezhnev's speech went thus: "What we now have in the Soviet Union is an advanced, mature socialist society. Major changes of fundamental importance have affected every aspect of the social life of the country. The nation's economy has changed beyond recognition. Socialist ownership reigns supreme in the country. An integrated and powerful national economic organism now exists which is functioning successfully…. The country's social make-up has also changed. Our working class today constitutes two-thirds of the country's population…. The workers have become more active socially and the scale of their participation in administering the state has considerably broadened. The farmers, too, have changed. The collective farmer of today was born and grew up on a collective farm and his mental outlook has been formed in socialist conditions…The intelligentsia has become truly representative of the people and socialist in outlook…We now have equality of nations, not only in the legal sense, but in practice. All of our republics including those which used to lag behind economically and culturally, have now achieved a high level of development. The economies of the republics have, at the same time, become inseparable components of an integrated national economy. Underlying all these changes is the growing homogeneity of Soviet society. The firm alliance of the working class, the collective farmers and people's intelligentsia has become still stronger. Distinctions between the main social groups are being gradually erased…A new historical community, that of the Soviet people, has emerged."

"With the attainment of mature socialism and with the adoption of the ideological and political positions of the working class by all sections of the population our state, which was first firmly established as a dictatorship of the proletariat, has grown into a state of the whole people. All these processes taking place in the country's life have been and continue to be directed by the Communist Party, which has been the leading, organising and mobilising force of our society ever since the October Revolution…"

"Finally, the international position of the Soviet Union and the entire social and political make-up of the world have also changed drastically. The capitalist encirclement of the USSR has come to an end. Socialism has become a world system. A powerful socialist community has emerged. The positions of the world capitalism have been substantially weakened. Dozens of young states opposed to imperialism have sprung up on the territories of former colonies. Our country's international prestige and influence have grown immeasurably. As a result, the world balance of forces has been completely altered..."

"On the basis of their achievements the Soviet people, under the Party's guidance are now carrying out new tasks: the creation of the material and technical foundations of communism, the gradual transformation of socialist social relations into communist relations, and education of the people in the spirit of communist consciousness. Such in brief, have been the major changes in our society and in our country's life since 1936. They are the main reasons and prerequisites for drawing up a new constitution of the USSR."[29]

Thus, the official explanation for understanding the constitutional reforms were mainly the maturity of the USSR as a country along with all its organisms, which naturally had outgrown the scope, provided in the 1936 constitution and, therefore, naturally needed updating. Interestingly, no shortcoming with the earlier constitution was highlighted—rather all the necessary changes recommended were attributed to the growth and upward mobility of the multinational society towards mature socialism, heading towards communism. In fact, no indication of the alarming economic crisis or the challenges posed by the nationalities or the increasing corruption was ever admitted. The regime under Brezhnev felt confident, or at least posed so, so that the state was moving steadily towards more and more growth, success and harmony. There had been 400,000 suggestions found from general public on the basis of which there had been 150 amendments which apparently might seem to be a substantial achievement of the people. Moreover, Article 52 guaranteed Soviet citizens 'freedom of conscience, that was the right to profess any religion or none ....'; Article 108 which introduced the principle of popular referendum. The constitution also referred to the right to housing which was new and unique, there was the guarantee of the right to health protection—a definite extension from 1936 Constitution which had only proclaimed the right to maintenance in case of illness or disability.[30]

But in the major political sphere the role of the Party and its overwhelming domination was not reduced in any sense. Thus Article 6 reasserted 'the CPSU is the force which directs and guides Soviet society, the nucleus of its political system...and of social organisation'. Moreover, regarding the federal structure, there was no change with the logic: "Comrades, the Soviet Union is a multinational state. Experience has fully confirmed the soundness of the basic elements of the federal structure of the USSR. There is no need, therefore, to introduce any major changes in the forms of our Soviet socialist federation."[31]

In the Articles 70, 71, 72, 73, 74 and 75 the status of the Federal states and their position vis-a-vis the USSR was described. At the beginning, Article 70 stated, 'The Union of Soviet Socialist Republics is an integral multinational state formed on the principle of socialist federation as a result of the free self-determination of nations and the voluntary association of equal Soviet Socialist Republics. The USSR embodied the state unity of the Soviet people and draws all its nations and nationalities together for the purpose of jointly building Communism." The right to free secession was mentioned in Article 72. There were some other rights of the Republics on decision making, such as approval of the budget, determination of the state borders of the USSR and approval of changes in the boundaries between Union Republics, etc. But at the end of Article 75 it was clearly stated, "The territory of the Union of Soviet Socialist Republics is a single entity and comprises the territories of the Union Republics. The sovereignty of the USSR shall extend throughout its territory."[32]

In the propaganda literature by Boris Topornin specially highlighted the Article 70 no more as a principle—but as a guide to success. The author explained, "The formula—the USSR is a multinational Union state—reveals the nature of the Soviet federation at the present stage, which witnesses the further internationalisation of the life of society and the intensive process of rapprochement between Soviet nations and nationalities. It testifies to the community of state and public life, to the common goals and strivings of all Soviet nations and nationalities. In economic terms this unity includes the economies of all Soviet Republics."[33] This type of statement reveals as to how far the issues like federalism had been taken for granted in the regime of the 70s that no more constructive thinking or experimentation was added to it. Rather the regime became satisfied in thinking that this rather complex question had its solution in communism.

The same intonation of resolving the issue could be traced in the speech of Brezhnev in his Report on the draft constitution. Here the General Secretary clearly stated, "Thanks to the consistent pursuance of the Leninist nationalities policy we have, simultaneously with the building of socialism, successfully solved the nationalities question, for the first time in history."[34]

Once again, the verbal promise on the political rights and freedoms of Soviet citizens had very little material viability as was stated quite matter of factly by Brezhnev, "It goes without saying, comrades, that the draft constitution proceed from the assumption that the right and freedoms of citizens cannot and must not be used against our social system and to the prejudice of the interests of the Soviet people.... Every Soviet citizen should clearly realise that, when all is said and done, the main guarantee of one's rights is the strength and prosperity of one's homeland. To this end every citizen should be aware of his responsibility before society and conscientiously fulfil his duty to the state and the people."[35]

Thus, all the rights and provisions made in the new Constitution of 1977 was nothing but formal and verbal promises in the name of the people which in reality left them with little options regarding the choice of their future. Rather, care was taken to protect the existing order.

The Economic Experience

The economy of Soviet Union was showing signals of crisis in general from the 70s but there too the economy of Central Asia had its own dimension—unique and complex. The pattern of Central Asian economy was markedly different from the rest of the USSR—especially from mainland Russia—before the Revolution. Traditionally the main form of economy in Central Asia used to be agriculture and stock-breeding. The Soviet system along with the revolution brought many new economic projects to this region. The agricultural productivity increased in leaps and bounds, collective farming (Kolkhoz), scientific methods and modern technologies brought mounting success in terms of output compared to her past. But, still, there remained drawbacks that created complexities because, in spite of marked growth in terms of her past, Central Asia lagged behind in comparison to the general economic progress of the USSR. Moreover, the growth was rapid in agriculture—the traditional economic activity of the zone. But in industry, the picture was not at all similar. In industry, the lack of progress compared to European Russia was glaring. The Brezhnev era stressed particularly on technological progress to increase industrial productivity and, therefore, did not or could not touch upon the specific requirements of Central Asia in the 70s. Rather, on part of the government, there was the tendency to make sweeping comments that the achievement of the USSR in economic sphere was great and the achievement of Central Asia in this sphere was unthinkable compared to her past backwardness. Western critics of Soviet system on the other hand flatly blamed the Soviet economy for being oppressive and exploitative about Central Asia as according to them Soviet occupation of Central Asia was just another form of colonialism. However, the real problems of Central Asia were somewhat different from both these extremes. And that came out of rational investigations by modern scholars who took up this issue in terms of genuine problems on part of both the centre and the region to bring parity in economic productivity and standard and weighed Moscow's conscious responsibility in the lopsided yields of the Revolution's achievement, from a rational perspective.

To start with, one might investigate the position taken by the Soviet government by analysing Brezhnev's own speeches during the early 70s. In one of them entitled "*The Unbreakable Unity and Fraternal Friendship of the Peoples of the USSR—A Great Gain of Socialism*" Brezhnev proudly stated, "Let us recall for a moment the state of the outlying national areas of the country at the time of the Revolution. In economic development Central Asia and Kazakhastan were on a level quite usual for colonial countries. Poverty, disease and ignorance were the lot of the bulk of the population."[36]

In the same speech Brezhnev continued, "The efforts of the party and the state over a period of many years yielded remarkable fruit. Look at Central Asia and Kazakhstan today! You will find not only first-class cotton fields in Uzbekistan and Turkmenia, the once fallow lands of the Kazakhs under crop, flowering orchards and new cattle-breeding farms in Kirghizia and Tajikistan. Today, these Republics are famed for a host of big, modern, beautiful cities, like Tashkent, Alma-Ata, Dushanbe, Frunze and Ashkabad. There you will find large centres of metallurgy, mining and heavy industry, like Jezkazgan and Karaganda, Pavlodar and Navoi, first-rate power and water installations like the Nurek hydro-electric power plant and the Karalum canal. Central Asia and Kazakhstan have became major producers of oil and gas, chemicals and modern machines. Since the formation of the Union, Kazakhstan's industrial output has increased 600-fold, Tajikistan's over 500-fold, Kirghizia's over 400-fold, Uzbekistan's about 240-fold and Turkmenia's over 130-fold. The gross cotton crop in Uzbekistan has gone up 120-fold and in Turkmenia 90-fold.

Kazakhastan now produces almost 30 times more grain than it did in 1922."[37] In another speech, while assessing the "results of the Five year period and the Main Objectives of the Party's Economic Policy" Brezhnev discussed at length the "Results of the Ninth Five-year Plan" without any specific reference to any zone and more or less provided a picture of all-round success and growth both in industry and agriculture. Similarly, while discussing the thrust areas of the ensuing 'Tenth Five-year Plan' Brezhnev stressed over and over again on scientific methods to increase productivity in various spheres. And while discussing the strategy on agriculture he only once mentioned the name of Central Asia and Kazakhstan to highlight the need for improved irrigation in this region.[38]

But, that the real picture of USSR's general economy was not at all so impressive became amply clear in retrospect. The official speeches depicted an illusory picture of the entire state of the socialist economy which in reality was undergoing great trouble during the period concerned. When there was the telling need for all-round economic reforms in all spheres, the long and abortive years under Brezhnev only provided ritual lip service to revolutionary ideals and let the economy stagnate till it reached the verge of collapse. Interestingly, the regional newspapers in Russian language also reflected the same confidence in the path followed by the Soviet government and the CPSU. For example, a number of new articles published in *Kommunist Tajikistana,* as late as in 1983, repeatedly stressed the contribution of the Party in the successful development of the republic's economy—with special emphasis on agriculture (collectives). For example, there were articles entitled *K Noveem Rubedsham* (meaning towards New Boundaries) which in detail dealt with the achievements of the collectives in fifty years experience. The article also touched upon the contribution of electro-energies in the progress of economy but repeatedly harped on the training of discipline, work atmosphere, etc. but over and above the thrust remained on the collective. The article ended with the note: "Collective Union commits timely implement of the plan towards the order and delivery of manufactured articles in total conformity to the nomanklatura". The article concluded by stating, "In fulfilling the resolution of the Plenum of the Central Committee of CPSU of May, 1982, collective union would carry on for future expansion of such kind of economy."

Another news report in the front page of Kommunist Tajikistana entitled *In the Soviet ministry of Tajik SSR*, assessed the role of Tajik

Soviet ministers in fulfilling the state's plans on economic and social development. Tajik SSR and the State budget and Tajik SSR through the year 1982. The article claimed that the state budget could bring 104 per cent profit (*Gosudarstvennoy budzhet vipolnen po dokhodam na 104, prodcenta*).[39]

All these claims, even after the death of Brezhnev, implied the deep rooted conviction about an imaginary progress while the reality faced not only stagnation but a serious crisis in Soviet economy from the 70s onwards.

Strong critics of the Soviet system like J. Keep claimed that all the information and statistical data provided in Soviet government records were exaggerated and false.[40] In support of his argument he stated, "From 1987 onward several Soviet economists openly questioned official statistics. Selivenin and Khanin caused a sensation by stating that since 1928 the national income had grown by a factor of only 6.9 not 89.5 as had been claimed."[41] In fact, for our purpose, it would be rather unnecessary to enter into such debates as it has been already proved that the Soviet economy was not in a very healthy state and needed all-round reforms. Although this was provided to the system by perestroika but the weak and unstable system failed to sustain the effort and ultimately collapsed. The reason for mentioning the general economic deterioration and crisis is only to create a clear backdrop for assessing the economic crises of Central Asia as a part of Soviet regional economy during the time concerned—a time when 'only patchwork repairs were attempted to the centralised system of planning and resource allocation'.[42]

In spite of repeated Soviet claims of harmonious development, the reality showed glaring disparities and those disparities were even more blatant in Central Asia. Sovietologist Boris Z. Rumer openly stated, "The conflict between regionalism and centralism in the economic development of the USSR is a contradiction that neither theory nor practice has been able to resolve in the 70 years that the Soviet state has been in existence."[43] In general the picture of Central Asian economic activities concentrated on agriculture and that also cotton cultivation. In this particular cash crop two neighbouring states of Central Asia, Uzbekistan and Tajikstan could excel. In fact, Uzbekistan used to produce 67 per cent of the entire cotton grown in the Soviet Union while Tajikistan produced 11 per cent of the same.[44] The other republics of Turkmenistan, Azerbaijan, Kirgizia and Kazakhstan put more emphasis on stock breeding—a traditional

Central Asian occupation inherited from the pre-revolutionary past. But there were also the introduction of extensive cultivation of virgin lands, especially in Kazakhstan.

But regarding industry a marked similarity could be found in all the republics. The major industries in the entire region were oil refineries, natural gas, chemical production, fertilizers, carpets, textiles, silk, ginneries and canneries, etc. But, undoubtedly, the major economic activity of Central Asia was agriculture in the pre-revolutionary days and that remained unchanged in the post-revolution era. According to Boris Rumer, "Central Asia produces approximately 95 per cent of the USSR's raw cotton and cotton fibres, 15 per cent of its vegetable oils, 100 per cent of its machinery and equipment for cotton growing, more than 90 per cent of its cotton gins, a large quantity of looms and equipment needed for irrigation."[45] But from 50s and 60s the discovery of oil and gas resources as well as hydro-electric power in this region brought a new dimension towards energy development and scope for new industrialisation that increased the potential for its economic development. In Tajikistan, the famous Nurek hydroelectric industry was founded in 1959. Rumer opined, that with this newly tapped source, Central Asia should have come up as one of the most promising regions of the USSR and could have got rid of her exclusive reliance on cotton.[46] But in reality, this sector of industries did not become as successful as the potential had seemed to promise. Rumer further investigated and found that, "Industrial development in Central Asia has lagged noticeably behind than as compared to other parts of the USSR. Approximately 80 per cent of the national industrial production and energy consumption is located in the European zone, although this area is poorly supplied with resources. Conversely, Soviet Asia has the bulk of resources but only a small share of industrial production."[47]

Ajay Patnaik in his book on Central Asia, however, provided a better picture of the state of affairs regarding industries.[48] He repeatedly stated, "By almost all measures of economic growth Soviet Central Asia underwent rapid economic changes. The republics of Central Asia benefited from the inter-republic redistribution of national income disproportionate to their contributions.[49] Again, elsewhere, he stated, "The growth of aggregate volume of industrial production cautioned to be very fast in Central Asia. Since the 1960s, Central Asia entered a new phase in its industrial development."[50] Patnaik also highlighted the success of mechanical industries in Uzbekistan and non-ferrous metallurgy in Tajikstan.[51]

But both Rumer and Patnaik have agreed on one point—that the industrialisation in Central Asia had its own complexities and could not solve the socio-economic and cultural problems of a traditional society which was forced to undergo a rapid transition under the new regime. Both of them highlighted the rapid growth of population in the entire zone which turned out to be a glaring problem in the USSR because the Asian Muslims under the Soviet state were rapidly outnumbering their Christian Slavic (Russian and non-Russian) brothers.[52] Though this was an issue that went beyond the purview of economic affairs, but it definitely had its effect on a developing economy. The problems of employment became glaring and the dependent population in Central Asia was comparatively more than in any other part of the Soviet Union. Thus, it was rather the dynamics of development itself that brought more and more complexities which the given system could not envisage. Rumer stated, "Another important feature of Central Asia's backwardness is the disproportion between its share of population and its share of national income. If the regional statistics of national income are taken seriously, then the fact that the region's share of population is twice as great as its share of national income can only mean that labour productivity is sharply lower in Central Asia."[53] But Rumer further investigated and opined that it was the method of calculation followed by Moscow that had put Central Asia in a disadvantageous position for the production in this zone mainly included raw materials or half-finished, half processed consumer items (especially cotton), whereas the fully processed items received much better evaluation but the credit of that part went to other regions and Central Asia was deprived of her due recognition. Boris Rumer stated, "Soviet Method of indices show that the Central Asian labour productivity was lower compared to other regions. But there was a difficulty in computing national income for particular regions is that many products are finally used outside the regions in which they are produced. According to this method, regions with industries of consumer goods have accordingly a higher index for national income while regions producing more intermediate products (serving as raw materials or semifinished components for final manufacture) find themselves disadvantaged: This has happened to Central Asia."[54] By way of explanation of this opinion Rumer took up the item of cotton. He wrote "The industrial processing of one ton of raw cotton yields 3400 hecters of cloth, 94 kgs of vegetable oil, 6 kgs of soap and so forth. The crucial difference is the rate of turnover tax imposed at the various stages: 410 to 600 rubles is added to the products obtained from the industrial processing of each ton of raw cotton, whereas 1260 to 1700 rubles is added to the products obtained from the industrial processing of each ton of raw cotton. Obviously, if a more significant part of the cotton raised in Central Asia were also processed there, the region's national income as well as its share in the total national income of the USSR would be greater."[55]

Ajay Patnaik also highlighted the fact that rapid industrialisation demanded 'too much influx of European labour to Central Asia and the disproportion in the ethnic composition of the industrial occupations, it reflected poorly on the rational use of resources, natural as well as labour. Only 7 per cent of the cotton produced by Uzbekistan was processed in the republic, the rest was shipped to distant areas which faced both urban and rural labour shortage. At the same time Central Asia brought from outside a good deal of output, the production of which could be organised in Central Asia itself."[56] Thus industrial development, being inadequate and lop-sided, brought disparity within the Central Asian society and discontent among the population about the regime. Ajay Patnaik also observed, "The labour force was ethnically divided along sectors of the economy, Europeans dominating skilled industrial occupation and the Central Asian light and food industry and agriculture. This brought about ethnic differences in earning and living standards. Thus economic progress, after a short run of success was no more considered a miracle that could eliminate inequality between peoples."[57]

Thus, there was the problem of industrialisation. As a result of the lack of infrastructure, even the limited industrialisation did not or could not be of use to the local population because, given their lack of expertise, the industrial sectors were dominated by Russians and other Europeans. Moreover, Central Asia had its own unique dimension of rapid population growth for which the states needed more labour intensive occupations. These problems could not be solved by initiating heavy industries because 94 per cent of the unemployed in the region were women, mostly rural and unskilled and therefore immobile and incapable of working in capital intensive industrial branches located in big cities. Rather, it was easier to employ such unskilled women in light and food industries and therefore, their increase in employment in this direction would have been more beneficial for Central Asia. But the necessities of Central Asia did not harmonize with the general spirit of the Soviet economy whose priority was heavy industry and gigantic constructions. But Central Asia could have served well as a good base for cotton industry where it remained only as a producer of raw materials throughout the Soviet experience. While Uzbekistan used to produce 70 per cent of the USSR's cotton fibre (white gold was the epithet), she had only a negligible share in textile output –2.7 per cent in 1940, 3.7 in 1960, 2.8 per cent in 1970 and 2.7 per cent in 1980.[58] The explanation provided behind such planning was that the proximity to the consumer world was more important for textile industries than to the source of its raw materials because, "shipment of raw cotton was cheaper than shipment of textiles."[59] This kind of logic implied that every decision used to be taken in broad terms—whether it suited the economy of the USSR or not. And if in the process, the regional economic interests were neglected, the matter was simply overlooked. This was the case with Central Asia. Ajay Patnaik concluded, "As a result, almost all of Central Asia's cotton had its utility for industries in other regiosns but not for the region itself. Industries that were important for the country's national economy were developed and transfer of labour resources from other regions to Central Asia was considered desirable and positive, labour use, like the use of any other resource, was considered purely from this overriding perspective in which the interest of the USSR's national economy was given paramount importance over any other interest—regional, local, ethnic or any other interest."[60]

Therefore, the picture in general in Central Asia was of a rural over-population which could not get distributed in the urban industrial sectors. Rather industries attracted a substantial number of outsiders as officials and skilled workers. This had created the complexities for the entire economy of the zone during the Soviet period that induced the feeling of alienation from the centre. Moreover, limited industrialisation invited urbanisation of a cosmopolitan nature where non-indigeneous population was more and this brought a mixed urban culture to the cities while the rural sectors remained free from external influences. This, once again, brought the differences within the region and created a sense of hierarchy within the indigenous population. People residing in urban territories, keeping in touch with the higher officials and Russian and other more advanced outsiders, began to experience a kind of alienation from their own rural less advanced counterparts. Throughout the years of stagnation under the later Soviet era (ensued from post World War II stage), this small group of local urban elites, closely attached to the Russian and other aliens helped the centre to maintain the status quo.

As Alastair Mcauley[61] analysed, "As has already been pointed out, decision making in the USSR was very centralised. This was particularly true of the economy. Decisions about which plants to build and where they should be sited were made by the so called industrial ministries; these were located almost exclusively in Moscow. This had definite—and mostly unfortunate—consequences for the development of the economies of individual republics. There were certain general policies on location, designed to ensure a degree of regional self-sufficiency and to economise on the use of transport. These were the responsibility of the All-Union and republican planning committees (gosplans). These bodies were responsible for drawing up annual and five-year plans. In practice, however, these policies were often ignored. Gosplan proved to be weaker, in this respect at least, than the industrial ministries. Rather, it appears that an important, if not the primary consideration, was control: ministries—and, indeed, planners generally preferred to deal with a few large plants rather than large number of small ones. The logic of planning thus reinforced all the other forces in favour of so called gigantomania. As a result, the Soviet economy was characterised by an excess of large plants and a dearth of small or medium sized ones in comparison with other economies at similar levels of developments."[62] An ideal example of such gigantomania that led to a vast fiasco was the Nurek aluminum industry in Tajikistan, which will be discussed at length later in this chapter. However, the basic trend of Soviet economy did not go in tune with the Central Asian requirements and therefore, the region, like many other non-Russian areas, remained neglected. Alastair Mcauley called this problem of incompatibility 'structural distortion' which the region had to bear with as a part of 'economic legacy of socialism' even in the post Soviet period.[63]

The post-Brezhnev era up to Gorbachev made no difference to Central Asia because both the tenures of Andropov and Chernenko were very shortlived. And even if Andropov could locate some of the very basic problems of the Soviet economy in general, he could neither take the risk of an allround economic reform, nor did he get the time to concentrate on such a large scale plunge. As far as Chernenko was concerned, he neither had the vision nor the courage to take up any new initiative. Therefore, the economic crisis of Soviet Union kept on increasing rendering an even more difficult situation for Central Asia.

In fact the issue of succession in Soviet leadership was a difficult one with various strands of complexities, within the bureaucracy, the party and all other branches of ministries. Therefore, it took time for Andropov to establish and reassess the general situation—which was really quite depressing at that stage, especially the general economy was almost at the verge of collapse. As, Seweryn Bialer observed that during the short spell of 'Andropov's interregnum', "The press openly reported serious shortages of food and consumer goods and pervasive bureaucratic foot-dragging. It said straight forwardly that economic plans remained unfulfilled and a major share of allocated investments frozen, and that waves and income would not rise without a significant improvement in labour productivity."[64] Though initially with his enthusiasm and discipline Andropov seemed to make the subjects expectant about bringing change for the better, yet, given the complexities of circumstances and his limited tenure, almost everything remained unfulfilled. Bialer concluded, "The Soviet elite now looks back to Andropov as a leader with great but unfulfilled promise."[65] And the shortest regime of Konstantin Chernenko left no mark in the Soviet polity, not to speak of the Central Asian region. Chernenko was a man of mediocre talent in every standard and rose to the final stage of leadership at an old age and therefore neither had the energy, nor the vision to embark on any drastic reform. Rather, the tenure of Chernenko marked the end of a generation of Soviet leadership who in the name of status quo initiated stagnation and always provided lip service to the socialist ideals and allowed the system to decay and above all, they were sceptical about any drastic reform measures in economic sphere for they knew that this would surely turn the situation out of their control.

The Tajik Experience

However, given the lopsided emphasis of the Soviet economy and the disadvantageous position enjoyed by Central Asia throughout the Soviet period therein, one could locate the position of Tajikstan as the poorest of Central Asian republics and one of the most neglected region in the whole of USSR. Again, if investigated separately, one can find many interesting divergences within Tajikstan itself. There too, the role of political influence and economic affluence depended on the proximity to the central leadership. In fact, the gravest mistake in the regional division of Tajikstan in the Soviet period was the lopsided distribution of industrial and commercial urban sectors. According to

Bolshaya Sovietskaya Encyclopaedia, the regional distribution of Tajikistan is shown in the table below[66] :

Region	*Size*	*Population*	*No. of Settle-ments*	*No. of Cities*	*No. of semi-urban settle-ments*
Gorno Badakhshan	63,700 sq. km.	112,000	6	1	–
Quliab Oblast	12,900 sq. km.	432,000	8	2	6
Leninabad (Khojent)	26,100 sq. km.	1,00,8000	12	9	20
Other regions under the Republic	40,400 sq. km.	1,75,5000	15	6	21

The above table shows the marked difference in development in terms of urbanity. Industrialisation of Central Asia, which began during the Tsarist period, followed quite an uneven pattern of distribution. Unfortunately, the emphasis remained the same during the Soviet phase when the nearer goal of rapid industrialisation preceded the far reaching goal of socialist achievements. As a result, the regions with more economic potential and prospect came to the limelight, whereas, the remote and naturally barren regions were left neglected. Though the so called fortunate regions also had their own dissatisfaction regarding the incomplete character of industrialisation, yet the presence of industries brought urbanity and a kind of socialisation that affected the political attitude of the people attached to the respective regions.

The most fortunate region in this sense was the north and north eastern Tajikistan, which is commonly known as Khojent—although Soviet authority named it as Leninabad. In the description of Barnet R. Rubin, "Most of the Republic's industrial investment went to Khujand and the Hissar valley near Dushanbe. Massive irrigation projects on the Amu Dariya and its tributaries transformed the arid southern areas, formerly mainly the nomadic pastoralists, into parts of the Central Asian cotton bowl. By 1991, Tajikistan produced 117 of the Soviet Union's longstaple cotton."[67] Another big zone in the north was the *Quliab oblast* where the capital Dushanbe was situated. This region being the central zone of the state received concentrated attention and all the big industries were also mostly concentrated around Dushanbe. Of them the most remarkable was the gigantic hydroelectric station at Nurek, a small township a few miles from

Dushanbe. Boris Rumer stated that, "The main economic advantage for creating an industrial centre here was the hydroelectric potential of the area: it has approximately 50 per cent of the hydroelectric resources in Central Asia and 8 per cent of the total in the USSR. Another favourable factor was the presence of natural mineral deposits (sodium chloride, limestone, certain rare metals)."[68] But, once the project was taken up in Nurek during the time of Khrushchev, it was found that the cost of transporting hydroelectric energy towards Tashkent, where it was necessitated, would be too costly for topographical disadvantages. Therefore, it was decided that the energy would be used in South Tajikistan and therefore a South Tajik Territorial Production Complex was created with a chemical combine at Yavan and an aluminium factory at Regar. But even then the plan did not seem to be fruitful as 'Despite the energy-intensive nature of chemical and aluminium production, it is admitted that, even with the Regar and Yavan projects, a considerable amount of Nurek energy will remain unused. According to the estimate, this unused remainder may be as high as 20-25 per cent of total capacity."[69] Boris Rumer assessed, "In 1984, the plant's losses amounted to 33 million rubles and the next year they climbed to 48 million rubles." Rumer further continued, "People at the plant say that their aluminium costs more than the gold extracted from the bottom of the Zeravshan River…. Ironically, until recently, this whole enterprise was proudly exalted in the Soviet press as the embodiment of "the aluminum industry of tomorrow" and was regarded as the most advanced industrial enterprise in Central Asia."[70] Thus, the huge industrial plan often proved to be great fiasco, as Nurek, yet a false image of huge productivity was maintained just to give an eye-wash to the region and its inhabitants. Dyker further analysed, "…… Nurek could perhaps be seen as a 'bribe' to the Tadzhiks, as a move in foreign policy, or simply as a result of the good blat of the Tadzhik leaders."[71] Nurek was shown as a huge project with a great deal of investment in order to satisfy the native nomanklatura. To them Nurek was a prestige symbol. But such costly and abortive symbols could not provide any direction to economic development. Again, there were many other industries like the Ordzhonikidze mechanical engineering factory, Kanibadam Cotton seed oil manufacturing factory, ginning factories at Kirovabad, Leninabad, Kanibadam, etc. all of which showed lack of technology and inadequate investment that led to 'dwarf-workshopism'[72] in the existing industries making production suffer significantly. But, however defective and dissatisfactory the Tajik industrialisation might have been, it brought urbanity in the surrounding zones and the local elites flourished from these so-called comparatively fortunate zones. Taking advantage of their fortunate position the people of Khojent-Quliab turned themselves into a privileged community under the Soviet govt. The simultaneous growth of industry and town gave them opportunities to participate in modern professions, materially improved life style, and above all, a new secular education. But this had two very interesting consequences. On the one hand, their relative prosperity made them alien to their less developed Tajik counterparts, while on the other, they could establish an amiable relation with the Russian and Uzbek people, residing in Tajikistan, mostly working as the government officials, due to similarities in socio-economic status and a common way of thought. Actually, a large number of Russian officials were appointed in professional and political departments of Tajikistan in order to supervise and conduct the process of development. And this policy was criticised under the title "Russian big-brotherhood".[73] Even though criticised by outsiders, the "big-brotherhood" could not make the people of Khojent-Quliab alien to the Soviet system. Rather, this region remained most loyal to the Communist cause, even after the disintegration in 1991. Actually, in spite of the presence of Russian bosses, in professional life or as government officials (Second Secretary, etc.), people of these region started experiencing important political powers and positions. All the topmost Tajik leaders of different generations like Bobojan Gafurov, Zhabar Rasulov, Rakhmon Nabiev hailed from this region. This region consistently provided a class of local elites who had good understanding with the Soviet officials (Russian or non-Russian outsiders) and ensured loyalty to the central authority of Moscow. Apparently, this fulfilled the Bolshevik aspiration of mutual trust and internationalistic (Mezh Natsionalnaya) friendship. But in a negative sense it alienated this handful of highly educated and prosperous Tajiks from their own fellowmen in the less fortunate regions of the country.

The most stubborn opposition to the fortunate northerns were provided by the inhabitants of the Gorno-Badakhshan region of the south. The treacherous mountains of the Pamir made this region the most difficult place for habitation. The modern technologies of Soviet system did not or could not remove the natural difficulties of this region. The thin population of this geographic zone maintained their age-old tribal way of life in spite of the socialist revolution and the presence of a long term socialist regime. The Soviet system made hardly any difference to these people in terms of economy, society or polity. Therefore, they remained faithful to their traditional culture. Quite naturally, religion played an important role in their life and thought. Compared to the Tajik people of other regions, the Pamiris, Ismailis, Garmis and other tribals of this region were much more faithful to Islamic principles. The communist teaching of denouncing religion as an unnecessary deterrent to socialism probably did not touch their conscience. They, in their underdeveloped surroundings remained untouched by such socialist propaganda. Discontent in this area grew out of a sense of being neglected and underdeveloped throughout the Soviet era. Therefore, once the veil of Soviet rule was lifted, this region became hell bent to find out a more dependable ideology as an alternative to communist ethos. In the process they came to imbibe the most coarse, almost fanatic, branch of Islam.

In between the elite north and the tribal south, one can locate the position of the Qurgan-Tyube region. Economically this region was quite prosperous. The population here had a mixed character. In fact, if seen statistically, this area was inhabited more by the non-Tajiks than Tajiks. Traditionally, this area was inhabited by the Uzbeks. But, after the creation of Tajikistan as a separate SSR, the Bolshevik government took a conscious policy of artificially grafting the Tajik populace to provide Qurgan-Tyube with a Tajik look. The modern habitation pattern of Qurgan Tyube was a result of Soviet policy of forceful emigration from one place to another in between 1930 and 1960. From within Tajikistan, there came people from Quliab as well as from Garm in the south. They were mainly made to emigrate for the need of manual labour in cotton cultivation and processing.[74] This attempt of artificial interaction did not work well. Because the Tajiks here suffered from two genuine complexes. Firstly, they could not overcome their bitter experience of getting uprooted from their own land. Secondly, in spite of being Tajik and staying in Tajikistan, they experienced the feeling of being outnumbered by the Uzbeks in this particular area. Therefore, although not much economically deprived, the Tajiks of this region could not remain faithful to the communist regime. Therefore, one can see that during the turmoil of 1991 there arose the Islamic Renaissance Party—whose ideology showed a mixture of democratic principles along with the moderate fervour of Islam.[75]

IV

Considering the multidimensional politico-economic factors related to the Soviet republics and their relation with the centre, scholars tried to assess the character of the Soviet state from different perspectives. There are two diametrically opposite views about the nature of the Soviet Socialist state. From the Western point of view the Soviet system seemed like an empire in her dealings with the non-Russian territories and also in her unopposed authoritarianism (posed by the CPSU) all over her territories. For example, J. Keep, R. Conquest, Dmitri Volkogonov and the other anti-Soviet scholars openly condemned the Soviet system as an imperial practice. Their anti-Soviet perspective can be seen in the very titles of their books. For example, the book by J. Keep is entitled *Last of Empires*, while one of R. Conquest's edited volume has almost an identical title *The Last Empire* and Volkogonov named his book *The Rise and Fall of the Soviet Empire*.[76] It seems that all of these authors, along with many others like A. Bennigsen, T.R. Harmstone and Wimbush, wanted to stress the problems of the non-Russian nationalities, minority nationalities and so on who were completely overshadowed by the mainstream political forces led by White Russia. But the Soviet intellectuals still tried their best to fight back this criticism and wanted to show how the Soviet Union fulfilled all the republican and federal characteristics within the system. Victor Shevtsov's book titled *The State and Nations in the USSR*, published from Moscow openly denied the Western view, "Some Western writers try to prove that union republics have no genuine statehood by arguing that these republics do not own their territory, mineral resources, farm land, and so on, and that to these writers, is incompatible with sovereignty."[77] Then he gave a list of rights enjoyed by the Union Republics and highlighted the ways through which the Constitutional reforms of 1977 further enhanced this autonomous character of the republics. Yet, he had to admit that, "It is, nevertheless, an essential distinguishing feature of a Union republic that it is a sovereign state and simultaneously one of the subjects of the Soviet federation; the USSR. Having become members of the USSR, the Union republics have voluntarily transferred some of their rights to the Federation, but that does not mean at all that they have circumscribed their sovereignty. It means merely that the Union republics, in full conformity with the Constitution of the USSR and their own Constitutions, exercise their state authority within the limits of the powers reserved to them."[78] This restricted sovereignty and the expected conformity to the Central authority implied the limited autonomy of the union republics. And the attempt by Soviet scholars to counter the Western argument during the mid 70s and 80s implied that the Western viewpoint posed a challenge to the integrity of the USSR and the pro-Soviet authors had to turn quite overtly defensive about the Soviet State System.

Though the Soviet claims of federalism and republicanism were to be rejected for the all pervasive party domination and overwhelming position of the centre vis-a-vis the union republics, would it be logical to call the Soviet state an 'empire'? For, the Soviet system, with all its shortcomings and unfulfilled promises of socialism and revolution had its base in each union republic, and could bring about a partnership with the new kind of local elites and could, therefore, maintain the power base till the revolution (Perestroika) began from above. The control of the centre, apparently, seemed overbearing for the republics. Yet, considering the decline of Moscow's leadership from the later part of Brezhnev era till Gorbachev, one can assume that the regional leaders had found enough breathing space in their internal affairs. Central Asia was politically quite peaceful before the break-up of the Soviet Union and most of the republics did not even welcome the prospect of complete independence in 1991. Thus, a kind of partnership between the local power base and the central authority in Moscow worked hand in hand. But, the most damaging aspect of this power equation was the tendency towards inertia and stagnation that got reflected in the thoughts and actions of the generation of leadership both at the centre and the republics.

Thus, the Soviet regime reflected a kind of partnership between the Russian and regional nomanklatura where the position of the Russian leaders was quite distinct in terms of the operating power-hierarchy. This partnership underlying the Soviet system was hegemonic where the participation of the non-Russian republics was conditioned by their allegiance to the centre (hegemon). Lacking in overt political aspirations for independence and still economically backward, Central Asia got naturally overshadowed by the overwhelming presence of a Soviet polity that was largely superimposed by Russian identity.

Four

Religion: The Determining Factor in Central Asian Identity

In the history of Central Asia, Islam became the most prominent religion from the medieval period and became a regular element of Central Asian Culture as well. Throughout the medieval period Islam developed spontaneously and penetrated popular psychology which affected social norms, behavioural and cultural patterns of Central Asia in a major way. But again, such a spontaneous exfoliation of Islam assumed several forms. For example, there was the development of Sufism along with the mainstream sunni creed, while in some places of Tajikistan the Ismaili cult was prominent. Thus Islam was far from being monolithic even at the height of its easy growth in Central Asia.

Thus, well before Tsarist expansionism was to reach Central Asia, Islam was ingrained in the socio-cultural matrix of the region. Although Central Asia experienced the domination of an alien culture from the time of Russian imperialism, the main challenge to Islam came along with the Soviet regime. Soviet authorities, being committed to Marxist socialism and determined to create *Novie Sovietskii Chelovek*[1], however, could not remain sympathetic to the idea of any religion having independence to the extent of spreading its idealistic outlook. Moreover, as a part of their mission, they took active part in removing superstitions, prejudices and social discriminations which had developed as a part of Islamic rituals and practices. The changes demanded by the Soviet authorities in the sphere of Islamic practices were explained by their principle of secularism. Thus, from its very inception, the Soviet system encountered difficulties with a few minor and some formidable religious beliefs and practices of Central Asians whose broader implications were not revealed until the collapse of the Soviet order.

But it would be fallacious to surmise on the basis of the objection in principle to the persistence of religion, that attitudes to Islam throughout the Soviet regime's history remained unchanged.

Atheistic propaganda was an important part of the Soviet system that disturbed the faith of all religions—Islamic or non-Islamic, residing under the Soviet umbrella. Nevertheless, the extent of the propaganda and the stringency of suppression of religious performances varied according to the personalities of Soviet leadership and the constantly changing demand of the time. Mehrdad Haghayeghi in his book *Islam and Politics in Central Asia* had studied the changing position of Islam under different phases of communism.[2] The phases were arranged chronologically into nine categories:

(1) 1917 to 1920
(2) 1921 to 1927
(3) 1928 to 1938
(4) 1939 to 1953
(5) 1954 to 1960
(6) 1960 to 1964
(7) 1965 to 1978
(8) 1978 to 1984
(9) 1985 to 1990

Phase one and two signified Leninist policy, phase three and four implied Stalinist policy and from phase five started the post-Stalin policies with the religious issue becoming very significant in the Khrurchev era. Phase five and six reflected Khrurchev's policy whereas seven and eight implied Brezhnev era and the interregnum upto Gorbachev's regime. Phase nine signified the Gorbachev era and the end of the Soviet state in this region when religious revival became a very common characteristic of all Central Asian states.

During the preparatory stage of the Bolshevik Revolution, Muslim Nationalism was protected and encouraged by the party leaders in order to bring the vast masses of Muslim faith living in Central Asia and Transcaucasia under revolutionary hegemony.

In order to win the support of the Central Asian Muslims, some kind of symbolic gestures were made, for example, the Koran of Usman, which had been confiscated at the time of the Tsarist conquest of Samarkand, was returned to the Muslims.[3] But, the moment there came up the question of sharing power with the local Muslim organisation, the Soviet system began to show unwillingness and incompatibility between the two ethos. By 1918, the Bolshevik policy towards Islam got reversed from a liberal stand point and there were many excesses done by the Russian Cadres of the Bolshevik party which culminated into heightened atrocities like profaning of mosques, shooting of clergy, confiscation of land given for religious endowment, closing of Shariat courts and the abolition of religious schools.[4] As a result of these unexpected atrocities done by the Russian Socialist Cadres, there was a protest movement in Central Asia named '*Basmachi*'[5] from 1918 onwards. The newly born Soviet government then had to handle the *Basmachi* challenge on the one hand and had to take up war communism as an all round policy on the other. At this alarming stage of the crisis, a two fold policy towards Islam began to develop from 1921 onwards. There was an effort to restore trust among the general Muslim psopulation by returning the confiscated Waqf property, reopening mosques and Islamic schools and resuming Shariat laws and, secondly, attempts to include more Muslims into the party also increased. Once this assimilation process could succeed in ensuring a substantial amount of Muslim support, the policy of eradicating Islamic influences from law courts, education and social practices began with increased intensity. The intention of these measures were reformative, yset their implementation made them appear quite repressive. Along with these, a new dimension of atheistic propaganda was added to justify all the anti-Islamic measures as a part of socialist development. The institutions like Commissariat of Justice, Commissariat of Education, Communist Youth League (Komsomol) and so on were given the responsibility of this propaganda. There were regular publication like *Khoda-Syzlar, Allah-Syzlar*, etc. where "Islam was frequently depicted as an antisocial, antifeminist, intolerant and xenophobic religion with barbaric and unhealthy customs.[6]

The next stage began with the change of leadership from Lenin to Stalin. The first phase of Stalinist era was marked with a more vigorous anti-Islamic campaign. It was during his time that Muslim Communist leaders like Sultan Galiev, etc. were purged from the Bolshevik party for allegedly joining the *Basmachi* movement. But, actually, by this time, the indigenous national leadership of Central Asia began to get disillusioned with the Bolshevik socialist doctrines as they found no room for nationalism or Islam in the new ideology. Thus incompatibility of Islam and socialism (Bolshevik) began to grow from this time onwards. In a part of the Soviet state, the amount of repression began to increase to remove the evil influence of their religion which according to them was a vehicle of medievalism and therefore needed to be abolished for the success of socialism. Along with printed propaganda, a League of Militant Godless was created whose task was to incorporate more and more Muslim members and convince them in favour of atheism, and against Islamic belief. Thus, attempts were made on both institutional and ideological levels to get rid of the Islamic influences.

But this was not a consistent government policy of the Soviet government which could be explained in terms of socialist ideology and principle. The moment Soviet Union entered the World War II, a qualitative change could be seen in the attitude towards Central Asian Muslims, for the support and loyalty of this region was needed in order to survive German onslaught. Therefore, the second phase of Stalinist era saw conciliatory gestures towards the Muslim believers of this region. Moreover, the official clergies were engaged in order to encourage patriotism with religious fervour among the general population of the region. For example, Rasulayev began his patriotic propaganda in 1941, as "Chief of Central Council of Islamic Religious Centre in the USSR" by asking the Muslims to support the Soviet war efforts.[7] Such motivated efforts to utilise religion at times of emergency was not very fruitful in this region and some 6,00,000 Muslims were deported to Siberia being accused of treachery at the end of the war. But, after the war came to an end, interestingly, Stalin did not revive the earlier stringency towards Islam—rather experiment with some token liberal gestures, for example, reopening of the Mir Arab madrashah in 1952, the publication of Koran and Islamic skepticals were allowed from 1948, some Islamic rituals like hajj to Meccah, etc. were resumed. Rebuilding of mosques was also gradually started and was allowed upto 3,000 in number, which had remained about 1700 in the pre-war stage, according to the official estimate. Thus, ruthless suppression was replaced by some apparent gesture of sympathy and acceptance of autonomy. Side by side, Stalin took up a more subtle method of propaganda whereby the process of eradicating religious influences (Islamic) continued unabated. The League of Militant Godless was dissolved. In its place the "All-Union Society for the Dissemination of Political and Scientific Knowledge" or *Znanie* (Knowledge) came into existence with the solemn task of removing Islamic influences from the Socialist path of progress in Central Asia. M. Haghyeghi opined, "And by 1948, a number of branch organisations under the auspices of *Znanie*, had been put in place all across Central Asia, utilising a wide range of propaganda techniques such as lectures, films, literature, posters, radio programmes and so on."[8] Soviet government's attitude to all religions including Christianity was officially the same. But as Islam, as an organised religion and guiding principle of the Soviet Muslims always acted as an all encompassing ideology in contradiction with Soviet Communism—Islam was always taken as a challenge.

With Krushchev there began the post-Stalin era in Soviet history which was marked with des-Stalinization in every respect of social, political and other state affairs. However, de-Stalinization did not imply a thaw in the religious sphere. Although Khrushchev's religious policy was not solely directed against Islam, but was equally applicable to Christian church and clergy, it brought to the Central Asian Muslims a bitter experience with the Soviet government after the short breathing space they enjoyed in the post-war period. Along with the pre-war devices of closedown of churches and mosques and control over pilgrimage, etc. there was introduction of some new methods of antireligious propaganda. For example, all the traditional social ceremonies, like, marriage, birth, funerals began to be replaced by 'secular Marxist rituals'. "A substitute for the Christian baptismal ceremony was concurrently introduced. It was called the "name-giving ceremony" at which the child was presented with a medal with its name on one side and a picture of Lenin's on the other."[9] Secondly, laws and measures were used against religious practices thought to be harmful for the socialist way of life. For example, religious activities which were or could be harmful to health, which could result in non-participation in social activity, or which could result in non-keptical of civil duties or 'entice' any minor into any religious organisation, were all prescribed by Article 227 of the Criminal Code, under pain of 'five years' imprisonment or exile. Special attention was given to the education of the children at their home and, therefore, families were visited by authorities to control and remove religious atmosphere from private life as well. With the removal of Khrushchev, in 1964, there again came a reversal in the Soviet religious policy. At least, there was an acknowledgement of mistakes done on the anti-religious front, and although the closed mosques were not reopened some of the imprisoned clerics were released.

The next stage in Soviet religious policy marked a new line of experimentation of a more complex and multidimensional variety. On the one hand propaganda continued on the socialist and atheist education in order to offset religious faith and tradition, on the other, various statistical surveys were organised to find out the actual number of believers still attached to Islam. Another interesting aspect of this propaganda process was to embrace the issue of women's emancipation which was a positive outcome of atheism and scientific socialism. Along with these, there were also amendments in laws to clarify the position of the state vis-à-vis religion. But the most striking feature of the religious policy of the Soviet regime of the 70s was to make a tacit alliance with the Soviet Islamic authorities—presumably the more progressive section of them—and utilise them in strengthening the regime's practical power base. Here the role of Islam in the contemporary world politics came as an added incentive to make the Soviet government more cautious to chalk out her foreign policies. Due to the centrality of the Cold War—the Soviet authorities' choices of allies often had to be made in terms of anti-US moves. As a result, they often came to support Islamic forces, for example, in Iran or Afghanistan. This brought a new dimension in Soviet religious policy because this led to ambiguity and dichotomy in her domestic and foreign policies regarding Islam. Thus, there began an era of confusion and ambivalence regarding the issue of accommodating Islam in the Marxist-Socialist framework. This was undoubtedly, a qualitative shift from the politics of the earlier generations of Soviet leadership and must have had widespread and complex impact on the psychology of the different variety of population in Central Asia.

To start with the laws, the Soviet Constitution had traditionally guaranteed 'freedom of religious worship and freedom of anti-religious propaganda' in Article 124 of the 1936 'Stalin' Constitution which was slightly altered in the Article 52 of the 1977 Constitution whereby, "Citizens of the USSR guaranteed freedom of conscience, that is religion, and to conduct religious worship or atheistic propaganda. Incitement of hostility or hatred on religious grounds is prohibited. In the USSR, the Church is separated from the state, and the school from the church."[10] In fact, as early as 1966, just after coming to the leadership, Brezhnev introduced three laws to clarify the position of the state vis-à-vis religion. First, article 142 of the Criminal Code identified six categories of offences which included collection of taxes for religious purposes and incitement of religious superstition among the masses. The second law made the above offences punishable for three years imprisonment. The third law dealt with the restrictions on religious associations and gatherings. A series of amendments to 1929 "Law on Religious Associations" took place in 1975 which intended to increase central control over religious activities. However, the amendment of 1977, which is cited above, had a significant change of expression, i.e. the term "anti-religious" was replaced by "atheistic" which according to M. Haghayeghi was a marked shift towards compromise.[11] But one must remember that these laws in Soviet system embraced both Muslim and non-Muslim (mainly Christian) followers and could not signify any special treatment towards the Muslim Central Asia. Laws only showed the general trend of the system and their continued faith in atheism and scientific socialism.

Therefore, to assess the Soviet authorities' attitude towards Islam in this phase, one should take note of the propaganda activities in the region concerned. Although the general guiding principles and purposes of this propaganda were strikingly similar for all faiths which were, to restrict religious practice, especially in the demonstrative forms, to prevent children and young people from being imbued with religious tenets or from being taught religious rites, the experimentation on atheistic propaganda in various forms becamè a serious problem for the largest non-Slav population of the Soviet regime, who followed Islam as their religion. Thus, the patterns of propaganda in the Soviet Central Asia became an interesting case-study for later scholars. Interestingly, the propaganda methods followed here were more intense. Use of print-media, along with audio-visual aids, appointment of direct officials known as agitators,[12] holding societies for the dissemination of political and scientific knowledge, etc. were some of the official initiatives to do away with the influences of Islam.

There were various journals titled *Nauka i Religia* (Science or Religion), *Vàprosy Nauchnogo Ateizma* (Question of Scientific Atheism), *Islam V USSR* (Islam in the USSR), which carried host of articles criticising the religious attachments, with special emphasis on Islam as an incompatible force to move along with socialism. This literature at this stage was not confined to theoretical exercises; rather, the more practical, immediate objective issues were taken up to make the agitations more effective. One article in *Pravda Vostoka* titled *Sotsialnyi Progress i ateizm by, I Dzhabbarov*, criticised the stereotype scholastic approach of 'quotation-mongering, superficial comment and formalism, but demanded that atheistic propaganda should 'take into account the dialectical unity of objective circumstances and subjective factors' and be reinforced by 'a complex of socio-economic and cultural measures."[13] At this stage stress on superstitions related to religious rites became the target of attack than the faith itself. The propagandists throughout the USSR were told by the 1979 CPSU

Central Committee decree *On the Further Improvement of Ideological and Politico-Educational Work* that there was much still left to be done in educating the *Novie Sovietskii Chelovek* and the decree laid down guidelines for improving the form of propaganda activity.[14] Along with ensuring a high scientific level, the decree stressed on reinforcing efficiency, specificity and link with life and the solution of economic and political tasks. In addition, the decree called for 'a systematic purposeful and uncompromising' struggle to remove the many obstacles to the creation of the New Soviet Man. In order to eradicate those 'ugly relics of the past that are often still prevalent' in their society like thriftlessness and wastefulness, drunkenness and hooliganism, bureaucratism and a callous attitude to people, violations of labour discipline and public order[15] was needed. In 1981, Brezhnev himself outlined the decree at the 26th CPSU Congress in the section of his report devoted to the strengthening of the material and spiritual bases of the socialist way of life and the forming of the new man.[16]

From this time, a kind of self-critical approach could be found among the propagandists to locate the short-comings of the previous agitation and activities. For example, the *obkom* secretary of Gorno-Badakhshan *oblast* of Tajikistan A.I. Babaev in the 15th Plenum of the Tajik Party Central Committee resolution noted, "...the core of ideological work is the formation of a scientific world outlook among the masses, their education in the ideas of Marxism-Leninism and the assertion of Communist morality..." and added, "As a result of the shortcomings of work in this direction, survivals of the past surface in the behaviour and consciousness of a certain section of the population."[17] Measures were taken to increase scientific knowledge as a positive force to eradicate the unscientific impact of religion, namely Islam from the region. The president of the Tajikistan Academy of Sciences and Chairman of the board of the republic's Znanie Society, M.S. Asimov, called at the same plenum for the publication in Tajik of *Nauka i Zhizn* (Science and life) which had supposedly attained popularity in other republics, among other things as a platform for scientific atheist propaganda."[18]

There arose discussions about the 'forms and methods' of ideological education and atheistic propaganda' and instructions were imparted to the party activists and the agitators to show 'a tactful attitude to the working peoples' needs and concerns.[19] The editorial of *Pravda Vostoka*, an Uzbekistan daily, stressed that the atheistic propaganda was 'individual work with believers'. In order to win popular minds the implementing of secular rituals, holidays and traditions were highlighted as an alternative to religious participation especially social festivals like birth, marriage, etc. In conclusion, the editorial stated, that the anti-religious education should be, 'more deeply thought out, richer and more interesting.'[20] The Kirgiz SSR daily complained, "Many organisations of the party, Soviets, trade unions and Komromol have not reviewed questions of atheistic education for years; they occupy themselves only feebly with the introduction of socialist rituals and do not ensure a strict and consistent implementation of Leninist principles on the attitude to religion.'[21] This realisation of inadequacy on part of the propaganda scheme, in the late 70s, resulted from some external factors which would be discussed in the later part of this chapter. Irrespective of the external scenario, the self-assessment of the Soviet regime came to reveal the hopelessly limited success of atheism after fifty years of propaganda. It was found that the number of believers was markedly high and religious faith could not be replaced by imparting scientific knowledge.

Faith in religion was much more deep rooted social phenomenon which could not be removed even from the Christian believers as such. For the Soviet Muslims, whether in Central Asia or elsewhere, the religious attachment seemed irremovable by propaganda activities.

The authorities, to their consternation, were compelled to acknowledge the reality of the growth of religious beliefs among the younger generation—those born in the post-revolution eras. So, one could no longer talk of the superstitions of bygone ages, currently found only among the aged and the uneducated people committed to an unthinking tradition. And there too, the Soviet authority itself had accepted that the religiosity among the Muslim people was comparatively higher. Y. Roi stated, "The fact that recently the Soviet Establishment has openly admitted that even intelligentsia in the Muslim regions is contaminated with religious prejudice (see below) has not led to any basic change in the propagandists' approach. Yet, recognition of the increase in religiosity as a whole within the Muslim population, and particularly of religion's growing appeal to the young and the educated making it more and more difficult to contend that the problem is limited to pensioners, keptica and 'backward elements', has led to an attempt to employ more sophisticated method of anti-religious propaganda and intensified efforts to implement it."[22] Different sources, provided different statistics of the number of religious believers within the Soviet system. Radio Moscow, in an

English-language broadcast (30th March, 1972) stated, "The word Muslim relates to a certain religious belief. ...Over the 60 plus years of Soviet-government, religion has declined sharply in this country, and although we have no figures..., it would be hard to imagine more than 10 per cent of the once Muslim population actually being religious today.[23] But interestingly, a research on the state of religion and the effectiveness of atheist measures in Tajikistan reveals that no less than 46 per cent people openly admitted their preference to participate in the religious festivals, instead of secular festivals. There were thus anomalies and confusions regarding their achievements in atheism, even within the Soviet sources. Michael Rywikin, in an article keptical, "Again statistical data are both spottly and unreliable. Soviet sources estimate percentages of believers from as high as 45 per cent in the remote Kara-Kalpak ASSR to as low as 20 per cent (with another 20 per cent list as 'in between' that is mildly religious) in more modernised areas of Uzbekistan. These figures compare with only 10 per cent believers and 20 per cent 'in between' reported for such traditional Russian Orthodox areas of Russia proper as Penza and Voronez. Among the educated classes the gap is said to be even larger: between 1 per cent and 1.5 per cent believers among the Russians along the Volga river as against 10-15 per cent in Muslim areas."[24] Thus, the Soviet sources not only admitted the presence of substantial number of Muslim believers compared to the Russian Christian believers, but also began to show concern on to how to combat this danger. Therefore, new strategies were chalked out in the methods of atheistic propaganda. Interestingly, the authorities held their inadequacy responsible for the limited penetration of atheism and scientific knowledge, rather accepting the force of religion more lasting and deeply ingrained in popular psychology and culture. In spite of the acceptance of substantial number of believers, scholars like Rywikin and Yaacov Ro'i opined that the Soviet source always provided an inflated number of the 'non-believers'. In Rywikin's analysis "However, it must be borne in mind that Soviet sociologists list among the non-believers those who only 'perform Muslim rites' and those who 'perform Muslim rite under the influence of their relatives, an approach aimed at overestimating the number of atheists."[25] Thus, even Soviet writers and specialists at this stage came to acknowledge the presence of 'Islamic survivals' in the Central Asian republics and keptica that "Communist upbringing" still would have a long way to go before they could create the *novie Sovietskii chelovek*.

After this somewhat open surrender the propaganda took a sharper focus whereby there began an attempt to distinguish religious attachment from national identity consciousness of the Muslim people. At least in Central Asia. Yaacov Ro'i notices, "The party and its propagandists found the connection between religious and national sentiments in the Muslim areas to be particularly disturbing."[26] Therefore, by the end of 1970s, Soviet atheistic propaganda could concentrate on the point of identity and The 25th Congress and the Central Committee decree combined the atheistic and internationalist propaganda in their agenda, putting special attention to dissociate religious identity from national identities. The *obkom* secretary of the *Osh oblast* of Kirgizhia wrote, "Some people suggest, that a person who observes Islamic rites, demonstrates thereby "respect" for his nation, and in deviating from them insults it."—this he found "a profound fallacy, a viewpoint that is foreign to us. We debunk such opinions, doing everything to make people see the difference between national traditions and religious prejudices."[27] Another Tajik expert in this field, Dadabaeva similarly stated that "there was a tendency to consider 'deviation from religious sites a deviation from national traditions" which were applied especially in the observance of "the rites of Muslim nuptials and Circumcision."[28] In June 1980, the First Secretary of the Turkmen Party, M.G. Gąpurov more explicitly stated, "religious beliefs have played and still play an anti-humanist, reactionary role in alienating and polarising nations. It should be borne in mind that national and religious survivals supplement, support and nourish each other". And in 1981 Pravda Vostoka boldly stated, "Socialism has utterly refuted the bourgeois nationalist thesis that some form of religion is a necessary element of the people's national life. On the contrary, under socialism, there is a gradual withering away of the religious (element) and a steady development of the international (element)".[29] Therefore, religion, especially Islamic religion was not only a mediaeval hangover of feudal culture, which sanctioned various exploitative and unscientific customs and rituals, but it was a living threat to the development of Soviet entity for it had a tendency to combine with national identities of the Central Asian people. To prevent this development, another strategy in the propaganda programme was taken which was to monitor the family atmosphere of the children and conscious attempts were made to protect them from any kind of situation which might introduce such illusory identity in their innocent minds. Here the attention was naturally turned towards their mothers as the primary mentor of the children and a special attention was given on the atheistic education of Muslim women of Central Asia.[30]

The official propaganda took special care in order to dissuade women from the overwhelming influence of religion, especially Islam during the 70s and 80s. For it was found, although secular preaching were at times favouring the position of women in the society by putting an end to polygamy and such other practices and allowing her to take up her own career, most of the women still preferred to follow at least some of the tenets of Islam and thereby were still belonging to the category of 'believers'.

Although in general Soviet studies, sociological or anthropological, majority of data on believers were not gender-specific, no data was foolproof. What actually intrigued the Soviet scholars of 70s and 80s was the fact of the allegiance of markedly higher percentage of women than men to Islam in spite of the generally discriminatory anti-feminist spirit of Islamic law and the conservative social customs supported by it. While the figure suggested that 70 to 80 per cent Soviet believes were women, the rate was expected to be higher for Islamic areas.[31] Naturally, reasons were sought for this over religiosity amongst women. The first and foremost reason provided was the lack of participation in the 'social-production' outside home. M.A. Tolmacheva in her article *The Muslim Women in Soviet Central Asia* stated, "The proportion of believers among those removed from the sphere of socialised production rises dramatically."[32] She, moreover, studied that the proportion of believers in skilled occupations was found to be six times lower than among those in unskilled jobs (20% and 3.2%). But here one thing must be kept in mind. In Central Asia, there were a substantial number of 'outsiders' (Russians and so on) working among the skilled employees. Therefore, the data might become misleading, if a ratio of only indigenous people was gathered out of the information from the workplace.[33] However, these scholars tried to relate the role of employment, outside home, in reducing womens' faith in Islam. Tolmacheva, in the same article quoted a statement of a working woman of Ashkabad: "I have six children, and if I don't work Allah will not feed them." In the same article the role of education in eradicating the influence of Islam was also studied. It was accordingly found, "Those with higher and junior-college education provided the bulk of atheists and non-believers (up to 100 per cent); those with elementary education or less—the bulk of believers."[34] S. Dadabeva, the director of the Scientific Atheism

Department of the Philosophy Faculty of the Tajik SSR Academy of Sciences who made serious efforts to make the atheistic propaganda useful for the women of Central Asia, also wrote that women usually became victims of the preachings of *mullahs* and *ishans* because, not all of them took part in 'social production'. She located the reasons for the non-participation of women outside home, in the lack of kindergartens and crèches, rather than inherent conservatism. But she also highlighted the fact that in residential areas, the educational work was lax. That too contributed to the attachment to and conformity to tradition—attachment to Islamic belief and practices."[35]

But M.A. Tolmacheva, tried to highlight some reasons other than educational backwardness and lack of financial independence. In explaining women's recourse to Islam, she stated, "On the other hand, besides the lingering influences of traditions, the destruction of severe curtailment of coercive aspects of the regulatory function of Islam in the Soviet Union not only resulted in pursuing Islam into a 'back corner' of interpersonal relations and individual spirituality: it also, by removing the worst abuses of women, made the religion of Islam into an often conforming, socially accommodating and culturally appealing alternative to what as has been now recognised in the USSR..."[36] For example, she cited the new positive attitude in the family to the birth of girls, although the desire for the couple to have a son still prevailed. Moreover, the pro-natal policies of the Soviet state and the Russian cult of motherhood could come together with the traditional respect for the aged and orthodox Muslim directive to venerate the mother (Hadith), to promote the cause of Islam as longstanding defender of women's interests. Thus, glorification of motherhood played a role to combine the traditional force of Islam with the Soviet form of scientific socialism. Another aspect which was characteristic of Central Asian Islam was the local cult of female spirits denoting the spheres of fertility, ancestor and hearth spirit or the traditions of female saints like Ambarona, Bibi-Seshambe, etc. which could situate the Central Asian women in the Islamic tradition in a comparatively more respectable position. Thus, the local forms of religious practices and rites did not always put women of Central Asia in a very disrespectful position or act solely as a coercive force. At times of distress or to seek peace in general, women found the teachings of Islam or their interpretations in local forms quite comforting. In the localised practices of Islam, popularity of *ishans* were very effective as faith-healers, dispensers of amulets and talisman and as custodians of the holy places like Shah-i-Zindeh in Uzbekistan, Tomb of Sultan Vais Baba in Turkmenistan, etc.[37] Very interestingly, the believers in Central Asia were not very well informed about the meanings of the religious customs or ceremonies, but enjoyed them with active participation. Similarly, women continued to use the amulets or magic designs without often knowing their meanings. Tolmacheva observed, "Very few, even among men, knew Arabic to be able to read written amulets, although the Arabic characters for "Allah" are widely recognised even by the illiterate. And these Arabic characters were believed to possess protective powers. And more specific to Central Asian Islam—there was the popularity of amulets—certain types of wood which supposed to contain magical power. These were sold at a comparatively high price by Soviet standards and the majority of the buyers of these amulets were women. The reasons for such dependence on unscientific powers were usually related to fertility, childbearing and illnesses of the children. Tolmacheva concluded, "And finally, each child's illness, specially in rural families, tend to perpetuate women's belief in evil spirits and the evil eye and promote their spiritual dependence on amulets, saints, pilgrimages, prayer and sacrifice." In spite of readily available medical assistance, their dependencies continued.[38] Thus, Islamic religion at the local level was an essential component of popular culture and did not always followed the formal directives of official hardline of Islam. Therefore, S. Dadabaeva, who was an active participant in the socialist system, and a citizen of Tajik SSR observed minutely that religion was a "complex social phenomenon, with traditions, rites and festivals formed over centuries, that in the part permeated people's mode of life and psychology" which along with the new method of education give rise to "split" personalities "with knowledge ensconced on the one side and conviction on the other". But, Dadabaeva did not take a defeatist attitude while accepting the reality. She suggested on "forms of atheistic work which (would) influence a person's emotional world", and therefore the struggle against religious survivals "has to be variegated, and cannot be reduced purely to educational activities and the unmasking of religious ideology or be restricted to influencing the believer's reason."[39] Dadabaeva also admitted the fact that, many women in Tajikistan, Uzbekistan, etc. were housewives, and therefore, played a greater role in the upbringing of their children than their European (Russian) counterparts and there are indeed more believers among them.'[40] Atheistic propaganda among women, therefore, received a new acceleration at this stage. 'Special Universities' had been set up in Kirgizia's Osh *oblast*, catering mainly for housewives, with lectures on child education, running the household and health. The Komsomol's girls brigade was supposedly very effective in this new method of propaganda which was directed to be 'individual work with believers', instead of confining into impersonal formal lectures.[41] The new intensity of atheistic propaganda was found in its height in Tajikstan in 1980, that within six months of time there were 4000 lectures held on atheism aided by practical—scientific conferences, question answer evenings and film lectures.[42] Prava Vostoka editorial of 23rd October, 1981 emphasised the need to increase the use of visual aids like cinema, television and theatre for successful propaganda work on atheism.[43] However, Turkmenskaya Iskra, in its editorial on 3rd July, 1981, suggested in a spirit of compromise that the campaign against religion should be directed against 'what is old and keptica' while preserving some 'good traditions, like hospitality, respect for older people and the collective celebration of family events by the entire village."[44] Thus a tune of compromise with the collective spirit of Islam on part of the official journals and newspapers indicated a new approach towards religion in the of Soviet system.

Reassessing Aethism

The notion of complete eradication of Islam as a natural outcome of socialist developments was no more hoped or preached. Neither could the authorities hope a steady decline of religious attachments of the Muslim people in the normal course of socialist developments, nor could they expect that a rigorous atheistic propaganda activity would help the process of erasing Islamic attachments. Therefore a tune of compromise crept in the official voice. *Pravda Vostoka* warned that although the very existence of the 'socialist society' in the USSR created a tendency for religion gradually to wither away, this did not mean that the process would happen by itself under the passive influence of socio-economic changes and the growth of culture and education. It was necessary to wage a constant struggle against religious beliefs. There could be 'no talk of relaxing the ideological struggle against religion'.[45] But while the focus of this statement was to emphasise stronger and more effective atheistic propaganda, the acceptance of the presence of the religion could not be overlooked. Interestingly, most of the propaganda literature, including the more sensible one (i.e., Dadabaeva's article), held the inadequate methods of propaganda responsible for the overwhelming survival of religion in the Central Asian territories. But, the Soviet position vis-à-vis the rational forces in Islam had begun to undergo a definite transition from this time onwards which was born out of a two fold dilemma. The first was the indigenous experience of a more lasting influence of Islam which the theoretical tenets of scientific socialism found almost impossible to eradicate. The other was an interesting and complex world situation developed out of the anti-American Islamic revolution in Iran under Khomenee and the Afghan socialist revolution and the Soviet support offered to these traditionally Islamic forces as part of the great game with USA. As a result of these combined forces, the religious policies during this period showed much ambivalence and dependence on the officially sanctioned posts of Islam in Central Asia. The most noticeable instance here was the 'Report of Mufti Ziyautdinkhan ibn Ishan Babakhan, Chairman of the Muslim Religious Board for Central Asia and Khazakhstan over the formal meetings held at the World Religious Conference under International Preparatory Committee of the USSR.[46] Babakhan made a long speech for lasting peace, disarmament and just relations among nations. But he dealt with all these issues from a very secular standpoint and religion was provided with a marginal lip service and the egalitarian principles of Islam and all other religions were highlighted. He stated that the regular calling of inter-religious peace making conferences at regular intervals (1952, 1962, 1969, 1973, etc.) was a good move on part of the Soviet government for bringing world peace. But more than that he had keptic on completely political conferences where attempts were made by 'the Muslims of Soviet Union' to solve various international issues.[47] Babakhan mentioned, "The 1970 International Conference on the problems of strengthening world peace and settling the Middle East conflict; the 1973 International Conference in Tashkent on the political settlement of the Middle East crisis and the necessity for immediate withdrawal of Israeli troops from the occupied Arab territories; the scientific conference in 1974 on the 12th century of the birth of the great mujtahid, Aba Abdulla Mohammed ben Ishmael Bukhari, the compiler of the Sunna of Mohammaed (may Allah bless him) which had as its theme "Imam ali Bukhari and the contemporary world;" the 1976 International Conference dedicated to the 30th anniversary of the Muslim Religious Board for Central Asia and Kazakhistan, which gave close attention to the problem of consolidating peace and strengthening friendship amongst the peoples of the world."[48] Thus, he summarised the attempt under Soviet banner to solve the questions related to Islam or the Muslim world outside the Soviet territories. Then he went on to discuss the purely political issue of détente and its contribution in enhancing peace. "The deepening of the process of détente is undoubtedly the primary condition of the attainment of lasting peace. Few sensible people now-a-days would disagree that the relaxation of international tension is the decisive factor in the modern world situation. The 1970s, will go down in history as an epoch in which the pernicious consequences of the cold war with its atmosphere of distrust, alienation and confrontation were gradually overcome.[49] He then made separate speeches on disarmament, human rights, ecology, population, migration and finally appealed to the tasks of religions to bring 'Just Relations among Nations'.[50] Thus, important secular political—even military issues—were discussed under the banner of religion, that also Islam, in the USSR, by this time, which was remarkable in terms of Soviet religious policy, especially towards Islam. On the task of just relations among nations he stated, "We religious workers are deeply committed to the teachings of our religions concerning the establishment of just relations among people and in international relations, and for this reason we must give special attention to the problems which we have been discussing with the aim of establishing true justice in relations among peoples. Our religious convictions forbid us to close our eyes to any acts of injustice. We must properly assess in this respect not only the contributions of all religions as a whole, but also the contribution of each particular religion. We must appeal to government, government agencies and all people of good will, demonstrating our own good intentions to them and urging the establishment of truly just relations among all nations."[51] Thus, not only the opinion of the supreme authority in Islam in USSR was sought in secular issues, but even the role of Islam in propagating peace and justice were sought after. This indicated a new process which was undoubtedly different from the earlier position of steadfast atheism. Here the notions of peace and justice and other humanitarian notions in Islam were stressed and highlighted as a positive force for socialism and the publication of this speech along with the host of propaganda literature implied some kind of truce between the atheistic Soviet authorities and the formally recognised strand of Islam in Central Asia.

In order to understand the shift in approach on part of both the Soviet authorities, as well as the official strand of Islam in the USSR, one would need to study the contemporary world scenario and position of Islam in global perspective in the 1970s. Actually, there had been a growing trend of Western propaganda, juxtaposed to the Soviet propaganda on Islam, which seemed overtly sympathetic towards the Muslims of Soviet Union for their lack of independence to observe their religious practices. This literature also stressed the fact that Muslims in the Soviet system suffered under Russian big brotherhood just like the Third World had suffered under colonial imperialism. This was actually an intellectual bi-product of the cold war in a bi-polar world. The scholars of this category had narrated the Soviet experience in Central Asia as a linear continuation of the earlier Tsarist regime. Almost every scholar of this group had described the Central Asian Republics as colonies of mainland Russia. These scholars were bitterly critical about the forceful suppression of Islam in Central Asia. Alexander Bennigsen had been one of the most formidable protagonists of this school.[52] In Bennigsen's account, Central Asia was deeply distressed by and thoroughly discontented with the Soviet experience and the suppression of Islam was the foremost reason of their anger. As Islam provided the strongest anchor to hold traditional life in Central Asia, the Soviet government was bent upon eliminating its influence root and branch. According to Bennigsen, Islam and the Soviet system were based on two completely incompatible ideologies that ruled out any scope of compromise between them. In one of his earlier works, *Muslim National Communism in Central Asia,* he discussed in details about the early Muslim Communist leader Sultan Galiev and his followers—their policy, strategy and principles. Here he had fully supported Galiev's view that Central Asia could never be able to bring about communism under the Soviet Socialist system dominated by Russia. For the Muslim Communists needed to proceed towards socialism without disregarding their faith in Islam. In this context he said, "East is not west, Muslims are not Russians ...."[53] Interestingly, here the term 'Muslim' implied Soviet citizens of Central Asia whose unsurpassable distance with the Russian Citizens was caused by their religious distinctiveness. In this Bennigsen could be accused of reductionism in believing and reducing the difference between the orient and the oxident in terms of the Muslim and non-Muslim attachments. Authors like Bennigsen and Allworth had repeatedly emphasised the special role of Islam among Central Asian Muslim communities. They, therefore, held the suppression of religion in Central Asia to be the gravest error of the Soviet government.

Similarly, they criticised the destruction of mosques and monasteries and confiscation of properties from such religious institutions, which had formed part of the socialist programme of USSR. To these critics, irrespective of other factors, the discontent around the suppression of Islam was enough to arouse distrust about the Soviet system. These scholars also believed that the scope of Islam was not limited to religious character. Islam was a world wide force, a force which was not weaker than any other ideological force in action (undoubtedly they implied the Marxist socialism as a contender). Bennigsen and others, moreover, tried to relate Central Asian Islamic attachments to the Pan-Islamic movements of the world. Islam was not only a collection of rituals, practices and festivals, but it was the strongest ideology which formed the ethical backbone of the Central Asian people.

To combat this ideological onslaught from outside world, the Soviet policy on Islam had undergone a marked evolution. In their ideological battle against Western critics, the Soviet regime embarked on a new strategy to placate the official strand of Islam in favour of the Soviet government to put up a new line of defence. In fact, the Soviet government, though in a very restricted form, sanctioned some religious institution and officials to operate at the individual level. This limited sanction always fell short of the demands and expectations of the Muslim Central Asia. The keptical religious organisations slowly began to take clandestine forms. Interestingly, many of the sufi saints and their followers, being unrecognised by the Soviet authorities took to underground activities and often got merged with extremist groups and practiced subversive activities. The Soviet government, on the other hand, felt that to curb the extremist and subversive forms it would be wise and expedient to win the faith of the officially accepted, moderate and peaceful Islamic leaders who still believed that as 'Soviet Muslims' they could gain both materially and spiritually. Thus, an article published in *Nauke i Religia* countered the Western propaganda as well as the reactionary Islamic forces outside the Soviet world. The author wrote, "Western propaganda betrays its secret hopes for the beginning of something like "a political Islamic operation" against the Soviet regime whereas the reactionaries in the Islamic world elsewhere discussed "bluntly of the need to create such an opposition" to build strong bridge," to the Muslims of the Soviet Union "According to the logic which Muslim reaction wishes to impose on believers, fidelity to Islam obligates Muslims in the socialist countries are automatically in political opposition."[54] But the Soviet author could proudly put forth the case of the Chairman of the Muslim Religious Board for Central Asia and Kazakhstan, Mufli Ziautdin Ibn Ishan Babakhan, who could claim quite strongly that he was a Soviet patriot and lectured on behalf of the Soviet regime, although belonging steadfast to the traditional tenets of Islam.[55]

The official Soviet stand began to highlight the material achievements of the Soviet Muslims remaining within the Socialist system, without losing their freedom of religious worship. Yaakov Ro'i insisted that, "The implication is that the Soviet Muslims have adopted the materialistic belief system of Soviet society as a whole without sacrificing their freedom of religious worship. This contention is invariably put forward when Soviet Muslims make the Hajj (the pilgrimage to Meccah), when Soviet religious functionaries travel abroad, and when their foreign counterparts visit the USSR."[56] An important journal titled *Muslims of the Soviet East* began to be published from USSR which wanted to highlight 'a thriving Muslim Community' that upheld the traditional Islamic way of life in the Central Asian region.[57] "Thus the new trend paid lip service to religion and refrained from any open split with it."[58]

There was another more concrete reason, other than ideological war with the West, behind this remarkable shift in position from this time onwards (late 1970s). This consisted of the Soviet support provided in favour of the revolution of 1978 in Iran, closely followed by that of Afghanistan. The case of Iran was of a purely Islamic nationalist revival under Khomenee removing the Shah who was a puppet of America. And as per her commitment to the Cold War rivalry Soviet Union found this as an opportunity to extend Soviet sympathy to the outside world and that too to a traditional Islamic zone. Yaakov Ro'i observed, "The apparent discrepancy between the reactionary role traditionally attributed by Moscow to Islam (and, indeed to all religion) and the major role played by Islam and the clergy in the Iranian revolution—of which the Soviets approved—bred a very extensive literature that was intended to explain how in fact Islam came to play a revolutionary role in Iran."[59] The explanations went on in different directions, for example, one version stated that Khomeni used the dogma and tradition as an effective weapon against the tyranny of the Shah and 'Westernisation'. A senior political commentator on Near Eastern affairs, Leonid Medvedenko stated, "an anti-imperialist revolution under the banner of Islam has been carried out in Iran—its economy and politics are being cleansed of the roots of American neo-keptical and a number of progressive reforms are underway."[60] Medvedenko further stated that 'the neo-colonialist (US and the West) have begun building bridges between different faiths and seek to promote mutual understanding allegedly to "defend them from the godless" (USSR)...The plans of contemporary imperialism aim precisely at alienating the Moslem states from the socialist world."[61] But Y. Roi indicated that this was a use of 'mirror theory', whereby, the Soviet scholars indicated the position of USSR while describing their adversaries.[62] There was no qualitative difference between the position of USA or USSR regarding the issue of Iranian revolution; for USSR proved herself equally opportunist by supporting Khomenee as USA did by promoting the Shah in favour of Western capitalism. The question of ideology was brought only to substantiate the action and there the protagonist of Soviet doctrines felt the urge to explain the official gesture with precaution. The shift in action and gesture brought the need for explanation. Another commentator, Pavel Demchenko, took up the material grounds for the popular support for Shiaite clergy to justify the movement in terms of socialist perspective as opposed to American capitalism. He pointed out that the clergy benefited from the dissatisfaction of the petty and middle bourgeoisie who actually suffered with the influx of Western commodities and the cosmopolitanism of Iran's big bourgeoisie the provocative luxury of the Shah's court and the way of American standards in culture which conflicted overtly with the material and moral values of the "traditional" bourgeoisie, artisans [and] residents of poverty-ridden outskirts, yesterday's peasants who had migrated to the cities and populated slum areas.[63] In another view, the basic trends in contemporary religious life consisted of three stands, traditional, modern and revivalist. Of these, the revivalist trend was the strongest and combined the elements of both traditionalism and modernism. This trend mostly suited the mood of the masses and influenced the political ideology towards radical movements. The credo of revivalism has "the omnipotence of god, democracy and justice."[64]

The position of USSR became even more indecisive regarding Islam with the Revolution in Afghanistan in April, 1978 which had introduced a Marxist regime there but that was not anti-Islamic. The Soviet regime provided their wholehearted support to the new regime and sided with them in their fight against the opposition. But, interestingly enough, both the groups, pro and anti-revolution, were putting stress on their faith in Islam. And here the position of the Soviet state was precarious. For in Iran USSR was providing lip service from outside. But, in Afghanistan, not only was Islam accommodated within the Marxist-Leninist revolutionary regime, but their geographical proximity to the Central Asian territories of the Soviet regime, especially Tajikistan, made the situation very complex for the Soviet government to take a clear and decisive stand in this development. Yaakov Ro'i analysed, "Afghanistan was not only the first Muslim country outside the USSR to undergo an avowedly Marxist-Leninist revolution—a Muslim country where religion played a major role in every day life—but it was also a country that bordered on the USSR's own Muslim republics and was now overrun by Soviet troops. From the point of view of the Soviet Union's own domestic requirements, religion in Afghanistan had to be given similar treatment to that meted out to the Muslim areas of the USSR."[65] Though the change of regime could only make a verbal promise of establishing Marxist-Leninist yet Islamic state in Afghanistan—how these characteristics could be keptical in reality remained questionable. The Soviet intelligentsia began to depict the combination as impracticable. The article by K. Kniazev *The Difficult Path of the Afghan Revolution* in *Agitator* argued that while the April revolution showed 'the point of departure...for the downfall of the absolute rule of the tribal aristocracy and the Islamic religious elite,' but still, 'difficulties in implementing 'progressive reforms' continued to be 'aggravated by the existence in the Democratic Republic of Afghanistan of deeply rooted religious survivals and manifestation of tribal discord."[66] Afghanistan with its unique combination of Marxism and Islam brought the gravest challenge to the Soviet power which made the ambivalence of Soviet religious policy inexplicable in terms of ideology. Ironically, the change of regime in Afghanistan made Soviet power apprehensive about her own Muslim people of Central Asia very transparent. Although Mufti Ziautdin Babakhan provided his lip service on behalf of the Soviet Muslims to welcome the revolutions in Iran and Afghanistan for "their profound solidarity with the peoples of Iran and Afghanistan who are struggling in the cause of building the just society."[67] However, in the face of reality, these formal declarations seemed very inadequate to maintain the rising tide of Islamic revivalism in the Soviet Central Asia—where geographical proximity brought a natural inclination to develop similar Islamic movements by removing the artificial banner of atheism. From this time onwards, Islam was not only a religious faith, not even the most active component in the formation of national identity; it was now a geopolitical force—threatening the threshold of the Soviet Socialist Republic.

Therefore, the indecisiveness of the Soviet position vis-à-vis the Islamic movement in the neighbouring countries became apparent. The cautious lip service to the newly established Islamic governments of Iran and Afghanistan began to fade away in front of the serious apprehension of Islamic revival in the Soviet regions, who were especially closer to Afghanistan geographically, such as Tajikstan. Moreover, there was the constant threat of US propaganda in favour of such spirit of revival as a part of cold war. The head of the Institute of Oriental Studies, E. Primakov expressed his view that, "At present the USA is indeed particularly interested in this deformation of the Islamic movement ... first .... To try to direct political activity in Iran against the Soviet Union, and second .... To use the green flag of Islam to set up a front of struggle against the Afghan revolution."[68] Primakov also provided his own analysis of this religious revivalism and its politicisation. In his perspective, "The Islamic movement as a whole clearly cannot be seen as a single entity. It comprises several trends. There is a radical trend which is strongly charged with anti-imperialism. And there is, as it were, a bourgeois-landowner trend which is loaded with a large charge of anti-communism and anti-Sovietism."[69] But, the fact that the apprehension of Islamic revivalism and its impact on the Soviet system was very alarming at this juncture could be surmised from the host of Soviet literature and articles written on the theme which revealed the utmost attempt on part of the pro-government intellectuals to differentiate the situation of the Soviet Muslims from their other counterparts who got involved in such revivalist movements. Such were the writings of A. Vasileyev's, *Islam in the Present Day World* or S. Aliev, *Islam and Politics*[70] which stressed the prevalence of the pre-capitalist mode of life in those countries, the illiteracy of the majority of their populations and the overbearing presence of the Islamic way of life and traditions, customs, etc. as the reasons behind the politicisation of Islam in those countries which, according to the official Soviet claim, were absent in the USSR. Thus, by literary arguments, there were attempts to keep Soviet Muslim regions away from the purview of the revivalist current.

But, these attempts of indirect propaganda seemed quite weak as could be understood by the apprehension of the Secretary of the

Azerbaijan SSR Communist Party, Geider Aliev who demanded a more effective security measures in that republic in 1980, explaining the need in terms of "the increasingly complex international situation, especially in the region of the Near East in states immediately adjacent to the southern borders of our country."[71]

But in spite of the utmost attempt on part of the Soviet government to prevent the revivalist spirit of Islam in Central Asia, it continued to develop throughout the 70s and increased in the 80s as evidenced by the limited sources of information. Irrespective of the officially approved strand of Islam, *Sufism* had a very popular base in this region which continued from medieval days. And out of the pressure of atheistic propaganda, whose attack was more severe to these sectarian brotherhoods, it turned to clandestine movements. The two popular branches of *Sufism*, the *Yasaviyya* and the *Nagshbandiyya* and their adherents were marked as worshippers of obscurantist cults. Thus, the mutual intolerance of these two forces, the Sufi religious cult and the Soviet atheism led to the development of a 'jihad' psychology among the clandestine sufi adherents. These underground forces began to re-strengthen themselves with the rising extremist fervour of Islam. Theirry Zarcone in his article *Sufi Movement: Search for Identity and Islamic Resurgence* stated, "In places, where the persecution against kepti was most severe, the Sufi orders organised themselves underground, the task which was facilitated by its hierarchical structure and adopted fully for such type of opportunities."[72] In another keptic's analysis, "Although officially persecuted during Stalin's time, these Sufi brotherhood continued to have the dynamism and vitality to survive the Communist onslaught."[73] Thus, there were also ground preparations continuing inside the Soviet soil, when the trend of Islamic revival began to pour influence from outside. The same article described, "By the late 1960s, the Long Haired *Ishans* were active in trying to prevent the youth in the region from joining the Young Communist movement (Komsomol), to attend illegal religious schools and evade the military draft. This process of defiance to official atheism continued through the 1970s and the Soviet invasion of Afghanistan allowed these Sufi groups to emerge stronger, and often as a sop to their influence over youth in the Central Asian region, they were allowed "limited" religious practice."[74]

Thus, in the changing dynamics of late 70s and 80s, Islam acquired a very complex dimension in Central Asia. Here again, the situation of Tajikstan was the most precarious because this state had close ethnic and religious connections with both Iran and Afghanistan. Being the only Persian-speaking people of Central Asia, they shared a similar identity with the Iranians but there too there was a difference in sectarian terms as the Tajik people, with the marginal exceptions of the Ismailies, were Sunnis whereas Iran followed Shiaism. However, the turmoil in Iran and the Soviet approach to that must have created a mixed feeling among the Tajik people in religious terms. Moreover, the effect of Revolution in Afghanistan closely followed by the Civil War and active Soviet participation in it was much more serious on Tajikstan than any other place of Central Asia because of the commonly shared border between Tajikstan and Afghanistan. The influence of the Afghan Mujahidins began to increase here which became apparent after the demise of the USSR when Islam emerged as a readymade, alternative ideology to communism. The ground for such revivalist movement was being created through the inadequacy of the officially allowed strand of Islam, the vacillations in the Soviet outlook reflected in various literature, the discontent created and maintained by atheistic propaganda, and suppression. At this juncture when external influence in the same direction began to pour in and the Soviet authorities' attitude to the extremist Islam varied according to their Cold War strategy, a possible background for a massive upheaval was silently created. Although, the growing religiosity of the Central Asian Muslims primarily resulted from the need to produce an indigenous identity consciousness as opposed to the abstract and unreal image of a 'new Soviet man' and the disillusionment with the Marxist-Leninist alternative to Islam and its socio-political connotation, the emergence of Islam as an extremist geo-political force had a tremendous potential to influence the large proportion of dissatisfied and confused people of the region in favour of militant Islam as an effective alternative.

In fact, faced with the changed world view, the Western critics also seemed slightly confused in assessing the character of Islamic movements in Central Asia. For example, Alexander Bennigsen, in his article *Islam in Soviet Union*, in *Change and the Muslim World*, published in 1981, wrote about Central Asian Islam, "It is a conservative creed that is undergoing a process of traditionalist revival similar to that which is found today in many other phenomenon that owes nothing to influences from abroad". However, Bennigsen himself in his article *Islam in Retrospect* in *Central Asian Survey 1987* contradicted his earlier view by stating, "It is more probable that the Islamic revival in Central Asia in 1986-87...Is a direct consequence of the victorious resistance of the Afghan Mujahidins waging a holy war against Russian unbelievers."[75] Thus, the authors of the Western school also seemed confused and vacillating in deciding the role of external influence on Central Asian people towards religious revivalism.

Thus, the situation of Soviet regime in the 70s and 80s depicted an era of indecision, ambivalence and vacillation from every perspective. The regime was facing or getting prepared to face challenges from outside and from within—the threat of the religious and nationalist uprisings in the Central Asian and some other non-Russian Muslim populated provinces was only one aspect of it. The brief tenure of Andropov and Chernenko saw some inadequate and limited attempts to regenerate the spirit of the Soviet identity and culture removing the so called parochial perspectives which arose in different spheres for several reasons through the mixed experiences of the Brezhnev era. But the introduction of perestroika opened the floodgate for all the anti-Soviet forces and here Islamic revivalism received a special impetus to replace the communist ideology and the power vacuum in real politics. The detailed discussion of the impact of perestroika on Islam in Central Asia would be taken up in the chapter six of this thesis. But in order to round up the current discussion, one can direct the attention towards the marked shift in the attitude of the Western Soviet-critics. The authors of this school were so long overtly sympathetic to the suppressed Islamic communities of Central Asia, till the Soviet Socialist Republic survived. But with the demise of the Soviet regime their approach towards Islamic revivalism became skeptical, the original optimism tending to slide into apprehension regarding Pan-Islamic movements. The Post-perestroika chaos in Central Asia did witness large scale politicisation of Islam. Influences from other parts of Islamic world tended to converge at this point. Therefore, many scholars became skceptical about the future of Islam in this region—whether Central Asia would join any modern Pan-Islamic movement and identify themselves as close allies of non-communist Muslim states, like the states of Middle East, Afghanistan, Pakistan, etc.[76] In fact, once this weak and uncertain region got global exposure, many strands of Islamic fundamentalism from other parts of the world contented to capture the power vacuum. In this backdrop, the pulls of Islam in Central Asia became a very serious issue, probably the deciding factor for her future. But, there too, politicisation of Islam had its own dimensions. Over and above, the synonymous use of modern national identity and modern Islamic identity of the Central Asian people constituted an obvious misrepresentation of facts. That these two identities shared overlapping elements could be accepted only with the understanding that both had their important spheres of autonomy as well. Here Islamic identity formed only a single element in the complex composition of the national entity. Again, the full scope of Islamic identity, might have had elements that went beyond the national dimension—such as Pan-Islamism. The Central Asian attachment to Islam as a phenomenon received increasing importance in both Soviet and Western viewpoints with the changed world perspective. The intensification of the tension caused by the extremist fervour of Islam in the surroundings affected Soviet policies and their critics' attitude towards the people of Central Asia. Thus, Islamic revival in Central Asia was seen more as a response to the external factors, than as a movement from within—and the position of Central Asia, independent of either Soviet or external Islamic influences, was not assessed in its full scope. Some scholars in the post-perestroika phase tried to highlight this aspect, without denying the forceful presence of clandestine Islamic societies and an inclination of a substantial part of the population for extremism. According to them, the presence of rational and moderate Islam was not totally absent in the region. Rather the presence of the latter could be found in the experience of Central Asia as early as 1917 (May)—i.e., even prior to the Bolshevik Revolution and even before the experiences of communism combined with atheism. This was the clear and articulate statement of Mehmet Emin Rosulzade in the First All Muslim Congress of Russia, held in Moscow on May, 1917. Rasulzade was a delegate from Azerbaijan who combined a firm adherence to Islam with a rational approach to it. He said, "No doubt, Islam, like other religions of the world, has created a certain bond among its adherents. Yet this is not a national bond, it is an international bond...Just as there is no such thing as 'Christian Nation', so there is no 'Muslim Nation'. Islam is a huge international 'building' encompassing separate 'rooms' for the Turks, the Persians, the Arabs and other national ethnic groups."[77] Unfortunately, the pressure of atheism and the forceful dynamics of geopolitics sidelined this rational trend.

However, religious revivalism was not a unique feature of Islamic regions in the USSR. The growth of Russian Nationalism (during the 70s), an intellectual trend based on nostalgic sentiments, had an overt tendency to fuse orthodox Christianity with the spirit of nationalism.

J.B. Dunlop stated, "The fusion was particularly observable among the authors contributing to the *Samizdat* journal *Veche* which appeared from 1971 to 1974."[78] And this spirit of Christian revivalism was not felt in an isolated pocket among a handful of Russian intellectuals. This too had a broader base with various nationalities embracing it with a strong fervour. Dunlop in another article stated, "Even more unsettling from the regime's point of view is the symbiosis of religion and nationalism that has been observable in Lithuania, Georgia, Armenia, the western Ukraine and recently, in Russia itself; the specter of such a fusion, or of a Pan-Islamic movement in Central Asia, is also worrisome."[79]

Thus, the heightened religious fervour of Central Asian Islam could be studied from the general Soviet perspective as well—where the ineffectiveness of the artificial doctrines of atheism seemed completely useless in front of the ever growing discontent among the citizens of various nationalities. To this discontent, may be added the evidence of each nationality embracing their respective traditional religion as an emotional anchor to put up their challenge against the Soviet regime.

Five

Role of Language in the Identity Formation of Central Asia

Soviet Union started its socialist experiments as a mult-lingual and multi-cultural State where Central Asia formed a wide zone of distinctive linguistic and cultural identities. The people of this Asiatic zone were different from those of European Russia in their ethnic-origin, culture, heritage, religion and language. Therefore, the official process of 'drawing together' leading to 'fusion' always faced a force working in the opposite direction to highlight local or regional identities in their histories. Here the difference of language had an important role to play. Language was a very important element which contributed to the identity formation of the people of Central Asia. In fact, language should be granted to be an elemental component of identity consciousness for any community not to speak of Central Asia alone. The natural, sentimental attachment towards one's own vernacular might be regarded as a common characteristic, deeply rooted within human culture. This sentimental bond, however, might become intense under circumstances where political independence was conditioned, economy was monitored and socio-cultural existence was constantly interrogated and revised by some alien authority. In such circumstances language might turn into a useful tool in the political movements aspiring for autonomy or independence. But the Soviet language policy was full of complexities and ambivalence where apparent sympathy and encouragement towards the regional languages were combined with the special emphasis on the necessity of learning the Russian language. Therefore, the reaction on part of the non-Russian subjects was also variable, mixed and complex. Here, the position taken by the Central Asians, in general, showed their remarkable attachment to their own respective languages and consciousness as a separate cultural entity.

The principal language of Central Asia was Turkic with the exception of Tajik, which was a dialect of Persian (Indo-Iranian root). The influence of the Russian language began to pour in this region during the time of Tsarist expansions, but at that time, there was no systematic drive for enforcing the Russian language upon these people *en masse'*, nor were there attempts to change the indigenous system of education of these people by the Russian imperialist government. Though with Tsarist imperialism, the use of the Russian language started with great vigour at the official and formal levels of interaction, the target of the Russian imperialism was not to spread education among general masses. The experiment with the language policy therefore did not crystallise firmly in the Tsarist phase. Rather, the Soviet government, from its very inception, took up conscious attempts to increase the importance of the Russian language as the 'Lingua franca'. Therefore, in education and official use, the absolute necessity of Russian was made very clear from the very outset. Thus, all non-Russians were practically forced to learn Russian as the official language of the state (USSR) and this brought the practice of 'bilingualism' to Central Asia as well.

Interestingly, however, in theory the Soviet government had shown serious concern for the development of all regional languages, promoted vernacular schools and modes of education, and also bestowed due respect for the preservation of linguistic distinctiveness of the people. But such an apparently liberal dispensation could scarcely fit into the existing complex practical situation. The regional languages became the rallying point for regional identity consciousness, especially in backward regions where people were forced to learn Russian for practical purposes and yet refused to accept the secondary status of their own mother-tongue in the existing social order.

In policy the Soviet system never showed disrespect towards the regional languages of Central Asia. Shams Ud Din, an Indian scholar on Central Asia stated, "Soviet language policy was conceived as an important ingredient of Marxist-Leninist nationalities policy which was originally intended to assimilate the different ethnic peoples belonging to different religious cultural streams."[1] Thus, the role of language was seen as a vehicle to communicate amongst different language groups. But ideally speaking that was not supposed to damage the autonomy of the regional languages. In fact, V.I. Lenin, in an extremely thoughtful essay, written prior to 1917, titled *Is a compulsory official language needed*?[2] attempted a balanced enquiry about the problem of a multilingual state. In this essay, Lenin vehemently criticised the concept of imposing Russian as the official language, although he supported the cause of voluntary extension of the Russian language amongst non-Russian people. He had the confidence that a language as popular as Russian would not have to be imposed by force. Rather, the non-Russian citizens of the future Soviet world would be eager to learn the language for their own benefit. He openly stated that, "people whose conditions of life and work make it necessary for them to know the Russian language will learn it without being forced to do so. But coercion will have only one result; it will hinder the great and mighty Russian language from spreading to other national groups, and most important of all, it will sharpen antagonism, cause friction in a million new forms, increase resentment, mutual misunderstanding and so on."[3] Thus, Lenin expected the 'mighty Russian Language' to become the dominant formal language of the state and also expected the non-Russians to learn it spontaneously. But what he opposed was the imposition of the same language from above. As he clearly stated, "...we, of course, are in favour of every inhabitant of Russia having the opportunity to learn the great Russian language. What we do not want is the element of coercion... a compulsory official language involves coercion, the use of cudgel. We do not think that the great and mighty Russian language needs anyone having to study it by sheer coercion."[4] This very expectation of Lenin showed his modest pride in Russian as a developed and necessary language leading to belief regarding voluntary submission of other languages to the former's supremacy as a natural outcome. Thus the Russian language was expected to be the natural link language among different cultural communities, apparently damaging the development of other minority languages in the state.

Thus, the role of regional or local languages was to highlight regional or national identities, whereas the Russian language symbolised the great union of all nationalities under the supra-national banner of Soviet identity. These two faces of the Soviet language policy from the very outset were bound to create tension and dichotomy in reality—for the task of assimilation was bound to clash with the sphere of autonomy and flowering of local languages as a symbol of autonomy. The language policy of the USSR was supposed to follow the Leninist principles throughout its tenure, though there were definite changes, shifts and turns in the process according to the demands of reality. But, undoubteldy, the language policy of the USSR was an inseparable part of her nationality policy and, therefore, each and every gesture in the direction of languages contained some connotations favouring the nationality policy, transcending autonomy, and leading to the greater goal of socialist assimilation (fusion).

The Soviet language policy, therefore, could be divided into three distinctive phases, namely, the Leninist, the Stalinist and the post Second World War0, and pre-glasnost phases. The Leninist phase, which was the preparatory phase extending from 1917 to 1925, had fixed the basic foresight of the language policy. Lenin, with his pragmatism, could realise that the task of the Soviet regime in the sphere of language would be a difficult one, for it had established its sway over a wide and diverse ethno-cultural zone with multi-lingual subjects. These languages could be basically divided according to slavic and non-slavic origins, which, once again, corresponded to their ethno-national background. Thus, Lenin preferred to use the language policy as a tactical weapon for the solution of the nationality question. Thus, the three main targets fixed by Leninist language policy were: one, to remove the psychological barriers between slavic and non-slavic peoples; two, the use of Russian as a national link language and third, on the contrary, the development of the languages of different ethno-nationalities or minority languages, slavic or non-slavic with due care.[5] The Bolshevik linguistic policy during Lenin's life time and beyond was that ethnic groups should be educated in their native language. But for that, the practical hindrances were many. Illiteracy was widespread, with rates approaching 100 per cent in some regions. Many languages did not have a written script. Language planning in the 1920s, therefore, was devoted in the main to obtaining linguistic data in the field, and deriving alphabets and orthographic systems which would develop writing systems for languages which did not have them before. The role of Russian as the official link language remained steady throughout the Soviet period which became an irresoluble issue of tension between the official language and the languages of the titular nationalities and began to foment discontent in every ethno-national communities at different stages of history at different levels.

However, Central Asian language policy became effective from the Stalinist era. Theoretically, Stalin did not deviate much from Leninist principles and stressed the need for the development of regional languages and literature. Writing in June, 1930, in *Deviation on the National Question*, Stalin clearly indicated his intention to follow Lenin's footsteps in this regard, ".... Lenin never said that national differences must disappear and national languages become fused into one common language within the boundaries of a single state, before the victory of socialism on a world scale." And he also added, "I have always maintained, and continue to maintain, the Leninist view that is the period of the victory of socialism on a world scale, when socialism has been consolidated and has become a matter of everyday life, the national languages will inevitably fuse into a single, common language which, of course, will be neither Great Russian, nor German but something new."[6] Though this kind of expectation for a new language emerging out of a fusion of all these centuries old languages seemed quite absurd from national ethno-linguistic perspectives, this view-point at least did not over-emphasise the inevitable supremacy of the Russian language. But with the passage of time the prospect of world revolution got rapidly annulled. Stalin's new theory of 'Socialism in one country' replaced the original call of a new world language. Reality witnessed the indomitable growth of the Russian language as the language of the entire USSR. The Central Asian SSRs, therefore, had no other option but to endure the dominance of an alien language.

The imposition of the Russian language, however, was not a one time simple solution of the Soviet language policy. There were various experiments on the regional languages as well. The first official step taken regarding the Central Asian languages was the change of scripts. The indigenous Arabic and Persian scripts were replaced first by Latin and then by Cyrillic scripts to bring uniformity in the whole state. The authority used two excuses for making this change—first, to remove printing hazards, and second, to lessen the difficulty of learning two different scripts by the children. In the process the spontaneity of the languages suffered. But it was noticable that the transition from Arabic or Persion scripts to Cyrillic was intervened by a phase of Latin alphabets to bring an appearance of neutrality. The outright imposition of Cyrillic script was avoided (probably consciously) since the "(C)onnotation it had with tsarist imperialism were undesirable".[7] Though, there was no attempt by the Tsarist regime to impose Cyrillic script on the Central Asian languages, the introduction of this script from above might have caused discontent for the people who, being still unsure of the new regime, might have taken this script as a symbolic extension of Russian domination and cultural encroachment. The New Turkic alphabet in the Latin script came to be known as New Alphabet. The language planning in the 1920s and 1930s, therefore, was very much a matter of language construction, construction of new alphabets, new writing systems, new vocabularies and the new usage of different languages. Once again, the move for the replacement of Latinised alphabets by Cyrillic scripts began which characterised the language policy of the late 1930s and early 40s. A list of new arguments were placed in favour of the new shift. There were unresolved difficulties inherent in the New Alphabet; there were excuses of typographical errors hampering printing; and there was another stronger argument that the children had to endure the unnecessary burden of learning two scripts, one for the native language and the other for Russian. The official Soviet explanation for this switch to Cyrillic was a response to the democratically expressed wish of the Soviet people,[8] while the critics of the regime took this as a barefaced manifestation of cultural imperialism.[9] Shams Ud Din also stated, "While the Soviets claim that the objective of the changes in script of Central Asian languages was promotion of peoples languages and culture, it was, in reality, directed to achieve two significant political goals: (i) To cut the Soviet Muslims from their cultural heritage and religious bonds and (ii) to promote differntiation among various sub-ethnic groups on linguistic basis."[10]

However, the intention of the Soviet regime on the language issue could not possibly be explained in any of such straight-jacket analyses—for the entire process was complex, experimental and therefore, to some degree indecisive. The post-Stalin stages especially began to show the surfacing of multi-dimensional complexities arising out of the ambiguous language policy where the regime got exhausted by the ever widening gap between ideology and practical direction of events on the issue.

The most important applied field of language policy could be seen in the sphere of education. The Soviet government took remarkable initiative to eradicate illiteracy as part of their socialist programme. The objective was sought to be realised by rapid introduction of a number of schools in all parts of the Soviet Union.

Central Asia became a focul point in this project of imparting education to a comparatively backward region with an overwhelming presence of mediaevalism and religiosity in local, indigenous education system that prevailed prior to the coming of the Soviet rule. So, the manifestation of Soviet language policy here consisted of the alteration of local and Russian languages in the curriculam of school education. The first non-Russian secular schools started in this region from the late 1920s. In 1924, the Soviet state, on the whole, used to publish text books in as many as twenty five languages. And within a decade, by 1934, the number had risen to 104—which apparently might seem to be an astonishing achievement. By 1938, in Uzbekistan alone 22 languages were taught—which was undoubtedly a remarkable success of a multi-lingual policy. Brian D. Silver, therefore, admitted the Soviet achievement in this sphere of local language education at the beginning of his essay "One of the most, notable achievements of Soviet nationalities policy has been the liberal provision of native-language schooling for over 50 nationalities." [11]

In 1938, however, there was a clear shift in policy with the imposition of Russian as a compulsory subject within the school curriculum. From this time onwards, the superior position of Russian in comparison to other languages used in the SSR became evident. Thus, the reality saw a rather rapid imposition of the Russian language as the compulsory state language without even caring for the non-Russian opinion about the issue. The optimism of Lenin's theory of spontaneous acceptance was quickly denied. This definite departure from Lenin's ideal got even more widened in the post-Stalin phase under Khrushchev when, in 1958-59, a new device on education announced that education in the mother tongue would no longer be compulsory and the parents could choose the language of instruction for their children.[12] This was a severe blow to the national language school education, as the Russian language medium schools would attract the parents for more viabilities and opportunities in real life for their children. This act, though apparently providing democratic choice for the citizens to decide their children's education method, actually destroyed the Leninist precept of the necessity of compulsory mother-tongue education. This policy of Kruschev era saw wide-spread acceptance of the Russian language by the parents for practical purposes. This was, definitely, a severe blow to the regional language schools, which increasingly failed to attract candidates willing to study in their mother tongue. Thus, however wrong the tendency might have been, it kept on increasing. This 'freedom of choice' was rather 'coercive' as most of the non-Russian parents felt constrained to enrol their children in Russian language schools. The number of enrolments definitely began to decline in national language schools from 1960s onwards and it continued in the same direction in the Brezhnev era. But one must not forget that the national language instruction schools continued to exist in the USSR and also in RSFSR, and even in Russian medium schools native languages of other nationalities were taught as separate subjects. But the unquestionable supremacy of Russian in the hierarchy of languages was established for "Russian was the most important language, since it was the language spoken most widely throughout the Soviet Union and indeed in terms of its range of functions was a language of world-wide significance, at par with languages like English and French."[13] Michael Bruchis also highlighted the attitude of Russian experts regarding the superior position of the Russian in the language hierarchy of USSR. He stated, "the leading role of Russian over the other Soviet languages was justified in a thesis advanced by Iu. Desheriev, one of the most active proponents of the official language policy. Desheriev asserted with characteristic ambiguity that each people has the 'sovereign right to use its language within the bounds of its vital interests. Similarly another writer argued, 'Soviet reality shows that languages can have equal rights but not always equal value'. Another thesis held that, in the conditions of bilingualism, a 'division of labor' among languages could be observed."[14] Therefore, the indirect pressure of switching over to Russian medium school proved insufficient for the programme—Russian became the second major language in every national language school and Khruschev himself refered to Russian as the 'second mother tongue'. Serious attention was given to the method of teaching Russian and efforts were made to turn this attention successful in school curriculum. For this the Research Institute for the Teaching of Russian Language in the national school was set up in 1968. The increasing tendency of Russian domination found another marked manifestation in a number of government directives in 1975. In 1975, under the auspices of the Ministry of Enlightenment and the Ministry of Higher and Secondary Specialist Education of the USSR, an "All Union Conference" held at Tashkent took some vital decisions, for example:

(i) Extend the provision of Russian as an optional subject in all higher and secondary educational establishments.
(ii) Produce 'model' text books and materials for use in primary, secondary and higher education.
(iii) Produce 'model' syllabus for programmes of 'intensified Russian instruction' (Uglulennol izuchenie russkogo yazyka) in national schools.
(iv) Organise by the end of the first quarter of 1976 measures for the organisation of Russian in national Kindergartens of the Union republics.
(v) Begin the teaching of Russian in the first class in the national schools of those republics where it was still being taught only from the second year onwards.
(vi) Request school supply authorities to launch a programme of equipping schools with language laboratories and audio-visual aid centres ('kabinaty russkogo yazyka').
(vii) Increase the extra-mural use of Russian.
(viii) Increase the number of schools offering, 'intensified Russian instruction.'[15]

Such an elaborate and well thought out programme to promote Russian language education in the mid 70s, somehow, implied the limited expansion of the language, so long among general non-Russian Soviet people. Moreover, the venue of such a convention being chosen in the Central Asian capital of Tashkent might have indicated the need to bring that particular zone within the orbit of Russian influence to a greater degree.

Actually, the non-presence of adequate data on the ratio of Russian and national language school enrolment kept these questions unanswered. Still, the attempts from above showed the intensification of the Russian language as an instrument for supra-national unification in the name of Soviet patriotism. The 'Novie Sovietskii Chelovek' needed to be trained in one language, one method and one curriculam. The further recommendation on the Russian language instructions included demands for the introduction of Russian in the first year of schooling and even in the kindergarten—thus Russian became an open contender of one's mother tongue from the very beginning of basic education. The process also initiated the centralisation of Russian language teaching under the control of NIIPRYaNsh in the name of standardisation and promotion of 'model' programmes. In 1979, in extension of the same policy, the Ministry of Enlightenment and NIIPRYaNsh published jointly a 'Model Programme of Russian Language for the Secondary National School' which contained aims, objectives, methods, contents, etc. for every school year from I to X. Thus the gradual increase in the imparting of Russian language was a symbol of overcentralisation tainted by a political and ideological motto to bring unity of thought and ideas and principle among the pupils, as the future citizens of the USSR. All children in their growing period ought to be taught to appreciate the unique significance of "Russian as the language of inter-ethnic communication, the language of socialism, the language of Lenin, the language of the great Russian people."[16]

Thus, the ever accelerating spread of Russian language naturally led to the marginalisation of local language education. Moreover, another interesting character of Soviet education policy from its very inception was the gradual decrease in the number of vernacular institutions in secondary, higher or technical institutions. In fact, the Kirgiz, Uzbek and other union-republican institutions for higher education were to follow certain directives to use Russian from the second year to impart knowledge in social sciences and general subjects. All course work and diploma work were instructed to be written in Russian.[17] Thus, those who were willing to take up higher studies, could not comprehend a career without a sound command over Russian.

The language policy of the Soviet government had been severely criticised by some Western scholars who considered the Soviet rule in Central Asia as a colonial rule in the guise of socialism. The attempts to introduce and spread the Russian language was alleged to be a clear attempt of Russification and cultural aggrandisement. Even the apparently benevolent gesture shown towards the Tajik community to get autonomy on the basis of linguistic distinction was also criticised by historians like T.R. Harmstone who believed that the intentional separation of Tajik from the mainstream Turkic language of Central Asia was no more than a method of divide and rule.[18] In the name of providing autonomy to the people and their language, the authority actually tried to fracture the overall common identity of the Central Asians. Again, the imposition of the Cyrillic script upon other Turkic languages was also seen as a blatant evidence of racial arrogance of the ruling class. Harmstone also noticed that, "Thus the knoweldge of Russian became a necessity for any Asian who wanted to progress up the political, economic and cultural ladder."[19] This was how the Russian language symbolised as the passport for better job (white collar) and provided higher socio-political status for the non-Russians which also included Central Asian people.

In the midst of this heavy handed campaign of Russification, a minor tactical retreat on the language front was sounded by Brezhnev at the 26th party congress in 1981. On that occasion, he urged that the linguistic and cultural needs of migrant workers in the Soviet Union be cared for. This sympathy for the internal diaspora probably indicated a kind of encouragement for the Central Asians and Transcaucasians to move towards Siberia. His sympathy was, however, a lip service for the migrants because, as J. Dunlop suggested, "Brezhnev was surely aware that migrants are more apt eventually to assimilate, linguistically and culturally, than "stay-at-homes", even though Islamic peoples have historically been less likely to assimilate than others."[20]

Bilingualism in Central Asia

In spite of being a sufferer under the general Soviet language policy like any other non-Russian nationality, the Central Asian Republics had shown markedly different reactions to the policy and its outcome—and thereby turning the characteristic regional attachment to their respective mother tongue into an inseparable component of their identities. Here too, there were differences traceable between the attitude of the rural and urban masses in their susceptibility towards the lure of the Russian language. According to some partial data for the period between 1960 and 1965, it appeared clearly that the rural people were relatively reluctant to switch over to Russian language schools whereas their urban counterparts were very prompt in embracing the Russian medium education. This was evident especially in the cases of Kazakh and Azerbaijan republics. But at the same time, the enrolement of Uzbek pupils in the Russian medium schools was negligible in the 1960s.[21] The Soviet initiative to hold the conference of NIIPRYaNsh in Tashkent in 1975 might probably be explained as a conscious attempt to bring this zone under direct Soviet control where the rapid spread of Russian language would be a necessary precondition. In spite of such attempts, and partial acceptance of the Russian language for practical purposes, the Central Asian people in general did not lose their attachment to the vernacular. Brian D. Silver noticed, "The linguistic behaviour of the titular nationalities of the five Central Asian union republics of the Soviet

Union illustrates that when groups with distinctive language and cultural traditions come into contact with one another, very complex linguistic adjustments can occur.... Central Asians display an interesting response to the conflicting pressures to learn Russian as an aid to upward social mobility and to maintain traditional languages as a sign of identity with the ethnic group. while remaining strongly attached to their national languages, they are simultaneously moderately attracted to Russian as a second language."[22]

Another sphere of Soviet centralised administration that demanded sufficient command over Russian language, was the army. Here the non-Russian recruits had to learn Russian at least to obey the commands. The Soviet Muslims, Central Asian or otherwise, faced much difficulty in learning the *'lingua franca'* as part of military discipline. Paul B. Henze observed, "Russian is the exclusive official language of the Soviet military, and substantial encouragement and pressure are extended to bring non-Russian recruits to a workable level of understanding Russian. A Muslim who wishes to have a career in the Soviet armed forces must, of course, acquire fluent Russian; but very few do...Many of these learn only enough Russian to understand commands. Among themselves they used their own language(s). The Soviet armed forces do not appear to function as a 'melting pot' for Soviet nationalities. Though Muslim recruits—especially those of rural origin—usually emerge from service knowing more Russian than when they entered, they also come out with their own Muslim national identity strengthened because most of them will have experienced active and passive forms of discrimination to a much greater degree during military service than in their native republics."[23] Thus, the army remained a sphere where interaction between Central Asian Muslims and the Russians were compulsory and the necessity of the Russian language as a formal medium of communication became an absolute imperative.

It was found especially in the case of Central Asia, that the practical importance of the Russian language was accepted and the indigenous intelligentsia, who largely faced the dilemma of native versus Russian language, found its solution in bilingualism. Unlike many other non-Russian nationalities, the Central Asians seldom elevated Russian as their mother tongue (*rodnoi yazik*) or as the second mother tongue; rather, they preferred to call it just a standard second language'. The preference of the Central Asians in this issue could be clearly identified from the census data of 1970 and 1979. From 1970 onwards a new question was added in the census questionaire about the knowledge of Russian or any other language used in the USSR as a second language, following the question of one's nationality.

Along with *rodnoi yazik*, therefore, '*Svobodno vladet*' or fluent command became a new criterion in the language issue. In 1970, the overwhelming attachment of the Central Asians to their respective mother tongues could be surmised from the 98.9 per cent or more claiming to maintain the native language as the national language, whereas, 87.0 per cent of the entire non-Russian population of the USSR could stick to such claim.[24] While 11.6 per cent of the entire non-Russian population of the USSR claimed Russian as a native language, only 1.1 per cent of Central Asians claimed so.[25] It is clear from suçh statistical evidence that among all non-Russians, the Central Asian nations were particularly sensitive about the centrality of their native language, and accordingly, strongly resistant of accepting Russian as the national language.

In fact, the claim of fluency in Russian as a second language was also relatively low in Central Asia compared to other parts of the USSR. Other than the Kazakhs, of whom 41.6 per cent claimed fluency in Russian, the other four Central Asian states showed not more than 19.8 per cent of the population claiming command over Russian as second language in 1970. This was markedly low compared to the general score of such category in USSR being 37 per cent. Brian D. Silver commented, "Although language is not the only important symbol of ethnic identity among Central Asians, the very persistence of attachment to the mother tongue suggests that it is certainly a significant symbol of ethnic identity."[26] "Among the principal Central Asian nationalities," observed Michael Rywikin, "the proportion of those who declared themselves fluent in Russian" in the 1979 census varied—every fourth Turkmen, every second Kazakh, Uzbek and Karakalpak, and every third Kirgiz and Tajik."[27] The 1979 census brought another set of statistical data on bilingualism, and the positions enjoyed by the native language in comparison to the Russian languages in Soviet Union showed interesting developments for the central Asian provinces. There was a marked rise in the percentage of fluency in Russian among the Central Asians but the preference for native language as national language remained almost unchanged. The picture would be clear from the table below:

		Total Population	*NlasL1*	*RasL1*	*RasL2*
Uzbeks	1970	9,195,093	98.6%	0.5%	14.8%
	1979	12,455, 978	98.5%	0.6%	49.2%
Kazakhs	1970	5.298,818	98.0%	1.6%	41.8%
	1979	6.556,442	97.4%	2.0%	52.3%
Azerbaijan	1970	4,379,937	98.3%	1.3%	16.5%
	1979	5,477,330	97.8%	1.8%	29.5%
Tajiks	1970	2,135,883	98.5%	0.6%	11.6%
	1979	2,897,697	97.8%	0.7%	29.5%
Turkmen	1970	1,525, 284	98.9%	0.8%	15.4%
	1979	2,027, 913	98.7%	0.9%	24.9%
Kirgiz	1970	1,452,222	98.8%	0.3%	19.1%
	1979	1,906,271	97.9%	0.5%	29.3%[1]

Thus, in terms of bilingualism, the seventies seemed to be a successful decade for the spread of the Russian language in Central Asian provinces. But the marked growth of fluency in Russian did not take a natural direction towards the acceptance of Russian as the first language. Therefore, Michael Kirkwood assessed that "It would seem from a consideration of the data that Soviet linguistic policy to date has been rather successful. On the one hand the numbers of non-Russian claiming fluency in Russian is increasing and on the other, retention rates for the mother tongue are impressively high".[29] Brian D. Silver also expressed his strong conviction that "My central thesis is that the advent of widespread bilingualism does not herald the eventual abandonment of the national languages for Russian, but may be viewed instead as a stable form of accomodation between ethnic groups."[30] But the high rate of attachment to mother tongue in Central Asia was not the only reflection of ideological attachment or cultural bond. There were some very practical, material reasons behind this peculiarity. Moreover, even within Central Asia, there were marked variations regarding the attitude towards the Russian language. These material conditions were limited urbanisation, low level of education, lesser exposure to the Russian language and culture (especially in case of women) and so on. There was a marked difference in the general fluency in Russian among the urban and rural Central Asians, because the standard of education was definitely higher in urban areas and, therefore, the standard of teaching of the Russian language was also better in urban schools that produced pupils better equipped in the second language. Moreover, the rate of formal education was higher in urban society, compared to the rural areas, which led to the diferences in command over Russian. Moreover, Brian D. Silver opined, "Yet the more extensive knowledge of Russian among Central Asians residing in urban areas can be almost entirely accounted for by the difference in the per centage of Russians' presence in the two residential settings. This evidence suggests that the amount of interethnic contanct is far more important in the spread of Russian among the Central Asian population than is the quality or extent of formal instruction in the Russian language."[31] Another interesting dimension of the Central Asian bilingualism was found in sex differences. The women here, because of lesser exposure to the outer world, had relatively lesser command over Russian compared to women of other provinces who worked outside the household and had opportunities of greater interaction with the Russian language. In 1970, 24.3 per cent of Central Asian males completed Secondary Education, whereas 13.4 per cent of the females achieved the same fate. Moreover, their restriction to household work gave them little chance to develop fluency over Russian. Another scope of interethnic interaction was, as we have seen, the military service, where again, the women usually had no access. Thus, in general, the Central Asian women had markedly lesser access to the Russian language compared to their male counterparts. This was also because the women's participation was lesser even in regular educational curriculum and could therefore avoid the compulsion of learning the state-language.

Though the response of the pressure to accepting Russian as the second language varied between urban and rural sectors and between gender, there was a practically uniform and negative response to the attempt to foist Russian as the mother tongue, cutting across urban-rural and gender distinctions.

Because of the lack of detailed data on bilingualism, the general Central Asian attitude towards Russian could not be found before 1970s. But the negligible per centage of Russian fluency in the four Central Asian states, other than Kazakhstan, implied a marked limited expansion of the Russian language in this ethno-cultural zone. The census report of 1979, however, provided quite an optimistic picture regarding the spread of the Russian language in almost every republic. Yet the nominal acceptance of Russian as the mother tongue implied their strong attachment to the native language as a symbol of identity. Interestingly enough, the meagre number of the Central Asians who had switched their national language from their mother tongue to

Russian, supposedly lost command over the national language. Yet, probably, for the Central Asians, this switching of the national language did not imply elevation in socio-cultural status. It implied rather an actual incapability to maintain command over the language concerned which would lead to a natural alienation from one's own ethno-national people.

However, different languages used in the USSR, had a wide range of variety in their witten forms. From a genealogical perspective the languages of the USSR were divided into five categories:—

(i) The Indo-European languages which included Slavic, Iranian, Baltic, German—i.e., Romanic, Armenian and Indian languages.
(ii) The Altaic languages which included Turkic, Mongolian and Tungus Manchu languages.
(iii) The Uralic languages.
(iv) The Iberian-Caucasian languages.
(v) Other languages.

Among these the major Central Asian languages stemmed from the Iranian and Turkic group of languages. Characteristically, these two groups of languages, namely Iranian and Turkic in their various forms and dialects made up the vernacular of the Soviet Muslim population. The Iranian group included the Tajik language of Central Asia, which was a form of Persian with a well-formed script unlike other languages of this group namely Ossetian, Kurdish and the Tati which were provided with literary forms during the Soviet period. The rest of Central Asia followed different versions of the Turkic language. Shams Ud Din commented, "Despite the Soviet policy of creating differentiation and formation of new languages and dialects have retained their basic core".[32] This non-assimilative character of Central Asian languages was not necessarily the reflection of the self-conscious national identities of her people. The natural character of these languages carried some kind of resistance towards external encroachment or influences of other types of languages. This was more evident in the case of the Turkic language. Andree F. Sjoberg in an article observed, "As a result of my research on Uzbek and some other Altaic languages, as well as the Dravidian family in South India, I developed the thesis that, other things being equal, languages with an agglutinative structure are more resistant to external forces for grammatical changes, and are apparently slower to change internally ....”[33]. Therefore, in spite of the longdrawn influence of the Russian language which started from the Tsarist period and constantly increased during the Soviet period, there was little encroachment of Russian into Uzbek or other Altaic languages. Isolated Russian words entered the language but it never penetrated the grammatical structure. Thus, the limited influence of the Russian language on the native language structure probably did not signify any ideological resistance towards the alien language, but only the natural characteristic of the indigenous languages, resistant to accommodate influences from a technically different kind of language.

The case of the Tajik language was markedly different form the Turkic experience, for Tajik was a version of Persian which had a more ancient heritage in Central Asia (being once the court language) than Turkic. But throughout the medieval period, there was constant interaction between these two patterns of languages (Turkic and Persian) which resulted in greater changes in the Tajik under Turkic influence whereas, because of the characteristic rigidity of the Turkic (Uzbek) language, the Tajik influence on these languages was superficial and limited.[34] The natural intermixing of the Uzbek and the Tajik communities representing the Turkic and Persian language groups came under Soviet intervention when the Soviet authority began to show some overt attention towards the Tajiks in order to promote them as a separate language group and as a separate nationality. The disorganised character of different dialects of Persian was consciously brought under the banner of the newly revived Tajik language, and a conscious process of transformation and enrichment continued which meant in practice. “the replacement of the Arabic socio-political vocabulary by that of the Marxist—Leninist, Russian and intenational classics.”[35] Thus a kind of artificial alienation from the neighbouring Uzbek community began on the excuse of language distinction in the Soviet period. But, interestingly enough, in spite of linguistic distinctinctions the close contacts and interactions between these two traditional neighbouring commuinities continued almost unabated throughout the Soviet period. However, Harmstone and other Western scholars described this segregation of the Tajik community from the rest of Central Asia as a deliberate process of divide and rule. According to this view in the name of giving autonomy to these people and their language, the Soviet authority actually tried to fracture the over all common identity of the Central Asians. But this view seems suspect for in that case the uniformity introduced in the scripts of all Central Asian languages remains inexplicable.

However, the Soviet encouragement from above helped the growth of Tajik as a modern language with a glorious past. Before the breakdown of the USSR, the Tajik SSR contained 31,000 general schools, 86 vocational and 39 specialised secondary schools, 10 higher educational institutions. The Republic used to publish 70 newspapers and 865 journals and had 1700 libraries which, taken on face value, appeared to be quite a marked achievement.[36] But at the same time, the encouragement of the Tajik language as a branch of the Persian or Iranian group, brought a kind of affinity between the Tajik nationalists and the Persian speaking nationalities outside the USSR—namely Iran and Afganistan—which, once again, had a complex geo-political dimension because of the geographical proximity of Tajikistan with these two out and out Islamic states.

Whatever the encourgement to local languages had been, their role was always regarded as secondary to the official language. The concept of '*Sovetskii narod—novaya istoricheskaya obstchnost*' was clearly associated with the conviction of '*velikii ruskii narod*' as the pioneer of the regime and there the language of the 'mighty Russians' received the highest score in the hierarchy of languages. Most intriguingly, the Soviet language policy was not only resented or opposed by the non-Russians for its dominating character, but a section of the Russian intellectuals, known as Russian Nationalists, who became vocal at the end of Brezhnev regime, were also bitterly critical of Soviet language policy. According to them, the policy had destroyed the high standard and originality of the Russian language by making it a vehicle to serve a certain ideology and too easily accessible to the various strands of non-Russian communities.

J.B. Dunlop stated, "Contrary to what is often believed, even by specialists, Russian nationalists were not happy with the campaign of Russification that was pursued by the Brezhnev and Andropov regimes. Indeed, even such an ardent foe of Russification as Ivan Dziuba, author of the seminal study, *Russification or Internationalism* (1965), singled out Russian notinalist writers Vladimir Soloukhin and Leonid Leonov for strong praise as principled opponets of Russification." The protagonists of this idea despised the Russification of the borderland and lamented that in order to become the state language, "…… Russian language represents no more than a kind of emasculated and cliché-ridden Esperanto." Valery Tishkov, a scholar very closely attached to the Soviet regime, during the time of turmoil, also openly accepted that "Ironically, this very process of disseminating socialist Soviet Cuture also produced dissatisfaction amongst ethnic Russians themselves, on the part of the intelligentsia—primarily writers. To many of them it signified a 'loss of one's roots' and abandoning the traditions of Russian folk (primarily peasant) culture."[37]

In the 1988 Plenum of the USSR Union of Writers, the question of the Russian language as a vehicle of communication for other nationalities was subjected to serious discussions in the light of glasnost. The speeches of the Russian representatives from Moscow and elsewhere strengthened the fact that the non-Russians needed the medium of Russian for their own correspondence and not for any other benefit enjoyed by the Russians, and lamented the degradation of the language as 'Russian esperanto'. Thus the speech of Maiia Ganina stated, "Because of historical reasons the unifying language of the Soviet Union is Russian. Armenians talk to Uzbeks, latvians talk to Georgians in some sort of 'Russian esperanto' which has a vocabulary of form one hundered to five hundred words, maximum a thousand. While Russian has more than two hundred thousand words!" She moreover continued, "I could only have written one thing, that let's suppose that Georgian or Lithuanian or Uzbek became the state language, the main language, instead of Russian. My "Great Russian pride" would not suffer from this at all! The opposite, in fact. After struggling to learn five hundred words and the essential grammar, I would take great comfort in the thought that now my native Russian had finally become a zone of preservation and would become once again as pure as it had been in the beginning, as pure as we can suppose Armenian and Georgian are today. No longer would people encroach on the complexity of Russian, on the ancient words it contains which can't be understood by those who out of two hundred thousand words know five hundred and think that the remainder aren't necessay."[38] Michel Kirkwood also mentioned that, "There were references to 'Russian esperanto', insinuating that Russian was becoming ruined by the influx of localism in the speech of many non-Russians, that many non-Russians operated on a vocabulary of some 500 words and that the problems of national languages in the national schools arose primarily as a result of over-centralisation in matters of policy formation."[39]

Thus, not even the Russians were whole-heartedly satisfied by the development of the Russian language as the language of the entire

Soviet land. This implied the artificiality of the Soviet indoctrination which removed spontaneity from the language itself and turned it into a dispassionate medium for communication, while the literature with a rich and mature heritage also suffered a retreat. This was realised by the group of Russian nationalists who were the political counterparts of the ethno-nationalist agitators of other nationalities in the USSR. The writings, paintings and other cultural exposure of this category of nationalist scholars showed a kind of nostalgic trend to go back to the pre-industral (implying pre-Soviet) values of life. The grandparents were depicted with great care as symbols of some old but valuable ethos willing to percolate down to the future generation of grandchildren while the artificial, anti-nature insensitive character symbolised the upholders of the existing regime by the authors like Raspution or Chingiz Aitmator (a kirgiz author) in their respective novels *Farewell of Matera* and *the White Steam Boat.*[40] Gerhard Simon commented on Aitmatov's works and their impact on Soviet society, "One of the novels by the Kirgiz Chingiz Aitmatov revolves around preserving the memory of the past. People without memory became slaves. It is necessary to preserve the old Islamic cemetry threatened by space technology as well as the memory of the terror the Stalin era caused. Only a living collective memory (i.e., history) can protect man from the total manipulation threatening him"[41] But Aitmatov's novels are no isolated instances of nostalgia, rather a part of the general trend developing among the nationalites, both Russian and non-Russian. Michael Rywikin observed, "The 1970s saw a "blossoming" of historical novels. In Uzbekistan alone such works as Abil Yaqubov's *The Treasure of Ulugbek,* Mirmuhsin's *The Architect,* Pirimqul Qairov's *Starry Nights,* and the first two volumes of Mirzakalan Ismaily's *Fergana before the Dawn* not only addressed themselves to the area's rich historical past but also reintroduced Chagatai expressions. Mamadali Makhmudov's *Immortal Cliffs* placed in the late ninethenth Century, stressed the theme of Central Asian Turkic unity in the face of the Russians. In Kazakhstan voices have been heard contradicting the "barbarian image" attributed in old Russian literature to Asian invaders (even the Igor Tale has not been spared). Finally, in the 1980s, the powerful voice of Chingiz Aitmatov, a novelist form Kirgizia who writes in Russian and reached the top of Moscow's literary establishement, proclaimed his allegience to this "Asian heritage". Thus, Aitmatov's attempts were seen here as the point of maturity and climax of a general process using historical backdrop as a reminder of one's original roots. Rywikin also obsrved similar tendencies in the Tajik literature of the contemporary period as expressed in Tajik poems. "In Tajikistan the traditional wealth of Tajik-Farsi poetry has been used to glorify its historical past at the exclusion of foreign implantations. The best poems by Mirza Tursunzade, a pro-Russian literary official, are still devoted to his own *Vatan* (homeland). Another poet, Laiq, writes about 'the thieves who stole not only the property but the heritage of our ancestors."[42]

Language Politics Turns Serious

More alarming was the response of general people to this kind of writings—which indicated a kind of popular exasperation in the artificialitv and dogmatism of the Soviet regime at the end of the 70s. Thus, the regime was heading towards a rupture, was evident from the developments in hindsight. In view of this great change (perestroika), the domination of language became one of the most pressing issues among the various nationalities within the union who had grown tired of the regime and became desperate for some kind of a break. One must recognise the fact that, the resentment of Central Asians was relatively less towards the language domination than some on other parts of the USSR, namely Ukraine, Georgia, Estonia, Moldavia, Latvia, Caucasus and so on. Interestingly the knowledge of Russian of these people was relatively higher compared to their Central Asian counterparts. Therefore, there was resentment towards the Russian language domination at the fag end of 70s in these non-Russian regions. These people were otherwise relatively advanced and for them mastering a command over Russian was no more a major problem, which actually signified the language issue being taken up as a matter of prestige and symbol of identity. Therefore, Tishkov considered the technical hazards of multilingualism and the hegemony of Russian language as a mechanical issue, completely different from the growing tendencies of 70s and 80s, in different provinces—which, according to him, was 'politics of language—or rather using the language attachment as a political instrument.[43]

The growing discontent and insipid yet strong forces of resentment against the Russian language domination, probably inspired a kind of reform in the sphere of language in 1984, after that of 1978-79. But these measures were completely overtaken by the advent of glasnost and perestroika and therefore had no lasting impact on the Soviet language policy. Glasnost led to the opening up of discussion on languages in different fora which brought out different views on the expected status of regional languages and the readjustment between Russian and local languages of different communities.

The last official attempt to concentrate focus on Russian language could be found in 1985, when there was a conference held in Dushanbe (capital of Tajikistan) on the teaching of Russian in native schools.[44] But from 1986, the scene began to change. There began a tendency from below to highlight the local languages. For example, in Kazakhstan the people started demanding the improvisation of teaching standard of both Kazakh and Russian, with special emphasis on Kazakh. Similar stronger demands of linguistic autonomy also began to arise in Estonia, Moldavia and Ukraine and other parts of the crumbling state of USSR. From this time onward, the debate over the necessity of Russian as the unavoidable part of bilingualism began to increase in all the nationality areas. The Central Asian territories were also part of this heightened tension over language identity. A contemporary article by E. Bagramov stressed the invincible role of Russian language in the future path of development while giving an apparent lip-service to the 'legitimate' demands of flowering of local languages. At the same time he warned against the 'artificially dramatised linguistic processes' and 'linguistic chauvinism'. Thus, the claims of Bagramov were authoritarian but the intonation seemed conciliatory which implied a markedly changing scenario.[45] A very interesting perspective developed among the Soviet scholars on language policy during the perestroika-glasnost period to assess the importance of bi-lingnalism among the Russian people of the USSR residing inside the RSFSR and in the union republics. This was an attempt to mellow down the blame of Russian domination among the titular nationalities. An article by M.N. Guboglu written in 1987 seems quite relevant in this context. Guboglu refused to accept that Russian language domination in the USSR was in any sense an enforcement from above. "Russian—natural—language bilingualism in the USSR is not dictated "from above". Its development and function shows with particular power the real need of all peoples of the USSR, joined into one friendly, fraternal family to have reliable instruments of communication." He then made a detailed study to show that the Russian people also got inclined towards bi-lingualism and showed interest to learn another language from the 70s. "In the 1970 census 3,876,668 Russians indicated that they were fluent in a second language, and another 203,769 indicated a native language other than that of their nationality."[46] In support of Guboglu's view, Maiia Ganina's speech can be cited: "Like the majority of Russian intellectuals, I was raised from childhood with the awareness that hatred of any nation first of all destroys the person who hates. Wherever I went, on business trip to Uzbekistan, Kazakhstan, khakasia (sic.), Lithuania, and so forth, I always learned a hundred or hundred and fifty words and phrases, so as to be able to talk and ask for things."[47] But, it is interesting to note that the same author who was so satisfied about herself while learning about hundred words of a native language, seemed quite disturbed by the limited vocabulary of Russian language (about five hundred words or so) of the non-Russians for general correspondence. Thus, even among the intellectuals with rational understanding of the situation, lack of balance in attitude to Russian and non-Russian languages remained evident. Guboglu, however, at the end of his article openly admitted this short-coming on the part of the Russian nationals, as he stated, "However, since the elemental and organisational factors in no way operate in isolation from one another, the practical necessity arises of purposefully stimulating the development of each of the components contributing to bilingualism among Russians, skills, speech activity, and the psychological recognition of the need for a second language.

Yet it must be stated that our progress has been least visible precisely in this sphere—propagation of the languages of the native nationalities among non-natives. Moreover, the scholarly publications of some republics rarely mention the need for purposeful, convincing, and well-argumented propagation of the language of the native nationality. When efforts are being undertaken to create favourable conditions for learning the Russian language, it is quite right to raise the question of creating the appropriate conditions for representatives of non-native nationalities, including Russians, to learn the language of the titular nationality of the given union republic (offering lessons on radio and television, free and paid courses, making available special conversational aids, text books etc.)."[48] This kind of open admission on the part of the Russian scholars definitely showed a slight shift in the position resulting from glasnost activities.

The next serious attempt to discuss about the language issue took place in a round table organised jointly by the Presidium of the Academy of Sciences of the USSR and the journal *Istoriia SSSR* in March 1987, where famous academicians from Estonia, Georgia, Moldavia, Uzbekistan, Kazakhstan, Kirghizia, Belorussia and other regions took part, including important figures like Yu.V. Bromlei, Yu.V. Arutunian, L.M. Drobizheva and so on. There were mainly too strands of opinion arising out of the discussions. The centrists like Bromlei, etc. preferred status quo, whereas the representatives of republics like Robakidze opposed that outright. The pragmatic analysts like Arutunian stressed on the complex reality like the problems of migration, deportation, and demographic imbalances between western and eastern regions, town and country areas and the like.

However, the ensuing years experienced growing polarisation between the centre and periphery over the language issue—all the republics now started turning adament to establish their respective mother tongue as the official language of the republics—replacing Russian. But the attitude to Russian, however, varied widely among nationalities because of practical predicaments. The language issue became very sensitive during these years of transition. Tishkov stated, "The centre was viewed as a stronghold of the communists—supporters of 'denationalised' or even 'anti—national' culture; As a backlash, such Russian nationalist rhetoric caused resentment among the non-Russian population. Thus, a painful and emotional discourse has developed around language and culture issues since the beginning of perestroika."[49]

Realising the changing direction of the changing tide, the CPSU accepted that "the official status of a republican language was a matter of prestige for that republic. "They made conditions which would help preserving the Russian language in its precious status. In order to succumb to the newly developed scenario, it was announced that Russian should have equal rights and status to the titular languages of individual republics. But, in this policy the status quo was little changed. The 'de facto' role of Russian remained unchanged though there were some alteration in the de jure status of the local languages. But this hardly affected the real scenario.

From 1989, many titular nationalities of union republics had already started to reject the official Soviet culture and ideology, and the Russian language began to be considered as a symbol of oppression. In June 1989, Uzbekistan announced Uzbek to be the state language. Similar claim was made by the Tajik government in favour of Tajik in July the same year. Both these republics, however, announced Russian as the main language of inter-ethnic communication. Even after making open announcement in favour of the languages of the titular nationalities, the link with the Russian language could not be severed once and for all. This was because the practical problems had to be kept in mind during such shift in the official language. The entire economy and the commercial contacts so long depended on the Russian language—the decades long process could not be done away with by a single stroke. Therefore, the language as a prestige symbol might be changed overnight as a state policy—but the language in everyday use for communication with the non-nationals, not necessarily Russians, in any republic being Russian continued to be endured. Shams Ud Din highlighted this role of the Russian language, "An important outcome of Soviet language policy has been the development of Russian as a language of communication particularly between the Slavic and non-Slavic people. Some Soviet scholars term it as the second mother tongue, second native language or simply second language; others, particularly Central Asian scholars perceive it as an international language, thus putting it in the same category as they put their international European languages, such as the French, German and English languages. Moreover, they dislike to contrast it with their native languages or see it as a rival to them."[50] The Russian language, to the Central Asians appeared as a medium of communication with the outside world and they preferred to keep it as the language of work place—so that the possibilities of clashes between the Russian language and the native language might not occur.

However, to come back to Soviet language policy which was an integral part of the nationality policy, its evolution through different phases of development actually showed that the main objective of the policy was to bring a greater unity of the Soviet people by transcending all local parochialisms, and thereby creating an all encompassing Soviet identity. To achieve this end the Russian language and culture were wrongly used.

However, it is common to find many multilingual countries caught in tension over the primacy of any particular language, and in most cases the language of the majority or the language of the more powerful and advanced community tends to overpower the rest. The same tendency was found with the 'mighty Russian language'. A kind of Russian hegemony over other languages gradually developed showing scant concern for the popular sentiments of the non-Russians. Here the Central Asian subjects suffered the same fate of being marginalised and their languages being relegated to a secondary status.

Actually, the fact that the Central Asians could not internalise the Russian language was as much consistent with the reality as the fact that they could neither completely ignore its practical relevance and material opportunities. Valery Tishkov wrote quite confidently, "It is a well-established phenomenon in sociolinguistics that language disparities and unequal statuses are not solely the result of politics and elitist efforts: they are also the results of the total numbers of speakers and of language communication dispositions at the regional, national and global levels. English, French, Russian or Chinese will always be more privileged than other 'smaller' languages, as a language serves as a vehicle for inter-ethnic and outside world communications. And there are no rational reasons for this to change as a result of new inflamatory propaganda. Nor are there any real competitors capable of replacing the Russian language in this role."[51]

However arrogant this statement might seem, one has to accept the reality. In the post-perestroika period, there were attempts to revive the regional languages, renaming Russian names of cities, streets, rivers and so on. In Tishkov's expression, "This process became an expression of 'internal self-defining' in the system of cultural symbols…"[52] In the independent Central Asian States, the regional languages such as Tajik, Turkic, etc. began to be used in formal official correspondence. Yet, they could not bid farewell to the Russian language. The practice of bilingualism prevailed, for in spite of their independence all these states were members of the CIS, sharing a common platform. Russian language was the only communication link amongst these different states. Another interesting development in the language equation that took place after the demise of the USSR was the changed status of the Russian diaspora residing in substantial number in every republics. Tishkov observed, "Millions of Russians have suddenly found themselves in an ascribed position of being ethnic minorities, whereas they used to consider themselves part of the dominant Russian-speaking cultural linguistic milieu of the Soviet Union."[53] Thus, a long-drawn process of linguistic reshuffling and re-adjustment ensued which affected the respective linguistic communities as well.

Although "practically all non-Russian nationalities found themselves to be cultural-linguistic minorities of the Russian-speaking USSR,"[54] none of the Central Asian languages became obsolete during the seventy years domination by an alien language. In everyday use all local languages survived. Again unlike the hard-core official sectors, where the knowledge of Russian was compulsory, in agriculture and other handicrafts the basic medium of language remained the mothertongue. Moreover, discussion on the prospect and future of the local languages, research on their evolution, and encouragement for composing literature and drama in local languages were part of the Soviet policy throughout the Soviet period. However inadequate these measures might have been to compensate the domination of Russian mainstream education, it helped in the flowering of the languages and kept them alive. Local languages prevailed along with the spread of Russian as a formal language. These inadequate attempts by the Soviet authorities, however, marked the difference between the Soviet and the colonial language policies. These gestures of respect and attempts to revive the status of the non-Russian languages brought a different dimension in the Soviet policy. This limited dispensation however failed to counter the overwhelming presence of Russian and its domination over the people of Central Asia, and the post-glasnost demands for linguistic autonomy gave vent to the suppressed discontent over the issue.

In the phase of transition from 1989 to 1991, the language issue got prominence as a news item. There were plenty of articles, interviews and statistical data collection on the question of monolingualism, bilingualism and multilingualism. Most of the Central Asians had responded in favour of bilingualism.[55] They usually provided priority to their mothertongue but preferred Russian as the language for wider communication. Such a balance in their approach towards the language question could be struck only when the imposition of the external authority was withdrawn. Probably, Lenin imagined this kind of voluntary acceptance of the Russian language by the non-Russian members of the Soviet state. Unfortunately, this became possible only after the demise of the Soviet republic.

The most balanced and thoughtful view from amongst the Central Asian intellectuals was probably provided by the Kirghiz scholar Chingis Aitmatov on the issue of bilingualism and autonomy of national languages. In an article in Literaturnaya Gazeta he stressed the need for compulsive acquisition of the respective territorial languages for the nationals of that territory. But at the same time he urged the people to accept that Russian was already the de-facto official language of the Soviet Union and whether it was given the constitutional designation or not hardly affected its position in reality.[56] The same author in another article in the same journal a year later entitled *Zhivi Sam i dai Zhitch Drugim* (meaning, live and let live) most persuasively argued that the languages in a multilingual society must learn to co-exist like the starlets in the milky way.[57] But how far this analogy could be realised remained a test for the future. Only time would prove the tenability of such a theory of mutual co-existence. But one should not forget that domination of Russian in the Soviet regime was not merely a domination of a language or its scripts. Rather, it was one of the instruments in the hands of the mainly Russian party-state bureaucracy to establish their high-handedness over the backward communities of Central Asia. Once the dimension of racial and bureaucratic arrogance was removed, the people of central Asia could reconcile themselves to the presence of the Russian language without much debate, for it served the purpose of communication with the external world including Russia. The revival of the local languages which were manifested in the renaming of cities, streets, rivers and institutions, were no more than a symbolic gesture of independence. Once more, the deep primordial attachment of the people of Central Asia to their vernacular came to be politically used by the new authorities to arouse national consciousness, with full knowledge of its practical and operational limitations as a medium of communication vis-a-vis the outside world.

Six

Role of Ethnic Factors in the Development of Multi-Layered Identities in Central Asia

Ethnicity is one of the most vital and inalienable component in the development and crystallisation of identity consciousness of any community or people at any time and space. Needless to say, the importance of these factors vary according to the change of environment or context. The Soviet Central Asia provides a very interesting case study on ethnic identities and their evolution, relations, compromises and complexities evolved during various phases of the communist regime till their independence in 1991. Interestingly, during the recent period of crises, ethnic issues often became angular and seemed decisive in the reorientation of the national identities of the five titular nationalities of the republics (namely, Uzbek, Tajik, Kazakh, Kirgiz and Turkmen). However, throughout the period of Soviet rule, the Central Asians could show quite a remarkable loyalty to their specific ethnic attachments and maintained some of their particular ethnic traits and values which were quite incompatible with Soviet teachings.

Ethnicity, as a very important socio-anthropolgical phenomenon, was recognised in Soviet scholarship. In fact, ethnic factors were quite carefully dealt with by scientific methods. Often ethnic identities were studied as the most important part of national identities. Again, in some cases, ethnic and national issues appeared as synonymous. Therefore, the indecisiveness and dichotomy regarding the perception of nationalities in Soviet theory also percolated in the Soviet concept of ethnicity and its growth, without however affecting the basic concept of merger (*Slianie*) of all identities into the great melting pot of Soviet identity. The coexistence of ethnic exclusiveness along with the supposed supranational Soviet entity was explained in terms of Marxist dialectics. Thus, the blossming of nations was expected to draw them closer, culminating finally in the fusion. The same theory seemed applicable in the cases of different ethnic groups residing in each national republics of this multinational conglomeration.

In fact, Central Asia could provide a most fascinating case study in this regard because their linguistic and religious exclusivity gave them the scope to develop strong ethno-national characteristics subject to regional variations. In spite of the Soviet goal of promoting social homogeneity by encouraging convergence of ethno-national categories, there were some distinct governmental policies that made ethnic distinctions prominent in this multi-ethnic land. In fact, the glaring difference between the ethnic Russians and the non-Russians, especially non-Slavs in terms of socioeconomic advancement, educational and other progress were repeatedly highlighted in Soviet speeches, essays and articles. The distinctly backward ethnic categories, therefore, had the task of catching up with the ethnic Russians in terms of modernisation and progress. In the 70s, the immediate goal was fixed on ethnic equalisation, not convergence. It goes without saying, that the expected way to equality for the less advanced nationalities lay in the blindfold following of the Russians as a role model. However, the major ethnic divisions according to ancient cultural roots in the USSR showed four major varieties:

1. European/Slavic: Russian, Belorussian, Moldavian and Ukrainian
2. Baltic: Latvian, Lithuanian, Estonian
3. Transcaucasian: Georgian, Armenian, Azerbaijani.
4. Central Asian: Uzbekistani, Tajikistani, Turkmenistani, Kirgiz and Kazhakh.

The Central Asians, thus, belonged to a major ethnic typology and, being demographically numerous, formed a substantial ethnic category, though not monolithic in character. Before going into the studies of ethnic variation inside Central Asia, however, one must take account of the relations between the ethnic Russians and the indigenous ethnic categories of Central Asian republics.

One very important feature of Soviet ethnic policy was the strict mention of national categories of each on passports. Here, the national categorisation was done according to the parental ethnic origin. Only in case of mixed parentage, the person concerned could choose either of the parent's nationality. Thus, ethnic identities were important in all Soviet records concerning the personal identities of their citizens. Rasma Karklins stated, "The identification of nationality is standard practice in virtually all official papers in the USSR, be they personal identity card, applications forms, job records, or else. Conversationally this is referred as the fifth point since the item '*natsionalnost*' typically appears fifth in row after other standard items of personal identification such as name, gender and year and place of birth."[1] Once declared, the nationalities of the citizens were permanently decided, a practice that definitely encouraged the individual's conscious ethnic self-identification. In another way, this policy, however, gave some kind of permanence to ethno-national distinctiveness as well which counterposed the Soviet thesis on assimilation. Another very regular question attached to any identity issue was language. In case of non-Russians, the spread of *lingua franca* or the Russian language was always tested. Even if a non-Russian, for example an Armenian or a Georgian accepted Russian as his second mothertongue, his nationality could not be transferred to Russian on the basis of such linguistic loyalty. Here, once again, more importance was attached to ethnic origin in deciding one's nationality. But in case of a mixed marriage between a Russian and a non-Russian, the Russian nationality was preferred by the off springs as that would definitely help in their upward mobility in career and society. Thus, ethno-social processes with their multidimensional perspectives continued under the Soviet regime, where the superior position of the Russians vis-a-vis other nationalities appeared very apparent both in policies and in practice.

Thus, a cross-current of attitude and behaviour on the part of different ethnic groups was traceable in the Soviet context. Given the scope and limits of the Soviet ethnic and nationalities policy, the Central Asians in general showed quite a distinct position which made their primary commitment to their ethnic roots quite evident. Usually, neither the feeling of inferiority complex nor the lure of better career prospect could sever their ethnic attachments. The ethnic loyalities of the Central Asians remained remarkably strong during the entire Soviet era which was reflected in the writings of both Soviet and Western scholars. But, whether this ethnic attachment prevented them to acquire the Soviet identity remains questionable. Given to its specific parameters, how far the Soviet system allowed ethnic identities to grow on their own remains another area of contest. However, in Central

Asia, the ethnic exclusiveness was an accepted fact, but the attitude of the ethnic-Russians residing in the Central Asian soil also showed remarkable distance from the indigenous people which proved that ethnic insularity was not an attribute of traditional or conservative communities alone.

There was a substantial number of Russian residents staying in each and every Central Asian republics during the Soviet phase, as party recruits or engaged in industrial production and other professional jobs with which the traditional Central Asian society was not used to. This Russian population in each republics was a minority except in Kazakhastan, where the proportion of indigenous and Russian population was compatible. However, though being a minority, these Russian people enjoyed quite a high status in the republics because of their white collar jobs and influential positions in the CPSU. According to a statistical report on the ethnic composition of each Central Asian republics just after the demise of the USSR (precisely 1991-92), the Russians comprised of 36 per cent of the total population in Kazakhstan, 21 per cent in Kirgizstan, 8 per cent in Tajikistan and Uzbekistan and 10 per cent in Turkmenistan.[2] Other than Kazakhstan, in all republics the Russians comprised a fairly small minority. But, interestingly enough, though being a minority, staying in the regional republics there was seldom any effort on part of the Russians to learn the languages of the titular nationalities. Rywikin pointed out, "The European settlers (implying the Slavs, mainly Russian, Ukrainians, Belorus, etc.), for their part, show no interest whatsoever in learning local languages and consequently in getting acquainted with local cultures, and this despite the presence of those languages (as electives since Khrushchev, as required subjects before) in school curricula."[3] There was very little initiative on the part of the so called progressive nationalities as well to get acquainted with the language and culture of the Asian nationalities. The task of 'drawing together' was seen as a one way traffic where the titular nationalities would keep moving closer to the Russian model, superimposed by the new Soviet culture. Valery Tishkov, a Russian scholar himself, and quite closely attached to the Soviet bureaucracy, openly admitted after the demise of the Soviet system, that, "In the former USSR, Russians enjoyed for decades the comfortable status of a people dominating all the major socio-cultural areas. The Russian language and culture were reference points for all culture that was transmitted forcibly from the centre to the periphery via the educational system, the mass media, party and government structures, and especially via the system of training managerial and intellectual elites, and military service. Under these circumstances, Russians residing in the union republics had no overwhelming motivation to learn the languages of the titular nationalities and integrate into the non-Russian ethno-cultural environment."[4] Most of the Russian settlers in the Central Asian republics came with the Soviet settlements and maintained their Russian cultural profile in somewhat aggregated forms. But, interestingly, as Tishkov pointed out, there were some Russian residents in Central Asia who came to settle in this zone much before the revolution and they were better acquainted with the languages, culture and every day life of the indigenous peoples, and are less condescending.[5] The natural process of 'drawing together' between peoples of different roots took place in a better way through the natural course than under the guidance of the Soviet values enforced from above. However, the majority of the Russian population who became residents of the regional republics during different phases of the Soviet rule always kept a safe distance (even culturally) from the local ethnic population. This distance, could be made out distinctly from the study of marriage records where marriages between the Central Asians and ethnic Russians were seldom found. Thus, a mutual ethnic-cultural gap was maintained on part of both the communities. Tishkov admitted that "Although there were intensive inter-ethnic contacts and a high level of linguistic Russification in all former Soviet republics, in this region the Russians and the titular population kept a cultural distance from one another and were in effect isolated communities with their own social niches and circles of every day contacts. Mixed marriages between Russian and people of the local nationalities were and remain rare. Marriage between Russians and Ukrainian Germans, Tatars and Koreans are much more frequent."[6] This implied that the non-indigenous population of Central Asia, mainly Europeans, could mix better within themselves, and gave little effort to interact with the indigenous communities of the region. The Russians staying in this zone always had a feeling of superiority which distanced them from the indigenous population and the cultural gap between Europe and Asia remained glaring. Alexander I. Motyl bluntly stated, "Simply put, the Russians are hegemonic socially."[7] Some other scholars alluded the Russian presence during the pre-Soviet and Soviet period to that of the missionaries, once preaching orthodox Christianity and European culture, later replacing by it a more articulated and organised

Soviet doctrinaire communism and Soviet culture.[8] However, the attitude of the Russian residents of Central Asia had to change drastically since with the demise of the Soviet Union they all suddenly turned into minority diasporas in each of the tilular national republics. Even Tishkov's seemed apologetic intonation while discussing the present condition and future possibilities of these Russian people. Tishkov stated, "There is indeed, a growing awareness among Russians that if they want to stay in the newly emerged, sovereign states of Central Asia, they must know their languages much better than they do now. This is corroborated by the answers given by Russians living in Tashkent to the question: what is the preferable way of improving inter-ethnic relations in Uzbekistan today—that Russians learn Uzbek or that Uzbeks learn Russian better? Thirty-six per cent foavoured the first against half that figure who favoured the second. True, over one third of the respondents were unable to decide one way or the other."[9] The changing attitude of the Russians implied their recognition of a change of status which reinforced the fact of their hegemonic role in the previous system. Barner and Hody also pointed out,"In the union republics (and in other ethnically based political subdivisions), the titular nationality was usually the primary ethnic group, and all other ethnic groups were subordinate. The Russians were officially the dominant ethnic group throughout the USSR and did not hesitate to claim their status as the senior partner in ethnic relations, no matter where they happened to be located."[10]

However, another very interesting development in the ethnic sphere began to accelerate from the 60s and 70s in the Central Asian territories that drew attention of both Soviet and Western experts. This was the ethnodemographic pattern of the Soviet Muslims with high rate of population expansion while the Slavic population growth began to fall in an alarming rate. There developed a very attractive Western thesis that the growing Muslim population in Central Asia and other parts of Soviet Union might out-number the dominant Slavic majority and turn the ethno-demographic equation upside down in the near future. This trend of declining population among the Slavs and the growing population of the Soviet Muslims began to draw attention of the specialists from the late 70s and early 80s. An article by V.I. Kozlov dealt in detail about the population issue in the USSR between 1959-79. According to the table provided by Kozlov, the size and growth of Russian and Central Asian population in thousand and in per cent are as follows:[11]

Nationality	*1926*	*1939*	*1959*	*1970*	*1979*
Russians	77,791.1	99.591.5	114,113.6	129,015.1	137,397.1
Kazakhs	3,968.3	3,100.9	3,621.6	5,298.6	6,556.4
Uzbeks	3,904.6	4,845.1	6,015.4	9,195.1	12,456.0
Turkmens	763.9	812.4	1,001.6	1,525.3	2,027.7
Tadzhiks	978.7	1,229.2	1,396.9	2,135.9	2897.7
Kirghiz	762.7	884.6	968.7	1,452.2	1,906.3

Increase of Population in Per cent

Nationality	*1926-39*	*1939-59*	*1959-70*	*1970-79*	*1959-79*
Russian	28.0	13.7	13.0	6.5	20.4
Kazakhs	21.9	16.8	46.3	23.7	8.1
Uzbeks	24.1	24.2	52.8	33.0	102.5
Tadzhiks	25.6	13.6	52.9	35.7	107.4
Kirghiz	16.0	9.5	49.9	31.2	96.8
Turkmen	6.3	23.3	52.2	33.0	102.5

But, Kozlov's concern about the diminishing demographic figures extended to Baltic citizens as well as other Slav categories of Belorussians, Ukrainians along with the Russians. Kozlov regretted, "Between 1959 and 1970, the number of East Slavs (Russians Ukrainians and Belorussians) grew by 18.8 per cent, i.e., their rates of increase were lower (by almost half, in the case of the Ukrainians) than the USSR average. There is a reason to expect that these peoples rates of natural increase in the near future will diminish even further, and that this diminished growth will not be compensated by their (primarily the Russians') absorption of other nationality groups through ethnic assimilation.

In his speculation for the year 2000, Kozlov argued that this demographic trend would grow unhindered as the mothers of the would be generation twenty year ahead were already born and it would be difficult, rather impossible, to increase their numbers. By the year 2000, the number of Uzbeks may reach 25 million, exceeding the Belarussians almost 2.5 times; in their demographic potential (the number of children born) the Uzbeks by that time may have surpassed the Ukrainians."[12] Now whether such speculations were motivated by apprehensions of Uzbek nationalities surpassing the ethnic-Russians in the coming years remain unclear. However, such detailed survey and hypothesis on ethnic pattern by Soviet intellectuals made it clear that ethno-national identity of the Russian and non-Russian nationalities and their proportional growth did matter to the Soviet regime though in theory, the claim was to transcend these parochial attachments.

Writing much later, Valery Tishkov also mentioned the high proportion of population increase in the Central Asian zone as a striking contrast to the growth of Slavic and Baltic people. As he gave the statistics, "From 1979 to 1984, the Russian population in the USSR increased by 5.6 per cent, Ukrainians by 4.2 per cent and Belorussians by 6 per cent. During the same period, population growth among the Azerbajainis was 24 per cent, Uzbeks and Turkmens 24 per cent, Kirgizia 32 per cent and Tajiks 45 per cent. In another writing, mentioned previously, Tishkov discussed the decreasing proportion of Russian population in Central Asia and the causes behind this trend: "According to the 1989 USSR census, the Russian population in the region numbered 9,500,000 and constituted 19.3 per cent of the overall population. Russians accounted for 21.5 per cent of the population in Kirgizia, 7.6 per cent Tajikstan, 8.4 per cent in Uzbekistan, 37.8 per cent in Kazakhstan and 9.5 per cent in Turkmenia." The reasons for such declining Russian population in the region were not only decreasing birth rate among the ethnic Russians; in Tishkov's view, immigration of Russians to Central Asia which began to decrease from the 70s and got almost stopped by the 80s was an equally important factor in decreasing the population growth rate of the Russians.[13]

Gerhard Simon stated, "After 1950, the people's birth rate and population growth progressed at dramatically different paces. The birth rates of the Slavic and Baltic peoples declined; at the same time, the birth rates of the Islamic peoples increased. Thus, they climaxed in about 1960 and then also began declining .... In the next decades, the population balance will continue to tip in favour of Islamic peoples because extremely strong age groups are entering child bearing age.... Already today, these demographic shifts have considerable effects in many different areas and will be even more noticeable in the future.[14]

However, it is often surmised that the extent of population increase among the Muslim Asians was an uneasy experience for the Soviet authorities. Especially, Western scholars began to put forth a popular thesis that the Muslim Asians outnumbering the European Slavs might change the balance of the Soviet world upside down. Victor Zaslavsky, however, strongly countered this possibility. Zaslavsky argued, "Many observers seem to attribute a special significance to the fact that the Russians will soon be a minority of the Soviet population, they forget that within the Tsarist empire they constituted less than 44 per cent of the population but still played the dominant role." Zaslavsky further explained that the demographic rise might not have any corelation with power politics and taken as a direct threat to a political system based on complex power equations. He thus opined, "The major defect with this type of argument consists in arbitrarily drawing a political conclusion from a demographic premise. Demographic growth is identified with growth of political activity, and the social power of a group is assessed solely on the basis of its size, without taking into account the level of organisation and the degree of control exercised by the group over resources. Sociological analysis does not warrant such a conclusion."[15] Another scholar Shams Ud Din looked at the problem of increase of Central Asian population vis-a-vis the Slavs (mainly Russians) from a distinctly different perspective. He highlighted the fact that compared to the decade of 1959-70, there was a relative fall in the growth rate during the decade 1970-79 in Central Asia. He admitted that in spite of the declining growth rate, the Central Asian ethnic population had a considerably higher birth rate than that of the union average. It is this comparative scale always used in measuring the Central Asian demographic trend, which tends to bring an elusive picture of population exodus in this territory. In his calculation, "According to the census of 1979 the Soviet Muslims constitute about 16.5 per cent of the total population of the USSR and at the most it will rise to about 20 per cent by the year 2000 when the Soviet Muslim population is expected to reach 64 million. According to Feshbach, the Soviet Union estimates that the population of Russians will increase from 137 million in 1979 to 140 million by the turn of the century. In other words, they would continue to enjoy the status of being the largest nationality group. Therefore, all projections of changing the population balance in favour of the Soviet Muslims are extremely exaggerated having no basis at all."[16] However, the demographic ratio between the Russians and the Soviet Muslims (mainly Central Asians and Tatars) being such a debated issue implied that the dynamics of ethnic polarity existed in Soviet psychology as late as 80s and 90s. This factual reality and the importance it received in both Soviet and Western scholarship completely destroyed even the conceptual credibility of the theory of 'fusion'.

Ethnic Diversity in Central Asia

The major five ethnic categories of Central Asia can be understood from the names of the republics. Other than these five titular nationalities, namely Uzbek, Tajik, Kazakh, Kirgiz and Turkmen, there were some minority nationalities and so also some ethnic sub-groups within each nationality. This made the ethnic composition of the region extremely complex, delicate and at times confusing because of overlapping identities. Mehrdad Haghayeghi pointed out, "Far from monolithic, the Central Asian ethnic make-up has been a colorful mix of the Iranian, Turkic and Mongolian races who were joined by the host of other ethnic groups during the Czarist and later the communist era, of which the Slavs continue to play a prominent yet potentially destabilising role."[17] As the role of the Russians had already been assessed, now the focus would be turned to the other indigenous elements.

To begin with, the ethnic patterns of the titular nationalities never worked as homogeneous compartments. There was a great deal of intermixing and exchange of population within and amongst the Uzbeks, Tajiks, Kazakh, Kirgiz and Turkmen tribes. Ashoke Mukherjee wrote, "The boundaries of individual states, therefore, were more administrative than historical, a fact which is extremely relevant in any appreciation of the geopolitical and geocultural entity of the region."[18] The titular nationalities had two broad ethno-linguistic background—Turkic and Persian. The Turkic group had nationalities consisting of Uzbek, Kirgiz, Kazakh and Turkmen while the Tajiks had Persian roots. Once again, though being Turkic, there were major differences between the Uzbek and the three other nationalities. The Uzbeks claimed a glorious medieval past (though they were not given the right to glorify it during the Soviet rule) which was traced to imperial Samarkhand and Timur and had already inherited an indigenous urban culture much before the Russian invasion in these territories. The Kirgiz, Kazakh and Turkmen ethnic identities were comparatively less prominent, with nomadic lifestyle and without much historical figures or heritage to cling to. These ethnic disparities surfaced during the post-Soviet phase, when search for identities began and the over-enthusiastic Uzbek nationalism often spilled over the other Turkic region with an acclamation of having memories of holding them under Uzbek sway during its glorious past. The only republic which was, in fact, dissociated from Uzbekistan during the formative phase of the USSR on the basis of linguistic differences was Tajikistan.

But Uzbek-Tajik republics throughout the Soviet era were closest neighbours and the most interactive ethnic categories in Central Asia. Once again, though the Tajiks were apparently a homolinguistic group residing inside Central Asia, they formed the richest conglomeration of various distinct and mixed ethno-tribal categories. Shirin Akiner mentioned, "The Tajks exemplify the complexity of the Central Asian heritage since, unlike the other large ethnic groups that now inhabit the area, they are Iranian-speakers, not Turkic. They represent the development of one of the early layers of Central Asian civilisation, predating the advent of the Turks." She also added at the same time that the Uzbek-Tajik proximity and close interaction implied an easy relation between the two major (prominent) ethnic communities, "The history of Tajikistan is particularly bound up with that of Uzbekistan, for the two areas are not only contiguous, but have often been governed by the same rulers and subject to the plains of Transoxiana for generations of conquerors from the south and the east."[19] Akiner's insight is noteworthy here. She found sharing the memories of common misfortune of external conquests equally important as recollection of the glorions past. Slightly extending this thesis upto the advent of the Russians followed by Soviet accumulation of the entire zone, the collective memories must have helped the people of various ethnic roots to share a common fate.

However, apart from the titular Asian ethnic groups, each of the republics here had other Asian ethnic minorities, for example:

- Karakalpaks—majority living in Uzbek SSR
- Uighurs—majority living in Uzbek SSR
- Dungans—majority living in Kirgiz & Kazakh SSR
- Baluchis—majority living in Turkmen SSR
- Afghans—majority living in Turkmen SSR & also in Uzbek & Tajik SSR
- Jamshids—majority living in Turkmen SSR
- Gypsies/Maghat—They are scattered but majority now in Uzbek SSR. (meaning fire worshipper)
- Kipchaks—non-Uzbek people of Ferghana Valley
- Kuramas—included with the Uzbeks
- Pamiris or Mountain Tajiks—majority living in Badakhshan ASSR of Tajikistan
- Yagnobis—living mainly in Tajik SSR[20]

This long list of minority nationalities of Asian origin residing within different titular nationalities helps in visualising a colourful ethnic map of the region with both bold and mild contours. To take up the case of Tajikistan's ethnic composition in details, an ever increasing number of categories were recorded in census reports of 1926, 1937 and 1989 consecutively:[21]

Tajik	*Non Registered Names Included into Official Category*		
Official Name	*Census 1926*	*Census 1937*	*Census 1989*
	Aratorcy, gornye, Tajiki, gorogcy, Tajiki gornye	aratorchy, gal'cha, gornyeTajiki, gorogcy, pamircy,Tadzhik vakharcy, vakhi, vukh, khajbari, khik, ishkashimcy, inskoshumi, sredneaziatskie zygane, dzhugi, kashkari, lyuli, mazang moltani, shugnancy, baredzh, bartangcy, mundzhancy, oroshorcy, reshancy, rushni khugnoni, khufey, shugni, yagnobcy, yazgulyamcy, zgamit, yuzdom.	Todzhik, chagatai, kharduri, kardivi, darvazi, vanchi, vandzh, goroncy, pamirskie Tajiki, pripamirskie Tajiki, badzuvey, badzhujey, badzhavidzh, badzhuvedzh, barvozcy, barvozidzh, bartangcy, bartangidzh, bartangi, vakhancy, khik, vakhi, vakhidzh, gundcy, gundedzh, gundi, ishkashimcy shikoshumi, ishkashimcy, shikoshumi, ishkoshumi, mundzhoni, oroshorcy, roshorvidzh, rushancy, rushchoni, rykhen, sarykol'cy, sarikuli, khufcy, khufidzh, shakhdarincy.

The ever increasing ethnic categories in record only emphasised the growing ethnic consciousness of the Tajik people in spite of their being members of a society with developed socialism where all these identities were supposed to get blurred into the grand melting-pot of Soviet identity. However, in the Tajik case, these huge ethnic categories formed various regional allegiences and gave birth to distrinctly different ethno-political group identities.

To take up the issue of ethnicity in general, it was found that all the titular nationalities of all Soviet territories had this kind of non-registered names to offer during the census in Central Asia. In some cases such names increased during the 1937 census (eg. Kirgiz, Uzbek) and again decreased in the census report of 1989. In cases of the Kazakhs and Turkmen there were marginal increase in the names from 1937 to 1989. Thus, the Tajik experience remains unique with its huge increase in varieties that implied the complexity of the ethnic distribution of this geographically diverse and territorially small republic. Valery Tishkov, however, expressed his doubt about the credibility of these names of communities as ethnic groups as he cited a number of examples where ethnic identities were artificially imposed on the people of different groups of confused identities. In his own language, "A new structure of ethnic identities began to be imposed in Central Asia after the 'national-territorial delimitation' of the early 1930s, when a new political-administrative map of the region was drawn up for local 'socialist nations'. Large-scale membership recruitment into ethnonations began throughout the country, gradually replacing regional, religious, clan and other group identities". Tishkov also added, "A famous ethnographer Yelena Peschereva, who was active in establishing ethnic and republican borders in Central Asia, confessed at the end of her career that during the first Soviet census she 'had given birth to thousands of Tajiks by simply registering them as such, so as to suit the purposes of the committee of national-territorial delimitation. Even more Tajiks were registered as Uzbeks."[22] Thus, in Tishkov's view, ethno-national identities were imposed upon various people in order to bring national-territorial cohesion for political and administrative purposes and, therefore, ethnic consciousness was not always the most authentic and natural attribute of the Soviet people. Tishkov did not give too much importance to ethnicity even in post-Soviet society. Rather, he found a never-ending and ever growing process of confusion over identification of people according to ethno-national boundaries. He wrote, "a kind of hierarchy of ethno-national units of the Russian *matrushka* doll type."[23] Reflection of the same image is found in the writing of Ahmed Rashid concerning the post-perestroika chaos among the Central Asian nationalities. "The national question had become the mirror image of the painted Russian dolls —after opening the top doll, one finds successively smaller and smaller dolls inside."[24] Regarding Central Asian ethnic scenario, Tishkov also highlighted the role of a strong religious bond (namely Islam) across ethnic, regional and national categories.[25]

In any case, the reflections of different intellectual opinion regarding Soviet ethnic policies have to be discussed substantially. Here the writings of some famous Soviet ethnographers during the hey-days of Soviet rule will uncover the Soviet ethnic policies and their impact on different 'ethno' groups residing in this multi-ethnic zone of Central Asia. Before going into the detailed survey of Soviet ethnographic research documents, one might take into account the general opinion of Gerhard Simon about the postures taken by these intellectuals. He highlighted the disparity between theory and the outcome of research by Soviet scholars stating, "Thus, Soviet researchers confirm the main findings of comparative research on nationalism and simultaneously refute two important ideological postulates and expectations: that the increasing intensity of inter-ethnic contacts would cause independent national self-consciousness to level off, and that the new intellectuals, who were socialised by the Soviet education system, would stop identifying with their national traditions, languages and national characteristics and adopt only all Soviet values, attitudes and behaviours. Soviet socialists find that international collectives and living and working intensively with various ethnic groups do not necessarily promote friendship among the peoples. On the contrary, these situations can create friction and conflict that would not arise as long as the milieu remained nationally homogenous. Multi-national collectives can be expected to produce positive effects only if 'there is already a history of favourable and long-lasting contacts.'[26] The position of this intelligentsia was somewhat unclear usually for their cautious behaviour, projected in their writings. Simon threw a number of questions about the stand-point of this government-aided intelligentsia of the Soviet system: "To what extent did the new national intelligentsia become a genuine part of Soviet society and influence its policies? How loyal are they to the whole state and the political power system? How developed is their desire for autonomy, and where does it lead them? Are these new elites a threat to the whole state, or are they smoothly integrated into the "new historical community of men—the Soviet people?"[27] Though specific and direct answers to such questions are not available, the study of a host of research articles by Soviet scholars like Bromlei, Arutunian or Drobizheva on ethnographic and nationalities issues provides a direction, not contrary to, but at least independent of propaganda postulates.

In one of her selected articles, L.M. Drobizheva started with the need of education to broaden the popular minds in favour of assimilation. Education was viewed as a very effective instrument in this process. She stated, "It is not only a fund of knowledge, which substantially broadens one's understanding of the world, one's own and other peoples and their place in the historical process, but also a purposeful training which can be used to fortify in men's consciousness friendly attitudes towards other peoples."[28] The role of education in eradicating parochialism and cultural backwardness was also highlighted, "And although education in and of itself is not a guarantee against inter-nationality tensions, national prejudices are often associated, not only in social science literature but also in ordinary people's minds with a certain degree of cultural backwardness."[29]

Drobizheva also stressed the scope of cultural interaction and the totality of socio-political and cultural information about the people of other cultures being important for overcoming prejudices. In this, the Central Asian region with its fast changing conditions provided an excellent example,

To quote Drobizheva *in extenso:* "In regions with a rapidly changing and more dynamic cultural environment, the spread of total cultural information, as well as education, has had a more pronounced impact on overcoming national prejudices among people.

"Thus, among Uzbeks who read literature of a more serious psychological content, watch television, either selectively or regularly, and know Russian in addition to their native language, the number who have friends belonging to other nationalities and exhibit a positive attitude towards inter-nationality relations (including informal relations) is one and a half to two times higher (both in urban and rural areas) than among those who do not have such cultural habits."[30]

Central Asians, backwardness and lack of exposure were repeatedly highlighted in inter-ethnic, inter-cultural or internationality relations in comparison to the Georgians or Moldavians who were much smoother in their behaviour towards and accpetance of other nationalities. But the reason for this easy inter-mixing according to Drobizheva was better cultural exposure. At the same time, Drobizheva admitted that the trend in marriage differed from the general attitude of friendliness. Regarding marriage the attitude was not so easy going for both Transcaucasians and Central Asians. As she wrote, "In

Transcaucasia and Central Asia attitude toward nationally mixed marriages are most often dictated not by the degree of friendly feelings toward other nationalities, but by deeply rooted traditions of marrying within the national group. Among the peoples of these regions, therefore, greater exposure to cultural information, as also rising levels of education, do not affect attitudes towards relations at the workplaces, although relations within the family are, on the whole, more closely linked to culture."[31]

Thus, there was an open admission of the limits of educational or cultural exposure to change in attitudes regarding the traditional institution of marriage. In fact, the Soviet ethnographers made detailed study on mixed marriages as an index of inter-ethnic fusion throughout the period. In Central Asia the scope of mixed marriage with the European counterparts always remained limited. There were detailed works on the Central Asian marriage patterns, family and life-styles in the Russian journal *Sovetskaya Etnografia* throughout the 70s and 80s which showed a mild compromise between academic research and political commitment to contribute towards the making of the broad supranational Soviet identity. The two opposite currents of national exclusivity and inter-nationality interactions were seen as part of Marxist dialectical movement. However, in the course of investigation, all the elements of national culture or self-awareness were studied in detail with full academic commitment. Drobizheva, herself, in another article on National self-awareness stated, "A concrete study of national self-awareness is complicated above all because it is difficult to find indications that are appropriate to each of its elements. Even among one people, it may show up as pride in historical figures and war heroes, it may accumulate around the anniversary of a major historical event, or it may concentrate on the celebration of a song or the name of an athlete who had won world acclaim...... At the individual level, national self-awareness will vary not only depending on age, but also on the particular situations in which a person may find himself. All these nuances must be taken into account in both studying and interpreting the phenomenon of national self-awareness".[32] She also found that ethnic roots worked as an important criterion in defining national self-awareness. But the importance attached to it by the different people of various nationalities varied. Drobizheva wanted to emphasise the role played by popular attachment to ethnic heroes or famous figures of the past and present to boost up ethno-national self-awareness of different nationalities.

Therefore, in her field survey she included a question about each respondent's choice of his or her favourite outstanding cultural figures. In her record Drobizheva maintained, "Of course, in their choices respondents in all republics named writers, scientists, composers and artists not only of their own nationality, but also some who had made contributions to Soviet and world culture. Again, there is no evidence that the base for relating to folk achievements is decreasing; on the contrary, not only are outstanding artistic works of the past becoming the possession of ever-broader masses but even contemporary ethnic artistic culture is acquiring universal recognition and becoming an object of pride. These folk values and achievements are by no means limited to artistic culture; economic accomplishments, exploitation of valuable national resources, scientific discoveries, etc. also rank with them."[33] Thus, there was a tacit protest against the Western criticism of destruction of folk culture by the imposition of one single Soviet culture. On the contrary, by admitting the importance of local cultural and artistic activities at the local ethnic level, some kind of respect was shown to the ethnic communities and their age-old traditions. At the same time, it was recorded that these traditions were not to be over emphasised as a determining factor in national self-awareness. The role of economy and progress was harped on while discussing the direction of national interests. Ethnic attachments or cultural expressions were taken as much milder components in the development of a people's national awareness. She wrote, "Of course, it is primarily cultural figures who are involved in folk music ensembles created to revive and spread popular dances and songs, in disseminating artifacts of the material culture—whether that be a headdress or old areas of a city restored in the traditional style—and in the preservation of former geographic names as ethnic symbols. But we do not think that the polularity of these things can be explained solely in terms of people's need for a variety of impressions, or a tendency away from the standardisation of modern life. All these phenomena, if they really undergo mass dissemination, exercise a consolidating function, and behind them are ethnic interests based on social needs of one type or another."[34] Drobizheva, thus tried to put ethnicity in hierarchical terms with other materially more important factors like economy and social needs. But once again, she felt that the ethnic feelings were not a static phenomenon, it could develop and get more articulated by using modern education, "Ethnic self-awareness is also stimulated by such factors as education, which gives people an idea of the history of their own and other people, their language and their culture; by an attachment to literature, and the information provided by the mass media, which helps the individual to assimilate social experiences; and finally by expanding direct contacts of individuals of different nationalities, facilitating inter-ethnic comparisons."[35]

Yu. V. Bromlei and N.I Kozlov in an article titled *To The Study of Present Ethnic Processes. In the Sphere of the Spiritual Culture of the People of USSR*[36] discussed the role of ideology, emotions, social psychology, art, architecture, songs, music and other visual and performing arts to promote ethnic-national attachments. Beginning with a firm conviction of internationalism, these authors, nevertheless, admitted the strong presence of ethnic-national distinctiveness in different spheres of life of different communities of people. According to Bromie and Kozlov, Ideology, as generally known, is most closely interrelated with social psychology. In the Soviet society ideology and politics of proletariat internationalism paved the way for the formation of a qualitatively new, internationalist psychology.

But it should be taken into account that psychology is more conservative than ideology; former national and psychological settings continue to exist as remnants, even, when the factors causing them are already gone off the stage. It should not be forgotten—remarked L.I. Brezhnev—that the nationalistic prejudices exaggerated or perverted manifestation of national feelings—are extremely vital, tenaciously held in the psychology of people, who are not sufficiently mature in political terms."[37] Thus, at the very beginning of the article, there was open admission of the fact that ethno-national attachments worked more on psychological and emotional basis than as a rational ideology. The article subsequently unravelled the various forms and facts of these emotional and psychological behaviour promoting such attachments. Here, like Dorbizheva, Bromlei and Kozlov also admitted the obvious development of national pride attached to great personalities like scientists who contributed to the development of civilisation. "The national affiliation of the scholars acquires a special significance in these cases, when they make outstanding discovery; their fame to one or another degree is extended to the appropriate ethnos, by enhancing the national pride."[38] Ethnographers thus emphasised the role of history in building national consciousness. The combination of past memories working together to help a different ethnos to come closer and develop the notion of internationalism to counterpose the overt and covert ideas of national discrimination was highlighted as well. However, the development of national consciousness and internationalism were regarded as simultaneous processes helping each other without cutting across mutual interests.

The role of art, both visual and performing, in the promotion of national self-consciousness was treated with special attention in this article as these were seen as expressions of human psychology and emotions that could inspire such attachments. It is stated about art that "The fact is that it reflects reality not all-embracing but selectively, and not as a mirror copy, rather in refraction through the prism of peculiarities of the character of its creators and performers, their creative abilities and aspirations, their social settings. As a result of this, the work of art may be dedicated both to the typical one and also to the rare one, both to the national as well as to international; the ethnic specificity may be emphasised or passed over."[39] However, though the role of art with its own characteristic power of emotional influence was accepted yet the commitment of these authors to Soviet socialist ideology inspired them to see art as an effective instrument for the spread of this ideology. "Just like the social sciences art also remains under strong influence of ideology, depending on which it may accelerate the ethnic processes or put a break on it; break apart the peoples or bring them closer. Precisely because of this formulation and development of the Soviet art, it passed into the struggle led by our party against nationalist, formalist and similar negative trends."[40] Thus the various forms of art were taken seriously to influence the popular emotionalism in favour of international harmony as well as for the maintenance of national distinctiveness. Here the role of drama, theatre, cinema and television network, etc. were strongly emphasised for they were vehicled through language. "These forms of visual art, particularly connected with language and fiction, are often guided by it; it is known that many literary pieces of work penetrated to the broad masses indirectly, through printing and owing to their screening or theatrical adaptation for stage. In comparison to theatre, film, using shooting on location and in the studio, possesses far greater potentialities of representing the realities in its ethnic forms; these potentialities (and on the whole ethnic aspect of film art) increased after the advent and in the course of development of film with sound-track, in which national language is used—often with its dialect specificity."[41] The national or regional character of art can be distinct even without the use of language and these forms of art with their deeper emotional appeal could act as equally or even more effective instruments for ethnic, local, or national consciousness. "Painting and sculpture on the one hand, music and choreography on the other are ascribed to the forms of art, which do not show direct link with language and literature and cannot be taken in by the audience, so to say, directly, irrespective of linguistic affinity. The music possessing tremendous power of emotional influence upon the deep layer of psychology, takes a distinct place in social and cultural life of the people. Being genetically related to folk arts, song and music reflect the peculiarities of melodies, tunes, etc. of specific ethnic characteristics almost as equally strongly as language. At the same time, with different people, similar musical phenomena, connected with both cultural adoption as well as consequent uniformity of socio-economic pattern, way of life, uniformity of natural conditions, etc. developed on its own. Choreography and dance also belong to very old and steady forms of folk art. Analysis of the development of choreography starting from the folk dances to the stage ballet gives the opportunity to explain not only peculiarities of traditional dances of the people of the past but also to track down the ways of expansion of interconnection between choreographic cultures of local groups and people."[42] Songs possess both the advantages of linguistic and non-linguistic art—because it combines languages along with the expression of melody and therefore has a greater appeal to mass psychology.

However, in the last part of the article, the authors emphasised that with the socialist Revolution all the nationalities got greater exposure to practice and perform their own forms of art and could maintain their characteristic features along with interactions with other nationalities. Here, the role of religious prohibitions or restrictions in the free development of art is also highlighted as the "paintings and sculptures of Muslim people did not depict image of human beings."[43] This kind of prohibitions was taken as part of cultural specificity or peculiarity. The development of national art, literature and culture in their sum total was taken as the development of the Soviet culture which, with marginal combination of socialist ideology formed an emotional message that percolated through popular psychology. As the appeal of visual and performing arts could spread easily in popular minds, it became an easy and effective process to draw different communities of people into the inter-ethnic and international integration with the Soviet socialist ideology working at the backdrop. The authors concluded in an optimistic note, "In the given connection before the Soviet science there remains a number of tasks. In deciding one of them, related to the elucidation of degrees of mass acceptance of mastering national and international art in various forms, first steps are already taken. To decide others connected, with the intrinsic mechanism of various forms and separate works of art on ethnic consciousness, inter-nationalities contacts, etc. is, to a significant extent, a matter of future. And in our view, ethnographic science and disciplines related to it are called for playing the main role in it."[44]

However, this dual presence of ethnic-national and international feelings among the people varied from one context to another. The consciousness about one's own ethno-national position vis-a-vis the others were clearer with the urban educated people in Soviet view. Drobizheva showed a kind of polarity between the two types of people—one group, concerned more about ethnic identities, preservation of ethnic culture, symbols and way of life while the group with a wider outlook could look beyond this micro-identity and situate themselves in the broader world view. She stated, "A general Soviet self-awareness and Soviet interests are combined with their ethnic counterparts."

Thus, the gradual disappearance of specific ethnic traits from cultural and everyday life and the emergence in people of common human and common Soviet features is reflected in the set of national identification symbols and in the weak content of national and group autostereotypes."[45] Without denying the historical roots of culture and tradition, Drobizheva, from her commitment to the Soviet standpoint, argued that with time and experience, national heritage of different people gets enriched—the new Soviet world outlook only broadens and enriches a national entity instead of countering the national self-consciousness based on ethnic roots and tradition. "The historic past of a people cannot disappear...and we cannot speak here of any sort of disappearance of "grounds". On the contrary, they are capable of growing stronger. This does not ignore the fact that national interests more often than not coincide with common Soviet interests.

"Thus, the objective base of national self-awareness does not disappear, it simply changes. Indeed the foundation for its continued growth expands. As noted in Communist Party documents: "The economic and cultural progress of all nations and nationalities is inevitably accompanied by the growth of national self-awareness."[46]

In this way, Drobizheva tried to bring harmony between the awareness of historic roots and the dynamics of socio-economic developments during the 'developed phase of Soviet socialism'. There was this attempt to show the enrichment and fusion of the two apparently opposite pulls of past and present, in the nationality areas. In her conclusion she stressed the given socio-economic conditions which she felt was enough to provide opportunities not only for the growth of rich national awareness but was also conducive for the development of 'amicable inter-ethnic relations'. But the essay ended with a warning towards extremist nationalist tendencies that might take turn towards disintegration. This fear of 'split up', once again, indicated the lack of confidence in the forces of fusion, claimed otherwise. Rather the very subtle yet recognisable alarm ringing in her study probably gave the faint indication of a future rupture and made an appeal to the intellectuals of the society to prevent such mishap from taking place. As she stated, "Our conclusion was that with the favourable socio-political conditions in our country, national self-awareness does not hinder the development of amicable inter-ethnic relations. It can serve as a basis for strengthening both national and general Soviet patriotism. The task of society is to see to it that unfavourable social situations do not arise that could cause a hyperbolisation of national self-awareness and split our peoples. The task of future research is to study ways to prevent such situations, as well as to explore ideological factors and the psychological mechanisms of development of national and general Soviet consciousness and their channeling into a positive inter-ethnic interaction."[47]

The process of interaction leading to cultural fusion was highlighted in many theoretical works side by side with the admission of the fact that the cultural autonomy of various ethnic groups was maintained as well. Here the Central Asian republics with their ethnic peculiarities received special attention of Soviet ethnographers. G.P. Vasileva's article in *Sovetskaya Etnografia*, entitled, *Some Tendencies of Development of Modern National Tradition in the Material Culture of Central Asia and Kazakhstan*[48] discussed in details about the characteristic features of food, dress and household habits of the Central Asians with special emphasis on the national and inter-national feelings involved in their day-to-day performances. The article started with a notion of harmony between national and Soviet characteristic traits in various spheres of life and culture. "The ethnic processes that are going on among the people of USSR at present, have got quite a complete theoretical comprehension to a number of different Soviet scholars. The most characteristic among them, as known are, the unifying processes which in its turn, are divided into intra-national and international (processes). The last one means coming together of individual nations, integration of their culture into a common Soviet one." Vasileva believed that for this kind of double-fold processes, a balanced combination of old traditions with new concepts were needed as she continued, "Further the processes of internal national development of each individual nation and processes of coming together of nations among themselves imply on one hand use of spiritual and material values accumulated by earlier generations and on the other hand refutation of old traditional ones and putting together of new norms and components of culture suitable to the modern perceptions of people."[49] Vasileva then proceeded to find out the areas of cultural autonomy and combination in general life-style of the people of Central Asia. She took up dress and costumes as the first area of her study and observed, "Elements of traditional dresses with urban European forms are combined to an equal degree in the modern national costumes of the people of Central Asia and Kazakhastan. The costumes with old fashioned elements are gradually getting outdated for they are not suitable for the changed conditions of life." Thus, fashion and tradition both depended more on convenience. It was observed, "As everywhere, the traditional features are less in gent's costumes and the dresses of the youth and also in the dress-style of the urban people. Old people, particularly the women in the rural areas, are maintaining the traditional dress, which sometimes carries remarkable difference in the neighboring provinces. The increased level of people's prosperity, growth of culture and expansion of international contacts are visible in the diverse kinds of dresses. For example, the overwhelming majority of the people have both national and equally Europeanised dresses."[50] The role of dresses as symbols of ethnic roots could be traced according to the occasions of their use. "A considerable section of the population use the traditional dress as the ceremonial dress. It is worn in different official meetings where it is necessary to emphasise the nationality such as during the parades, theatrical representations etc. The traditional national costumes to a remarkable degree have got revived. Some half-forgotten elements of dresses, for example, girls' cap with fur brim, or the pointed velvet hat of the Kirgiz, almost out of fashion since as long as the 20s of our century, have become an indispensable part of the theatrical national costume though in day to day life it is hardly used at present."[51] She also cited examples of a particular attire becoming a national symbol during the Soviet phase, such as the '*tus-tuppe*' of the Uzbeks which could become the Uzbek gent's national head-dress during this period. Vasileva observed that "Before the revolution it was in fashion only in one region (small city of Chust of Namangan oblast) where both Tajiks and Uzbeks wore it, but during the years of Soviet power it expanded to the whole of Uzbekistan…tus-tuppe is an inseparable part of the Uzbek national costume. It is worth noting that this cap is widespread also in Tajikistan and during the last ten years it is also worn in other parts of Central Asia." Vasileva cited some other similar cases also—"During the past two decades, the short quilted robe made of black satin has become most popular in Uzbekistan and Tajikistan, which was mainly characteristic of the people of the Ferghana valley. It is worn by both old and young male folks and gradually it is replacing all the traditional robes."[52] Thus, she wanted to stress that the ethnic processes in the direction of national symbolism as well as cultural fusion were going on under the Soviet rule.

Regarding the influence of the combination of traditional past and economic affluence of the socialist present upon the construction and planning of the dwelling houses, Vasileva wrote, "The socialist reforms, growth of economic prosperity and cultural level of the people led to the removal of the differences between city and rural settlements, their living conditions in the city and in the rural areas. There is very small difference in the outer structure and planning techniques of dwelling places of most peoples of Central Asia. The cause behind this is the climatic condition, similar construction materials and the same techniques of construction related to it…But it did retain the local variant of dwelling places. Along with the new common planning, the traditional planning continued—in preservation of the local dwelling places."[53] Vasileva observed that ethnic characters of the houses were more prominent in the interior, in the décor and also in the style and organisation of the household. "On the whole, a style is maintained in the interior which meets the habits, day to day practices, tasks and norms of behaviour of each people." Here too, it was found that the furniture of the rooms were usually newly manufactured ones with some traditional trappings, while the rooms of the old people were usually furnished in strictly traditional style. She further observed that, "The walls and floor are decorated in an intense national style; keeping of utensils, etc. were also done in traditional pattern. Keeping of things had a typical ethnic-national style."[54]

Next to dwelling places, Vasileva discussed the extremely interesting sphere of food habits where national flavour and content was often enriched by external ingredients and style. "Extremely interesting and very evident are the tendencies of development of food habits of Central Asia and Kazakhstan, strictly maintaining their ethnic specificity. On the whole, they are analogous by tendencies of food habits, but different from other people of our country."[55] She found that the food style of the people with nomadic background was markedly different from sedentary people with a long and settled background. For example, the Kazhakhs and Karakalpaks with nomadic background had their most favourite dishes made of wheat, while for some semi-nomadic Turkmens' and Uzbeks', most favourite dish was made of *Jugar* (joar). Again, in northern Tajikistan and Uzbekistan, most of the popular dishes were made of rice. However, there were also exchanges of some dishes across the ethnic communities resulting from cultural interactions."[56] A very interesting attribute of the existing situation was that "The ritual dishes also bore ethnic traits." The same food was used for absolutely different purposes, for example, "Chelpek a kind of lipeshka (flat cake fried in oil)—is prepared by the Turkmen on the occasion of birth of a child, or during marriages, whereas for the Uzbeks and Tajiks they are made usually for funeral banquet."[57] She also noticed a number of Russian influence on the cooking style and addition of ingredients in the Central Asian cooking from the Soviet era. "Many vegetables appeared in Central Asia with the advent of the Russians—potato, cabage, tomato, etc. which got widely incorporated in the list of food of the local people only during the Soviet period."[58] Again it was found by Vasileva that the national character of any dish did not always depend on its traditional root. "It is interesting that, dishes, adopted two-three decades back from the neighbouring people started to be considered as their own and national. Such dishes of the majority of Central Asians and Kazakhs are 'Manti' and 'Lagman'.[59]

In the conclusion to her article, Vasileva honestly admitted the national and international, ethnic and inter-ethnic material cultures were in the process of constant development, change and fusion. "The national traditions in costume, interior, food, folk decorative and applied art of the people of Central Asia and Kazakhstan are still being maintained and are developing. Preservation and development and in some cases even revival of ethnic traditions are connected with the emergence of national republics, with the awakening of pride for their own national culture. At the same time, in the dwelling places of the region studied, except the interior and also in the costume of the people of some oblasts clear traits had been observed towards erasing of the national specialities...."[60] At the end she stated that material culture is even more difficult to obliterate, compared to spiritual culture of a nationality and ended her essay with the firm conviction that "As it seems to us, the ethnic functions of the useful traditions will be maintained and developed so long as the nations will exist."[61] Thus, as far as the cultural life was concerned, the Soviet writings did not appear as too inconsiderate towards the ethno-national traits. Rather, such research work showed sufficient recognition and respect for regional specificities in manifestations of material culture and the autonomy of its functioning and through the simultaneous process of intermixing of different cultures (especially European) under the Soviet regime.

In Soviet intellectual writings on the army it was attempted to boost up the Soviet identity of the local nationals across their ethnic categories. Here 'Soviet patriotism' was highlighted repeatedly to acknowledge the contribution of the soldiers coming from different parts of the USSR. Especially during the Afghan crisis, the ethnic segments of Central Asia were extensively used by the Soviet state in the war primarily due to their geographical proximity with Afghanistan. The local Central Asian newspapers glorified the heroic deaths of those young soldiers as Soviet martyrs. This was an important sphere of fusion where ethno-national identities were sought to be dissolved in the propagated faith of Soviet patriotism. In fact, for Tajik soldiers, the fight with the Afghan Mujahidins could be depicted as a fight within a broad ethno-lingual community between peoples who happened to be citizens of two neighbouring sovereign states. For, a substantial number of Mujahidins were Tajiks or Persian speaking by origin and many of them were successors of the deported Tajik *Basmachi* leaders or victims of Stalinist purges. In fact, the Afghan-Tajik border during the late 70s became a cause of tension for the Soviet security system because of constant inflow of cross-border terrorism associated with many other troubles (religious fanaticism, drug peddling, etc.) In such a scenario, the gallant service of a Tajik soldier in favour of the Soviet government against the Afghan enemies made a very strategic intervention in order to maintain the notion of great Soviet patriotism. Thus, the story of El' Murod Alovakov's sacrifice was published in Kommunist Tajikistana with great respect. El' Murod, of course, died during the battle. Interestingly, his story ended with a sentimental note to his ethno-lingistic lineage, "And how could you forget? A year ago E. Alovakov had a son, whom he named sherafgan. A pretty name translated into Russian it means "Afghan tiger".[62] Thus, writing even as late as the perestroika period, the Soviet correspondents could not take a stand on either of the identities firmly—the attempts of combining both and promoting each was an illusory ideal to which they were committed to. Therefore, the intellectual writings appeared vexed and often self-contradictory in their conclusions, though the specialists mostly had undergone serious and tedious research, fieldwork or data collection on ethno-demographic or ethno-national issues. The article by A. Dashdamirov on 'Soviet patriotism' brought out distinctly the Soviet position, expectation and anomalies about the national and supranational loyalties of its citizens. He stated, "the patriotism of the Soviet man is the true embodiment of the dialectical unity of national and international elements in the life of our society and the life of the individual."[63] In fact, he ulogised the Soviet patriots as a new category in human history, "The formation of the Soviet man—a patriot and internationalist—serves as a touchstone of the maturity of our society and a measure of the solidarity of the Soviet people as a qualitatively new, historic community of people,"[64] In spite of such proud comments he had to admit that Soviet patriotism was threatened by internal evil forces even as late as in 1982! "The struggle against distortions of patriotic values, against attempts to inject into Soviet patriotism elements alien to its nature and to insinuate into modern social consciousness backward, conservative petty—bourgeois and patriarchal ideas under a "patriotic" mask, continues to be relevant. A false understanding of the "purity" of national culture, remote from any concern for its fruitful development, and advocacy of obsolete forms of culture and way of life under the banner of preservation of traditions—how remote this is from the ethics of socialist internationalism, how incompatible with the nature of true patriotism!"[65] Thus, it is clear that patriotism with ethno-national overtone was completely disapproved by the mainstream Soviet scholarship. Such abberations, however, were not denied outright. Rather communist education was repeatedly endowed with the responsibility of strengthening and rebuilding Soviet patriotism all over the USSR.

However, the Soviet scholars and researchers used to emphasise more on the cultural, educational and other important social practices and institutions as material culture, marriage, family, the role of art, etc. as these themes apparently had lesser possibilities of clash with the idea of greater Soviet identity. For the Central Asian region, these characteristic trends which reflected their traditional community practices, formed an important part of their national behaviour and ethnic patterns. Many Western and other experts also took account of these ethno-national behavioural and institutional perspectives of the Central Asian people, as this way of life apparently made them look markedly different from their European counterparts in the Soviet union. Central Asia, as a broad culture-zone attracted scholarly attention of both pro-Soviet and anti-Soviet categories. It is, however, established by the scholars of both extremes that in order to understand and explain the ingenuity and uniqueness of Central Asian people, their traditional way of life with conventional institutions has to be studied from an ethnographical perspective.

To take up the 'family' as an institution, Central Asia showed both her own uniqueness and some common characteristic traits across categories. Usually, families followed the old patriarchal pattern of a broad based joint structure where more than two generations lived under one roof. This had some serious socio-economic and political consequences in the Soviet system. Large families were associated with traditional values and high birth rate. In comparison, the ethnic Russians and other European nationalities like Ukrainians, living in Central Asia, on an average had a distinctly different notion or pattern of family planning. Ajay Patnaik observed that "The average family size in Central Asia was about six, as compared to the European republics where the average size of the family was only three in 1979. In indicators like children/woman ratio, children living with the mother, fertility ratio, expected and ideal number of children, etc. the Central Asian republics were well ahead of other republics."[66]

The average expectation of children was five or six and this mind set did not change through the decades of Soviet teachings. Patnaik stated, "Research conducted in 1985 showed that among married women between 18-44 years of age, as many as half among Uzbeks and Tajiks and three fifth among Turkmen were expected to have 6 or more children. This was in contrast to only 0.3 per cent among Russian women in the above age group."[67] This tendency to have larger families implied an indigenous ethno-demographic trend of this region that gave rise to major demographic tensions for the Soviet authorities. It seemed that with time the Soviet Muslims of different ethnic segments would collectively surpass the Slavs in numerical strength.

However, the alarm raised on the demographic boom in Central Asia, was also probably an exaggeration as statistics showed that the growth rate began to decline in these territories from 70s onwards. Anyway, what remained static was probably the mother's psychological inclination to have many children which actually implied a natural commitment to tradition and love for age-old conventions. Shams Ud Din has cited several practical reasons for the acceptance of larger families by the women of Central Asia. In his opinion, "Several factors, such as, poor family planning, practice of early marriages, low employment of Muslim women in organised sectors of Soviet economy, a greater per centage of marriageable persons and an extremely high ratio of rural population among the Soviet Muslims seem to contribute to higher birth rates among the Soviet Muslims."[68] Among the Central Asian families, the Tajiks had the highest rate of growth. L.F. Monogarova in her article entitled, "Structures of modern urban family of the Tajiks (on the basis of surveys conducted on the cities of Ura-Tyube and Isfara[69]) dealt in details about the tendency towards larger families among the Tajiks. She also emphasised the traditions of having many children in Tajik families whose number of children often crossed eight (in some families even more than ten). She further noted, "Tradition does not allow mothers, if there is no other helper in the family, to balance the maternal duties and running the household with work in production."[70] Monogarova also admitted that the increase in average longevity of people in general under Soviet health protection also had some role to play in the increase of population. But still, the high birth-rate was the major cause of the marked increase in the Central Asian population. She also highlighted the opinions of A. Saliev and V.V. Pokshishevskii in support of her view.[71] The high birth rate was more visible in the rural regions, compared to the urban centres. This was because in rural areas the ethnic character of the indigenous people remained pure and ethnic traditions more alive. In V.V. Porkshishevskii's explanation, birth rate in the rural area was markedly more for they maintained ethnic tradition much better than in the city. In his opinion, "the ethnic tradition of bearing many children was a determining trend, but it was also necessary to take into account the role of such factors as the recent increase of the marriage age and improvement in the cultural level of the spouses, the actual status of a woman in the family and social life and also such socio-economic factors as the level of employment of a woman in social production, influence of urbanisation in general, which rendered and renders decreasing impact on fertility.[72]

Larger families in rural sectors had another interesting effect in the socio-economic sphere. The evergrowing rural population began to face problems of unemployment, but showed unwillingness to leave their abode to migrate outside for job. The Soviet ethnographer Arutunian showed that there was an inverse relation between migration and family size in rural areas. This inertia to move out of the traditional family protection affected the economic growth of the region quite adversely for this created an unnecessary burden on rural sectors while the urban industrial sectors had to borrow workers from European parts of Soviet union. This created a very complex ethnic equation in the zone. While there was population pressure from within, the general apathy towards migration to urban industrial sectors made the influx of Russian and other skilled workers necessary for industrial activities. This caused a feeling of ethnic distinctiveness between urban and rural populations of Central Asia as well. Rural life contained stronger traditional values and frame of mind while urban life had to discount many ethnic characteristics partly for the faster dynamics of urban life and partly for compulsive intermixing with the people of other nationalities. Ajay Patnaik stated, "Family size differentiation was also influenced by the socio-occupational structure. Urban white-collar employees indicated lower preference for bigger family than either manual urban workers or rural workers. Similarly, collective farmer's families revealed a higher preference for bigger families as compared to any other occupational categories."[73] However, this traditional type of family structure later created problems in political and economic sphere as this trend remained somewhat incompatible with the Soviet concept of inter-national interaction and mobility. From late 70s, onwards, local demands began to increase the scope of placements for the local people and a kind of discontent towards the non-indigenous people also began to surface. For, these people, being more skilled and capable, were tougher competitors whom the Central Asians did not want to face in the professional sphere.

This problem of manpower mobilisation had become quite a serious issue for the state policies. There were academic researches on the labour supply trends where findings showed Central Asia to be quite inflexible. One such Russian text was by L.V. Ostapenko and A.A. Susokolov which dealt in detail the prospects of labour mobilisation from Central Asia to other parts of USSR, especially to the rural areas of RSFSR where there existed an agrarian labour shortage. They called the Central Asian zone a 'labour surplus' area. But the fact that the 'labour surplus' zone was not conducive to the concept of migration was a well known fact to the scholars. They stated, "One approach to the solution of the problem of labour reserves in the Non-Black-Earth zone sometimes considered is the possibility of attracting part of the rural population from republics with a high birth-rate, sometimes called labour-surplus areas. Since this involves contacts not just between regions, but also between peoples, the consideration of ethnic factors in such recruitments is very important from a practical point of view."[74] They proceeded in the same essay inquiring about this patterns of ethnic migration: "The question of why the migration mobility of a number of indigenous populations of the Central Asian and Caucasian republics is so low is widely considered in the scientific literature, with various opinions expressed..... Familiar social and natural surroundings, the moral and economic support of relatives and friend, a reduced likelihood of psychological stresses (a common companion for rural migrations to large cities) all slow resettlement to the city, even within one's own republics."[75]

Thus, the institution of the family in this ethnic zone played a much more important role than it did in the rest of the USSR. Another specific feature that made this zone appear static and averse to mobility was the role of the women population. The women of Central Asia did not, because of over-burdening families, could not, participate in productive labour of the region. In statistical calculation this lot of womenfolk constituted a 'labour-surplus'—i.e., capable labour not engaged in productive economy. This work force, though capable of work, was virtually immobile because of their family commitments and protective upbringing and also lacked any professional career orientation. Ajay Patnaik harped on this point, "Family in Central Asia retained many of its traditional characteristics and restricted the mobility of women, both for education and for jobs. This affected the rural migration process." Women often worked as the unskilled rural labour force in cotton picking (which was a seasonal and temporary job). Patnaik explained, "Their (women) lack of education or low level of education and their status in the family prepared them least for migration. Not only were fewer girls trained, but even after being trained fewer were allowed to operate machines in the collectives."

Sujan Bridger pointed out that "in Central Asia women graduates of rural vocational-technical colleges were unable to make a full time career as machine operators and rarely sought jobs in towns, prefering to stay in the villages to work as manual agricultural workers."[76]

The uniqueness in Central Asian family pattern becomes even more prominent with the study of their institution of marriage. The most striking feature of Soviet Central Asians was marriage within ones own ethnic-natinality. Even if there were mixed marriages, the pattern of inter-ethnic marriage showed that the mixed marriages took place within the broad Central Asian ethnoses, rather than with the ethnic Russians and other Slavic or European communities staying in their territories. There is no full Soviet index published on the details of inter-ethnic marriages. Therefore, information about this complex issue remains incomplete. However, Prof. Shirin Akiner has provided some data on the general rate of mixed nationality marriages in each Central Asian republics in 1959 and 1970. From this list of data, the attitudinal trend towards mixed marriage in the whole region could be surmised:[77]

	Total Coverage Mixed Marriages 1959/1970	*1950/1970 Urban*	*1959/1970 Rural*
Uzbek SSR	8.2% / 10.9%	14.7% / 18.4%	4.7% / 5.7%
Turkmen SSR	8.5% / 12.1%	14.9% / 20.0%	2.5% / 3.4%
Kirgiz SSR	12.3% / 14.9%	18.1% / 20.9%	9.2% / 10.6%
Kazakh SSR	14.4% / 20.7%	17.5% / 23.8%	11.9% / 17.1%
Tajik SSR	9.4% / 13.2%	16.7% / 22.3	5.5% / 6.5%

The above table shows a distinctly variable ethnic-marriage trend in each national republic with the general rate of mixed marriages being minimum in Uzbek and Tajik SSR and maximum in Kazakhstan. But this data could not distinguish the marriages within Central Asian nationalities and Slavic or other European nationalities. But one consistent feature of mixed marriages in each republic was the higher ratio of mixed marriages in urban areas. As there were conglomerations of other nationalities more in urban areas the scope of mixed marriages was automatically more in such places. We have noted earlier, the rural sector provided the peaceful abode of traditional values that promoted marriage and family building within homogenous categories. Even within cities, mixed marriage instances were rare in old blocs, as it was studied by Monogarova in details on Ura Tyube and Isfara.

"In national content, overwhelming majority of the Tajik families living in old blocs are single national ones. Thus, in Ura Tyube, in the old blocs, studied out of 215 families, only one is mixed national (husband Tajik, wife Tatar). In the micro region of Fabrichnaya, there were five mixed national families in which the husband was Tajik and wife Russian, in one, husband Tajik wife German, in five, husband Tajik, the wife Tatar. Thus, there were only twelve mixed national families out of one hundred and thirty two families—(9%).[78]

However, marriages in Central Asia even in the 70s and 80s, were not usually a matter of free choice—especially for girls. Parental consent in marriage was almost mandatory. This had encouraged two major tendencies—one was early marriage and the other, marriage within the same nationality. In cases of mixed marraiges, Central Asia followed some norms of its own that implied the prevalence of regional ethnic characteristics. Here religion—namely Islam—played an important role. Even in case of inter-ethnic marriages, it took place usually within the co-religionists of other titular nationalities. Rasma Karklins observed, "Again, this community oriented proclivity is strongest among Soviet Muslim groups. In these few instances where Tadjiks, Uzbeks, Kazakhs, Azari, Ingushi and so on, intermarry, they typically marry another Muslim." Karklins further doubted whether such marriages can at all be classified as inter-ethnic. Rather, such marraiges looked like an intra-community affairs within a macro ethno-cultural zone.

She stated, "In some of these cases it is even questionable whether it is accurate to talk of 'mixed marriages' since many of the current national subdivisions and designations represent creations of the Soviet periods and remnants of the pre-Soviet all-encompassing Islamic identity survive. This is especially true for the smaller groups of the northern caucasus and the indigenous people of Central Asia."[79] For example, such intermarriages used to take place in Central Asia between the Kazakhs and Tatars, or Uzbeks and Tajiks. Similarly, the other pattern of ethnic intermarriage that used to take place in Central Asian soil was between the Russians, Ukrainians and Belorussians and other Slavic groups residing in this territories as migrant populations. Thus, even ethnically mixed marriages showed a tendency to maintain some kind of cultural or linguistic affinity in general. Karklins opined, "....the Slavs have been at the forefront of the migratory population movement in the USSR and intermarriage is much higher among migrants than among residentially rooted groups."[80] However, both the Soviet ethnographic research and Western detractors of the Soviet system had taken up the issue of inter-ethnic marriage as a cornerstone of Soviet ethnic tendencies and directions. In fact, a very popular method of Soviet ethnic studies was to survey the attitude towards mixed marriages which was supposed to reflect the general attitude regarding the mental tolerance for inter-ethnic and internationality intermixing. Of these, the study of Arutunian on the Tatar ASSR was the most exhaustive from which some general conclusions were drawn by Karklins. As women rejected intermarriages more frequently than men, age or occupation usually played a more complex role. Generally, older people opposed mixed marriages, but some categories of young people also showed vehement opposition to such prospects. From the occupational stand point, usually the townspeople favoured the prospect more than the rural folk but there were exceptions in attitude as well.[81] Thus many other relative factors like religion, gender, age, occupation, linguistic viabilities, all played their respective roles in the issue of 'ethnic intermarriages. Though the case study was made about a specific community of the Tatars, who lived in an authonomous province within Kazakh SSR, the findings seemed generally applicable for the rest of Central Asia as well. Arutunian in another article admitted that no universal characterisation of ethnic relations or ethnic behaviour could be made within the Soviet Union, that could prove an improving ethnic interaction leading to an unprecedented socialist harmony. In Arutunian's observation, "A given technique may lead to different and sometimes even directly opposite results in different social groups. The question of the role of the milieu is extremely urgent in this connection." He admitted openly that the more ethnic contacts were supposed to improve ethnic relationships but the effect of contacts was not the same for all people. People from different contexts and backgrounds responded quite differently to similar ethnic contacts. As he observed, "for people engaged in physical labour (for whom it is only cultural differences that interfere with ethnic mutual understanding), such contacts must necessarily serve as a powerful stimulus to cultural integration, and thereby improvement in ethnic relations. However, contacts among professional and para-professional peoples, among whom competitive strivings exist in mixed environments, by no means necessarily result in similar consequences."[82] Interestingly, this open admission by Arutunian also indicated the position taken by the Soviet intellectuals, not as propaganda activists, but rather as confused academicians who have failed to specify any common ethnic behaviour for any part of the entire multi-ethnic territories of the USSR. So, it would be wrong to surmise that all Soviet intellectuals have tried to stress the unreal claim of *sblizhenie* and have undermined the role of ethnic exclusivity or unique characteristics found still strong in many titular national communities.

Moreover, in the official Soviet claim, ethnic intermarriage was often shown as an ideal example of ethnic fusion, which, once again, was a myth created to support the notion of evergrowing friendship of the Soviet people at the stage of developed socialism. But, instead of fusion or blurring of ethnic feelings in such cases, either of the marriage partner's nationality appeared prominent and dominant. This was indirectly encouraged by the Soviet passport requirements where the choice of nationality was left to the sibling from either of the parent's nationalities. In another table provided by Drobizheva, it was found that 24 per cent-30 per cent of different occupational groups of Uzbeks expressed their objection or disapproval of the notion of ethnic intermarriage.[83] Therefore, mixed marriages, instead of bringing harmony and equality, indirectly induced a tacit hierarchy of national status within such mixed marriage families. Among the Central Asians, it was found that as Central Asian women were mostly prevented to marry outside the ethnic community, loss of national identities seldom happened with them.[84] Monogarova cited one example where a Tajik woman married a Russian. This woman herself was born of a mixed parentage, the father being a Tajik and the mother a Russian. But, Monogarova also noted that, "She, however, chose her father's nationality."[85] Thus, in spite of mixed marriages for two generations, the ethnic attachment to the Central Asian roots remained quite strong.

In Central Asian ethnic communities another interesting feature connected to marriage was a lesser divorce rate. This once again reinforces the presence of much stronger traditional values within the families here. Thus, family as an institution, played quite an important role in this society and turned the society resistant to alien or outside influences to a remarkable degree.

Though Central Asia practiced a kind of cultural insularity and ethnic exclusiveness, the ethnic behaviour of the elites, who were part of the Soviet administration in the republics or were close to them, seemed to show a marked difference in attitude. Here intra-ethnic and inter-tribal relations became conflict-laden as a natural corrolary of power politics. Thus, it was found that within Central Asia, the Uzbeks, being numerically the largest ethnic nationality and politically closer to the centre, tried to dominate and control the general political direction of Central Asia. Again, if seen within a particular nationality, the Tajiks show the widest and the most interesting variations in political participation bearing overwhelmingly ethno-regional connotations. Seweryn Bialer analysed, "Ethnic identification and aspirations could, and to some extent already do, bridge the social divisions of occupational interests and class distinctions. Moreover, already today they are the only example where the interests of one segment of the Soviet political elite coincide with a social stratum latter. This representative function served by segments of the minority political elites for their native social groups is still very limited and tenuous, but in the eyes of the central, primarily Great Russian political elite, it is probably the most dangerous trend, because in many respects it repeats the nationalist threats to them in Eastern Europe."[86] But at least in the case of Central Asia, till the onset of perestroika no such overt pressure on the central authorities can be traced. Rather, the elites enjoyed their elevated social status that resulted from the power and authority they exerted in their respective regional territories. In fact, these elites working with the Russian and other Slavic population or engaged in power politics or in white collar jobs in the region, consequently alienated themselves from their own native folk.

Ethnicity, therefore, appeared to be quite a complex component of national identity, as it did not work in water-tight compartments and all ethno-national or ethno-regional categories were influenced by various cross-currents of other relevant factors such as religion, politics, economy, regional disparity urban-rural discord and so on. This intra-ethnic polarity got sharpened during and after perestroika or at any rate, began to receive more attention form this time onwards. For with the removal of the all- encompassing binding of the Soviet yoke a need for reorientation in the national identity formation was badly felt. Here ethnic identities supplied a rudimentary element in national identity formation and was also used as a tool to mobilise different groups of people in favour of some kind or other political factions.

Before looking into the real impact of perestroika on Central Asian ethnic politics it is necessary to survey the change of intellectual positions regarding Soviet ethnic politics. Interestingly, the academics, who were mostly writing throughout the 70s and 80s with a pro-Soviet stand suddenly shifted their position in favour of 'more democratisation' in the sphere of ethnic polices. This sudden shift implied their urge to keep themselves in tune with the changing scenario. A new article by Drobizheva entitled *More Democracy* raised the issue of ethnicity in the changing context as it was written in 1988. There was ritualistic mention of the enormous achievements of the USSR, for she reminded all, "No one can deny what the peoples of our country have achieved."[87] Yet she openly admitted, "In bringing democratisation into being it is important to take account of the preparedness for it among various groups of the population. This means national groups as well. That it is true is demonstrated at least by the fact, that in ethnosociological surveys in the middle of the 1970s and beginning of the 1980s (that is, before restructuring), in listing the most important problem for the country, about one-fifth of the population named the further democratisation of society."[88] More importantly, she highlighted the regional variation in the demands for democracy "At the same time, there were more Estonians who considered this a necessity than there were Uzbeks or Moldavians. This means that it is important to find and make use of those forms of democracy which correspond to the traditions of the people. It is known, for example, that among the Russian people there were traditions of the *obshchina*, while for the Uzbeks the *mahale* plays a big role even now. But in order to have the possibility of using nationally specific forms of democratisation, the republics must have the right and be oriented to the democratic realisation of democratisation itself."[89] Thus, the specific necessities of each different regions were openly admitted and the discontent arising in the initial phase of restructuring was regarded as a result of "the insufficient democratisation of the past."[90] This kind of honest confession was unimaginable in the Soviet literature before the advent of perestroika-glasnost.

Yet, at the same time, Drobizheva was quite optimistic and assimilative in her thoughts. Commenting on the inter-ethnic tensions in the sphere of employment she insisted: "Competition to occupying scarce places appeared in the labour sphere. Psychological restructuring was necessary. People of the basic native nationality in each republic must, of course, consider that their national identity in and of itself does not give any special right to advancement, with Russians, Ukrainians, and people of other nationalities who have assisted the development of the peoples must always remember that they are working with people of equal status."[91] It came out from her writing that the projection of inter-nationality disputes were getting pointed on the issue of unemployment for both the people of titular nationalities and the migrant populations everywhere came to disapprove each others position with equal indignation. The 'national chauvinism' which was marked as an evil from Lenin's time had survived the entire seven decades of Soviet rule but came to be admitted honestly by the Soviet academicians only after the onset of the glasnost. Drobilizheva claimed that the situation of Soviet Union was still better than many other parts of the world facing similar problems of restructuring, for, in the Soviet state laws 'prohibit' nationalism and chauvinism. Yet, that this was nothing more than empty statement is easily discerned from the rest of her article. For, she kept on providing suggestions about plausible ways of interaction between nationalities, harping on the need for cultural interactions to prevent bitterness among nationalities. "People of other nationalities could come to the celebration, to watch the dances, to hear the songs, to try the dishes of another people. Unfortunately, in the recent past the celebration on such holidays has not been encouraged among us, while their spontaneous appearance has even caused alarm."[92] Here, the revival of the '*nauroz*' festival in the Central Asian republics and the governmental acceptance of it as the local 'new year festival' may be cited as an example.

Ethnic Faultlines in Central Asia After Central Asia

Valery Tishkov, in his detailed analysis on the ethnic and national issues stressed the fact that ethnicity and nationalities had different dimensions. Ethnicity on its own provided only group solidarity while ethnic nationalism always had a political goal which tended to challenge the status quo. Ethnic engineering or giving directions to ethnic consciousness was therefore a task of the politicians, particularly in a trouble-torn multi-ethnic state. Tishkov, though being quite candid about the short-comings of the Soviet system could not denounce the system in its entirity or hold it responsible for the unfolding of discontents amongst the nationalities. In his view, "Socio-economic indices and statistics on living standards show that only Central Asian republics experienced serious developmental gaps compared with other republics. These republics were followed by Russia and Moldavia, with the Baltic, Armenian and Georgian republics representing the highest standards."[93] Thus, unequal development and the consequent suffering of the people of Central Asia was the result of nothing more than the shortcomings of the Soviet policy effect. Therefore, in spite of so many divergencies, differences and dichotomies which existed in docile form and surfaced during perestroika, Tishkov could stick to his belief, that "The emergence of the 'one community of Soviet people' doctrine in the country was no accident: the overwhelming majority of Soviet citizens shared the same (or very similar) social, political, and even cultural values. On the other hand, differences in cultural traditions, industrial development, demographic behaviour and political culture managed to survive all through the Soviet period."[94] Actually, the Soviet system till perestroika-glasnost kept on experimenting with the nationality question where ethnicity played an important role. Whether the authorities deliberately encouraged the studies on ethnicity as a sub-national factor to down-play the role of nationality was not very clear. But, it is true that the Soviet system, with its superimposed Soviet identity, could not or did not overshadow the ethno-national identities completely. It only arranged them in a hierarchical basis—putting the Soviet identity above the rest. That is why Seweryn Bialer stated, "The freedom afforded to non-Russian nationals in the Soviet Union—territory, language, cultural heritage, symbols of statehood, indigenous elites—are clearly circumvented. Moreover, and more importantly, behind those freedoms and privileges lurks the reality of extreme centralisation, where key political and economic decisions are being made not in the respective national centres but in far away Moscow. Ergo, these freedoms are "formal": they do not have a meaning; they are insignificant in themselves."[95] Therefore, the task of reorienting the identities was little more than a reshuffling of their arrangements and positions, hitherto stated in a hierarchical order. Here, ethnicity, being a strong form of distinctiveness, came to occupy a more prominent position. This might lead to opportunistic use and even misuse of the ethnic identity for political purposes—but how far this politicisation process consciously used ethnicity as an effective tool and how far it was brought within the political sphere as an obvious and inalienable part of identity politics—will probably remain a topic for academic debates for long time to come.

Perestroika produced intra-regional, often intra-republican tension while redefining and re-organising the state powers. Ethnic clashes mounted in the areas of ethnic plurality like Central Asia. Within Central Asia, an acute ethnic crisis ultimately took the form of a protracted civil war in Tajikistan. However, the impact of perestroika upon general ethnic categories and in the forging of new ethnic-equations in Central Asia has to be assessed before passing on to the case of Tajikistan.

Perestroika created a new era of enforced independence in Soviet Central Asian republics from the political and economic standpoints. A number of party officials were replaced on charges of corruption or were simply made to retire. Instances of corruption came to be admitted formally by the authorities and these major changes from above resulted in popular indignation that gave rise to major riots and political unrests. These popular out-bursts, if seen from an ethno-regional standpoint, can be divided into two types. The first was the indigenous ethnic population versus the Russian and other outsiders which was depicted in the Alma Ata riots in 1986. The other type unfolded within the Central Asian nationalities themselves, as was reflected in the Ferghana riot in Uzbekistan in 1989. There were again divisions within this intra-Central Asian feuds namely, inter-tribal or inter-nationality clashes on the one hand, and intra-nationality ethno-regional clashes within a republic, on the other. The Tajik case provided the ideal example of the last category of ethnic clashes. However, Mehrdad Haghayeghi wanted to make a simple categorisation of such clashes on the basis of religious identities. From his perspective, the first type was depicted as a clash of "Muslim versus non-Muslims" and the innumerable varieties of internal strifes as "Muslims versus Muslim."[96]

However, distinction along religious lines might complicate the problem even more, because the issues concerning all riots were based either on economic and political resentment or by ethno-national power distribution dynamics where the role of religion was nothing but an additional mobiliser. The first variety of uprising, which was heralded against the ethnic-Russians, was the initial outcome of perestroika when Russians were replacing indigeneous rulers or representatives. The purge of Kunaev (dealt in details in the chapter six) provides a suitable illustration of this category. But as the perestroika years continued, other types of rivalries leading to bloody civil war began to increase. Thus, in 1989, a number of such clashes took place in different parts of Central Asia. The Ferghana riot, for example, between Uzbeks and Meshkhetian Turks broke out on the 3rd of June, 1989. The reason behind this clash was basically economic disparity. The Meshkhetians were relatively better-off than the Uzbeks of the Ferghana valley. The unemployed Uzbeks were somewhat convinced that the problem of unemployment would be resolved if the economically secure Meshkhetians could be removed. Thus, a purely economic problem received a strong ethnic character in the ensuing riot. The Uzbek political parties like Birlik also provided support to the Uzbeks to organise a riot claiming the removal of the Meshkhetians who became the residents of the region since 1944 under Stalin's policy of shifting and reshuffling the ethnic segments from one place to another. Meshkhetians hailed from Gerogia but were Turkish by ethnic origin. There arose another similar conflict over the Osh *oblast* of Kirgizia where the Uzbeks residing in Osh demanded reconsideration of their status. The population of Osh included a substantial number of Uzbeks who seldom thought themselves a part of Kirgizia. These Uzbeks, at the time of turmoil, established an Uzbek organisation named Adalat (1989) whose main aim was to oppose the implementation of Kirgiz language law but later began to claim autonomy. The Kirgiz government was not prepared to succumb to such a pressure. Moreover, a Kirgiz national organisation named Osh *Aymaghi* began to demand redistribution of land among the Kirgiz in Osh—which was bound to affect the position of the Osh Uzbeks. This led to the outbreak of violence between the two ethnic groups, and it continued with increasing complexity that consequently affected the Uzbek Kirgiz relations to a large extent. In fact, with the unleashing of perestroika and its associated political dynamics, Uzbekistan appeared to be a real potential force aiming to conceive a new hegemonic role in Central Asia to fill in the existing power vacuum. These conflicts in Ferghana or Osh reflected as much the Uzbek claim of authority as it revealed the strong opposition of other Turkic people to admit the role of the Uzbeks as the self-appointed leaders of the rest of the Turks in Central Asia. M. Haghayeghi openly admitted that these intra-tribal discords shattered "the myths about the gathering strengths of pan-Turkism or pan-Islamism in the region. Once again, ethnic identity had superseded Islam as the final emotional arbiter of human conflict,"[97] Again, when seen objectively, all such ethnic disputes had very concrete material reasons behind them. The ethnic conflicts, in retrospect, seem mostly indecisive, never-ending tug of war on limited political opportunities and inadequate and rapidly dwindling economic resources.

However, the dominating tendency of the Uzbek nation over the rest of Central Asia was not a sudden development emerging out of post-perestroika chaos. Rather, this trend was backed up by a long history of prominence enjoyed by the Uzbeks throughout the Soviet period which made them quite self-righteous to claim the authority to hegemonise the entire multi-ethnic zone of Central Asia. Thus, the Uzbek entity developed at three levels, national, supranational and subnational. The supranational claim was definitely strengthened by the Soviet encouragement, but the Uzbeks had some material advantages to claim such a position as well. For example, Uzbeks were numerically the largest nationality residing in Central Asia, their number almost equalling the sum total of the rest. Secondly, it was the only Central Asian state which shared borders with each of the other four republics. This central position and numerical strength added to their political prominence for decades and gave them a sense of self-acclaimed arrogance over the rest. This sense of dominance was not, however, confined only to overpower the Turkic nationals of their immediate neighbourhood.

Here we come to the issue of Uzbek-Tajik conflicts—which took a much more serious political turn. The Uzbek government also took interest in the internal conflict of Tajikistan and initially encouraged the branch of Tajik IRP (Islamic Renainance Party) to open a branch in Samarkhand. The Uzbek revival party Birlik also supported this ultra-Islamic group., But as the internal condition of Tajikistan worsened, leading to a civil war between the two extremist camps (ultra Islamic and Communist old guard), Uzbek president Karimov decided to play safe and did not support the ulta Islamic movement so overtly. On the contrary, the branch of IRP and its leaders in Samarkhand were brutally repressed and thrown out of the republic. This kind of anomalous behaviour on the part of central Uzbek leaders naturally rendered inter-ethnic relations even more complex. Uzbek involvement in Tajik affairs had a long and complicated history partly for their being neighbours of two distinctly different ethno-cultural national origins and partly for the conscious nationalities policy embarked on them by the Soviet authorities in different stages.

In fact, the independent Tajik SSR was a creation of Soviet policy in 1929. For in 1924, Tajikistan started her Soviet life as an ASSR within the Uzbek republic. Their separation was effected on the basis of ethno-linguistic distinction. This was undoubtedly a decision 'from above' for neither the Tajiks, nor the Uzbeks had demanded such a division on their own. However, the grant of separate identity for Tajikistan was supposedly in keeping with the idea of self-determination of nations according to Soviet principles. But, scholars opposed to Soviet system criticised this as a conscious step to encourage disintegration in Central Asia.[98] Uzbekistan and Tajikistan were old neighbouring provinces with long experience of ethno-cultural interactions. The two important cultural centres Samarkhand and Bukhara were situated in this region of which both the nationalities felt equally proud. But when the separation took place, both these cities were kept in Uzbekistan while Dushanbe, a rather unknown city, without much pedigree and heritage, was made the capital of Tajikistan.[99] The meaning of Dushanbe is Monday. Burnet R. Rubin remarked, "Tajikistan's capital, Dushanbe, was a sleepy town named for the day (Monday) on which the market was open—which might imply as Olivier Roy has remarked that it was closed on Tuesday."[100] Thus, Soviet Tajikistan with her obscure capital started her journey into the modern era while Uzbekistan, from the very outset, received a better attention from Moscow's leadership. Starting from the redistribution of areas, the authority seemed definitely preferential towards Uzbekistan. However, their political demarcation as independent nations did not bring an end to the centuries-old interaction between the two people. Starting from intermarriages, various kinds of traditional interactions between them survived the entire Soviet regime. But along with the socio-cultural interactions, there remained a sense of tacit competitiveness between the two nationalities in the political sphere as well. Moreover, the political boundaries did not coincide with their ethnic distribution since Uzbekistan contained a number of Tajiks while Tajikistan also had quite a substantial number of Uzbeks residing there as citizens. The division of the two neighboruing communities into two separate republics could not turn them into two water-tight compartments. They still remained neighbours and followed the same process of give and take, only the political delimitation turned the situation more complex and uncertain for both.

A very interesting trend can be traced from the data furnished by Shirin Akiner about the Uzbek-Tajik percentage of population residing in each other's territory. It was found that the Uzbeks in Tajikistan always remained more than 20 per cent of the entire population—21.2 per cent in 1926, 23.0 per cent in 1959, 23.0 per cent in 1970. 22.9 per cent in 1979. The numbers of the Tajiks staying in Uzbekistan had markedly fallen from the initial period probably as a result of Stalin's policy of forced migration (in this case, grafting the Tajik population within the bounds of new geographical map of TSSR by uprooting them from their age-old domain in Uzbekistan). It is gathered from Akiner's data that in 1926 there were 18.4 per cent of Tajiks staying in Uzbekistan, but the number dropped to 3.8 per cent in 1959, remained the same in 1970, and marginally increased to 3.9 per cent in 1979.[101] However, V. Tishkov provided a very valuable insight in this Uzbek-Tajik ethnic redistribution during the initial days of the Soviet rule. Tishkov observed, "A new structure of ethnic identities began to be imposed in Central Asia after the 'national territorial delimitation' of the early 1930s, when a new political-administrative map of the region was drawn up for local socialist nations. Large-scale membership recruitment into ethnonations began throughout the country, gradually replacing regional, religious, clan and other group identities."[102] He stressed that before the Soviet intervention, no clear concept of broad ethnic or national belongingness existed among common people—not even among the Russians—small regional, clan or often village identities served as their primary identity. "It was the culture workers, the census takers, local administrators, and intellectuals who established the notion of 'real' ethnic affiliation or 'corrected' a 'wrong' one."[103] Thus, the naming of different categories of people, confused about their ethno-national origin, was taken to be the tasks of concerned officials and they used their discretionary powers to give ethno-national stamp to all the citizens enlisted in their reports. The experience of Yelena Peshchereva (mentioned earlier in this chapter) re-emphasises this conviction.

Kakhar Makhamov, the First Secretary of Tajik Communist Party Central Committee openly admitted during perestroika, "we clearly see the many problems and difficulties in ethnic relations. This heavy legacy of the past is the product of our reluctance to face the truth and we must overcome it together, by common efforts under the conditions of good will and dialogue. In Tajikistan we still encounter the results of the incompetent demarcation of the boundaries between the republics of Central Asia. The errors made long ago are still felt now. Some of these problems we can resolve ourselves but some we cannot. The tiniest of the problems is the following. Many Tajiks and some Uzbeks who reside in Tajikistan and Uzbekistan want to change the nationality shown in their passports since their entries were incorrectly made in the past. In November 1988, the governments of Uzbekistan and Tajikistan asked the USSR Council of Ministers for permission to do this, but it still has not been granted.... Together with the Uzbek leaders we do everything we can for strengthening and resolving the current problems. We have started a joint programme for developing the economic and cultural relations between our republics..."[104] This kind of confusion on ethnicity increased with time and the victims of such confused ethnic categories felt insecure in the late 80s. According to some Western scholars the division between Uzbek-Tajik nationalities was a motivated manoeuvre of the Soviet politicians. But if kept together, the two conflicting nationalities would have undoubtedly aggravated the ethnic collisions during and after the Soviet period. For, within Tajikistan there were so many strands of ethnic tensions that got reflected in political feuds and bloody clashes in the struggle for asserting power and self-interest. Remaining along with the Uzbeks would have aggravated the crises to a greater degree. The problem of Uzbek-Tajik tension got aggravated more because of the lop-sided opportunities provided to the two republics through which Uzbeks came to the time light overshadowing the Tajiks. P.L. Dash has tried to trace the historical legacy of such Uzbek supremacy thereby depriving the Tajiks of their due respect, "The Turkic Uzbeks who came to Central Asia from time to time as invaders of the Iranian people to displace them from the fertile river valleys of that region had succeeded in creating an uneasy coexistence. This continuing problem took a sharp turn towards exacerbation by the unreal territorial delimitation of Central Asia by the Soviet authorities who finalised the human and historical map of that region by subordinating the Tajiks to the Uzbeks in 1924. Although, Tajikistan acquired the status of a union republic in 1928, it remained much smaller in size, and much weaker economically. The perennial subordination of all other Central Asian republics, including Tajikistan, remained overshadowed by the Uzbek domination and continued to bring deleterious results of a misguided nationality policy. In the process of all nations striving toward their nation state formation, the one whose ego was badly ruptured kept the nationalist fervour enlivened beneath the placidity of an all-well appearance."[105]

Once unleashed by the programmes of perestroika, all these national and sub-national ethnic identities were let loose making the situation even more tense and indecisive. In Tajikistan national solidarity as a whole seemed too brittle a concept to hold the divergent self-seeking people together. Tishkov observed, "In a situation of political liberalisation, weakening state institutions, and the rising role of local initiatives, ethnic unrest in the USSR started not as a major political cleavage but as inter-ethnic riots and communal clashes directed mainly towards vulnerable 'double minorities' in national republics."[106]

However, with the overwhelming involement of Uzbekistan in a number of inter-ethnic riots, one misconception should not arise that there was a mutual harmony amongst the other four Central Asian republics. The Tajik-Kirgiz conflict over land dispute in Isfara region in 1989 created quite a difficult situation for both the governments. A 144 hector plot of land in the Kalinin district of Tajikistan was given to Batken district of Kirgizia thirty years back. As the Tajik population pressure intensified, need for more private plots was felt and the given plot of Kalinin district was claimed back by the Tajiks. When the Kirgiz constructed a cannal in this disputed land as part of land reclamation and the Tajiks knocked down its walls, the skirmish started. Similar disputes also spread to Vorukh and Chorkh in Isfara district and in Samarkandyk village in the Osh province of Kirgizia. Such border disputes between republics showed the presence of popular discontent between neighbouring people of two different nationalities despite years of super-imposition of a common Soviet identity. Ajay Parnaik stated, "Ferghana and Isfara incidents were indicators of the re-emergence of nationalism in Central Asia that could not be solved within the framework of simply redefining the powers of the Union and the republics. The new trends required deeper comprehension of the social and economic issues in Central Asia that threatened the relationship between the indigenous nationalities."[107]

The Ethnic Couldrion in Tajikistan

Coming back to the Tajik case, one finds the widest variety of ethnic disputes leading to extreme polarisation of the people of Central Asia in this republic. Interestingly, in case of Tajikistan, the ethnic characters had very interesting regional attachments which provided them with specific and deep-rooted political and ideological commitments—the one extreme being led by communist old guards while the other extreme was nurtured by the growing Islamic fundamentalists. In between these two extremes, there sprouted and developed a number of political parties with their own fixed agendas and goals, that were different from each other. Interestingly, in Tajikistan, each of these parties had an ethno-regional character that received political shape at the time of chaos and crises. This showed that in spite of the official Soviet attempts and claims of successively blurring ethno-national and ethno-regional markers through the Soviet identity, the ethnic identities, however distorted and motivated they might have been, remained quite strong and effective in this territory.

The Northern Tajikistan with its relatively more modernisation, urbanisation and closer attachment to Russian 'big brothers' turned communist in character. The majority of the Tajik Communist leadership for generations was usually provided by the Khojent-Quliab-Hissar-Leninabad (north) zone for decades. The Leninabad region in the north of the country occupied a privileged position. Throughout the regime the people of this region enjoyed the status of being the political, commercial and managerial elite. Khojent was most closely linked to Moscow within the power dynamics of Tajikistan. Quliab closely followed Khojent in this regard. Burnet Rubin has called this interdependence of the leaderships as "the Khujand-Kulab patron-cilient network"[108] However, this region constantly gave rise to communist leadership of mixed Uzbek-Tajik parentage throughout the Soviet regime. Two very prominent political figures of the past and the present Bobojon Gafurov and Rakhmon Nabiev respectively, hailed from Khojent. These two famous leaders only symbolised the ethnic legacy of the north-zone's political ascendency throughout the communist regime.

Southern Tajikistan provided just the opposite socio-political scenario since because of its mountain terrain, the region neither received much modernisation nor the influence of the Soviet Communists. The people of these regions could cling to their tribal ethnic identity more strongly and showed quite a variety of ethnic categories such as the Pamiris, Ismailis and so on. Garm district in the south had a different history of development—the people of this zone experienced more recent economic growth, especially in trade and marketing, and wanted to be come contenders of the north-zone in the political sphere as well. Rakesh Gupta has studied extensively the ethnic characters of the Pamiris, "The Pamir Tajiks include minority people speaking Wakhi, Shughni, Roshani, Khufi, Yazgulimi, Ishkashmi and Bartang, grouped in Gorno Badakhshan Autonomous oblast." The author studied the complex ethnic characters of other Tajik territories as well: "Another distinct group is formed by the Yaghnobis, direct descendants of the ancient Sogdians or Transoxians, who live in the Zeravshan river basin. Tajiks are mixed with Uzbeks and the Soviet participation has not led to segregation. Apart from the Russians there are the Tatars, Germans, Kirghis, Ukrainians and Jews."[109] The political party rising form this Gorno-Badakhshan area was named *Lal-i-Badakhshani* (or the Ruby of Badakhshan). This party had a definite Islamic agenda but, more importantly, it strongly demanded the redressal of this politically neglected and economically deprived zone.

The Qurgan-Tyube region is situated both geographically and, on liasis of status hierarchy, in between the elite north and the tribal south. Kurgan-Tyube zone belonged to the Khatlon region and provided the republic's most diverse and complex ethnic map. It had settlers from Quliab and Garm among the non-local Tajiks as a result of Soviet migration policy. But even otherwise, there lived a number of Uzbek and Tajik families in the Vaksh Valley who were resettlers in the zone from much earlier times (originating from Samarkhand and Ferghana). Moreover, "For centuries, the region was home to the Turkic Lokay, Kungrant, Katagan, Durmen, Yuz and other tribes. Here live also Uighurs, Turkmen, Arabs, Baluchis, Russians, Germans, Belarussians, Ukrainians, Ossetes and other ethnic groups."[110] The cosmopolitan population pattern here was a reflection of the Stalinist programme of forced migration. The people from Quliab and Garm were mainly emigrated for the need of manual labour in cotton cultivation and processing. The mixed population of this zone, with their complex attitude of disapproval of the Soviet regime went for the ultra-Islamic alternative. The most powerful and well-organised Islamic fundamentalist party IRP—Islamic Renaissance Party—had its main centre located in this territory. Other than internal ethnic distributions and its various impacts, the ethnic contiguity and solidarity of the Tajiks with their kin group staying in Afghanistan had a great role in fomenting ethno-political disturbances in Tajikistan. The constant inflow of the Mujahidins and their fanatic version of Islamic teaching made the situation in Tajikistan especially complicated compared to the other Central Asian republics. Beseiged ethnicity, in conjugation with a revivalist Islam, also had a role to play in the cross-border terrorism in that part of the world.

Aziz Niyazi observed from hindsight, "The wheel of violence and terror in Tajikistan was kept turning by all the conflicting sides with a fatal obsession, engendering feuds and quests for vengeance which will linger in that land for a long time to come. The political confrontation between new socio-political formations on the one hand and on the other, the heirs of a post-communist party and state system. But as the conflict developed, the ideology and party affiliations of its participants became irrelevant, giving way to interest of region and of clan."[111]

Seen from the ethnic standpoint, the Tajik south was a more complex region with varied ethnic tribes maintaining their traditional ways of life, religious beliefs and vision for the future which seemed incompatible with the Soviet Communist guide lines. The economic plight of the zone was also remarkable. A long term negligence on part of the authorities turned the population completely disillusioned with the existing communist representatives of Tajikistan. In fact, at the hour of turmoil, they tried to turn the wheel of power in their own favour. At least, they used the crisis to put up a legitimate claim to set up an alternative to the impersonal unIslamic communist regime. Their loyalty towards to traditional culture and religion was reflected in their political motto as well. For example, the Pamiris, who were a zonal ethnic segment living in the hills of Gorno-Badakhshan autonomous oblast, had their own ethno-religious prospective. They followed an Ismaili sect which was different form the common Sunni strand and the language of these people was also markedly different form the rest. Their dialect was regarded as 'mountain Tajik' to maintain a subtle distinction between them and the other, more advanced and more polished, groups within Tajikistan. There arose a political party named *Lal-i-Badakhshani*, which in general demanded greater autonomy for the entire Badakhshan, but also had a special claim to protect and defend the rights of the Pamiris. Judged by their nature, aim and demands this was not an extremist Islamic party like the IRP or the Islamic Renaissance party. These extremist outfits had their base in Kurgan-Tyube, but they also gathered their supporters from parts of the discontented south, especially the people of Garm, who quite expectantly, flocked to the IRP in search of an immediate redressal of their grievances. There were a good number of Badakhshanis within the IRP as well who wanted to put an extremist challenge to the Communist North. In fact, in the elections of 1991, the leader who contested the Communist candidate Rakhmon Nabiev was a Pamiri intellectual—a film maker called Davlat Khudanzarov. Thus, Islamic movements began to develop in different regions of Tajikistan with definite ethnic attachments. The IRP being the most forceful and ambitious of them, ultimately gathered the highest momentum and emerged as the most potent confessional outfit.

The ethnic character of the Communist North, the more advanced Khojent-Quilab regions, was also not homogeneous. Those areas witnessed more ethnic mixing because of urbanity. The presence of

Russian and other non-Central Asian ethnic categories made these regions apprehensive of any kind of Islamic revival. The regional leaders here themselves often came from mixed parentage, like Nabiev, who had both Uzbek and Tajik lineages. It seems that the commitment to the path of Communism was rather a matter of convenience than that of ideology for the cosmopolitan urban population of these territories of Khojent-Quliab and Hissar valley.

The factionalism within Tajikstan began to mount from 1990s as Tajik republic was made independent on 25 August, 1990. But far from joy, this 'sovereignty' brought enormous economic calamity to the region for the substantial subsidies from the centre were suddenly stopped. Meanwhile, the internal power-struggle within Tajikistan had also taken a serious turn. The intense struggle between Garm and Quliab came to be known as 'Hot February'. The 'Hot February' riots had a major implication for intensifying the regional alienation within the *nomanklatura* itself. A large number of officials from the district level were removed, for example, Gosplan Chairman Buri Karimov, culture Minister Nur Tabarov of Garm, Supreme Soviet Chairman Goibnazar Pallaev of Badakhshan. But the Quliabi official, Chief of the Political Department of Ministry of Interior, Abdulla Khabibov though found guilty of being involved in the riot was not dismissed. He was charged with a severe penalty. Aziz Niyazi commented, "In one way or the other, a marked tendency towards a split in the apparatus on a regional basis became apparent during those days. A shadow political alliance was built on the solidarity between sections of the Garm, Kuliabi and Badakhshani *nomanklatura*.[112]

Thus, the representatives of the party themselves were still quite sidetracked by the northern factions. This only implied that the situation of the ordinary people, the unaware and ignorant masses whose economic plight must have reached an unbearable stage at this time of political turmoil, were becoming increasingly restive. Therefore, popular unrest became a regular feature of these dissatisfied territories.

At times, some more farsighted and sensible northern leaders tried to bring the Southern representation into lime light. For example, after Hot February, Kakhar Makhamov became the head of the Tajik Supreme Soviet and when in August Tajikistan got sovereignty, he became the President of the newly independent state. In November he installed Kadriddin Aslonov, a Garmi leader, to take up the Chairmanship of the Supreme Soviet. Such token recognition, however, was far from meeting the expectations of these deprived regions. Aziz Niyazi stated, "The main invisible struggle was waged in the offices of highly placed people in the capital and the provinces. It was there that the *nomanklatura* alliances were concluded, the roles distributed and the fates of political adversaries decided. The enemy of one's enemy became a friend, and personal loyalty and local ties were at a premium. The rules of the political game were formed, and ideology did not play an essential role in them. The leaderships of various regions sought to have Kinsman-patrons in the highest echelons of power, an asset not only conducive to upward mobility and greater incomes, but also facilitating the region's economic development."[113]

1991 saw the polarity getting accelerated between the two major factions, communist and ultra Islamists, while the moderate Islamic groups like, DPT (Democratic Party of Tajikistan) or *Lal-i-Badakhshani* vascillated between the two extreme groups to come closer to the main power base. 1992 brought even more tension in the Tajik political scenario. Along with all other Central Asian republics, Tajikistan gave support to the anti-Gorbachev coup (putsch) of August 25 that exposed the latent discontent of the official strand of Tajik communist leadership for the challenges brought about by Gorbachev and his reforms. But as this coup failed, the internal polarity within Tajikistan got sharpened. As the communist party was banned by Yeltsin in Russia, a similar ban was announced on the Tajik communist party by Aslanov. Here the regional character of politicians became most accute. Aslanov being a Garmi himself, tried to utilise this opportunity to get rid of the communist old guards from power politics. Interestingly, satisfaction of personal power ambition did not dissuade Aslanov, one of the thinly represented Garmi leadership, from combating the more powerful northern faction. This indicated a stronger commitment to regional identity. Aziz Niyazi observed, "An anti-Communist campaign from Moscow found an echo in Tajikistan. The revitalised Tajik opposition, which the southerners had by that time begun to lead, resolved to get rid of Communist rule, and with it the northerner's monopoly of the top post in the state."[114] But this move did not last long as power-politics became even more intense—throwing entire Tajikistan into an irresolvable and ever complicating crisis. Barnett R. Rubin observed, "In September 1991, acting President Qadruddin Aslanov banned the Communist Party, as Boris Yeltsin had done in Russia, but communist parliamentary deputies overturned the ban, ousted the president and declared a state of emergency."[115]

To depict the strength of popular participation in this political turmoil Rubin stated, "Demonstrators outside the parliament building forced a reversal of the reversal. Under pressure, parliament agreed to organise a direct presidential election, which was held on 27 November."[116] Meanwhile, the Communist Party elites also strengthened their position by ousting Makhamov who tended to compromise with the demands of the south. Rakhamon Nabiev was selected at this stage to combat the steep battle against the IRP representative in the election. The opposition struck an alliance between IRP and DP—Rastokhiz whose candidate was Davlat Khudanazarov, a Pamiri from Badakhstan. Aziz Niyazi observed, "The *nomanklatura* power s truggle was being waged between blocs—Garm and Badakhshan on the one hand, and Khojent, Kuliab and Gissar on the other."[117] The result of this election showed Nabiev as victorious by securing 57 per cent of the votes while Khudanzarov received 30 per cent and the rest going to the other opposition candidates. However, the result of this election held in such chaotic sociopolitical conditions involved charges of definite irregularity. Khudanazarov complained of simple rigging. Anyway, the victory of Nabiev by whatever method, reinstated the communist old guards in their previous positions and also unleashed a vengeful policy of trial and removal of important opposition leaders. This offensive against the opposition neutralised any prospects of conciliation between the communists and the non-communists (different strands of Islamites aiming at different kinds of state systems). Thus the trials of the former head of the Rastokhez movement, Mirbobo Mirrakhimov and the DPT leader Shodomon Yusupov were fixed in spring 1992 and Kazi Akbar Tursunzoda, the official head of the Tajik Muslims, who was not a member of IRP, but had a strong independent voice, was dismissed for being untrustworthy. The opposition, of course, did not succumb to this pressure. They took up the challenge to fight back the old *nomanklatura* with greater support from their loyal support base in Garm and Badakhstan. Thus, Tajikistan took the preliminary strides as an independent state amidst a protracted civil war that only promised confusion, crisis and destruction.

However, did their regional variations along ethnic lines became apparent to the Tajik people only with the advent of perestroika and in its aftermath? The changing character of political candidature during the mid 80s proves that the problems of ethnic polarity and regional discrimination were surfacing. Even the communist leadership, apparently quite secure under the Soviet rule in 1985, began to include representatives from the usually ill-represented regions. Khakhar Makhamov's assumption of power as the First Secretary in 1985 saw the beginning of a revisionist approach on part of the Communist North to reverse the older policy of lop-sided representation. Under his rule, Giobnazar Pallaev, a Badakhshani became the chariman of the Supreme Soviet. More importantly, a Khojent man Abdurrakhmon Dodobaev was replaced by a Badakhshani Shodi Shabdolov. The Ministry of Interior was given to another Badakhshani Mamadayaz Nauzhuvanov and Buri Karimov, a Garmi became the head of the Gosplan.[118] In this way, Makhamov, a moderate Khojenti tried to correct the injustice done to the neglected regions by the communist power bloc. But, as it was found, Makhamov's measures were quite inadequate compared to the expectations and ambitions of the long deprived people of Garm and Badakhshan. Moreover, the unwarranted changes brought by perestroika and glasnost put the situation even more out of control. No scope for further piecemeal changes in a peaceful process was left. In fact, with the rapidly changing situation, no place for moderate communists were left even within the Communist Party itself. Makhamov himself was removed at a time of bitter struggle between the old guards and the aspiring opposition in 1991. Rakhmon Nabiev, a conservative Leninabadi, seemed the obvious choice to promote the communist cause at this hour of crisis. The leadership strategy at the top level aimed to keep portfolios like employment opportunities, housing and other material necessities under control in a situation of limited economic resources. Therefore, representatives from each region received followers from their same ethnic stock and ideological moorings. Thus ethno-regional relations seemed to have become quite mutually interactive. Barnet Rubin noticed, "The only links the protagonists in the capital had with the rest of the population were regional ties, which increasingly defined the contours of the war. Each side's regionalist ties solidified in response to the security threat posed by the other side."[119]

Another factor which had accelerated the crisis in Tajik policies was the external inputs coming from Afghan Mujahidins. Apparently, this Afghan influence seemed more religious than ethnic as it helped in the diffusion of Islamic fundamentalism through the southern borders of Tajikistan. This religious tie, undoubtably got strengthened by the bonds of ethnic commonality shared by the Afghan Mujahidins of whom a large number were ethnic Tajiks and shared the same langauge with the Soviet Tajiks. Abha Dixit in her article *Tajikistan: Engulfed by Flames of Afghan Civil War* stated, "The link between external support to religious parties in Afghanistan and central and southern Tajikistan was stabilised through the Mujahidin. Through the 1980s, the Afghan civil war was an adjunct to a larger goal of destabilising the Muslim republics of the Soviet Union".[120] In this view Tajikistan acted as a gateway not only for Islamic fundamentalism but also for the smuggling of arms, drugs and all other corrupting influences emanating at the time of Afghan civil war which created an atmosphere conducive for cross-border terrorism in the South Tajik territories—a zone which was even otherwise quite prone to disturbances because of its own economic and political reasons. According to K. Warikoo the Afghan factor turned Tajikstan into the 'Cockpit of Central Asia'.[121] This external Afghan influence seemed more worrying because it not only did provide strong Islamic indoctrination as an alternative ideology but it acted as a training camp for the young Tajiks and provided the radical groups with huge supply of arms, that brought the ground situation in a state of real war at the time of transition. Muriel Atkin, however, looked into the issue of Afghan influence from a slightly different perspective. She argued: "The degree of Afghanistan's disruptive influence on Tajikistan, in the form of Islamic 'fundamentalist' propaganda, arms smuggling and ethnic reparation, are controversial subjects on which there is more propaganda than reliable information. Some of the least credible information comes from certain supporters of the old Soviet order who are biased against Islam and Muslims. A prime example of this obsessive hostility is V.V. Petkel, who was head of the KGB in Tajikistan between 1985 and 1991; he warned that Tajikistan was threatened by hostile foreign forces, above all in Afghanistan. Given that allegations like these come from people who are not disinterested observers, the cunning and extensive subversion they depict ought not to be accepted unquestionably."[122] Though Atkin accepted the presence of cross border terrorism, smuggling and raiding for plunder, she did not take these as illustrations of political violence. To her, Tajikistan's proximity to Iran and Afghanistan was more of an ethno-linguistic and ethno-cultural nature, with limited geopolitical or strategic significance being attached to it by the Central Asians themselves.

This relation had remained somewhat suppressed under the long Soviet rule. At the end of Soviet rule, precisely from the perestroika period, these feelings began to get revived. Thus, Muriel Atkin did not see the links with Afghanistan solely as a negative influence on Tajikistan during the time of transition. In the context of newly independent Tajikistan the influences from the two neighboring countries, namely Iran and Afghanistan, seemed obvious. In Atkin's words: "With the collapse of the Soviet state, Tajikistan had to look abroad to fill that void. Political and economic groups in Iran, Afghanistan and many other countries have their own ambitions to play a role in Tajikistan. That does not guarantee that the republics' inhabitants will respond positively to all such efforts....Tajikistan's social and economic problems are so serious that whoever rules there will have to seek outside help. However, it is an oversimplification to assume that Tajikistan must necessarily fall into another country's orbit because of the cultural and religious similarities between them."[123]

To sum up the internal situation of Tajikistan at the moment of independence, Said Akhmedov stated, "In sum, the conflict broke out originally on partly political and religious grounds, the regional aspect being initially concealed. Political competition among parties and movements subsequently receded, although the opposition still uses political slogans of that competition. The channeling of political confrontation into a regional form was inevitable."[124] The forces of regionalism completely paralysed the central power turning the entire state into a fragmented' fiefdom', This indecisive factional politics reminded us of the medieval warlordism, a common scene in this territory much before the coming of the Soviet rule." Niyazi observed, "ocontinues to loom large in the republic's political life, shaping the behaviour of politicians and the sub-ethnic self-awareness characteristic of the Tajiks, whilst that same internally divided nature of the Tajik ethnic group means that the regional factor is ever present in politics. A strong sense of belonging to autonomous local subcultures serves among the Tajiks as an effective instrument in the hand of the power-hungry and prevents a consolidation of society."[125]

However, accepting the importance and influence of ehtno-regional factors in Tajik politics, one must admit the fact the these sub-national identities could not bring much positive results for the republic in the post-Soviet phase. Each and every region, with their respective geographic variations provided various professional and cultural scopes. The Soviet system with its apparent motto of equating all under socialist principles, could not make any qualitative change in these variations. Rather, the Soviet experience led to the politicisation of each region along suitable ideologies. A very old proverb of the pre-Soviet period remained quite relevant throughout the Soviet era: "The pamiris dance, the Qualiabis defend, Dushanbe produces and Khojent trades and rules."[126] However, these differences in professional and political life were no more taken for granted by the inhabitants of the regions with a relatively low profile and this was amply evident during the time of turmoil. Rather ethnic, regional and religious attachments had made this small, poor state even more vulnerable in the hands of the mutually hostile groups of people. Eden Naby came to a thoughtful conclusion about the role of ethnic factors in Tajikistan. Naby wrote: "The focus on ethnicity as a key to the understanding of Central Asian politics follows from the political importance of Soviet nationality policy in studies of Central Asia. With the breakdown of the Soviet Union, the assumption, that ethnicity would automatically translate into 'national' identity with the eponymous republics being transformed into 'states' is being challenged. The main challenge currently is evident in Tajikistan where there is a weak self-identification of regions with the Tajik republic. These regions do not wish to be transformed into a state on the terms hitherto dictated by Dushanbe. Islamic leaders have joined and indeed lead in the political struggle less as regional or ethnic figures but as religious leaders commanding respect across ethnic lines. Despite the homogeneity and, therefore, consensus possible under an Islamic umbrella, secular and Ismmaili competitiveness-threatens any unity forged by Islam. Appeals to Tajik ethnic components are heavily mixed with Uzbek components in nearly all respects expect language. Appeals to Islamic identity, too, may be defeated due to secular and Ismaili interests. Thus, a stalemate has emerged which—if nothing else—will lead to the hasty departure of non-Central Asians including the hundreds of Russian military families along the Afghan border and eventually, to a close working relationship with related people across international borders, especially in Afghanistan and Uzbekistan. In the short run, Tajikistan's significant economic problems can only be aggravated by the political stalemate as western aid and trade missions steer a wide path away from Dushanbe."[127]

A survey of the general role of ethnicity in the USSR and the intense form of ethno-regional politics in Tajikistan seems to bring out one common characteristic of ethnic identities. More often than not, ethnicity in Soviet Central Asia worked as an exclusive rather than inclusive force. Therefore, at the time of redfining national identities, strong ethnic attachments created more division instead of consolidating various groups of people together. The 'we-they' syndrome that began with the Slavs and other European diaspora was surpassed by the inter-tribal, inter-clan, inter-regional and inter-ethnic conflicts at the intra-national level. Ethnicity, therefore has to be realistically situated as a reality in this trouble torn soil, having both positive and negative consequences, instead of romanticising the scope of ethnicity as a force capable of resolving the identity disputes and power politics of this multi-ethnic and multi-cultural zone. Moreover, ethnicity cannot work autonomously in a politically complex and ideologically unsettled society. Ethnic identities primarily denote a form of anthropological classification. Therefore, the study of ethnic politics in Central Asia has been closely linked with ethno-religious, ethno-regional, ethno-cultural and ethno-linguistic identities of the region which involved complex interactions of a number of variables at different levels providing different results for specific cases.

Theoretically viewed, different ethnic categories, with their own characteistic features and peculiarities, can co-exist without much serious trouble. It is usually the manipulation of a political hierarchy working on economic disparity, that catapults an ethnic discord to the level of an irresoluble dispute. This is what has happened in the case of each and every ethnic dispute in post-Soviet Central Asia. Tajikistan's acute ethnic crisis also did not develop on its own, but resulted from other material causes. Tajikistan being the smallest Central Asian republic with highest density of population and lowest material resources was automatically exposed to all kinds of violent political unrests once the Soviet yoke was removed. These unrests sharply polarised the state, given the characteristic lop-sidedness in the distribution of economic and political opportunities in different ethnic regions or geographical territories throughout the Soviet regime.

Seven

Perestroika, Glasnost and the Change in Central Asia

The era of Gorbachev became synonymous with the two newly popularised terms, perestroika implying restructuring and glasnost meaning openness. The Soviet system had undergone a very elaborate reformation process under this regime which was shortly followed by the collapse of the entire system. However, in spite of the indirect responsibility of Gorbachev in the demise of the Soviet system, he was not usually blamed for it. Rather he received credit from many analysts as a harbinger of liberty and freedom to a mass of people who were tired of remaining under a hollow ideological framework and a crumbling economic structure. But while appreciating Gorbachev's achievements, one should remember his intentions as well. Neither did he wish to do away with the socialist doctrines, nor envisage the demise of the USSR as a state system. These two major consequences that followed perestroika were not consciously planned by Gorbachev, rather they resulted from the dynamics of events on which he lost all control. Thus, the era of Gorbachev along with its fascinating developments towards multidimensional reform programmes witnessed many more complexities over various issues which were not present in the initial scheme of perestroika. The nationalities question and its future in the USSR was one such issue, which even Gorbachov, being more concerned with the issues of economic revival initially overlooked. It was in the process of implementing perestroika reforms that he faced the heat on nationalities affairs and attempted a serious revision in the official outlook towards nationality policy. But once again, Gorbachev's perestroika and glasnost did not have uniform effect on all regions of the USSR. In Central Asia its impact was very unique from all perspectives. From economic to ideological, all changes had sharply distinct reactions in the Central Asian soil that brought the entire zone to an unexpected cross-road of political indecision, economic crisis and ideological vexation, which caught this region completely unprepared. Therefore, the study of Gorbachev's perestroika needs a particularistic orientation in order to assess its impact on Central Asian society. Even Gorbachev, the so called usherer of freedom, could not transcend the feeling of alienation towards the region and did not try to see the region from its own perspective in terms of economic and other material relations with the centre. Therefore, perestroika was not a very welcome event for the Central Asians unlike their Russian counterparts. They could not even rejoice in their independence like the Baltic republics because of their utter material and psychological unpreparedness. Glasnost only created an apparent opportunity to speak out that led to the surfacing of various cross-currents within the prevailing indigenous socio-political conditions. However, it was the forces of change which were unleashed during the perestroika years that suddenly brought the region into limelight in international affairs. Therefore, though unwarranted and coming from above perestroika became a watershed in the history of Central Asia with specific impacts on its economy, society, polity and ideology, which was distinctly different from the effects of perestroika in mainland Russia or in other multi culture zone of the earstwhile Soviet Union.

Mikhail Gorbachev came to be elected as General Secretary on the 11th March, 1985, after the death of K. Chernenko. Gorbachev's coming to power symbolised a great change in the character of CPSU leadership as he came from a comparatively younger generation and, therefore, was enthusiastic from the very inception to bring about necessary changes to the stagnant situation. This change in attitude implied a shift from the old and incapable leadership that followed from the era of Brezhnev both at central and regional levels and a system of status quo that had been taken for granted by the past leadership who were afraid of taking any new initiative in the mortal fear of unknown consequences. Therefore, the very inception of Gorbachev marked a new era in Soviet history for it bid a silent farewell to the old guards. Moreover, Gorbachev's selection by his colleagues, Gromyko, Aliev, Solomentsev, Kunaev and so on implied his popularity and aptness for the post. This spontaneous shift towards a younger leader itself showed the need for change surfacing from within the system. Gorbachev, took up the telling issues one by one in his scheme of restructuring. Some analysts felt that this shift towards the new generation of leadership was inevitable. "A gerontocracy, by definition, is unable to remain in power for an extended period of time. Finally, in March 1985, the elderly leadership was forced to permit a younger generation to take power. The post of General Secretary was passed to a person who was in his early fifties and was vigorous and able to truly lead. Mikhail Gorbachev, the new General Secretary, began with a whirlwind of activity designed to get the Soviet Union moving again. This implementation of his reform plans was helped by the fact that the members of the gerontocracy quickly began to lose power through death or retirement."[1]

Thus, Gorbachev came to power with great expectations on the part of his colleagues and took up the elaborate scheme of reforms as soon as he entered the office of the General Secretary. Gorbachev himself stated, "Perestroika is an urgent necessity arising from the profound processes of development in our socialist society. This society is ripe for change. It has been yearning for it. Any delay in beginning perestroika could have led to an excerbated internal situation in the near future, which, to put it bluntly, would have been fraught with serious social, economic and political crises."[2] In the same chapter, Gorbachev defined perestroika as a 'revolution'. He stated, "Perestroika is a word with many meanings. But if we are to choose from its many possible synonyms the key one which expresses its essence most accurately, then we can say thus: Perestroika is a revolution. A decisive acceleration of the socio-economic and cultural development of Soviet society which involves radical changes on the way to a qualitatively new state is undoubtedly a revolutionary task."[3] That perestroika meant revolution and a revolution from above was consciously admitted by its initiator, as he himself mentioned the term 'qualitative change'. But how that qualitative change could ensue without disturbing the given framework was something, which remained unclear in Gorbachev's thought, and, therefore, in practical field, his reforms failed to remain within the existing parameter. Perhaps, if we study his reports and speeches we see a shift. In the first year or two, he was talking of reform within the structure, and then he was almost suggesting capitalism under CPSU. An author like Dmitri Volkogonov, who was otherwise full of praises about Gorbachev had to admit this dichotomy in him (Gorbachev). In his analysis, "He wanted to restructure 'everything' without touching the socialist foundations of state ownership, the party's 'leading role', and the regime's Communist goals. It is not hard to see that these goals were not attainable. To restructure everything, and yet to leave intact the foundations laid by Lenin was logically impossibility."[4] But, Gorbachev, somehow, either could not realise or did not accept this fact. To Gorbachev, "Perestroika is a revolutionary process for it is a jump forward in the development of socialism, in the realisation of its essential characteristics."[5] The two major targets were to reinvigorate the dwindling Soviet economy by drastic measures instead of 'timid, creeping reforms'[6] and to encourage democratic principles in political sphere without disturbing the socialist framework. In the process of democratisation came the perspective of glasnost or openness whereby corruption and deviation from principle in all stages of Soviet history in all levels began to surface. Both these perestroika activities left their indirect impact on Central Asian republics.

First, to take up the issue of economic reforms the notion of combating corruption and sluggishness was encouraged. Gorbachev himself admitted both the initial progress and later stagnation in Soviet economy as he stated, "However, the Soviet union is a young state without analogues in history or in the modern world. Over the past seven decades—a short span in the history of human civilisation—our country has traveled a path equal to centuries" and pointed out, "At some stage—this became particularly clear in the latter half of the seventies—something happened that was at first sight inexplicable. The country began to lose momentum. Economic failures became more frequent...Analysing the situation, we first discovered a slowing economic growth. In the last fifteen years the national income growth rates had declined by more than a half and by the beginning of the eighties had fallen to a level close to economic stagnation."[7] With this conclusion Gorbachev took political initiatives to improve the economic standard. Gorbachev outlined the major themes of his economic reform agenda in a speech that he delivered on December 10, 1984, four months before he assumed leadership as general secretary. In this speech, he called for a programme of intensification (*intensifitcatsiia*), acceleration (*iskorennie*), openness (*glasnost*), and restructuring (*perestroika*).[8] In his initial days as General Secretary, Gorbachev concentrated on improving the economy in industrial and agricultural sectors by concentrating all economic related ministers into superministerial body. Planning and coordination was stressed and reorganisation was initiated in agriculture as well. The main target at this stage was to transform the stagnating command economy into a market economy.

Other than sluggishness and deficiency in the economy, underproductivity was also caused by rampant official corruption reflected in shortages and poor quality of consumer goods. However, this economic reinvigoration could not be taken up in isolation. He had to simultaneously fight corruption in political personnel and high officials and moreover, needed to bring about attitudinal change among people. Therefore, Perestroika became a complex process where one reform invited another. In order to combat corruption and ideological deviation he took the policy of purges and this led to tremendous uproar especially in the republics for the replacement of local officials by Moscow's representative. Though made on the excuse of corruption, this measure appeared as a blow to their nationalist sentiments. Actually, Gorbachev meanwhile had undertaken an elaborate administrative reform programme and announced democratisation in all spheres of Soviety society at the 19th Party Conference. The Conference also emphasised the need to overcome the prevalent bureaucratic centralism and to expose bureaucratic malpractices and to put an end to bureaucratic red-tapism. But at the same time the Conference stressed the need to maintain a nationwide centralised bureaucracy for the organisation of major state and administrative activites. Similarly, while speaking of democracy, Gorbachev never mentioned the way out from democratic centralism and one party rule. Therefore, the democratic and reform measures taken up by the centre could not bring much delight to the republics. Especially, the economically weak and dependent region of Central Asia seemed quite sceptical about the revolutionary developments of perestroika and glasnost.

The most glaring event in this regard was the Alma Ata riot of 1986 that resulted from the replacement of local Kazakh First Secretary, D. Kunaev by a Russian named Kolbin. This was not an isolated event of protest, but the first major blow from ethnic territories towards Gorvachev's reform programme that indicated the heightened ethno-national sensitivity of contemporary Soviet land in general. The change of a corrupt local personnel by a Moscow man symbolised the usurpation of republican autonomy by the centre. As Graham Smith opined, "Bringing in an outsider in order to reassert control over a republic economically crippled by elite corruption and mismanagement may have made rational sense, but for many Kazakhs, numerically out-numbered, and feeling socially vulnerable and economically deprieved in their own homeland, it showed the new regime as being totally insensitive to national sensibilities".[9] Thus, the incident of a Central Asian leadership being assaulted by Moscow for corruption seemed quite insulting. The attitude of the centre towards Kunaev was not an isolated measure to curb corruption; rather, it was the final blow to a process of change which had started a few years earlier. In fact, the old generation of First Secretaries from all the five republics were changed between 1983 and 1986—but the last replacement being a part of perestroika created such a violent reaction. However, the unravellling of corruption in the economy of this zone started with the death of Sharaf Rashidov, the First Secretary of Uzbekistan in 1983. The local secretaries of the oblasts were also rapidly replaced in order to control corruption—but this gave rise to much local indignation as this was seen as a kind of re-imposition of Moscow authorities in places where the people of the region become used to see their own personnel. The reflection of this discontent could be found in some glasnost papers which will be discussed later in this chapter.

At the same time one must remember that the purge of Kunaev was not an isolated step taken by Gorbachev. The number of enforced retirement of high officials reached more than hundred by 1989 which included important officials like Tikhonov, Grishin, Romanov and so on. But in European Russia this action did not receive an ethno-national character. The meaning of the same policy changed along with the change of contexts.

An apparently revised lip service to reforms could not bring enough confidence among the republics to trust the initiative of perestroika. Especially for Central Asia, where the economic standard remained low throughout the Soviet regime, perestroika did not bring much scope of prosperity. Therefore, there was no reason for the Central Asians, both the general mass and the elite leadership, to be much elated with the prospect of reforms in this direction. For, the long Soviet experience had brought them the realisation that the interests of Moscow often went quite contrary to the Central Asian interests, and Gorbachev in spite of his revolutionary zeal would not at any cost sacrifice the centre's interest for the republics, though, the promise of increased investment for machine building industries as well as increase in the prices of raw materials and fuels were two positive steps towards reinvigorating the Central Asian economy. Moreover, in 1987, Gorbachev spoke of investing an additional amount of 50 million rubles for housing constructions in the region. But all these moves fell short of the necessity and expectation of the zone. All these programmes were chalked by the centre and no further scope of economic autonomy could be envisaged in the Central Asian republics. Moreover, the official retrenchment leading to job shortages in this region came as a real threat associated with perestroika. Central Asia with its huge population, needed labour intensive industries to provide employment for all, while, the capital intensive and highly technological industries would have suited the central cities of RSFSR. John Anderson stated, 'And although the authorities did not publish the statistics till much later, it was becoming clear that the economic decline-population growth mismatch was producing de facto unemployment: 25.7 per cent in Tajikistan, 22.8 per cent in Uzbekistan, 18.8 percent in Turkmenistan and 16.3 per cent in Kirgiziya in 1986."[10] Surprisingly, no policy distinction could be found in the economic policy of perestroika considering the differences of need. Therefore, Central Asia had thin chances of recovery from her age old backwardness. Boris Rumer commented, "The predominance of a capital intensive policy means that an ever greater proportion of the investment allocation goes toward the producer sphere of the economy, and an ever smaller share to the non-producer sphere. The upshot is social stagnation and backwardness in comparison with other regions of the country."[11]

The general economic stagnation of USSR also had its reflection in Central Asia in an even more acute form. By the end of 80s, there emerged huge uproar against cotton mono-culture of the region for which Central Asia lost self-sufficiency in food grains. Moreover, the turnover in cotton was proving quite dissatisfactory in this decade. "In Uzbekistan the cotton harvest fell short of target by 300,000 tons in 1985, despite the reduction of the target from 6 million to 5.7 million tons."[12] Cotton being quite a thirsty crop used to drain up the limited water resources of the region. Water shortage came up as yet another telling issue of the area to which the centre paid no heed to. In fact, Gorbachev, by dropping the water diversion scheme (that aimed at redirecting Siberian river water to Central Asia) in August 1986, had seriously hurt the Central Asian sentiments for this scheme would have brought much scope of economic revitalisation of the zone. Gorbachev, giving priority to ecology over economy, got misunderstood. For the Central Asians felt deceived after all these years of raw cotton supply to Moscow. In fact, the intensive cotton cultivation led to the drying up of limited water resources—but the centre seemed quite harsh in rejecting the prospect of reviving water resources through river diversion. Thus, Gorbachev with his so called lofty ideals did not make much difference to the Central Asians since their claim ranked low on the priority list. Rather, there was an indirect instruction towards the region to become self-sufficient through a better use of their existing resources. This was quite an alarming condition for Central Asia, for this zone was so far not given any scope to turn self-sufficient, whether in heavy industry or consumer goods, or food crops, or in energy management. Though Central Asia had good potentials in energy resources and food crops, the Soviet economy did not encourage these aspects to develop, for its entire emphasis was to turn the zone into the cotton bowl of USSR. The production of this white gold had drained up all the resources, energies and water of the region so long. Therefore, perestroika message, instead of bringing a sigh of relief, brought a sense of indecision and tension about the future direction of the economy. Boris Rumer quoted the opinion of a Tajik economist, Rustam Mirzoev, "Social-economic research conducted by the economists of Central Asia permits one to conclude that one of the most important ways to solve the social-economic tasks of the region is to create labour-intensive, but not capital-intensive, branches of material production [primarily in industry]."[13] But no such special attention to larger investment schemes for Central Asia was taken up by the perestroika programme which could have really reinvigorated this backward zone blessed with so much natural and human resources. John Anderson also observed, "Overall, Gorbachev's redefinition of economic priorities did little to improve the situation of Central Asia and much to aggravate the region's sense of grievance. Having created a dependency relationship based upon a single crop, Moscow was now asking the region to be self-sufficient. Yet, as the all-union economy continued to decline, the likelihood of Moscow providing substantial help to the region was further reduced."[14] Thus regional discrimination became even more glaring with the perestroika reforms and this economic discrimination along with the retrenchment of officers on the charge of corruption affected the popular nationalist sentiments bitterly, and the Central Asian response began to surface in a hostile manner.

Thus, nationalist discontent leading to violent demonstrations kept on increasing through the perestroika decade. The Baltic region was much more vocal compared to Central Asia in this regard. The issue of ethno-national discontent became quite an universal phenomenon in the USSR of 80s. Therefore, the 'nationaity question' needs to be reassessed in the light of perestroika—glasnost. Shams Ud Din pointed out, "The emergence of ethno-nationalism and its violent manifestation in Nagorno Karabakh, Ajerbaijan, Armenia, Georgia, Latvia and Estonia has once again put the nationalities question on the high agenda of present Soviet leadership."[15] Gorbachev in his book "Perestroika" dealt with nationalities issues in a very moderate fashion. To quote his own expression, "Every national culture is a treasure which cannot be lost. But a sound interest in everything valuable which each national culture has, should not degenerate into attempts to shut off from the objective processes of interaction and rapproacment. It is also dangerous when the attitude of representatives of one nationality toward those of another betrays a lack of respect....I'd like to say once again that if negative phenomena emerge in this highly sensitive sphere of human relations, they emerge not just by themselves, but as a consequence of red tape, and lack of attention to people's lawful rights."[16] This luke warm stand, however, was not enough to deal with the burning issues of nationalities at this stage. In fact, the superimposed Soviet identity, now began to be questioned as the process of glasnost began to move ahead. The natural attachments to religion, language and ethnic origin began to surface in the politics of all nationalities which made the task of Gorbachev even more challenging. The 19th Party Conference held in June, 1988 followed by Mikhail Gorbachev's speech at the special session of the USSR Supreme Soviet on November 1988, gave the assurance of a special and thorough reexamination of the nationalities policy.[17] A realisation began to emerge that suppression of nationalities and perestroika could not go together. Yet Gorbachev was not ready to do away with the socialist framework of the state and therefore a notion of purification was included with an apparently lofty ideal of going back to Leninist perception about nationalities. In his essay on perestroika, Gorbachev wrote in 1987, "Lenin taught us to display extreme caution and tact in the nationality issue. There cannot and should not be any stereotyped pattern here. One thing is clear:when the fundamental interests of nations converge, when the principle of equality in everything forms the backbone of relations between peoples—and this is exactly how it is in Soviet society—then any emerging problem and misunderstandings can be settled, even in difficult situations. Of course, there are quite a few people in the West and, for that matter, in the East, who would like to undermine the friendship and cohesion of the peoples of the Soviet Union. But this is an entirely different matter and here Soviet land stands on guard, protecting the accomplishments of Leninist nationality policy."[18] By 1989, an extension of the same position put all blame on the thoughtlessness and inconsiderate position of Stalinist and post-Stalinist Soviet nationalities policy. As Gorbachev stated in his speech,"...indifference towards ethnic interests, the failure to resolve many socio-economic problems of the republics and autonomous territories, deformations in the development of the languages and cultures of the country's people, the deterioration of the demographic situation and many other negative consequences"[19] had caused the ethno-national unrests in different contexts of the Soviet soil. However, the special plenum on the Nationalities in 1989 reconstructed the nationalities policy as follows:

1. To transform radically the Soviet federation by investing it (constituent parts) with real political and economic content, which is to include republic's financial autonomy and self-financing (Khozraschet). Nationality republics, however, are not to have party organisations separate from the CPSU, and nor are other forms of social organisation to be constructed on nationality grounds. Nonetheless, greater autonomy for the republic's Communist Parties is proposed, which would include more organisational and financial autonomy,and greater control over cadre appointments.
2. The union republics are to be allowed to establish relations with foreign states and international organisations and are to be responsible for ensuring the country's defence, but the armed forces are to continue to be organised on an inter-ethnic basis.
3. Given that the Russian republic does not possess the administrative and party infrastructure of other union republics, it is recommended that additional bodies be established for it, including creating a bicameral supreme Soviet for the Republic.
4. The rights of the autonomous republics should be substantially expanded as well as the legal status of more minor nationality administrative units. But provision should be made for ensuring that 'the territory of an autonomous *oblast* or *okrug* cannot be altered' without the consent of the union republic's supreme Soviet.

5. Those nationalities expelled by Stalin from their homelands are to be fully rehabilitated.
6. Whether the language of the nationality of a namesake union of autonomous republic is to become the state language is to be left up to the republic.[20]

There were many similar recommendations made for the promotion of republican autonomy. In spite of the radically increased scope of federalism, the Party remained centralised. This led to the utmost lack of balance in a system, newly launched in a trouble-torn territory. And soon after the ensuing of this policy, the break up of the union started with the secession of Lithuania, closely followed by Estonia and Latvia. But once again, Central Asian republics, in spite of their discontent and disillusionment with the system, did not opt for independence spontaneously. This apparently inexplicable conduct on part of Central Asian republics could be explained in terms of their economic dependency, political immaturity and psychological unpreparedness to accept such a drastic change in their status. But the vacuum created by perestroika measures in ideological as well as political spheres gave rise to various internal movements to redefine the local identities on the basis of religion, language and ethnic compositions. Thus, perestroika had hardly any direct impact in the region, but indirectly it prepared the ground for the movements of local identities to become stronger as never before.

Glasnost Unveils

Another important aspect of Gorbachev's reforms was glasnost or openess, whereby many important documents, statistics, reports began to come in the open, the debates over several issues took place in current meetings and conferences and alongside this, the speeches of party leaders, deputies and other representatives began to get formally published. This was an unprecedented trend in the Soviet Union. The secrecy which was practiced over the years in internal affairs to suppress the truth from the general people and also from the outside world now gave way to open publication of facts, often admitting the shortcomings of the system. This was probably a more revolutionary trend so far as the political culture of the state was concerned. Therefore, though consisting of only a part of democratisation, glasnost became a very important aspect and came to be clubbed with the concept of perestroika. Tatyana Zaslavskaya observed, "Although democratisation represents only one component of restructuring, and openness only one component of democratisation, the concepts 'restructuring' and 'openness' are often used together as if they meant the same thing. This is understandable, for the development of openness has been the most important achievement of restructuring."[21]

However, as a result of glasnost, in nationality areas, various opinions towards the Soviet rule began to surface. Many articles on various issues began to appear on the contemporary Russian newspapers. One such article stated openly that "Nationalist feelings cannot be satisfied by theoretical abstraction or political postulates, it demands its realisation precisely in day to day life.... The rights are to be given not just to the autonomous republics, they must be genuine for each of its citizen".

"We have got used to assume that one or the other national wound, discomfort—is a consequence of only deep seated bureaucratism or red-tape and chauvinistic indifference (non only Russian) but also to the requirements of the minority people. Meanwhile, as it turns out to a less extent,the potentialities of the autonomous self-governments are restricted by the economic mechanism currently in force."[22] Thus, there was open admission about the faults and defects of the system followed so far and the complex and indeterminate future of the nationalities both under the titular republics and as scattered minorities. The economic constraint was recognised as one of the telling material reasons behind the incompleteness of national autonomies. Another article stressed the need to bring humanism in the sensitive issue of nationalism as it stated, "In the years of Stalinism, the national consciousness in theory and practice essentially was opposite to the international consciousness. Amidst a show of harmony a habit was steadily formed not to take note of the painful spot of development or explain them, say 'as survivals of capitalism in the peoples' mind" and causes likewise.' The same article complained about the suppression of national art and literature as part of propaganda and then resolved, "At present, it may be said with full confidence, that the restoration of the Leninist concpets of inter-nationalities relations is possible just through their humanisation, imparting new, modern look to entire Soviet federations."[23] On humanisation the author exposited, "what is humanisation of the federal relations? This first of all is complete elimination from them the administrative commanding method of the control of extraordinary restrictions and strengthening of mutual interests of the national republics in preserving and developing the Union of SSR."[24] Another article titled *Democratisation or Denationalisation* openly admitted the mistakes in Soviet perception as it stated, "If to expect that it is possible to resolve our problem on the basis of 'socio-democratic socialism' then one will have to acknowledge the mistake: by socialism we considered only our own version...."[25] However, this somewhat apologetic intonation underlying the writings implied a kind of revisionism in the intellectual platform so long reflecting mainly the tight, top-downward control of the party-state bureaucracy. But in none of these writings there was any indication of the ensuing break up of the union. Rather, ideas and explanations were formulated as to how to get over the previous mistakes and begin at a new plain.

But the reflections of the views of Central Asian representatives in the First Congress of Peoples' Deputies held in Moscow in May—June 1989 showed much sharper reactions towards the Moscow administration throughout the Soviet regime, and some of the speeches implied that for the Central Asian people the change of regimes basically made no difference. The people in general were equally disgusted with the Gorbachev regime and its reforms and as they now could speak out, the sense of deprivation and exploitation got out in the open. Mostly, the First Secretaries of the Central Committee and other similar representatives in leadership still spoke in favour of the Federation and welcomed the changes introduced by perestroika. For example, Abasmat Masaliev, First Secretary of the Central Committee of the Kirgiz Communist party said, "We believe that the further development of nations and ethnic groups must not be isolationist but should combine organically the independent interests of the republics with the interests of the union as a whole. The union will be really strong if it has strong republics and a strong centre and is based on the sincere trust and mutual respect between our nations." But there was also an honest admission of the inability on part of the formal governments to sustain power and discipline at the hour of transition from authoritarianism to democracy as he said, "...... The current democratic process is undoubtedly a significant achievement of perestroika. We must not, however, forget about the need for strengthening discipline. Unfortunately, our efforts in this field have slackened. It is no accident that democracy has brought with itself extremist groups that whip up the nationalist sentiments and purposefully undermine the authority of the Soviet state and the communist party, the party's policies and ideology."[26] Kakhar

Makhamov, the First Secretary of Tajik communist party central committee more categorically reiterated the concept of strong centre and strong republics. But his position reflected the worry about the future economic administration of the republic considering the perestroika notion of *khozrastoz*. He strongly opined, "Many press reports suggest that the so-called 'raw-materials' republics are quietly withdrawing from the concept of territorial economic independence. This is entirely untrue. We support the concept of self-financing and self-administration on the whole but believe that it can be realised only under the following three conditions.

First, there must be a reform of the system of wholesale prices and prices for raw materials.

Second, the concept must be realised simultaneously throughout the country.

Third, a legal foundation must be set up in the form of a law on the economic relations between territorial units in a federal state.

We shall not achieve our goals without satisfying these conditions.... In the nearest future 150,000 new jobs must be made in Tajikistan to give work to the ever increasing population. Since the amount of arable irrigated area in the republic per capita is only 0.11 hectre, the new jobs can be generated only in new industries...."[27] Thus, without openly defying the Moscow authorities, the Tajik Secretary articulated the actual necessity of the republic and also highlighted the economic difficulties as the major problem to overcome. The Turkmen secretary (First) Saparmurad Niyazov too highlighted the 'deficient economic structure' in his speech.[28]

But the approach of the deputies who were not directly involved with the republican administration was antagonistic and hostile towards the centre as was found in the small speeches of Mukhtar Umarkhodzhaev,[29] rector of Andhizan language Teachers' Training college of Uzbekistan and Pulatdzan Akhunov, Assistant school Headmaster of Andhizhan region (YCL member). The former speech made only the alarming statement of uncontrolled birth rate in the Uzbek republic and demanded on behalf of all cotton producing republics to increase the cotton wholesale price by 50 per cent. In fact, his speech created much turmoil inside the hall and after a little heated debate Pulatdzhan Akhunov managed to reach the platform and registered his protest in categorical terms: "I must table a protest. Only those deputies from Uzbekistan are admitted to the platform whose opinions are unanimous [and agree with those of the leaders].

I demand an opportunity to speak for the minority who have their own views on conditions in Uzbekistan. Why are we not allowed to tell about the catastrophic situation there? Uzbeks hoped that perestroika would allow them to get rid of the monoculture of cotton. Unfortunately, nothing is being done about that. The area under cotton must be cut by 50 per cent. I have much to say allow me to speak at the next session."[30]

The expression of bitter indignation on cotton monoculture and its negative impact was also registered by Adyl Yakubov, First Secretary of the Uzbek Writers Union, who lamented, "Hundreds of thousands of hectares of orchards, pasture and shady almond and walnut tree groves were mercilessly cut down to plant cotton. The country got its self-sufficiency in cotton and immense riches with it. But what did our villager, his wife and children get? Just twelve hours of hard work, under the sultry southern summer daily, without holidays or vacations. The numerous reports in the press on corruption in our republic give you a chance to calculate precisely how much each of the corrupt officials has stolen from the people. The officials must be punished...But what have our villagers got for their backbreaking toil? Our women work under scorching sun in fields sprayed with poisonous chemicals. This results in an increasing incidence of cancer, hepatitis, intestinal infections and gynecological disorders leading to higher death rates for women and children."[31]

This picture of terrible misery and injustice brought out in the open, the darker side of the propaganda story of successful yields of 'white gold' and also explained the rapid decline in targeted cotton produce in the zone during the perestroika years. This picturisation was definitely true for all the cotton producing states of Central Asia.

At the 9th sitting of the Congress in June, the famous author Chengis Aitmatov discussed in details about all the discrepancies with a special emphasis on language discrimination. He concluded his speech with an honest confession about all the wrongs done in the past and envisaged a better future for the nationalities based on better understanding between the centre and the republics. He declared, "Let us learn from the terrible lessons of our past to prevent any repetition of the same experiences. Constitutional guarantees must be worked out that protect absolutely deportations of any ethnic groups on any political, administrative or racial grounds, and provide equal justice for everybody. Each nation must have a homeland where its historical roots lies."[32]

Though the Central Asian republics had every reason for discontent and resentment toward the Soviet system, and though with glasnost much of their bitterness had began to surface, probably these republics were the most unprepared ones in the USSR to accept such an abrupt demise of the Soviet state. The unexpected demise of the USSR suddenly left them free to carve out their own destiny. Martha Brill Olcott commented, "Few people of the world have ever been forced to become independent nations. Yet that is precisely what happened to the five Central Asian republics......."[33] The statistical report furnished by Valery Tishkov on the results of the 17 March 1991 referendum on preservation of the Soviet Union showed overwhelming support in favour of the preservation in all five Central Asian states. The majority of voters preferred the maintenance of the USSR, whether in mainland Russia or in the republics. But there too, the percentage of Central Asian voters were markedly high. This distinction became amply evident from the statistics provided by Tishkov as used in the Table below: [34]

Name of Republic	*Voted Number*	*Turnont Percentage*	*Yes (Number)*	*Yes (%)*	*No (Number)*	*No (%)*
Kazakhstan	8,816543	88.2	8,295,519	94.1	436,560	5.0
Kirgizia	2,174,593	92.9	2,057,971	94.6	86,245	4.0
Tajikistan	2,407,552	94.2	2,315,755	96.2	75,300	3.1
Turkmenia	1,847,310	97.7	1,804,138	97.9	31,203	1.7
Uzbekistan	9,816,333	95.4	9,196,848	93.7	511,373	5.2
Russia	79,701,169	75.4	58,860,783	71.3	21,030,753	26.4
Ukraine	31,514,244	83.5	22,110,899	70.2	8,820,089	28.0

In fact, the August coup in Moscow which was anti-Gorbachev in nature was quite a welcome event in Central Asia as the leaders here thought that this might again bring back the status quo and would give protection to the old *nomanklatura* a who were feeling insecure and unstable with the unleashing of various forces of opposition in each of the republics. But the coup failed and the USSR got dissolved immediately after the event, leaving Central Asia completely perplexed and vulnerable in the face of the multi-dimentional challenges of that difficult hour.

This sudden change of status created tremendous indecision and uncertainty among the states at all levels, political, economic, cultural and ideological. This indecisiveness along with material crisis affected each and every stratum of the population of the entire zone. The superimposed Soviet identity was withdrawn at an hour when the local identities were in the making. At this hour of crisis, the anchorage of Islam seemed to be the most prominent alternative ideology for these people. To many analysts 'Islam' appeared as a 'common bond' for the entire Central Asian region which was to direct the future character of the republics. Their relations with the outer world was more complex with cross currents of several strands of Islam working simultaneously on the same soil. Moreover, ethnic unrest became a common feature for the entire region with Tajikistan experiencing the most acute form of civil war. After the removal of the Soviet identity, the local identities began to crystallise on the basis of three major components, religion (namely Islam), language (titular) and ethnic origin. Attachment to all these indigenous forms of identities had been there in the Central Asian soil throughout the Soviet experience. But because of the strict code of conduct under that regime, these characteristic features could not flourish to their fullest scope and spontaneity. The demise of the Soviet system created a double-fold crisis of power vaccuum and ideological vaccuum in the zone, which began to get fuelled by the already existing elements of local identities. On their own, these elements had enough potential to create mature indigenous identities. But in the uncertainty and tension of the given circumstances, different parallel trends of identity consciousness led to frequent clashes within the indigenous communities. This was probably because the acute political unstability added to terrible economic depression and increased social tension. In the period of heightened tension, religion and culture came in the purview of politics with a promise of rescue from the allround crisis.

The Collapse of the Soviet System and Central Asia

The Soviet Union entered a process of disintegration from 1990. The situation inside Central Asia was also very fluid with the rising tide of nationalism threatening the existing communist regimes of the republics. In fact, the years 1988-91 seemed to be extremely trouble-torn for these republics as there were frequent riots [Nagorno Karabakh in January 1988, Ashkhabad in May 1988, Ferghana Valley riot in June 1989, Dushanbe 1990 (February), battles over Osh between Uzbekistan and Kirghizia in June 1990] and unrest over several internal ethno-political issues. The local party and governments of the republics remained preoccupied with such disturbances but no spontaneous demand for secession could be heard from official republican authorities yet. Moreover, by an interesting coincidence, all the First Secretaries of the five republics were replaced immediately before Gorbachev's accession to power. After serving long tenures from pre-Brezhnev and Brezhnev eras, these veteran communist leaders either died or were ousted. Jabar Rasulov of Tajikistan, who remained in the chair since 1961 died in 1982, Sharif Rashidov of Uzbekistan was removed in 1983 on charges of corruption, Turdiakun Uzubaliev was forcibly retired in 1985 in Kirgizia, Mukhamadnazar Gapurov of Turkmenistan was retired in 1986. The process of transition was very much under the way when the replacement of Kazakh secretary D.I. Kunaev by Russian cadre led to riots in Alma Ata. This implied that the nationalist sensitivity of the region was very high strung at this hour of impending crisis. As the Perestroika decade moved forward, this heightened nationalist tension only got worsened whose reflections were found in several sporadic local upheavals. In spite of such growing socio-political unrests and total disillusionment with the perestroika-glasnost move from the centre, the Central Asian leadership could not yet envisage complete secession from Moscow like the Baltic states. Therefore independence came to these republics only as a byproduct of the downfall of the Soviet system. On 8th December, 1991, the presidents of the three Slav republics, Russia, Ukraine and Belarus, declared their new three member-union called the CIS (Commonwealth of Independent States), without even consulting the other republics. The unthoughtful action of these three major slavic states implied that the USSR henceforth ceased to survive.

This led to the forceful independence of the five Central Asian republics—the event to which many scholars provided a similar kind of interpretation. Shirin Akiner stated, "Thus, by default, without a liberation struggle or change of leadership, the Central Asian republics suddenly found themselves independent." Martha Brill Olcott stated, "That action by the three Slav presidents left Central Asian leaders with an unpleasant choice: they could go it alone—either singly or as a group—or they could shrug off the intended snub by their Slavic counterparts and agree to join the Commonwealth."[35] Bess Brown stated, "For the five Central Asian republics—Kazakhstan, Uzbekistan, Kyrgyzstan, Turkmenistan and Tajikistan—the collapse of the USSR and their *de facto* independence at the end of 1991 was an unexpected event for which no one in the new states was prepared psychologically, politically or economically,"[36] Considering the given unexpectedness of the situation, the Central Asian republics decided to remain within the CIS; for, making complete diplomatic and economic breach with the former mother country, namely Russia, would have been suicidal for them because of practical dependencies which were not very easy to get over. The economic crisis at that hour was most pressing given the prospect of a sudden withdrawl of all subsidies from the centre. As it is, Gorbachev's reforms proved to be quite unsympathetic to the miserable economy of the region and the zone was also suffering the brunt of the general depression ensued by the transition from command to market economy at this stage. Moreover, the internal dynamism of demographic multiplicity got reflected in ever increasing unemployment. Thus the region got independence at an hour of cumulative economic crisis and tremendous political chaos. The distress and despair of the general populace manifested in different variants of popular movements where Islam served as an indispensable component. But the revival of Islamic attachment raised various questions as to where this ideological shift (formally from Communism) would lead these nascent states to? What was the prospect of Pan-Islamism in a region that did not observe legitimate Islamic rites for half a century? What would be their relation with the Islamic states outside Central Asia (Iran, Turkey, UAE and so on)? What would be the result of both physical and psychological proximity to Afghanistan and so on? *Inter alia*, the question of religious fundamentalism had worried the scholars most at this stage. A very interesting shift in the attitude of scholars following the Western line of arguments could be traced from this time onwards. Instead of sympathy towards the followers of Islam inside Central Asia, there arose some kind of apprehension about the future conduct of these people. Islam was no more just any sentimental attachment or common bond of culture which held these people together against communist suppression. It was now seen as a decisive force destined to direct the geo-political dynamism of the entire Eurasia along with the Middle East.

In the post-perestroika phase, scholars took initiative to find out the development of the psychology of independent self-seeking amongst these people at a time of acute distress, chaos and indecision. Being freed from the Soviet yoke, indigenous self-seeking movements began to develop towards national consciousness. In this process Islam played a major role. According to some scholars Islam acted as the key idea around which the independent national consciousness of the Central Asian people began to crystallise. These authors highlighted the central role of Islam in reviving national identities of the ex-Soviet republics, although they dealt with other relevant elements in identity formation as well. The works like *Resurgence of Central Asia: Islam or Nationalism* by Ahmed Rashid,[37] or *Between Marx and Muhammad: The changing Face of Central Asia* by Dilip Hiro[38] are some of the more well known illustrations of this trend, whose emphasis on the role of Islam in reviving Central Asia become evident from the very titles of the books. While describing the situation in Tajikistan, Ahmed Rashid stated, "The green flag of Islam, with the Crescent and star and the Kalma or creed of Islam written in Arabic script, is the most potent symbol of the future in Dushanbe, the capital of landlocked Tajikistan."[39] Surprisingly, these authors have repeatedly over emphasised the over-arching role of Islam in unifying the whole region, in spite of being aware of the internal conflicts and bitter civil strifes between different Islamic parties inside Central Asia. Actually, once this weak and uncertain region got global exposure, many strands of Islamic fundamentalism from the outer world contested to capture the power vaccuum. In such, a fluid context Islam appeared as the deciding factor in the region's future. But the politicisation of Islam had its own dimensions. This was reflected in the creation of too many divergent political parties in the name of Islam who had different principles and goals thereby forcing Islam to contribute more in decentralising the political sphere, instead of unifying it into one unidimensional Islamic consciousness. Yet there are scholars who, without disregarding the tremendous spirit of Islamic revivalism, tried to see beyond Islam. These scholars tried to judge the situation on the basis of other factors that influenced the socio-political movements of the region as well and considered Islam to be one of the most essential components in the formation of national identities of the former Soviet-citizens of the republics. The works of Uwe Halbach,[40] Muriel Atkin,[41] , J.O.Voll,[42] Abha Dixit[43] , Burnet R. Rubin, [44] , Eden Naby [45] for instance dealt with the role of Islam in these territories in transition and found that Islam as a motivating force in the national consciousness and political characterisation of Central Asian states was not in any sense extraordinary. In Uwe Halbach's own expression, "...... the search for national and cultural identity of the Central Asian Muslims is not limited to the recollection of Islamic roots."[46] In fact, Halbach criticised the 'distorted perception on Religion of the Western scholars who had "an intense fixation on the Islamic factor"[47] Eden Naby, another scholar of this trend, assessed the role of Islam in promoting the future of Central Asia, in comparison with the role of ethnicity.

But whatever its attraction and impact, it is undeniable that some trends of Islamic fundamentalism had developed in Central Asia during this period of indecision. Of them, the most prominent was the Islamic Renaissance Party or *Partiya Islamskovo Vozrozhdeniya* (IRP in abbreviation). In fact, this party was founded during the Soviet period in 1990. But this was not an indigenous party of Central Asia. Operating from Moscow, it had three regional branches, of which Central Asia was one. In Central Asia, IRP acquired maximum subscription of Tajiks. This IRP wanted to get the power using the support of the deeply religious stratum in Central Asia and used the Islamic ideology as a counterpose to the still existing communist regime. Pinar Akcali observed, "According to the leaders of the party, the best way to protect the interests and rights of the Muslim people was to unite them. So, the all-union party, established itself as an organisation open to all Muslims of the former Soviet Union and aimed to unite all those who wanted to live in accordance with the requirements of the Qur'an and Sunnah. The IRP stood for the revival of the ideals of Islam, restoration of Islamic culture and the maintenance of Islamic traditions. The first paragraph of the party programme stated that the party was a religious organisation uniting Muslims who were actively propagating Islam, observing its rules and taking part in cultural, socio-political and economic life on the basis of the principles of Islam."[48] The study of Islamic fundamentalism in Central Asia, in its recent past, brought the most obscure state of the region, Tajikistan, into maximum focus. For here the fundamentalist developments were associated with external incitements from neighbouring Afghanistan and was posing a global threat. Moreover, this was the region where fundamentalist versus old communist forces clashed in a bitter and prolonged civil strife. Naturally, Sovietologists, historians, area experts, strategic analysts, all had concentrated their attention to Tajikistan to read the role of Islamic fundamentalism and its future in Central Asia. In Tajikistan it did appear to be the deciding factor for her future, but there too the limitation of this fundamentalism could be understood from the presence of a secular opposition (communist) that could fight back the rising forces of Islam in this unprecedented chaotic situation. However, while studying the situation of Tajikistan, authors have tended to show two basic trends. One group of authors, like Bess Brown, Martha Brill Olcott, Ajay Patnaik, K. Warikoo, wanted to identify the main reason behind fundamentalist growth in economic crisis, political immaturity and lack of modernisation. To them, perestroika, bringing an unexpected future to the zone, provoked the fundamentalist forces to emerge in such a major scale. K. Warikoo stated, "In 1991, subsidies from the former Soviet Union to Central Asia amounted to 24 billion roubles. Now the absence of hefty subsidies from Moscow is bound to push large sections of the fast growing population in Central Asia below the poverty line, which in turn would only exacerbate social tensions and discontent among the political leadership."[49] Warikoo had clearly distinguished the role of Islamic revivalism as part of nationhood and Islamic fundamentalism as "the negative and distabilising influence",[50] Bess Brown analysed, "The Tajik civil war originated in the hostility of a coalition of self-designated democratic, Tajik nationalist and Islamic opposition groups to the communist order that continued to reign in Tajikistan after the August 1991 coup in Moscow and the triumph of the Russian democrats."[51] At the end of the study, Brown concluded, "Tajikistan's economy was in decline before the country became independent; it worsened as a result of the political turmoil in 1992. Observers reported that Tajikistan's cotton crop, its major potential hard-currency earner, had been neglected while fighting raged in the cotton growing regions. One of the few points on which the conservative communists, who regained control of the Tajik government in December, and the democratic-Islamic opposition coalition agreed was that the country must attract foreign investment but to do so peace would have to be restored, and there was little prospect of an end to the civil war."[52] Ajay Patnaik quite strongly expressed his opinion about the nature and limitation of Islamic revivalism to provide an overarching identity to the Tajik people, leaving aside the prospect of whole Central Asia.[53] However, with time it was proved that some territories in Tajikistan became the seat of Islamic fundamentalism and there were specific, material reasons behind such developments. The stronghold of Islamic Fundamentalism was Kurgan Tyube region where the IRP was the most prominent, while the Gorno Badakhshan Autonomous Oblast in the Pamir mountain region had another variant of Islamic party *Lal-i-Badakhshani*, with an Ismaili orientation. The industrial and prosperous north zone of Khojent and Quliab were still under Communist influence. Thus, Tajikistan was riven by sharply polemical ideologies leading to factionalism.

Other than the fundamentalist trend there also was another, though not so prominent, milder variant of Islamic party, which was founded in 1989 by the Tajik writers and intellectuals, called the Rastokhez Popular Front. There was another similar kind of moderate Islamic Party, called Democratic Party of Tajikistan, founded in 1990. These organisations, while endorsing their faith in Islam and its revivalist spirit, decided to follow a democratic path in the political sphere and distinguished themselves from the fundamentalist uprisings.

The fundamentalist leaders of the IRP, namely Himatzade, Tursunzade and others repeatedly overstressed the steadfast faith of the Central Asian people in Islam. It was noted by Mohammed Sharif Himatzade on the eve of declaration of independence in Tajikistan, "For seventy five years the communists tried to wipe out the memory of Allah, but every Tajik today still remembers Allah and prays for the success of the party of Allah."[54] Yet, one must recognise the fact that at the hour of crisis, there arose moderate and democratic views to downplay the forces of fundamentalism and most remarkably, these forces were not attached to the communist *nomanklatura* either. This implied the fact that in between the two extreme forces struggling for power, there remained a milder and moderate variant of Islamic consciousness which wanted to proceed along democratic lines. It was, therefore, quite clear that in spite of the over-emphasis on Islamic fundamentalism in this territory, Islam was not a monolithic concept taken up uniformly by the general populace as an alternative ideology to combat the weak and distorted version of communism available in the entire zone. Most interestingly, among the five Central Asian states, only Tajikistan began as a communist regime, though, there the forces of Islam was the most vocal. Of course one should not attach too much significance to the communist principles of the communist leadership of Rakhmon Nabiev because it was the question of power that mattered in that hour of crisis and not principles. The Communist leadership used enough foul means and coercive methods to retain power and that kept the future of the state uncertain and protected the civil war. Rather, it was a kind of warlordism that continued in the region, sometimes in the name of Islam, sometimes in the garb of communism.

However, some scholars took up the issue of Islam irrespective of perestroika and Central Asia's unexpected independence and tried to show how it was a growing force in Central Asia from the 80s onwards which merely got openly recognised with change of outlook after perestroika and glasnost. Allen Hetmenek highlighted the number of riots taking place in Tajikistan in between 1986 and 1991, "The long series of demonstrations in the republic staged either by Islamic activists, as in Kurgan Tyube in October 1986, Kulyab in October 1989, a number of locations in Kurgan Tyube province throughout 1989, and in an undetermined site in February 1989, or with fundamentalist participation as in Dushanbe on February 24, 1989, and again in the same city in February 1990, were either overlooked, downplayed or not characterised as at least partially involving Islamic activism by specialists on Tajikistan or Central Aisa over all."[55] This trend towards Islamic fundamentalism only got intensified in the course of events. Even the comparatively moderate and democratic forces of Islam began to join the extremist programme of IRP in order to fight the communist regime. As Hetmenek pointed out, "Indeed, Rahmon Masov—an academician and until the autumn of 1991 a member of the governing presidium of one of these secular groups—the Rastokhez popular Front—revealed in an article in the Tajikistani newspaper *Narodnaya Gazeta* (people's newspaper) that he had resigned this position because his movement and the Tajikistan Democratic party, realising that they had too few members and too little power to confront the antocratic regime of Rakhmon Nabiev and the former communist party *nomanklatura*, compromised their democratic principles by entering into a coalition with the much stronger fundamentalist Islamic Revival Party and supporters of Kazi Akbar Turazhonzoda, the leading Islamic 'hierarch' of the republic and a widely respected public figure. Once involved in the anti-regime movement, the Islamic forces, in Masov's words became its 'mainspring'. Although the *Rastokhez Popular Front*, largely a movement of the intelligentsia, could field only 200 demonstrators, the Islamic Revival Party, having built up its infrastructure as an underground movement for well over a decade, was able to mobilise literally thousands of rural residents."[56] But the most remarkable incident was the shift of the Islamic—democratic party towards Nabiev, the Communist leader during the election in 1991. This shift in collaboration from one extreme to the other implied lack of commitment on part of the group. It became evident that the target for these people was rather to come closer to power than to Islam. But the extremist Islamic party too could not find a uniform goal for all Islamites. Though the IRP tried its best to set a 'common goal for the Central Asian Muslims', yet the prescribed norms of IRP showed an exclusive tendency, rather than inclusive. For example, noted Allen Hetmenek, that the party mainifesto of the IRP, as described by Sh. Abdullayev, a prominent leader of the group who was sentenced to jail for demanding theocracy in 1986, claimed again after coming out in 1990 that the Tajik Islam should be purified from all un-Islamic beliefs and practices which disregarded the indigenous pre-Islamic tenets of the region. Hetmenek read a clearcut tendency towards theocracy in the programme of IRP from 1990s, as he found, "With the passage of time, it became manifest that a theocracy was indeed a pragmatic objective of the Islamic Revival Party. Its chairman Mohammed Sharif Khimmatzoda, and vice-chairman, Davlat Usman, made this abundantly clear in public statements, still maintaining, however, that the route to this goal should not be through violent revolution but through a parliamentary regime and a referendum."[57]

At the same time Hetmenek highlighted the practical constraints for establishing a theocracy in the region because of the objection of the coalition partner of the IRP, the Democratic Party, whose leader Shadmon Yusupov referred to the advocacy of an Islamic republic as a 'delirium'.[58] However, that the notion of theocracy was not forced upon the people and was decided to be passed through parliamentary process itself showed the speciality of Tajik fundamentalism. More importantly, Ajay Patnaik highlighted that this party, though being the strongest in Tajikistan, did not envisage a 'supra-national' Islamic state for the Tajiks and was not prepared to do away with the national and ethno-racial identities by the all—encompassing 'common bond' of Islam. Ajay Patnaik stated that, "A number of Tajik intellectuals have expressed concern that any supra-national Islamic identity would be dominated by the Turkic speaking groups. Even one of the founders of the Tajikistan branch of the all-Union Islamic Revival Party (subsequently a separate party), Davlat Usmanov, showed no interest in creation a supra-national Islamic state. Apart from the fact that he considered such a state impracticable, Usmanov also saw it as undesirable. To him, it is significant that Muslims belong to different nationalities, and he thinks, "their national differences matter."[59] Again while giving an interview to a Russian newspaper, D. Usmanov made his opinion clear about establishing an Islamic state. He stated, "That (the character of the state) can only be decided by the people, and in no circumstances by the Party. We have no intention of attempting to establish a new system by force."[60] Thus Islamic revivalism had its impact limited by the clash of interests among different ethno-national and ethno-regional segments.

Moreover, the presence of Afghanistan at the border of the USSR as a free Islamic country who shared similar ethno-cultural heritage with the Islamic peoples of Central Asia had always been a cause of uneasiness and tension for the Soviet government and the Soviet republics of Central Asia. This uneasiness got heightened during the Soviet intervention in Afghanistan in 1979 in order to help a pro-Soviet faction to come to power. From that time onwards Soviet Union got entangled into a protracted conflict over the complex Afghan imbroglio where many Uzbeks and Tajiks fought on part of the Soviet government. At the same time, there was an opposite force unofficially working in the cross-border territories which percolated into and heightened the appeal of Islamic extremism in Soviet Central Asia.

The anti-Soviet faction of the Afghans in the Soviet-Afghan war called themselves 'mujahidins' which literally means soldiers for the cause of jihad. The Soviet regime being atheistic in principle was taken to be a land of the infidel and therefore the fight against the pro-Soviet camp was symbolised as a holy war or jihad by them. The influx of Afghan mujahidins was already a decade old phenomenon in Tajikistan when the turmoil of perestroika began in the mid 80s. The withdrawl of Soviet forces from Afghanistan in 1989 as part of Gorbachev's foreign policy brought a sudden change in the official Central Asian position towards the issue.

Here the situation of Tajikistan was the most vulnerable because of her geographical proximity as well as ethno-national linkages with the Afghan territories. In fact, the number of Tajiks residing in Afghanistan was more than the Tajik population of Tajikistan itself.[61] Barnet R. Rubin observed, "The conflict in Tajikistan developed out of two linked events: The dissolution of the Soviet Union as a result of the failed Moscow coup of 19th August, 1991 and the collapse of the Najibullah government in Afghanistan on 15 April, 1992." [62] Rakesh Gupta, Abha Dixit and many other strategic analysts, believed that the problems of Tajik civil war during the early 90s were accentuated to a large extent by the Afghan mujahidin influences. Writing in 1992, Abha Dixit had begun her article thus, "The Afghan civil war seems to have engulfed its first victim. Recent turmoil in the southern regions of neighbouring Tajikistan has given rise to fears that the area of destabilisation has increased dramatically"[63] Rakesh Gupta also prognosticated that, "It is the Iranians and the Afghans that may give the slogans for strengthening the cementing force of Islam now that the Marxist universal idea is discredited and on the retreat."[64] In fact, the presence of Afghan mujahidins willing to help any kind of anti-establishment uprising could be traced as early as

1980s. Their help was, of course, not limited to the provision of ideological encouragement in favour of Islamic state formation, but extended to material support such as supply of arms and amunitions as well as the organisation of an underground trade in drugs, etc. Thus, Afghanistan, the difficult neighbour of Tajikistan, which also shared a large number of ethno-cultural contiguity with the latter, made the situation far more complex. K. Warikoo observed, "And by the time the Soviet Union crumbled, an underground network of Islamic movements, arms dumped, and trained Islamic militants had positioned themselves in Tajikistan for launching the offensive to oust the remnants of the Communist system and establish an Islamic form of government. This is borne out by the subsequent events in Tajikistan which has witnessed the rise of the Islamic fundamentalist political parties and proliferation of armed bands resulting in bloody armed clashes between rival groups."[65]

At this hour of transition, Central Asia could have got overpowered by the traditional Islamic forces from Iran, Afghanistan and Pakistan, as was apprehended by many strategic analysts during the late 80s and early 90s. But Central Asian republics including Tajikistan still preferred to maintain their earlier bond with Russia as they all joined the CIS. Though this linkage was intended more for economic and strategic purposes than for any residual ideological hangover, this common bond of all Central Asian states indicated some kind of secular self-seeking without surrendering to any brand of available Islamic current. It also seemed quite interesting that the republic which was most prone to Islamic fundamentalism faced the gravest challenge from old communist *nomanklatura*. The other four republics also did not show any inclination to get entangled into the trouble-torn politics of Tajikistan. The apprehension of Islamic fundamentalism as a disturbing force could be sensed in the attitude of the Uzbek president Karimov as he stopped open correspondence between the people of the two centuries old neighbouring states, namely Uzbekistan and Tajikistan. The fundamentalist groups like Birlik, another unrecognised branches of the IRP in Uzbekistan, were strongly suppressed. The Kazakh republic under Nazarbaev or Turkmenistan and Kigizia under their respective rulers deployed a similar strategy towards any kind of extremist Islamic forces.

The very fact that the Islamic fundamentalism remained either as underground politics or as anti-establishment struggle implied the limited success of these forces. In spite of their strong network established and maintained secretly during the last phase of the Soviet rule, and the widening of their scope with the sudden and unexpected demise of the Soviet order, these groups could not fill in the power vacuum smoothly. They could only increase disturbances, put pressure and heighten tension in the whole region. Revival of Islam was an accepted phenomenon in the post-Soviet Central Asia, but the excesses of fundamentalist perceptions remained by and large superflous and therefore illegitimate in nearly every Central Asian Republic.

Eight

Quest for Identity Continues (Conclusion)

The identity politics of Soviet Central Asia thus reflect a very complicated scenario where various overlapping factors with their complex and contradictory pulls have made the situation completely indecisive. Apparently, the attempted superimposition of an artificial Soviet identity seemed to be the most unjust thing implemented on the Central Asian people from 'above'. As long as the Soviet Union survived, that identity never seemed to be very attractive or fulfilling for the people in general in this zone. Soviet identity at that time symbolised Russian big-brotherhood, economic exploitation, indirect disrespect to their religion and culture and direct threat to their attachment to the vernacular language. Throughout the Soviet history, Central Asian popular attitude showed a sincere attempt to maintain their indigenous identities, which always did not go in tune with the prescribed Soviet model. But at the same time, the Soviet system along with an imposed identity brought a number of material changes, which a substantial number of Central Asians did internalise. Therefore, the general attitude towards the Soviet rule was not one of outright rejection. There were indeed many areas of dissatisfaction and discontent which was quite understandable from the study of the complex context, in the previous chapters. However, when with an unexpected twist of history, this region was set free from the imposed Soviet yoke, it was found most vividly that their regional identities on their own showed no less complexity. This quest for identity on a new, uneasy platform thus begun, is still continuing.

The common tendency of Western scholarship was to see the development of Soviet identity and regional or indigenous identities as a dialectical process. Soviet identity, for its artificiality and imposed paramountcy was always seen as an obstacle to the growth of local indigenous identities of the republics. Soviet official stand on the other hand overestimated the level of acceptance of the Soviet identity in the non-Russian, as well as Russian regions. A very strong anti-regime attitude, firmly critical of the Soviet system, grew among the Russian intelligentsia from the late 70s who felt disgusted with the stagnation, corruption and lack of vision of the long Brezhnev era. Reflection of a similar attitude was quite normal among the non-Russian republics as well. Quite naturally, the discontent in the non-Russian areas took a different colour as the regime became apprehensive of secession. Yet, the similarity in the attitude of intellectuals in both Russian and non-Russian lands indicated the qualitative difference between a colonial empire and the Soviet multi-national state without denying the fact that the regime quite self-righteously claimed Russian superiority over the other races and thereby inculcated and encouraged the development of a kind of 'we-they' or even 'we versus they' syndrome among the non-Russian citizens. Here the Central Asian people in general seemed to be one of the most sensitive categories who were always eager to maintain their local identities. A very strong commitment to the indigenous culture, tradition, language and religion could distinguish them as a people or group of people engaged in a kind of self-preservation. Yet, at the same time, the attitude of these people towards 'Soviet' identity was not one of complete rejection. At least, in the later part of the Soviet rule, a kind of understanding developed where mostly the moderately educated citizens of the republics accepted the practical necessities of the Soviet attachments, the need of bilingualism, etc. Thus, though imposed from above, the 'Soviet' identity did percolate down to the popular mind with the passage of time and when it was once again withdrawn from above, republics had a mixed reaction. They could not rejoice in their unexpected independence. Rather, they tended to cling to the previous system, knowing fully well all its disadvantages. This apparent gesture of dependency resulted not only from political immaturity, but also from practical need and economic insufficiency. There was a feeling of helplessness on part of the Central Asian republics for being overtly dependent on the supply of food grains and grant of subsidies from the Centre, which suddenly got stopped with the demise of the USSR. In fact, an attitude of indignation towards the authorities (Moscow) began to surface during the perestroika years when the corruption in economic sphere began to be investigated and Central Asian cotton sphere seemed to be particularly inflicted by this evil. The Central

Asians began to react very sharply towards such accusations and took this as national insult (especially the Uzbeks). Intellectuals of all categories however had taken up a revisionist stand towards the regional republics or nationalities issues within the USSR and almost openly admitted that the Soviet state should have been more thoughtful in its dealing with the nationalities of the republics. However, the mistakes of more than half a century could not be corrected overnight and especially when such mistakes included lopsided economic planning which was the gravest political problem facing Soviet Union before its demise. In fact, economic reform was the primary reason for the initiation of perestroika. But even perestroika programmes failed to see the economic needs of the Central Asians from their perspectives. Therefore, the glasnost programme led to a series of emotional outbursts, which indicated mistrust on the regime. In spite of a large number of enlisted complaints against the regime, none of the speeches expressed any demand for independence. What they demanded was redressal—not desertion by the Centre.

However, as long as the Soviet state remained, the gravest challenge to the imposed Soviet identity was the Islamic attachment of the overwhelming majority of the population in the entire zone. The Western scholars strongly involved in the Cold War polemic or even otherwise preferred to identify these people with overlapping identities as 'Soviet Muslims'. In fact, the mouth-piece of the officially accepted strand of Islam in Soviet Union in the 70s, Mufti Muhammad Ziautdin ibn Ishan Babakhan also seemed quite comfortable with this 'Soviet Muslim' identity.

Thus, though the Soviet system tried to curb the religious influence in general and Islamic influence in particular by atheistic propaganda, the 'Muslim' identity remained strong enough to supercede all other national, regional, ethnic or linguistic attachments. However, the combination of Soviet and Muslim identities was unique as they had one marked commonness in them—both of them were supra-national in concept and therefore, encompassed a much broader territory with varied communities across ethnic, regional, linguistic or national compartments. The 'Soviet' identity also embarked upon a similar programme to accommodate different communities under its common umbrella without displacing the rest. Soviet system tried to accommodate national, ethnic, linguistic and regional identities to the extent and as long as they did not clash with the Soviet identity. The Soviet system even encouraged some of these identities as the linguistic identity of the Tajiks. But as long the Soviet regime continued in principle all these identities with their relative spheres of influence, were taken as subservient to the Soviet identity. Thus all the age-old socio-cultural attachments were dwarfed in front of the all-pervasive Soviet identity.

As long as the Soviet state continued, the Western critics showed much sympathy to these non-Russians, especially towards the backward and Muslim Central Asians. A hope remained ingrained in this literature throughout the Cold War state, that, given to themselves, these people would have flourished with all their indigenous facets in full form. A great disillusionment took place in this regard as the independence along with power vacuum and acute economic crisis brought tremendous confusion over different overlapping identities. This confusion at the time of indecision and political turmoil often led to collisions over ethnic, religious and other elements within the different communities residing in the vast region. The quest for identity at this hour of crisis did not seem to be a pleasant experience for the people of this broad multi-cultural zone.

The presence of several parallel identities is common in any given human community and in this Central Asia did not appear as an exception. But the tendencies of putting these identities in a hierarchical order with a sense of priority implied motivated use of identities for some other purpose—namely to acquire power. Thus different identities worked as essential components of power politics even within the indigenous people. Here Islam at the supra-national level and ethnicity at the sub-national level seemed to be the most potential elements in the identity politics of the region. Yet, none of these extremely sensitive attachments could bring an all encompassing cohesion in the entire region. On the contrary, these attachments, bringing emotional rigidity and irrationality, created deeper fragments at many places. Tajikistan was the most badly affected zone from this respect as the combination of various conflicting identities was the most unique in this smallest and poorest republic of Central Asia. Linguistic exclusivity and ethnic plurality, combined with various strands of Islam, created an extremely complex situation, aggravated more by the strong presence of the ex-Soviet (Communist) *nomanklatura* as a power bloc in Tajikistan. The problem of lopsided economic distribution on a regional basis had sharpened the polarity between different groups of people. The various groups who had so long enjoyed power and position as the Leninabadi group, people of

Quliab-Khojent-Hissar, and those who got overshadowed by the prominent section like the inhabitants of Qurgan-Tyube, and those who experienced outright denial of power and did not enjoy any economic benefit of the Soviet system like the Garmis, Badakshhanis-Pamiris and so on, all wanted to come to the limelight and became vocal during the time of this transition. For the Khojent-Quliab faction, the task was maintaining their power rather than the communist principles. For the rest it was the movement to snatch power in their own favour. But this power-game took an overtly ethno-religious character because of the use of these two strong identities to mobilise popular support in their own spheres by each leadership. Thus, in a complex situation, multi-layered identities were used against one another in order to accentuate the distinctions that led to sharp divisions along small territorial, regional, ethnic, even sub-ethnic lines. Thus the painful story of Tajikistan showed how the indigenous identities standing in juxtaposition caused fragmentation instead of consolidation within this newly independent state.

In fact, all the fifteen Soviet successor states faced the task of redefining their national identities from a new perspective. Each of them experienced several technical as well as practical problems in doing so. The five Central Asian republics also had to undergo this difficult process where religious revivalism and ethnic attachments along with linguistic distinctiveness (especially for the Uzbek and Tajik people) played decisive roles. Because of their exclusionist identities often tended to compartmentalise the nations instead of bringing cohesion. Thus, given to their absolute autonomy, each of the identities might have served the nation in a negative sense.

The extent of each and every identity ought to be carefully measured before blending them to compose a 'national' identity. At a time of excitement and chaos in Central Asia, an overdose of each element created imbalance in the composition of national identities. But, very interestingly, the revival of national identities did not imply any outright rejection of the Soviet identity. Rather, the mixed experience of the last seventy years under the Soviet rule was accepted as a *fait accompli*. In spite of the difficult relation with the dominant Russian big brothers, all the republics of Central Asia welcomed a formal link with the CIS. Within Central Asia, the power equation involved a sharp shift against the Russians residing in these territories. The question of 'Russian diaspora' became a new topic of discussion at the academic level. But at least, in Central Asia, in spite of the discrimination and domination by the Russians, the intolerance towards these non-indigenous Slavic communities were not as acute as their intra-tribal or intra-regional feuds.

As long as the Soviet regime existed, it was easier to blame the all-pervasive system for dwarfing the national and other identities of its people. The imagined authenticity of the Soviet identity based on a set of secular-socialist virtues imposed upon the entire USSR overshadowed the more intimate characteristics of this traditional society. The Soviet regime had genuine reasons to be blamed for its outright claim of creating the 'new Soviet man' committed to the socialist goal where all other attachments were supposed to become secondary. Independence of the republics from Soviet domination could prove that consolidation of national identities was a much more difficult process than it was thought to be. In their attempts to revive and create national identities, all the Central Asian states resembled many of the Third World countries inflicted by economic deficiencies and lopsided political power distribution. The experience of Soviet identity would work as an important memory in the future reorientation of these communities striving for a cohesive national definition. Therefore, with the demise of the Soviet system, Tajikistan found herself engulfed in a multi-dimensional complexity, where the creation of her present-day state-solidarity on the basis of past experiences became an immensely difficult task.

BIBLIOGRAPHY

Primary Sources (English)

Aitmatov, Chingis, Writer and Chairman of Kirgiz SSR's Writers Union, 155/4, *The Russian Empire: Its Nationalities Speak Out, The First Congress of People's Deputies, Moscow, 25 May to 10 June, 1984*. Edited and Translated by Oleg Glebov and John Crowfoot, Moscow, Harwood Academic Publishers, Apchur, London, Paris, New York, Melbourne, 1999.

Akhunov, Pulantdzan, Assistant School Headmaster Andhizhan Region, Uzbekistan (Young Communist League) 155, *The Russian Empire: Its Nationalities Speak Out, The First Congress of People's Deputies, Moscow, 25 May to 10 June, 1984*. Edited and Translated by Oleg Glebov and John Crowfoot, Moscow, Harwood Academic Publishers, Apchur, London, Paris, New York, Melbourne, 1999.

Andropov, Y.V., *Speeches, Articles, Interviews: A Selection*, Allied Publishers Private Ltd., New Delhi, etc. 1982.

Ataullah, Dodojon, (Interview) *Central Asian Monitor*, No. 3, 1995.

Brezhnev, L.I., *Socialism, Democracy and Human Rights*, Pergamon Press, Oxford, New York, Toronto, Sydney, Paris, Frankfurt, 1980.

Brezhnev, Leonid I., *Pages from his Life*, Allied Publishers Private Limited, New Delhi, Bombay, Calcutta, Madras, Bangalore, Hyderabad, 1979.

Brown, Bess., Central Asia: The First Years of Unexpected Statehood, *RFE/RL Research Report*, Vol. 2, No 1, January, 1993.

Brown, Bess., Central Asia, *RFE/RL Research Report*, Vol. 3, No 16. 22 April, 1994.

Brown, Bess., Central Asian States Seek Russian Help, *RFE/RL Research Report*, Vol. 2, No 25. 18 June, 1993.

Brown, Bess., Tajik Civil War Prompts Crack down in Uzbekistan, *RFE/RL Research Report*, Vol. 2, No 11. 12 March, 1993.

Brown, Bess., Tajikistan to Restore Presidency, *RFE/RL Research Report*, Vol. 3, No 31. 12 August, 1994.

Brown, Bess., Three Central Asian States Form Economic Union, *RFE/RL Research Report*, Vol. 3, No 3. 1 April, 1994.

Chernenko, K.V., *Socialist Peoples Power: Practical Prerequisites*, Novosti Press Agency Publishing House, Moscow, 1977.

Declaration of the Council of the Heads of the CIS Member States, *Strategic Digest* 23(6); June 1993.

FBIS–SOV–93–050, 17 March, 1993, End of Lawlessness Urged.

FBIS–SOV–93–067, 9 April, 1993, Abdullodzhanov Comments on Russia's 'Important Role'.

FBIS–SOV–93–119, 23 June, 1993, Prime Minister Interviewed on Economic Policy.

FBIS–SOV–93–119, 23 June, 1993, Tajik–Afghan Talks Held on Stabilisation, Refugees.

FBIS–SOV–93–130, 9 July, 1993, Tajik–Afghan Talks Held on Stabilisation, Refugees.

FBIS–SOV–93–156, 16 August, 1993, US Ambassador Meets Gorno–Badakhshan Representatives.

FBIS–SOV–93–163, 25 August, 1993, UN Envoy Favours Tajik–Afghan Summit.

FBIS–SOV–93–163, 25 August, 1993. People's Party Formed; Supports 'Evolutionary' Path,

FBIS–SOV–93–165, 27 August, 1993. Tension Persists on Afghan Border as Troops Rebuild,

FBIS–SOV–93–187, 29 September, 1993, Opposition Forces Reportedly Captures town.

FBIS–SOV–93–187, 29 September, 1993, Tajik Opposition Group Captured Along Afghan Border.

FBIS–SOV–93–188, 30 September, 1993, Abdullodzhanov Warns of Tough Economic Times Comining.

FBIS–SOV–93–188, 30 September, 1993, Opposition Commander Predicts Attacks on Dushanbe.

FBIS–SOV–93–202, 21 October, 1993.Troops, Killed in Battle With 'Islamic Opposition'.

FBIS–SOV–94–069, 11 April, 1994. Rakhmonov, Interviewed on Islamabad Visit.

FBIS–SOV–94–093, 13 May, 1994.Tajik, Refugees Return Home From Afghanistan.

FBIS–SOV–94–094, 16 May, 1994, Alimov Says Leadership Wants Peaceful Solution to 'Strife'.

FBIS–SOV–94–094, 16 May, 1994, More Nationals Return From Afghanistan.

FBIS, Vol. III (Soviet Union), 15 January, 1980, Ziautdin Mufti Muhammad., BABAKHAN.

Gorbachev, Mikhail, *Perestroika: New Thinking for Our Country and the World*, London, Collins, 1987.

Gorbachev, Mikhail, *Speeches and Writings*, Oxford: Pergamon, 1986.

Khrushchev, N.S., *Communist Construction and the Development of Revolution Theory*, Foreign Languages Publishing House, Moscow, 1961.

Khurshchev, N.S., *The National Liberal Movements, Selected Passages,* 1956–63, Foreign Languages Publishing House, Moscow, 1963.

Lenin, V.I., *Collected Works*, Progress Publishers, Moscow, Vol. 20, 21, 22, 23, 1977.

Makhamov, Kakhar, 1st Secretary of Communist Party Central Committee (territorial district Dushambe, Tajikistan) 153, *The Russian Empire: Its Nationalities Speak Out, The First Congress of People's Deputies, Moscow, 25 May to 10 June, 1984*. Edited and Translated by Oleg Glebov and John Crowfoot, Moscow, Harwood Academic Publishers, Apchur, London, Paris, New York, Melbourne, 1999.

Marx, K. and F. Engels, *Manifesto of the Communist Party*, National Book Agency, Indian Edition, April, 1993.

Marx, K. and F. Engels, *The First Indian War of Independence 1857–1859.* Progress Publishers, Moscow, 1959.

Marx, K., *Surveys from Exile: Political Writings*. Vol. 2, Penguin Books, London, 1973.

Marx, Karl and Frederich, Engels, *Collected Works*, Lawrence and Wishart, 1976, Vol.6–7, 8.

Masiliev, Abasmat, 1st Secretary of the Central Committee of the Kirgiz Communist Party territorial Deputy, Kirgizia) (speech) in *The Russian Empire: Its Nationalities Speak Out, The First Congress of People's Deputies, Moscow, 25 May to 10 June, 1984*. Edited and Translated by Oleg Glebov and John Crowfoot, Moscow, Harwood Academic Publishers, Apchur, London, Paris, New York, Melbourne, 1999.

Medvedenko, Leonid, *SWBI,* 30 January, 1980.

Niyazov, Sapurmurad (Speech), *The Russian Empire: Its Nationalities Speak Out, The First Congress of People's Deputies, Moscow, 25 May to 10 June, 1984.* Edited and Translated by Oleg Glebov and John Crowfoot, Moscow, Harwood Academic Publishers, Apchur, London, Paris, New York, Melbourne, 1999.

Olcott, Martha Brill, *The Soviet Multinational State, Reading and Documents*, M.E. Sharpe, Inc. Armonk, New York, London, England, 1990 (Translated Russian documents).

Soviet News, 5 July, 1989.

Stalin, Joseph, *Marxism and Nationalism*, Kanti Publication, Delhi, 1993.

Suslov, M.A., *Marxism-Leninism—The International Teaching of the Working Class*, Progress Publishers, Moscow, First Printing, 1975.

Topornin, Boris, *The New Constitution of the USSR*, Progress Publishers, Moscow, 1986.

Tuzumuhamedov, R., *How the National Question was Solved in Soviet Central Asia (A Reply to Falsifiers),* Progress Publishers, Moscow, 1973.

Umarkhodzhev, Mukhtar, Rector, Andhizhan Languages Teachers Training College, Andhizhan (national deputy – Uzbekistan) 155, *The Russian Empire: Its Nationalities Speak Out, The First Congress of People's Deputies, Moscow, 25 May to 10 June, 1984.* Edited and Translated by Oleg Glebov and John

Crowfoot, Moscow, Harwood Academic Publishers, Apchur, London, Paris, New York, Melbourne, 1999.

Yakubov, Adyl, 1st Secretary, Uzbek Writers Union, Tashkent (USSR Writers Union), 162, *The Russian Empire: Its Nationalities Speak Out, The First Congress of People's Deputies, Moscow, 25 May to 10 June, 1984*. Edited and Translated by Oleg Glebov and John Crowfoot, Moscow, Harwood Academic Publishers, Apchur, London, Paris, New York, Melbourne, 1999.

Ziyautdinkhan Mufti Ishan ibn., BABAKHAN, Chairman of the Muslim Religious Board for Central Asia and Kazakhstan (USSR), *Islam and the Muslims in the Land of Soviets*, Moscow, Progress Publishers, 1980.

Primary Sources (Russian Language)

News Papers Consulted

Bakinski Rabochi
Izvestia
Kommumist Tajikistana
Literaturnaya Gazeta
Nezavisimaya Gazeta
Pravda
Pravda Vostoka
Sovetskaya Kirgizia
Turkmenskaya Iskra

Secondary Sources (English)

Books

Akhmedov, Said., Tajikistan II: The Regional Conflict in Confessional and International Context, in Michael Waller, Bruno-Coppieters and Alexei Malashenko ed., Conflicting Loyalties and The State in Post-Soviet Russia and Eurasia, Frank Cass, London, Portland or, 1998.

Akiner, Shirin ed., Cultural Challenge and Continuity in Central Asia, Kegan Paul, London, 1971.

Akiner, Shirin., "Post-Soviet Central Asia: Past is Prologue", in Peter Ferdinand, Post-Soviet Central Asia, Pinter Publishers, London. 1994.

Akiner, Shirin., Islamic Peoples of the Soviet Union, Kegan Paul International, 1983.

Allworth, Edward., Central Asia: 120 Years of Russian Rule, Durham: Duke University Press, 1989.

Allworth, Edward., Central Asia: A Century of Russian Rule, Cambridge University Press, New York, (etc.) 1967.

Allworth, Edward., ed. The Nationality Question in Soviet Central Asia: Praeger, New York, 1973.

Anand, Jagjit Singh, M.P., Soviet Society and Communist Party, Sterling Publishers Pvt. Ltd., Year?

Anderson, Benedict., Imagined Communities: Reflections on the Origin and Spread of Nationalism, London: Verso, 1983.

Anderson, John., The International Politics of Central Asia, Manchester University Press, Manchester, New York, 1997.

Armstrong, John A., *Nations Before Nationalism*, Chapel Hill, N. C.: University of North Carolina Press, 1982.

Atkin, Muriel., "Tajikistan's Relations With Iran And Afghanistan", in Ali Banauzizi and Myron Weiner, ed. *The New Geopolitics of Central Asia and Its Borderlands*, I. B, Tauris, London, New York, 1994.

Banauzizi, Ali., and Weiner, Myron., ed. *The New Geopolitics of Central Asia and Its Borderlands*, I.B. Tauris, London, New York, 1994.

Bennigsen, Alexander & Wimbush, E., *Muslim National Communism in Central Asia*, The University Press, Chicago (etc.) 1980.

Bennigsen, Alexander., *Islam in the Soviet Union, Change and the Muslim World*, 1981.

Bergson, Abraham and Levine, Herbert S., *The Soviet Economy. Towards the yYear 2000,* George Allen and Unwin, London, Boston, Sydney, 1983.

Bialer, S., 'The Political System', in Robert F. Byrnes ed. *After Brezhnev,* Frances Pinter (Pub.), London, 1983.

Bialer, Seweryn., *Soviet Paradox-External Expansion, Internal Decline*, I.B. Tauris and Co. Ltd., London, 1986.

Bialer, Seweryn., *Stalin's Successors: Leadership, Stability and Change in the Soviet Union*, Cambridge University Press, Cambridge, London, etc., 1989.

Bloom, S., *The World of Nations: A Study of the National Implications in the Work of Karl Marx,* AMS Press, New York, 1967.

Bruchis Michael., "The Effect of the USSR's Language Polity on the National Languages of its Turkic Population" in Yaacov Ro'i ed., *The USSR and the Muslim World, Issues in Domestic and Foreign Policy*, George Allen and Unwin, London, Boston, Sydney, 1984.

Callinicos, Alex., *Marxism and the National Question,* East End Offset Ltd., London E 3, 1989.

Cohen, Stephen F., Rabinovitch, Alexander and Sharlet, Robert., ed., *The Soviet Union Since Stalin*, Bloomington, Indiana University Press, 1980.

Conquest, R., *The Harvest of Sorrow: Soviet Collectivisation and the Terror Famine*, Oxford University Press, New York, 1986.

Conquest, Robert, ed. *The Last Empire, Nationality and the Soviet Future,* Hoover Institution Press, Stanford University, 1986.

Conquest, Robert., Soviet Nationalities Policy in Practice, *Soviet Studies Series,* The Bodly Head Ltd., First Published in 1967.

Critchslov, Jones., *Nationalism in Uzbekistan: A Soviet Republic's Road to Sovereignty*, Boulders Co., Westview Press, 1992.

D'Encausse, Carrere. Helene, *Islam and the Russian Empire: Reform and Revolutions in Central Asia*, I.B. Tauris, London, 1988.

Dunlop, John B., 'Languages, Culture, Religion and National Awareness', in

Robert Conquest, ed., *The Làst Empire, Nationality and the Soviet Future*, Hoover Institution Press, Stanford University, Stanford, California, 1986.

Dunlop, J.B., *The Faces of Contemporary Russian Nationalism*, Princeton University Press, Princeton, N.J. 1983.

Dunlop, J.B., *The New Russian Nationalism*, Praeger Publishers, New York, 1985.

Dyker, David A., *The Future of the Soviet Economic Planning System*, Croom Helm, London and Sydney, 1985.

Ferdinand, Peter., *The New Central Asia and its Neighbours,* Royal Institute of International Affairs, Pinter Publishers London, 1994.

Fierman, W., ed., *Soviet Central Asia: The Failed Transformation*, Boulders, 1991.

Fletcher, William C., *The Russian Church Underground*, Oxford University Press, Oxford, 1973.

Gidadhubli, R.G., ed., *Socio-Economic Transformation of Soviet Central Asia*, New Delhi, 1987.

Gleason, G., *Federalism and Nationalism: The Struggle for Republican Rights in the USSR*, Boulder & Co. Westview Press, 1990.

Goldman, Marshal I., *What Went Wrong With Perestroika*? New York, W.W. Norton, 1991.

Great Soviet Encyclopedia, Macmilan Educational Corporation, 1980, USA, Vol. 23, 24.

Gross, J.A. ed., *Muslims in Central Asia: Expressions of Identity and Change*, Durham, 1992.

Haghayeghi, Mehradad., *Islam and Politics in Central Asia,* St. Martins Press, New York, 1995.

Harmstone, T.R., *Russia And Nationalism in Central Asia*, The John Hopkins, Press, Baltimore and London, 1970.

Harmstone, Teresa Rakowska, "Minority Nationalism Today: An Overview", in Robert Conquest, ed. *The Last Empire, Nationality and the Soviet Future*, Hoover Institution Press, Stanford University, Stanford., California, 1986.

Henze, Paul B., 'The Significance of Increasing Bilingualism among Soviet Muslims' in Y. Ro'I, ed. *The USSR and the Muslim World, Issues in Domestic and Foreign Policy*, London George Allen and Unwin, 1984.

Hiro, Dilip., *Between Marx and Muhammad: The Changing Face of Central Asia*, Harper Collins Publishers, London, 1994.

Hody, Cynthia A. & Carol Barner-Barry., *The Politics of Change*, St. Martins Press, New York, 1995.

Hosking, Geoffrey., *A History of the Soviet Union*, Fontana Press, Collins, 1985.

Hough, J.P., *Soviet leadership in Transition*, The Brookings Institution, Washington D.C., 1980.

Hough, Jerry F., *The Soviet Prefects: The Local Party Organs in Industrial Decision making*, Harvard University Press, Cambridge, Massachusetts, 1969.

Imam, Zafar ed., *Restructuring Soviet Society*, New Delhi, 1987.

Jalalzai, Musa Khan., *Central Asia, Political Situation and Economic Opportunities*, Polyglot, The Frontier Post Publications, 1980.

Karklins, Rasma., *Ethnic Relations in the USSR, The Perspective from Below,* Boston, Allen and Unwin, London, Sydney, 1986.

Kaushik, D., "Soviet Nationalities Policy in Central Asia", in R.G. Gigadhubli ed., *Socio-economic Transformation of Soviet Central Asia*, New Delhi, 1987.

Kaushik, Devendra., *Socialism in Central Asia: A Study in the Transformation of Socio-Ethnic Relations in Soviet Central Asia*, Allied Publishers Private Ltd. Bombay, New Delhi, Madras, Bangalore, 1970.

Keep, J., *Last of Empires*, Oxford University Press, 1995.

Kolakowski, Leszek., *Main Currents of Marxism,* Vol. II, Oxford University press, 1982.

Kolstoe, Paul., *Russians in the Former Soviet Republics,* Hurst & Com., London, 1995.

Lane, David., *Soviet Economy and Society*, Basil Blackwell, Oxford, 1985.

Lewin, Moshe., *Lenin's Last Struggle,* Monthly Review Press, New York and London,1968.

Lowrie, Donald A. & Fletcher William C., 'Krushahev's Religious Policy, 1959-1964', in Richard H. Marshall Jr. *et al.*, eds., *Aspects of Religion in the Soviet Union, 1917-1967*, Chicago, 1971.

Lubin, N., *Labour and Nationality in Soviet Central Asia: An Uneasy Compromise*, London and Basingstoke, 1984.

Mcauley, Alastair., 'Economies of Central Asia' in Yaacov Ro'i ed., *Muslim Eurasia: Conflicting Legacies*, Frank Cass, London, 1995.

Mcville, Andrei & Lapidus, Gail W., ed., *The Glasnost Papers*, Westview Press, Boulders, San-Francisco, Oxford, 1990.

Medvedev, Zhores., *Andropov,* Basil Blackwell, Oxford, England, 1983.

Motyl, Alexander J., *Will the Non-Russians Rebel? State, Ethnicity and Stability in the USSR*, Cornell University Press, Ithaca and London, 1987.

Munk, Ronaldo., *The Difficult Dialogue, Marxism and Nationalism*, Zed Book Ltd., 1986.

Niyavzov, Pavel., *Tajikistan*, Novosti Press Agency Publishing House, 1979.

Niyazi, Aziz., Tajikistan I: The Regional Dimension of Conflict, in Michael Waller, Bruno -Coppieters and Alexei Malashenko, ed., *Conflicting Loyalties and the State in Post-Soviet Russia and Eurasia*, Frank Cass, London, Portland or, 1998.

Olcott, M.B., *Central Asia's New States: Independence, Foreign Policy and Regional Security,* Washington, 1996.

Olcott, Martha Brill., with Lubomyr Hajda and Anthony Olcott, ed., *The Soviet Multinational State, Readings and Documents*, M.E. Sharpe, Inc. Armonk, New York, London, England, 1990.

Pandita, K.N., Language and Culture in the Politics of Tajikistan, in K. Warikoo, ed., *Central Asia, Emerging New Order*, Har-Anand Publications, 1995.

Patnaik, Ajay., *Central Asia: Between Modernity and Tradition*, Konark Publishers, Pvt. Ltd., 1996.

Pipes, Richard., *The Formation of the Soviet Union: Communism and Nationalism, 1917-1923*, Harvard University Press, Cambridge, 1955.

Rahman, Azizur and Ghai, Dharam., *Collective Agricultire and Rural Development in Soviet Central Asia*, London, 1979.

Raleigh, Donald J., ed., *Soviet Historians and Perestroika*, M.E. Sharpe, Inc. Armonk, New York, London, England, 1988.

Rashid, Ahmed., *The Resurgence of Central Asia, Islam or Nationalism*? Oxford University Press (Karachi), 1994.

Ro'i, Yaacov., 'The Impact of the Islamic Fundamentalist Revival of the Late 1970s on the Soviet View of Islam', in Y. Ro'I, ed., *The USSR and the Muslim World: Issues in Domestic and Foreign Policy*, London: George Allen and Unwin, 1984.

Ro'i, Yaacov., ed., *Muslim Eurasia: Conflicting Legacies*, Frank Cass, London, 1995.

Rothschild, Joseph., *Ethno-politics: a Conceptual Framework*, New York, 1981.

Rumer, Boris Z., *Soviet Central Asia, A Tragic Experiment*, Boston, 1989.

Rywikin, Michael., *Moscow's Muslim Challenge*, M.E. Sharpe, inc. Armonk, New York, 1990.

Rywikin, Michael., 'National Symbiosis: Vitality, Religion, Identity, Allegience', in Y. Ro'I, ed., *The USSR and the Muslim World: Issues in Domestic and Foreign Policy*, London: George Allen and Unwin, 1984.

Shams Ud Din, 'Soviet Language Policy: Change in Script of Central Asian Languages and its Impact on Nationalities Question', in Shams Ud Din, ed., *Perestorika and Nationalities Question in the USSR*, New Delhi: Vikas, 1990.

Shams Ud Din, *Secularisation in the USSR*, New Delhi, Vikas, 1982.

Sharma, R.R., *Soviet Central Asia: A Marxist Model for Social Change*, New Delhi: Macmillan, 1979.

Shevtsov, Victor., *The State and Nations in the USSR*, Progress Publishers, Moscow, 1982.

Simmonds, G.W., ed. *Nationalism in the USSR and Eastern Europe in the Era of Brezhnev and Kosygin*, Detroit, 1977.

Simon, Gerhard., *Nationalism and Policy Toward the Nationalities in the Soviet Union. From Totalitarian Dictatorship to Post-Stalin Society*, West-View Press, Boulders, San Fancisco, Oxford, 1991.

Smith, Graham., ed., *The Nationalities Question in the Soviet Union*, Longman, London and New York, 1990.

Smith, Graham., Law, Vivien, Wilson, Anadrew Borh-Annettee and Allworth, Edward., *Nation—building in the Post-Soviet Borderlands: The Politics of National Identities*, Cambridge University Press, Cambridge, 1998.

Spuler, Bertold., *Central Asia Under Russian Rule. The Muslim World: A Historical Survey*, Part IV, Modern Times, *Fascicule 1*, Translated and Adapted by F.R.C. Bagle, Leiden, 1981.

Tajik Soviet Socialist Rupublic, Novosti Press Agency Publishing House, Moscow, 1972. (Anonymous).

Tishkov, Valery., *Ethnicity, Nationalism and Conflict in and After the Soviet Union: The Mind Aflame*, Sage Publication, Landon, Prio and Unrisd, 1997.

Tishkov, Valey., Russians in Central Asia and Kazakhstan, in Yaacov Ro'I, ed., *Muslim Eurasia: Conflicting Legacies*, Frank Cass, London, 1995.

Volcogonov, Dmitri., *Rise and Fall of the Soviet Empire*, Harper Collins 1998.

Voll, John Obert., Soviet Central Asia and China: Integration or Isolation of Muslim Societies, in John L. Esposito, ed., *Islam in Asia: Religion, Politics and Society*, Oxford University Press, 1987.

Waller, Michael., Coppieters Bruno and Malashenko Alexei, ed., *Conflicting Loyalties and the State in Post-Soviet Russia and Eurasia*, Frank Cass, London, Portland, or 1998.

Warikoo, K., Cockpit of Central Asia: Afghanistan Factor in Tajikistan's Crisis, in K. Warikoo, ed., *Central Asia: Emerging New Order*, Har Anand Publications, 1995.

Williams, Christopher, and Sfikos, Thanaris D., ed. *Ethnicity and Nationalism In Russia: The CIS and the Baltic States*, Ashgate, Broofield, 1999.

Zarcone, Theirry., Sufi Movements: Search for Identity and Islamic Resurgence, in K. Warikoo, ed., *Central Asia Emerging New Order*, Har Anand Publications 1995.

Zasalavskaya, Tatyana., *The Second Socialist Revolution: An Alternative Soviet Strategy*, I.B. Tauris and Co. Ltd., London, 1990.

Zaslavsky, Victor., *The Neo-Stalinist State, Class, Ethnicity and Consensus in Soviet Society*, M.E. Sharpe, Inc. The Harvester Press, New York, 1982.

Journals

Abdukholikov, Yokubjon., The Social Condition of Rural Women in Tajikistan, *Central Asia Monitor*, No. 2, 2000.

Adams, Jan S., Institutional Change in the 1970s: The Case of the USSR People's Control Committee, *Slavic Review*, Vol. 37, 1978.

Adams, Jan S., Institutional Change in the 1970s: the Case of the USSR People's Control Committee, *Slavic Review*, 1978.

Akbarzadeh, Shahram., The Political Shape of Central Asia", *Central Asian Survey*, 16(4), 1997.

Akcali, Pinar., "Islam as a 'Common bond' in Central Asia: Islamic Renaissance Party and the Afghan Mujahidin", *Central Asian Survey*, 1998, 17(2).

Alici, Didem Mersin., The Role of Culture, History and Language in Turkish National Identity Building: an overemphasis on Central Asian roots, *Central Asian Survey*, 15(2), 1996.

Amalrik, Andrei., Will the USSR Survive Until 1984? *Survey* (Editor, Leopold Labedz), Autumn, No. 73, 1967.

Anderson, John., Constitutional Development in Central Asia, *Central Asian Survey*, 16(3), 1997.

Atkin, Muriel., The Survival of Islam in Soviet Tajikistan", *Middle East Journal*, Vol. 43, No. 4, Autumn, 1989.

Bennigsen, Alexander., Islam in Retrospect, *Central Asian Survey*, 1987.

Browning, Gary L. and Rogers, Thomas F., Chingiz Aitmatov's The Executioner's

Block: Through Dreams a Confrontation with Existential Good and Evil, *The Russian Review*, Vol. 51, No. 1, January, 1992.

Central Asia Review, Islam in Central Asia: Recent Soviet Writings, 1962.

Central Asia Review, Nationalism in the Soviet Muslim Republics, 1959.

Central Asia Review, The People of Central Asia: Past and Present Distribution, 1959.

Central Asia Review, The People of Central Asia: The Survival of Religion, 1959.

Central Asia Review, The Peoples of Central Asia: Cultural Development, 1960.

Central Asia Review, The Peoples of Central Asia: Social Customs, 1959.

Central Asia Review, The Basmachis, 1959.

Central Asia Review, The National Question At the XXIInd Congress of the CPSU, 1962.

Chakravartty, Sumit., Russian and Central Asia, *World Focus* 14 (34-38), March-April, 1993, Special Issue.

Clowes, Edith W., "Ideology and Utopia in Recent Soviet Literature", *The Russian Review*, Vol. 51, No. 3, July, 1992.

Daulet, Shafiga., The First All Muslim Congress of Reussia, Moscow, 1-11 May, 1917, *Central Asian Survey*, Vol. 8, No. 1, 1989.

Demchenko, P., Iran takes a new Road, *International Affairs*, Moscow, No. 10. October, 1979.

Dixit, Abha., Tajikistan: Engulfed by Flames of Afghan Civil War, *Strategic Analysis* 15(9); December, 1992.

Dyker, David A., Industrial Location in the Tadzhik Republic", *Soviet Studies*, Vol. 21, 1969-70.

Educating, Atheists., Fizika V Shkole, *Soviet Education*, iasp, A Journal of Translations, Vol. XVI, No. 3, January, 1974. (Anonymous).

Fisher, Wesley A., Ethnic Consciousness and Intermarriage: Correlates of Endogamy Among The Major Soviet Nationalities, *Soviet Studies*, Vol. XXIX, No. 3, July, 1977.

Foltz, Richard., The Tajiks of Uzbekistan, *Central Asian Survey*, 15(2), 1996.

Gitelman, Zvi., Are Nations Merging in the USSR? *Problems of Communism*, September-October, 1983.

Gooding, John, Perestroika as Revolution from Within: An Interpretation, *The Russian Review*, Vol. 51, No. 1, January, 1992.

Guangcheng, Xing., An analysis of the internal and foreign politics of the newly independent countries in the Central Asian region, *Foreign Affairs Journal* (26); December, 1992.

Gupta, Rakesh, Tajikistan: Locked Horns for Power", *Strategic Analysis*, 15(6); Sept., 1992.

Haberkern, E., On Roman Rodolsky as a guide to the Politics of the Neue Reinsche Zeitung, *Science and Society*, Vol. 63, No. 2, Summer, 1999.

Haghayeghi, Mehrdad, Politics of Privatisation in Kazakstan, *Central Asian Survey*. 16(3), 1997.

Hajda, Lubomyr., "Nationality and Age in Soviet Population Change", *Soviet Studies*, Vol. XXXII No. 4, October, 1980.

Halbach, Uwe., "World Politics and Indigenous Development in Central Asia", *Aussen Politik*, 43(4); 1992.

Harmstone, Teresa Rakowska., "The Dialectics of Nationalism in the USSR", *Problems of Communism*, May—June, 1974.

Hauner, Milan., "Central Asian Geopolitics in the Last Hundred Years: A Critical Survey from Gorchakov to Gorbachev", *Central Asian Survey*, Vol. 8, No. 1, 1989.

Hetmenek, Allen., "Islamic Revolution and Jihad Came to the Former Soviet Central Asia: the Case of Tajikistan", *Central Asian Survey*, 1993, 12(3).

Jones, Ellen and Grupp, Fred W., "Modernisation and Ethnic Eqalisation in the USSR", *Soviet Studies*, Vol.—36. No. 2, April, 1984.

Karpat, Kemel., "The Old & New Central Asia", *Central Asian Survey*, Vol. 2 No. 4, 1993.

Khodjibaeva, Moukhabbat., "Television and the Tajik Conflict", *Central Asia Monitor*, No. 1, 1999.

Kirkwood, Michael., "Glasnost: the National Question and Soviet Language Policy", *Soviet Studies*, Vol. 43, No. 1, 1991.

Kothari, Raj Kumar., "CIS in the nineties and beyond", *Link* 35(8), September, 13, 1992.

Kreindler, Isabella., "The Soviet Deported Nationalities: A Summary and Update ", *Soviet Studies*, Vol. 38, No. 3, July, 1986.

Lowy, Michael., "Marxists and the National Question", *New Left Review*, No. 96., 1976.

Medvedenko, Leonid., 'Islam: two trends", *New Times*, No. 13, March, 1980.

Mesbahi, Mohiaddin., "Russia and the new Muslim states: Change or Continuity?" *Central Asian Survey,* 12(2), 1993.

Mesbahi, Mohiaddin., "Russian Foreign policy and security in Central Asia and The Caucasus", *Central Asian Survey* 12(2), 1993.

Miller, John H., "Cadre Policy in Nationality Areas", *Soviet Studies*, Vol. XXIX, No. 1. January, 1977.

Miller. John H., "Cadres Policy in Nationality Areas", *Soviet Studies*, Vol. XXXIX No. 1., January, 1977.

Moses, Joel C., "Regionalism in Soviet Politics, Continuity as a Source of Change, 1953-1982", *Soviet Studies,* Vol. XXXVII, No. 2, April 1985.

"Moslems in The Soviet Union", *Asia and Africa Today*, No. 5, Sept. Oct., 1980.

Mukherjee, Asoke., "Ethnicity, Geopolitical Entity", *World Focus*, 14(3-4), March—April, 1993, Special Issue.

Muslims of the Soviet East, No. 3, 1978.

Naby, Eden., "Ethnicity and Islam in Central Asia", *Central Asian Survey*, Vol. 12, 1993.

Naby, Eden., "Bobodzhon Gafurovich Gafurov, 1908-1977", *Slavic Review* No. 2, June 1978.

Newth, J.A., "The 1970 Soviet Census", *Soviet Studies*, Vol. XXIV, No. 2, October, 1972.

Nourzhanov, Kirill., "Seeking Peace in Tajikistan: Who Is The Odd Man Out?" *Central Asia Monitor*, No. 6, 1998.

Nove, A., "History., Hierarchy And Nationalities: Some Observations on the Soviet Social Structure", *Soviet Studies*, Vol. XXIX, No. 3, July, 1977.

Olcott, M.B., "Central Asia's Catapult to Independence" *Foreign Affairs*, 71(3), Summer 1992.

Olcott, Martha Brill., "Yuri Andropov And The 'National Question'", *Soviet Studies*, Vol. XXXVII, no. 1, January 1985.

Olcott, Martha Brill., "The Basmachi or Freemen's Revolt in Turkestan, 1918-24", *Soviet Studies*, Vol. XXXIII, No. 3, July, 1981.

Palat, Madhavan K., "Forms of Union, Russian Empire and The Soviet Union", Address of the Sectional President, Countries Other Than India, Proceedings of the Indian History Congress, 52nd Session, New Delhi, 1991-92.

Polat, Abdumannob., "Karimov's Carrot And Stick Policy Towards Uzbek Muslims", *Central Asia Monitor*, No. 2, 2000.

Raeff, Marc., "What Became of the Liberal Tradition?—Comments on Samosoznanie", *Slavic Review*, Vol. 37, No. 1 March, 1978.

Rigby, T.H., "The Soviet Regional Leadership: The Brezhnev Generation", *Slavic Review*, No. 1. March, Vol. 37, 1978.

Ritter, William S., "The Final Phase in the Liquidation of Anti-Soviet Resistance in Tadzhikistan: Ibrahim Bek and the Basmachi, 1924-31", *Soviet Studies*, October, 1985.

Ro'i, Yaacov., "The Task of Creating The New Soviet Man: Atheistic Propaganda In The Soviet Muslim Areas, *Soviet Studies*", Vol. 36, 1984.

Rubin, Barnett R., "The Fragmentation of Tajikistan", *Survival*, (34-4); Winter, 1993-94.

Saunders, Harold H., "The Inter-Tajik Dialogue within The Framework of The Dartmouth Conference", *Central Asia Monitor*, No. 4, 1997.

Schaeberlein-Engel, John., "The prospects For Uzbek Nationl Identity", *Central Asia Monitor*, No. 2, 1996.

Shahrani, Nazif., "Central Asia and the Challenge of the Soviet Legacy", *Central Asian Survey*, 12(2), 1993.

Shirazi, Habibollah Abolhassan., "Political Forces and Their Structures in Tajikistan", *Central Asian Survey*, 16(4), 1997.

Silver, Brian D., "Bilingualism and Maintenance of the Mother Tongue in Soviet Central Asia", *Slavic Review* (Editor: James R. Millar, University of Illinois at Urbana Champaign), Vol. 35, 1976.

Silver, Brian D., "Ethnic Intermarriage And Ethnic Consciousness Among Soviet Nationalities", *Soviet Studies*, Vol. XXX, No. 1, January, 1978.

Silver, Brian D., "The Status of National Minority Languages in Soviet Education: an assessment of recent changes", *Soviet Studies*, January, 1974.

Sjoberg, Andree F., "Language Structure and Cultural Identity: a historical perspective on the Turkic Peoples of Central Asia", *Central Asian Survey*, 1993, 12(4).

Slider, Darrell., "A Note On The Class Structure of Soviet Nationalities", *Soviet Studies*, Vol. XXXVII, No. 4, October 1985.

Subtelny, Maria Eva., "The Cult of Holy Places: Religious Practices Among Soviet Muslims", *Middle East Journal*, Vol. 43, No. 4, Autumn, 1989.

Susokolov, A A., "The Influence on Interethnic Relations of Differences in the Educational Levels and the Number of Ethnic Groups in Contact", *The Soviet Review*, Vol. 18, No. 1, Spring 1977.

Tolmacheva, M.A., "The Muslim Woman in Soviet Central Asia", *Central Asian Survey*, 1993, 12(4).

Vasileyev, A., "Islam in the Present Day World", *International Affairs*, Moscow, No. 11, November, 1981.

Volobuev, P.V., "Perestroika and the October Revolution in Soviet Historiography", *The Russian Review*, Vol. 51, No. 4, October, 1992.

Zwick, Peter., "Ethnoregional socio-economic fragmentation and Soviet Budgetary Policy", *Soviet Studies*, Vol. XXXI, No. 3, July, 1979.

Secondary Sources (Russian Language)

Arutunian, Iu.V., "Ethnosocial Aspects of the Internationalisation of the Way of Life" (Etnosotsialnie Aspectii Internatisionalisatsii Obraza Zhizni), *Sovetskaya Etnografia*, No. 2, March -April, 1979.

Arutunian, Iu.V., "On Certain Trends in a Nation's Cultural Pattern", (O Nekotorikh Tendentsiyakh v Izmenenii Kulturnov Oblika Natsii), *Sovetskaya Etnografia*, Vol. 4, June-August, 1974.

Arutunian, Iu.V., "Social-Cultural Aspect of the Development And Mutual Raprochment of Nationalities in the USSR" (Sotsialno-Kulturniie Aspektii Razvitia i sblizheniya Natsii v SSSR) *Sovetskaya Etnografia,* Vol 3, May-June, 1972.

Arutuniyan, Iu.V., "On Some Tendencies in the Changing Cultural Patterns of The People of USSR at the Stage of Developing Socialism" (O Nekotoriikh Tendentsiakh Kulturnovo Sblizheniya Narodov SSSR Na Etape Razvitogo Sotsializma), *Istoria SSSR,* No. 4, July-August. 1978.

Bromlei, Iu V., "Ethnographical Studies in the Contemporary Nationalities Processes in the USSR", (Ethnograficheskoe Izuchenie Sovremennikh Natsionalnikh Protsessov v SSSR), *Sovetskaya Etnografia*, No. 2, March-April, 1983.

Bromlei, Iu.V., "International and National Trends in the Building of Socialism", (Enternatsionalnoe i Natsionalnoe v Stroitelstve Sotsializma), *Sovetskaya Etnografia*, Vol. 5, Sept.-Oct., 1977.

Bromlei, Iu.V., "Towards The Study of National Processes of Socialist Society in The Context of Ethnic History" (K Izucheniyu Natsionalnikh Protsessov Sotsialisticheskogo Obshestva v Kontekste Etnicheskoi Istorii), *Istoria SSSR*, No. 6, 1984.

Bromlei, Iu V., "Basic Tendencies of Nationalities Process in the USSR" (Osnovniie tendentsii natsionalnikh protsessov v SSSR), *Sovetskaya Etnografia*, No. 6, November-December 1982.

Bromlei, Iu.V., "International and National in the Making of Socialism", (Internatsionalnoe i Natsionalnoe v Stroitelstve Sotsializma), *Sovetskaya Etnografia*, No. 5, September-October, 1977.

Bromlei, Yu.V., Kozlov, V.I., "Towards the Study of Present Ethnic Processes in the Sphere of the Spiritual Culture of the People of USSR, (Izuchenioo Sovremennikh Etnicheskikh Protsessov v Sfere Dukhovnoi Kulturii Narodov SSSR), *Sovetskaya Etnografia*, Vol. 1, January-February, 1975.

Bruk, S.I., Gubolgo, "Ethnic-Social Aspects of Bilingualism in the USSR" (Faktorii Rasprostraneniya Dvuyazichnya i Narodov SSSR), *Sovetskaya Etnografia*, No. 5, September-October, 1975.

Bruk, S.I., Gubolgo M.N., "Bilingualism and Coming Together of Nations in the USSR" (Dvuyazichie i Sblizhenie Natsii V. SSSR), *Sovetskaya Ethnografia*, Vol. 4, June-August, 1975.

Cheshko, S.V., "Nationality Question in the USSR: The Conditions and Perspectives of its Study". (Natsionalni Vopros v SSSR: Sostoyanie i Perspectivi Izuchenia), *Sovetskaya Etnografia*, No. 4, 1988.

Dankovskii, Iu.V., "International Significance of Soviet Experience in Solving the National Problem", (Internatsionalnoe Znachenie Opita Reshenia Natsionalnovo Voprosa v SSSR), *Sovetskaya Etnografia*, Vol. 4, June-August, 1972.

Drobizherva, L.M., "National Self-Awareness: The Basis on Which It is Formed and the Sociocultural Factors Stimulating Its Development", (Natsionalnoe Samosoznanie: Baza Formirovaniya i Sotsialno-Kulturniie Stimulii Razvitiya) Sovetskaya Etnografia, 1985, No. 5, Russian text by 'Nauka' Publishers, compiled in, M.B. Olcott ed. *The Soviet Multinational State Reading and Documents*, M.E. Sharpe, Inc., Armonk, New York, London, England, 1990.

Drobizheva, L.M., "More Democracy", (Politicheskoe Obrazovanie), 1988, No. 3, translated article in M.B. Olcott ed. *The Soviet Multinational State Reading and Documents*, M.E. Sharpe, Inc., Armonk, New York, London, England, 1990.

Drobizheva, L.M., "The Drawing Together of Cultures and Inter-ethnic Relations in the USSR", (Sblizhenie Kultur i Mezhnatsionalniye Otnosheniya v SSSR), *Sovetskaya Etnografia* Vol. 5, September-October, 1977.

Drobizheva, L.M., "Role of Education and Cultural Perspective in Interpersonal Relations Among Nationalities (Dukhovnaia Obshchnost' Narodav SSSR), Moscow 1981, Russian Text 1981 by 'Mysl' compiled in, M.B. Olcott ed. *The Soviet Multinational State Reading and Documents*, M.E. Sharpe, Inc., Armonk, New York, London, England, 1990.

Dzhariilgasinova, R. Sh., "Theory of Ethnic Consciousness in the Soviet Ethnographical Science" (Teoria Etnicheskogo Samosozhnania v Sovetskoi Etnograficheskoi Nauke), *Sovetskaya Etnografia*, No. 4, July-August, 1987.

Ekkel, B.M., "An Index for Evaluating the Mosaic Character of Ethnic Settlement in the Republics, Karys and Oblasts of the USSR", (Opredelenie Indeksa Mozaichnost Natsionalnovo Sostava Respublik, Kraev i Oblastei SSSR), *Sovetskaya Etnografia*, No. 2, March-April, 1972.

Gorinov, M.M., "Alternatives in the Crisis Period of NEP" (Alternativii i Krizusii v Period NEPa), *Voprossi Istorii KPSS*, No. 1, January, 1990.

Gurvich, I.S. "Ethnocultural Drawing Together of the Peoples of the USSR" (Ethnokulturnoe Sblizhenie Narodov SSSR), *Sovetskaya Etnografia*, No. 6, November-December, 1977.

Gurvich, I.S., "Modern Trends In Ethnic Processes in the USSR" (Sovremenniye Napravleniya Etnicheskikh Protsessov v SSSR), *Sovetskaya Etnografia*, Vol. 4, June-August, 1972.

Iasnov, M.A., "Constitutional Autonomies In The Republic of Russian Federation" (Konstitutsii Avtonomnikh Respublik Rossiiskoi Federatsii), *Sovetskoe Gosudarstvo i Pravo*, No. 9, 1979.

Ismailov, Hasan., "Reply to the Soothsayers", *Nauka i Religia*, No. 1, 1980.

Iuvlei, Slavnyi., "Towards the 50th Anniversary of the Central Asian Republics", (K Priyatidesiatiletiu Obrazovania Respublik Srednei Azii), *Sovetskaya Etnografia*, No. 5, September-October, 1974.

Kassyanenko, V.I., "Some Questions Of Historiography in the Development of Socialism In The USSR". (Nekotorie Voprossi Istoriografii Razvitogo Sotsializma v SSSR), *Voprossi Istorii*, No. 8, August 1976.

Krukov, M.V., "Soviet Ethnografical Science Needs Restructuring" (Sovetskaya Ethnograficheskaya Nauka Nuzhdaetsya v Perestroike), *Sovetskaya Etnografia*, No. 1, 1988.

Kulichenko, M.I., "Leading Role of CPSU in Ensuring the Blossoming and Drawing Together of Nations" (Rukovodiyashaya Rol KPSS v Obespechenii Rastsveta i Sblizheniya Natsii), *Voprossi Istorii*, Vol. 2, 1974.

Kulichenko, M.I., "Socio-Economic Basis of Mutual Influence and Mutual Enrichment of National Culture in the Development of Socialism", (Sotsialno-Economicheskie Osnovii Vzaimovliyaniya i Vzaimoobogasheniya Natsionalnikh Kultur v Usloviyakh Razvitovo Sotsializma), *Voprossi Istorii*, Vol. 5, 1977.

Lushkevich, F.D., "Tradition of Inter-Family Relation of Uzbek—Tajik Population In Central Asia",(Traditsii Mezhsemeiniikh Sviyazii Uzbeksko-Tadzhikskovo Naseleniya Srednei Azii), *Sovetskaya Etnografia*, Vol. 4, July-August, 1989.

Markov, G.E., "The Socialist Way of Life and Problems of Ethnography" (Sovetskii Obraz Zhizni i Problemii Etnografii), *Sovetskaya Ethnografia*, No. 2, March-April, 1976.

Monogarova, L.F., "Structures of Modern Urban Family of the Tajiks: on the basis of cities of Ura-Tyube and Isfara" (Struktura Sovremennoi Gorodskoi Semii Tadzhikov) *Sovetskaya Etnografia*, 1982, No. 3, ISSNOO38-5050.

Ostapenko, L.V. and Suskolov A.A., "The Interregional Mixing And National Composition of Labour Resources" (Sto Natsii i Narodnostei: Etnodemograficheskoe razvitie SSSR) Moscow, 1985, Russian text compiled in, M.B. Olcott ed. *The Soviet Multinational State Reading and Documents*, M.E. Sharpe, Inc., Armonk, New York, London, England, 1990.

Pestiriakov, A.P., "Anthropological Studies of Some Groups of People of Tajikistan and Uzbekistan", (Antropologicheskoe Issledovanie Nekotoriikh Grupp Naseleniya Tadzhikistana i Uzbekistana), *Sovetskaya Etnografia*, No. 1 January-February 1975.

Pimenov, V.V., "Preparation of Professional Ethnografers: Problems of Restructuring" (Podgotovka Profesionalnovo Etnografa: Problemii Persestroiki), *Sovetskaya Etnografia*, No. 3, 1988.

Ponomarev, V.N., "Some Problems of Historical Experiences of the KPSS and Contemporary (Situation)" (Nekotoriie Problemii Istoricheskogo Opiita KPSS i Sovremnnost), *Voprossi Istorii KPSS,* No. 4, 1988.

Sdanko, T.A., "The Delimitation of Nationalities and States and Processes of Ethnic Development Among the People of Middle Asia". (Natsionalno-Gasudarstvennoe Narodov Sriyedi Azii), *Sovetskaya Etnografia*, Vol. V, September-October, 1972.

Shafir, M.A., "Mutual Relation Among the Highest Organs of Control of the Union of SSSR and the Union Republics" (Vzaimotnosheniya Viisshikh Organov Vlasti i Upravleniya Soyooza SSR i Soyoozniikh Respublik), *Sovetskoe Gosudarstvo i Pravo*, No. 1, 1983.

Smiikov, F.N., "To Educate With Appropriate Replenishment", (Vospitiivat Dostoinoe Popolnenie) *Voprossi Istorii KPSS*, No. 4, 1988"

Tammistu, K.I., "Peristorika Inter-National Relation and Language Politics" (Perestroika Mezhnatsionalnikh Otnoshenii i Yaziikovaya Politika), *Voprossi Istorii KPSS*, No. 1, January, 1990.

Tikhonov, N., "A Single Peoples-Economy in the Complex of Multinational Soviet State" (Edinii Narodnokhoziyaistvennii Kompleks Mnogonatsionalnovo Sovetskovo Sovetskovo Gosudarstva), *Kommunist*, No. 11, 1982.

Vasileva, G.P. "Some Tendencies of Developmets, of Modern National Tradition in the Material Culture of Central Asia and Kazakhstan", (Nekotoriie Tendentsii Razvitiya Sovremennikh Natsionalnikh Traditsi v Materialnoi Kulture Narodov Srednei Azii i Kazakhastana), *Sovetskaya Etnografia*, Vol. 3, 1979.

Vasileva, G.P., "Reflections of Ethno-Social Processes in the Material Culture of Contemporary Rural Families" (Otrazhenie Etnosotsialniikh Protsessov v Materialnoy Kulture Sovremennoy Selskoy Semi), *Sovetskaya Etnografia*, No. 5, 1982.

Vasileva, G.P., "Women of the Middle Asian Republics and Kazakhstan and Their Role in Transforming the Everyday Life of the Rural Population" (Zhenshinii Respublik Srednei Azii i Kazakhstana i nikh rol v preobrazovanii Bita Selskovo Naseleniya), *Sovetskaya Etnografia*, Vol. 6, November-December, 1975.

"We—The Soviet People" (Mii—Sovetskii Narod) (Anonymous) *Kommunist*, No. 12, 1982.

Zlatopolskii, D.L., "Development of Leninist Ideology on Soviet Federations in New Constitution of USSR" (Razvitie Leninskikh Idei O Sovetskoi Federatsii v Novoi Konstitutsii SSSR), *Sovestskoe Gosudarstvo i Pravo*, No. 4, 1979.

Endnotes

1. Introduction

1. Benedict Anderson, *Imagined Communities, Reflections on the Origins and Spread of Nationalism*, London: Verso, 1983, p. 15.
2. *Ibid.*, p. 28.
3. R. Tuzumuhamedov, *How the National Question was Solved in Soviet Central Asia* (A Reply to Falsifiers), Progress Publishers, Moscow, 1973.
4. *Ibid.*, pp. 24-26.
5. *Ibid.*, pp. 127-39.
6. *Ibid.*, p. 140-70.
7. *Ibid.*, p. 195.
8. *Ibid.*, pp. 195-96.
9. *Pravda*, 16 August, 1973, pp. 1-2.
10. *Ibid,*
11. Madhavan, K. Palat, *Forms of Union Russian Empire and the Soviet Union, Address of the Sectional President*, Proceedings of the Indian History Congress, 52nd Session, New Delhi, 1991-92, p. 875.
12. *Ibid.*, p. 885.
13. Bobajan Gafurov was the 1st Secretary of the Tajik SSR from 1946 to 1956 and remained the Director of the Academy of Science, USSR from 1956 to 1977.
14. *Op. cit.*, p. 885.
15. Bruno Coppieters, Form and Content in Soviet and Post-Soviet Nationality and Regional Policies, in Michael Waller, Bruno Coppieters and Alexel Malashenko ed. *Conflicting Loyalties and the State in Post-Soviet Russia and Eurasia, Frank Cass*, London, Portland, or, 1988, p. 18.
16. *Op. cit.*, p. 857.
17. *Op. cit.*, p. 25.
18. *Tajik Soviet Socialist Republic*, Novosti Press Agency Publishing House, Moscow, 1972, p. 7.
19. Michael Rywikin, *Moscow's Muslim Challenge*, M.E. Sharpe, inc. 1990, Armonk, New York, etc., p. 144.

20. Pavel, Niyavzov, *Tajikistan*, Novosti Press Agency Publishing House, 1979, p. 33.
21. Martha B. Olcott, Yuri Andropov and the National Question, *Soviet Studies*, Vol. XXXVII, No. 1, January, 1985, p. 107.
22. *Ibid.*, p. 109.
23. Alexander, J. Motyle, *Will the Non-Russians Rebel? State, Ethnicity, and Stability in the USSR*, Cornell University Press, Ithaca and London, 1987, p. 39.
24. M. Rywikin, *op. cit.*, p. 105.
25. L.F. Monogarova, Structures of Modern Urban Families of the Tajiks (on the basis of the cities of Ura-Tyube and Isfara), *Sovetskaya Etnografia*, 1982, No. 3, ISSNOO38-5050, pp. 20-23.

2. Socialism and Nationalism

1. Karl Marx and Frederich Engels, *Collected Works*, Vol. 6, p. 389, Vol. 7, p. 166 (Lawrence and Wishart, London, 1976).
2. Marx-Engels, *The First Indian War of Independence 1857-1859*, Progress Publishers, Moscow, 1959.
3. K. Marx and F. Engels, *Collected Works*, vol. 6, p. 503.
4. Ronaldo Munk, *The Difficult Dialogue, Marxism and Nationalism*, Zed Books Ltd., 1986, p. 21.
5. K. Marx and F. Engels, *Collected Works*, Vol. 8, p. 234.
6. *Ibid.*, p. 367.
7. Ronald Munk, *op. cit.*, p. 21.
8. *Ibid.*, p. 21.
9. E. Haberkern, On Roman Rodolsky as a guide to the Politics of the Nue Reinische Zeitung, *Science and Society*, vol. 63, No. 2, Summer 1999, p. 236-37.
10. K. Marx, *Survey From Exile: Political Writings*, Vol. 2, (Penguin Book, London, 1973), p. 45.
11. K. Marx and F. Engels, *Collected Works*, Vol. 6, p. 503.
12. *Ibid.*, pp. 502-3.
13. *Ibid.*, p. 495.
14. S. Bloom, *The World of Nations: A Study of the National Implications in the Work of Karl Marx* (AMS Press, New York, 1967), p. 59.
15. Karl Marx and Frederick Engels, *Manifesto of the Communist Party*, National Book Agency, Indian Edition, April, 1993, p. 57.
16. V.I. Lenin, *Collected Works*, Progress Publishers, 1977, Vol. 22, p. 154.
17. V.I. Lenin, *Collected Works*, Progress Publishers, 1977, Vol. 20, p. 397.
18. V.I. Lenin, *op. cit.*, (Item No. 16), p. 143.
19. *Ibid.*, p. 321.
20. *Ibid.*, p. 322.
21. *Ibid.*, p. 322.
22. Michael Lowy, "Marxists and the National Questions", *New Left Review*, No. 96, 1976, p. 97.

23. V.I. Lenin, *op. cit.*, Vol. 20, p. 23.
24. *Ibid.*, p. 24.
25. V.I. Lenin, *op. cit.*, Vol. 21, p. 414.
26. V.I. Lenin, *op. cit.*, Vol. 20, p. 442.
27. V.I. Lenin, *op. cit.*, Vol. 22, p. 147.
28. V.I. Lenin, *op. cit.*, Vol. 22, pp. 143-44.
29. *Ibid.*, p. 143.
30. *Ibid.*, p. 148.
31. V.I. Lenin, *op. cit.*, Vol. 23, pp. 29-30.
32. *Ibid.*, pp. 34-35.
33. V.I. Lenin, *op. cit.*, Vol. 22, p. 151.
34. *Ibid.*, p. 328.
35. *Ibid.*, pp. 146-47.
36. *Ibid.*, p. 146.
37. V.I. Lenin, *op .cit.*, Vol. 20, p. 281.
38. *Ibid.*, p. 281.
39. *Ibid.*, p. 282.
40. *Ibid.*
41. Leszek Kolakowski, *Main Currents of Marxism*, Vol. II, Oxford University Press, 1978, 1982, p. 401.
42. Joseph Stalin, *Marxism and Nationalism*, Kanti Publication, Delhi, 1993.
43. *Ibid.*, p. 6.
44. *Ibid.*, p. 3.
45. *Ibid.*, pp. 8-11, pp. 26-47.
46. *Ibid.*, p. 13.
47. *Ibid.*, p. 14.
48. *Ibid.*, p. 15.
49. *Ibid.*, p. 18.
50. *Ibid.*, pp. 71-77.
51. *Ibid.*, p. 73.
52. *Ibid.*, p. 76.
53. *Ibid.*
54. *Ibid.*, p. 77.
55. *Ibid.*, pp. 79-88.
56. *Ibid.*, p. 80.
57. *Ibid.*, p. 80.
58. *Ibid.*, p. 85.
59. *Ibid.*, "*The Policy of the Soviet Government on the National Question in Russia*", 1920, pp. 89-98.
60. *Ibid.*, p. 90.
61. *Ibid.*, p. 90.
62. *Ibid.*, p. 94.
63. *Ibid.*, p. 94.
64. *Ibid.*, p. 95.
65. *Ibid.*, p. 95.

66. *Ibid.*, p. 95.
67. *Ibid.*, p. 102.
68. *Ibid.*, p. 108.
69. *Ibid., Delivered at the 10th Congress of the Russian Communist party*, March 10, 1921. p. 111-21.
70. Moshe Lewin, *Lenin's Last Struggle*, Monthly Review Press, New York and London, 1968, pp. 43-63.
71. J. Stalin, *op. cit.*, p. 115.
72. *Ibid.*, 114-15.
73. *Ibid., Report delivered at the 1st Congress of Soviets of the Union of Soviet Socialist Republics*, December 30, 1922, pp. 135-44.
74. *Ibid.*, p. 135.
75. *Ibid.*, p. 140.
76. *Ibid.*, p. 175.
77. *Ibid.*, p. 196.
78. *Ibid., Rights and Lefts in the National Republics and Regions*, (speech on the first item on the agenda: The Case of Sultan-Galiev, June 10, 1923). pp. 197-209.
79. It was an indigenous movement for freedom in Central Asia arising just after the Bolshevik victory which was ruthlessly suppressed by the Soviet authorities as a counter-revolutionary uprising.
80. *Op. cit.*, p. 199.
81. *Ibid.*, p. 199.
82. *Ibid.*, p. 199.
83. *Ibid.*, pp. 201-02, 204.
84. *Ibid.*, p. 202.
85. *Ibid.*, p. 202.
86. *Ibid.*, p. 203.
87. *Ibid.*, p. 203.
88. *Ibid., Speech Delivered at a Meeting of the Students of the University*, May 18, 1925. pp. 235-50.
89. *Ibid.*, pp. 235-36.
90. *Ibid.*, pp. 239-40.
91. *Ibid., Extract from a Report Delivered at the 16th Congress of the CPSU (B)*, June 27, 1930.
92. *Ibid.*, Extract from the Report on the work of the Central Committee of the CPSU(B), Delivered at the 17th Party Congress, January 26, 1934. pp. 305-06.
93. *Ibid.*, p. 305.
94. *Ibid.*, p. 306.
95. *Ibid.*, p. 306.
96. *Ibid., Friendship Among the Peoples of the USSR—A great and Important Achievement*, p. 307.
97. *Ibid.*, p. 307.
98. *Ibid.*, p. 308.

99. *Ibid., On the Draft Constitution of the USSR*, p. 310.
100. *Ibid.*, p. 310.
101. *Ibid.*, p. 310.
102. N.S. Khrushchev, *The National Liberal Movements, Selected Passages, 1956-63*, Foreign Languages Publishing House, Moscow, 1963.
103. *Ibid., Every Assistance to the Struggle for National Independence*, p. 39.
104. N.S. Khrushchev, Speech at Soviet—Hungarian Friendship Meeting, July 19, 1963, *Pravda*, July 20, 1963. p. 43.
105. N.S. Khrushchev, Speech at a Luncheon for the President Head of the Govt. of the Republic of Ghana. July 11, 1961. *Communism—Peace & Happiness for the Peoples*, Moscow, vol., pp. 311-12.
106. N.S. Khrushchev, *An Account to the Party and the People—Report of the C.C., C.P. S.U. to the 22nd congress of the Party*, October 17, 1961, Foreign Languages Publishing House, Moscow, 1961, p. 134.
107. Lenoid I. Brezhnev, *Pages from His Life*, Allied Publishers Private Limited, New Delhi, Bombay, Calcutta, Madras, Bangalore, Hyderabad, 1979, Ch-III, p. 111.
108. *Ibid.*, pp. 110- 11.
109. *Ibid.*, p. 111.
110. *Socialism, Democracy and Human Rights*, L.I. Brezhnev, Pergamon Press, Oxfored New York Toronoto, Sydney, Paris, Frankfurt, 1980. *Speeches of Brezhnev* 1970-72, p. 56.
111. *Ibid.*, p. 59.
112. *Ibid.*, p. 59.
113. *Ibid.*, p. 57.
114. *Ibid.*, p. 34 (Report of the Central Committee to the 24th Congress of the CPSU, 30 March, 1971) L.I. Brezhnev, *Pages form His Life* Chapter III, p. 112.
115. L.I. Brezhnev, *op. cit.*, p. 34.
116. *Ibid.*, p. 68.
117. *Ibid.*, p. 68.
118. *Ibid.*, p. 68.
119. *Ibid.*, p. 69.
120. L.I. Brezhnev, Socialism Democracy and Human Right, op. cit. Speech at the joint celebration meeting of the Central Committee of the Communist Party of Uzbekistan and the Supreme Soviet of the Uzbek SSR, on presentation of the Order of Friendship Among Peoples, 24 September, 1973, p. 80.
121. *Ibid.*, p. 118.
122. *Report of the Draft Constitution of the USSR at the Plenary Meeting of the Central Committee*, 24 May, 1977, p. 152.
123. *Ibid.*, p. 153.
124. *Ibid., Report on the draft constitution of the USSR at the seventh (special) session of the USSR Supreme Soviet.* (the proposed constitution was adopted and came into force on 7 October, 1977), 4 October, 1977, p. 179.

125. *Ibid.*, Article, 'A Historic Stage in the Road to Communism', published in *World Marxist Review*, no. 12, December, 1977, p. 208.
126. M.A. Sustov, *Marxism Leninism—The International Teaching of the Working Class*, Progress Publishers, Moscow, First Printing 1975. p. 93.
127. J.B. Dunlop, *The New Russian Nationalism*, Praeger Publishers, 1985, New York, p. 13.
128. *Ibid.*, pp. 10-12.
129. J.B. Dunlop, *The Faces of Contemporary Russian Nationalism*, Princeton University Press, Princeton, N.J., 1983, pp. 143-46.
130. Y.V. Andropov, A Triumph for the Leninist Nationalities Policy, excerpt from a report to a meeting of personnel of the committee for state security under the USSR council of ministers on the occasion of the 50th anniversary of the USSR, Dec. 15, 1972, Speeches Articles, Interviews, A Selection, Allied Publishers Private Ltd., New Delhi, etc., p. 85.
131. *Ibid.*, pp. 84-85.
132. J.B. Dunlop, *The New Russian Nalianalism*, *op. cit.*, p. 16.
133. *Op. cit.*, 60th Anniversary of the Union of Soviet Socialist Republics, *Report at a joint jubilee meeting of the CPSU Central Committee, the Supreme Soviet of the USSR, the Supreme Soviet of the REFSR*, December 21, 1982, p. 151.
134. *Ibid.*, pp. 151-52.
135. *Ibid.*, p. 157.
136. *Ibid.*, p. 157.
137. Martha Brill Olcott, *Yuri Andropov and the National Question, Soviet Studies*, vol. XXXVII, no. 1, January, 1985, p. 112.
138. *Op. cit.*, p. 157.
139. K.U. Chernenko, Soviet Democracy Principles and Practices, *Socialist Peoples Power: Practical Prerequisites*, Novosti Press Agency Publishing House, Moscow, 1977, pp. 18-20.
140. *Ibid.*, p. 20.
141. *Ibid.*, p. 20.
142. J.B. Dunlop, *The New Russian Nationalism*, *Op. cit.*, p. 30.
143. *Ibid.*, pp. 31-32.
144. *Ibid.*, p. 33.
145. *Ibid.*, p. 34.
146. Zhores Medvedev, Andropov (Oxford England: Basil Blackwell, 1983), pp. 18-19.
147. Mikhail Gorbachev, *Speeches and Writings*, Oxford: Pergamon, 1986 Ch-II, pp. 187-204. Mikhail Gorbachev, *Perestroika*: *New Thinking for Our Country and the World, London*, Collins, 1987, pp. 17-122.
148. Mikhail, S., Gorbachev, Perestroika, *ibid.*, p. 17.
149. *Ibid.*, p. 18.
150. *Ibid.*, p. 21.
151. *Ibid.*, *The Union of Socialist Nations—A Unique Formation*, p. 118.

152. *Ibid.*, pp. 118-19.
153. *Ibid.*, p. 119.
154. *Ibid.*, p. 119.
155. *Ibid.*, pp. 120-21.
156. *Ibid.*, pp. 119-20.
157. *Ibid.*, p. 120.
158. *Ibid.*, p. 121.
159. *Ibid.*, p. 121.
160. *Ibid.*, p. 120.
161. *Ibid.*, p. 121.

3. Political Evolution and Economic Experience: Central Asia under the Soviet Rule

1. Boris Topornin, *The New Constitution of the USSR*, Article 72, Progress Publishers, Moscow, 1986, p. 250.
2. *Robert Conquest, Soviet Nationalities Policy in Practice*, The Bodly Head, London, Sydney, Toronto, 1967. p. 117.
3. Victor, Shevtsov, *The State and Nations in the USSR*, Progress Publishers, Moscow, 1982, pp. 132-33.
4. Dmitri Volcogonov, *Rise and Fall of the Soviet Empire*, Harper Collins pub. [Here Brezhnev was called 'Harbinger of Collapse] 1988. p. 318. Seweryn Bialer, Soviet Paradox-External Expansion, Internal Decline, I.B. Tauris and Co. Ltd. London, 1986. p. 57.
5. S. Bialer, *ibid.*, p. 43.
6. S. Bialer, The Political System, in Robert F. Byrnes ed. After Brezhnev, Frances Pinter (Pub), London, 1983. p. 2.
7. *Ibid.* p. 52.
8. J. Keep, *Last of Empires*, Oxford University Press, 1995. p. 206.
9. *Ibid.* p. 204.
10. S. Bialer, *Soviet Paradox, op. cit.*, p. 55.
11. D. Volkogonov, *op. cit.*, p. 318.
12. Kommunist Tajikistana, 4.1.83. p. 1.
13. Kommunist Tajikistana, 19.1.83.
14. Kommunist Tajikistana, 22.1.83.
15. *Pravda Vostoka*, 10.10.81, 20.12.79.
16. John, H. Miller, Cadre Policy in Nationality Areas, *Soviet Studies*, Vol. XXIX, No. 1, January, 1977. p. 4.
17. A. Leonov, *Kommunist*, 1971, No. 18, p. 51.
18. *Survey*, Vol. 20, No. 4, 1974, pp. 100-01.
19. Miller, *op. cit.*, p. 8.
20. John Anderson, *The International Politics of Central Asia*, Manchester University Press, Manchester, New York, 1997, p. 34, Miller, *op. cit.*, p. 8.
21. Miller, *Ibid.* p. 8.

22. T.R. Harmstone, *Russia and Nationalism in Central Asia*, The John Hopkins Press, Baltimore and London, 1970. p. 146-86.
23. Joel, C. Moses, Regionalism in Soviet Politics: Continuity as a Source of Change, 1953-1982, *Soviet Studies*, Vol. XXXVII, No. 2, April, 1985, p. 188.
24. Martha Brill Olcott, *The Soviet Multinational State, Reading and Documents*, M.E. Sharpe, Inc. Armonk, New York, London, England, 1990. p. 79.
25. *Ibid.* p. 79.
26. John Anderson, *op. cit.*, p. 36.
27. S. Bialer, Soviet Paradox, *op. cit.*, p. 54.
28. Dmitri Volkogonov, *op. cit.*, p. 278.
29. L.I. Brezhnev, Report on the draft constitution of the USSR at the Plenary Meeting of the Central Committee, 24 May, 1977, in *Socialism, Democracy and Human Rights*, *op. cit.*, pp. 152-54.
30. J. Keep, *op. cit.*, p. 200.
31. Brezhnev's Speeches, *op. cit.*, p. 160.
32. Boris Topornin, *op. cit.*, p. 250-52.
33. *Ibid.*, p. 136.
34. L.I. Brezhnev, *Socialism, Democracy and Human Rights*, *op. cit.*, p. 179.
35. *Ibid.*, p. 159.
36. *Ibid.*, p. 57.
37. *Ibid.*, p. 59.
38. *Ibid.*, p. 107-32.
39. *Kommunist Tajikistana*, 19.1.83 & 22.1.83.
40. J. Keep, *op. cit.*, pp. 223-24.
41. *Ibid.*, p. 223.
42. *Ibid.*, p. 222.
43. Boris, Z. Rumer, *Soviet Central Asia—A Tragic Experiment*, Boston, 1989, p. 1.
44. Musa Khan Jalalzai, *Central Asia, Political Situation and Economic Opportunities*, Polyglot, The Frontier Post Publications, 1980, pp. 132-54.
45. Boris Rumer, *op. cit.*, p. 28.
46. *Ibid.*, p. 46.
47. *Ibid.*, p. 43.
48. Ajay Patnaik, *Central Asia: Between Modernity and Tradition*, Konark Publishers Pvt. Ltd., 1996, pp. 64-70.
49. *Ibid.*, p. 64.
50. *Ibid.*, p. 65.
51. *Ibid.* p. 65.
52. B. Rumer, *op. cit.*, [Between 1970 and 1984 the Central Asian population grew by 44 per cent while its share of fixed capital in the social sphere shrank from 39.3% to 34.3%] p. 42. A. Patnaik, *op. cit.*, [...Growth in employment had not kept pace with the growth in population] p. 71.

53. B. Rumer, *Ibid.*, p. 31.
54. *Ibid.* p. 31-32.
55. *Ibid.* p. 35.
56. A. Patnaik, *op. cit.* p. 69.
57. *Ibid.*, p. 67.
58. B. Rumer, *op. cit.*, p. 72.
59. *Ibid.*, p. 73.
60. A. Patnaik, *op. cit.*, p. 69.
61. Alastair Mcauley, Economies of Central Asia in Yaacov Roi's, ed., *Muslim Eurasia: Conflicting Legacies*, Frank Cass, London, 1995.
62. *Ibid.*, p. 260.
63. *Ibid.*, p. 260.
64. Seweryn Bialer, *The Soviet Paradox*, *op. cit.*, p. 91.
65. *Ibid.*, p. 97.
66. *Great Soviet Encyclopaedia*, Macmilan Educational Corporation, 1980, USA, p. 84.
67. Barnet R. Rubin, "The Fragmentation of Tajikistan", Survival, (34-4); Winter, 1993-94, p. 94.
68. *Op. cit.*, pp. 50-51.
69. David, A. Dyker, Industrial Location in the Tadzhik Republic, *Soviet Studies*, Vol. 21, 1969-70, p. 497.
70. Boris Rumer, *op. cit.*, pp. 51-52.
71. David A. Dyker, *op. cit.* p. 505.
72. *Ibid.* p. 499, 505.
73. T.R. Harmstone, *op. cit,.* pp. 96-99.
74. John Anderson, *op. cit.*, p. 177.
75. Ahmed, Rashid, *The Resurgence of Central Asia, Islam or Nationalism*, Oxford University Press (Karachi), 1994. p. 177.
76. J. Keep and D. Volkogonov, *op. cit.*, Robert Conquest, ed. *The Last Empire, Nationality and the Soviet Future*, Hoover Institution Press, Stanford University, 1986.
77. V. Shevtsov, *op. cit.*
78. *Ibid.*, p. 121.

4. Religion: The Determining Factor in Central Asian Identity

1. Meaning "New Soviet Man"—a construct of the communist regime to imply a human being who would be above all parochialisms of nationality, regionalism and religion in order to melt into this broader identity of Soviet Socialist state.
2. Mehrdad Haghayeghi, *Islam and Politics in Central Asia*, St. Martin's Press, New York, 1995.
3. *Ibid.*, p. 16.
4. *Ibid.*, p. 17.

5. For detailed information about the *Basmachi* movement, see *The Basmachis, Central Asia Review*, 1959, p. 236-48. Martha Brill Olcott, The Barmachi or Freeman's Revolt in Turkestan, 1918-24, *Soviet Studies*, Vol. XXXIII, No. 3, July, 1981, pp. 352-69.
6. M. Haghayeghi, *op. cit.*, p. 22.
7. *Ibid.*, p. 27.
8. *Ibid.*, p. 28.
9. Donald, A. Lowrie and William, C. Fletcher, Khrushchev's Religious Policy, 1959-1964, in Richard H. Marshall, Jr. *et al.*, eds., *Aspects of Religion in the Soviet Union*, 1917-1967, Chicago, 1971, p. 139.
10. Yaakov Ro'i, The Task of Creating The New Soviet Man: Atheistic Propaganda in the Soviet Muslim Areas, *Soviet Studies*, Vol. 36, 1984, p. 42.
11. M. Haghayeghi, *op. cit.*, p. 35.
12. *Central Asia Review*, 1959, p. 112..
13. I. Dzhabbarov, 'Sotsialnyi Progress i ateizm', *Pravda Vostoka*, 20 December, 1979.
14. Yaakev Ro'i, *op. cit.*, p. 28..
15. *Pravda*, 6 May, 1974.
16. *Pravda*, 24 February, 1981.
17. *Pravda*, 4 July, 1982.
18. *Ibid.*
19. Y. Ro'i, *op. cit.*, p. 30.
20. *Ibid.*, p. 31.
21. *Ibid.*, p. 31
22. *Ibid.*, p. 27.
23. Yaacov Ro'i, The Impact of the Islamic Fundamentalist Revival of the Late 1970s on the Soviet view of Islam, Y. Ro'i ed. *The USSR and the Muslim World: Issues in Domestic and Foreign Policy*, London: George Allen & Unwin, 1984. p. 153.
24. Michael Rymikin, National Symbiosis: Vitality, Religion, Identity, Allegience, Y. Roi ed. *The USSR and the Muslim World: Issues in Domestic and Foreign Policy*, London: George Allen & Unwin, 1984, p. 9.
25. *Ibid.*, p. 9.
26. Y. Ro'i, The Task of Creating The New Soviet Man, *op. cit.*, p. 34.
27. *Ibid.*, p. 36.
28. S. Dadabaeva, Sama Soboi Ne Otmoret, *Kommunist Tajikistana*, 31 October, 1980.
29. Poryshat' uroven' patrioticheskogo i internatsional'nogo vospitaniya trudyashchikhsya', Turkmenskaya iskra, 15 June, 1980.
30. Dadabaeva, *op. cit.*
31. M.A. Tolmacheva, The Muslim Woman in Soviet Central Asia, *Central Asian Survey*, 1993, 12(4), p. 234.
32. *Ibid.*, p. 535.

33. *Ibid.*, p. 536.
34. *Ibid.*, p. 537.
35. Dadabaeva, *op. cit.*
36. M.A. Tolmacheva, *op. cit.*, pp. 534-35.
37. Maria Eva Subtelny, The Cult of Holy Places: Religious Practices Among Soviet Muslims, *Middle East Journal*, vol. 43, No. 4, Autumn, 1989, pp. 593-604.
38. Tolmacheva, *op. cit.*, pp. 542-43.
39. Dadabaeva, *op. cit.*
40. *Ibid.*
41. B. Ryspaev, *Sovetskaya Kirgiziya*, 16 September, 1980.
42. *Kommunist Tajikistana*, 31 October, 1980.
43. *Pravda Vostoka*, 23 October, 1981.
44. *Turkmenkaya Iskra*, 3 July, 1981.
45. *Pravda Vostoka, op. cit.*
46. *Report by Mufti Ziyautdinkhan ibn Ishan BABAKHAN*, Chairman of the Muslim Religious Board for Central Asia and Kazakhstan (USSR) in International Preparatory Committee for Lasting Peace and Disarmament, in Ziautdin Khan Ibn Ishan BABAKHAN, Islam and the Muslims in the Land of Soviet, Moscow: Progress Publishers, 1980, pp. 46-66.
47. *Ibid.*, p. 50.
48. *Ibid.*, p. 50.
49. *Ibid.*, p. 51.
50. *Ibid.*, pp. 58-65.
51. *Ibid.*, p. 65.
52. Alexander Bennigsen E. Wimbust, *Muslim National Communism in Central Asia*, The University Press, Chicago (etc.), 1980 Edward Allworth, *Central Asia, A Century of Russian Rule*, Cambridge University Press, New York (etc.), 1967.
53. *Ibid.* p. 48.
54. Hasan Ismailov, 'Reply to the sooth sayers', *Nauka i religia*, no. 1, (1980), pp. 40-43.
55. *Ibid.*
56. Yaacov Ro'i, *op. cit.*, p. 51.
57. *Muslims of the Soviet East*, no. 3, (1978), pp. 1-3 & 19-20. *Muslims in the Soviet Union, Asia and Africa Today*, no. 5 (Sept.-Oct., 1980), pp. 36-39.
58. Yaacov Ro'i, *op. cit,.* p. 157.
59. *Ibid.*, p. 160.
60. Leonid Medvedenko, 'Islam: two trends', *New Times*, no. 13, (March, 1980), pp. 23-25.
61. Leonid Medvedenko, *Radio Moscow's 'International observers at the round table* (27 January 1980/SWB 1, 30 January, 1980).
62. Y. Ro'i, *op. cit.* p. 159.
63. P. Demchenko, 'Iran takes a new road', *International Affairs* (*Moscow*), no. 10 (October, 1979), pp. 80-86.

64. Religion in the countries of Asia and Africa, *Narody Azii i Afriki*, no. 1 (Jan.-Feb.) 1980, pp. 40-54.
65. Ro'i, *op. cit.*, p. 163.
66. A. Kniazev, "The Difficult path of the Afghan revolution", *Agitator*, no. 3 (February, 1980), pp. 46-48.
67. Mufti Mohammad Ziautdin Babakhan, Radio Moscow in Arabic, 14 January, 1980/Foreign Broadcast Information Service, *Daily Report*, Vol. III (Soviet Union) (FBIS III) 15 January, 1980.
68. Evgenyi Primakov, 'When black is passed as white', *Literaturnaya Gazeta*, no. 11 (12 March, 1980), p. 14.
69. *Ibid.*, p. 14.
70. A. Vasileyev, 'Islam in the present day world', *International Affairs* (*Moscow*), no. 11, (November, 1981), pp. 52-54.
71. Geider Aliev's report in *Bakinskii Rabochii*, 25 December, 1980.
72. Theirry Zarcone, *Sufi Movements: Search for Identity and Islamic Resurgence, Central Asia Emerging New Order* ed. K. Warikoo, Har-Anand Publications. p. 64.
73. Abha Dixit, Tajikstan: Engulfed by Flames of Afghan Civil War, *Strategic Analysis* 15(9); December, 1992, p. 875.
74. *Ibid.*, p. 873-76.
75. A. Bennigsen, Islam in the Soviet Union, Change and the Muslim World, 1981, p. 123. A. Bennigsen, Ishan-in Retrospect, *Central Asian Survey*, 1987. p. 91.
76. Dilip Hiro, Between Marx and Muhammad: The Changing Face of Central Asia, Harper Collins Publishers, London, 1994, Ahmad Rashid, The Resurgence of Central Asia: Islam or Nationalism', Oxford University Press, Karachi, 1994. Rakesh Gupta, Tajikstan: Locked Horns for Power, *Strategic Analysis*, 15(6), September, 1992, pp. 519-537. Abha Dixit, Tajikistan: Engulfed by Flames of Afghan Civil War, *Strategic Analysis*, 15(9), December, 1992. pp. 873-81.
77. Shafiga Daulet, The First All Muslim Congress of Russia, Moscow, 1-11 May, 1917, *Central Asian Survey*, vol. 8, no. 1, 1989, pp. 34-35.
78. Dunlop, J.B., *The Faces of Contemporary Russian Nationalism*, Princeton University Press, Princeton, N.J., 1983, p. 36.
79. Dunlop, J.B., *The New Russian Nationalism, Georgetown University*, Washington DC, 1985, p.

5. Role of Language in the Identity Formation of Central Asia

1. Shams Ud Din, Soviet Language Policy: Change in Script of Central Asian Languages and its Impact on Nationalites Question, in Shams Ud. Din ed., Perestroika and the Nationalities Question in the USSR, New Delhi: Vikas, 1990, p. 72.
2. V.I. Lenin, Is a Compulsory Official Language Needed? *Collected Works*, Vol. XX, December, 1913, Progress Publishers, Moscow, 1977.

3. *Ibid.*, p. 73.
4. *Ibid.*, p. 72.
5. Shams Ud. Din, *op. cit.*, p. 74.
6. J. Stalin, *Marxism and Nationalism*, Chapter XXII, Kanti Publishers, Delhi, p. 293-94.
7. Michael Kirkwood, 'Glasnost: the National Question and Soviet Language Policy', *Soviet Studies*, Vol. 43. No. 1, 1991, p. 62.
8. *Ibid.*, p. 63.
9. T.R. Harmstone, *Russia and Nationalism in Central Asia*, John Hopkins Press, Baltimore and London, 1970, pp. 241-48.
10. Shams Ud Din, *op. cit.*, p. 72.
11. Brian D. Silver, "The Status of National Minority Languages in Soviet Education, "An Assessment of Recent Changes," *Soviet Studies*, University of Glasgow, Vol. XXVI, January, 1994, No. 1, p. 28.
12. M. Kirkwood, *op. cit.*, p. 64.
13. *Ibid.*, p. 64.
14. Michael Bruchis, 'The Effect of the USSR's Language Policy on the National Languages of its Turkic Population" in Yaacov Roi edited, The USSR and the Muslim World, Issues in Domestic and Foreign policy. George Allen and Unwin, London, Boston, Sydney, 1984, pp. 141-142.
15. Michael Kirkwood, *op. cit.*, p. 66.
16. *Ibid.*, p. 67.
17. *Ibid.*, p. 67.
18. Harmstone, *op. cit.*, p. 241.
19. *Ibid.*, p. 242.
20. John B. Dunlop, Language, Culture, Religion and National Awareness, in Robert Conquest; ed., The Last Empire Nationality and the Soviet Future, Hoover institution press, Stanford University, Stanford, California, 1986. p. 269.
21. Brian D. Silver, *op. cit.*, p. 38. Brian D. Silver, Bilingualism and Maintenance of the Mother Tongue in Soviet Central Asia, Slavic Review, Editor: James R. Millar, University of illinois at Urbana Champaign, Vol. 35, 1976, p. 406.
22 Brian D. Silver, *op. cit.*, p. 38.
23. Paul B. Henze, The Significance of Increasing Bilingualism among Soviet Muslims, Y. Roi, ed. *The USSR and the Muslim World*, *op. cit.*, p. 122.
24. B.D. Silver, *op. cit.*, p. 409.
25. *Ibid.*, p. 409.
26 *Ibid.*, p. 409.
27. Michael Rywikin, *Mascow's Muslim Challenge, Soviet Central Asia*, M.E. Sharpe Armovk, New York etc., p. 96.
28. *Ibid.*, p. 69.
29. *Ibid.*, p. 69.
30. B.D. Silver, *op. cit.*, p. 406.
31. *Ibid.*, p. 418.

32. Shams Ud Din, *op. cit.*, p. 80.
33. Andree F. Sjoberg, Language Structure and Cultural Identity: a historical perspective on the Turkic peoples of Central Asia, *Central Asian Survey*, 1993, 12(4), p. 557.
34. *Ibid.*, pp. 557-58.
35. T.R. Harmstone, *op. cit.*, p. 245.
36. K.N. Pandita, Language and Culture in the Politics ofTajikistan, K. Warikoo ed.. Central Asia, Emerging New Order, Har-Anand Publications, 1995, p. 95.
37. J.B. Dunlop, *op. cit.,* p. 271 Valery Tishkov, *Ethnicity, Nationalism and Conflict in and After the Soviet union: The Mind Aflame*, Sage Publications, London, Prio and Unrisd. 1997, p. 87.
38. From the 1988 Plenum of the USSR Union of Writers, Literaturanaya Gazeta, 9 March, 1988, Russian text @ 1988 by the USSR Union of Writers, in Martha Brill Olcott, Lubomyr Hajda and Anthony Olcott, ed. *The Soviet Multinational State, Readings and Documents*, M.E. Sharpe, Inc., Armonk, New York, London, England, 1990, pp. 358-359.
39. M. Kirwood, *op. cit.* p. 72.
40. J.B. Dunlop, *op. cit.*, p. 273-74.
41. Gerhard Simon, Nationalism and Policy Toward the Nationalities in the Soviet Union. From *Totalitarian Dictatorship to Post-Stalinist Society*, Translated by Karen Forster and Oswald Forster. Westview Press, Boulder, San Francisco, Oxforx, 1991, p. 290.
42. M. Rywikin, *op. cit.*, pp. 100-01.
43. V. Tishkov, *op. cit.*, p. 85-99.
44. *BBC Summary of World Broadcasts*; 12 October, 1985.
45. *Kirkwood*, p. 71.
46. M.N. Guboglu, Factors and Tendencies of the Development of Bilingualism among the Russian population living in Union Republics, Istoriia SSSR, 1987, no. 2. pp. 25-43 Russian Text @ 1987 by "Pravda" Publishers in M.B. Olcott ed. *op. cit.,* p. 263.
47. Speech of Maiia Ganina, in M.B. Olcoft, *op. cit.,* p. 358.
48. M.N. Guboglu, in M.B. Olcott. ed. *op. cit.,* p. 279.
49. V. Tishkov, *op. cit.*, p. 87.
50. Shams Ud Din, *op. cit.*, p. 83.
51. V. Tishkov, *op. cit.*, p. 100.
52. *Ibid.*, p. 104.
53. *Ibid.*, p. 98.
54. *Ibid.*, p. 97.
55. Na Kakom Yazike Govorit, Literaturnaya Gazeta, no. 37 (5259), 7. 9. 89. p. 3.
56. Chengez Aitmator, Literaturnaya Gazeta, 9th March, 1988.
57. Chengez Aitmator, Zhivi sam i dai zhitch drugim p o provodu prockta zakona o yazeekakh narodov SR, *Literaturnaya Gazeta*, 22. 11. 89., No. 47(5269).

6. Role of Ethnic Factors in the Development of Multi-Layered Identities in Central Asia

1. Rasma Karklins, Ethnic Relations in the USSR, *The Perspective from Below*, Boston, Allen and Unwin, London, Sydney, 1986, p. 31.
2. Mehrdad Haghayeghi, *Islam and Politics in Central Asia*, St. Martins Press, New York, 1995, pp. 202-06.
3. M. Rywikin, *op. cit.*, pp. 96-97.
4. Valery Tishkov, Russians in Central Asia and Kazakhstan, Yacov Roi ed. *Muslim Eurasia Conflicting Legacies*, Frank Cass, London, 1995, p. 297.
5. *Ibid.*, p. 298.
6. *Ibid.*, p. 298.
7. Alexander J. Motyl, Will the Non-Russians Rebel? *State, Ethnicity and Stability in the USSR*, Cornell University Press, Ithaca and London, 1987, p. 43.
8. M. Rywikin, *op. cit.*, p. 300.
9. Tishkov, *op. cit.*, p. 300.
10. Carol Barner-Barry Cynthia A. Hody, *The Politics of Change*, St. Martins Press, New York, 1995, pp. 96-97.
11. Martha Brill Olcott with Lubomyr Hajda and Anthony Olcolt, ed. *The Soviet Multinational State, Readings and Documents*, M.E. Sharpe, Inc. Armonk, New York, London, England, 1990, pp. 181-83.
12. *Ibid.*, pp. 187-88.
13. V. Tishkov, R*ussians in Central Asia, op, cit.*, pp. 290-92
14. Gerhard Simon, Nationalism and Policy Toward the Nationalities in the Soviet Union, *From Totalitarian Dictatorship to Post-Stalin Society*, Westview press, Boulders, San Francisco, Oxford, 1991, pp. 291-92.
15. Victor Zaslavsky, *op. cit.*, p. 119.
16. Shams, Ud Din, Demograplic Changes and Nationality Problems in Soviet Central Asia, Kazakhstand and Azerbaijan, in Shams-Ud-Din, ed. *Perestroika and the Nationality Question in the USSR*, New Delhi, Vikas, 1990. p . 97.
17. Mehrdad Haghayeghi, *op. cit.*, p. 166.
18. Asoke Mukherjee, Ethnicity, Geopolitical Entity, *World Focus*, 14(3-4), March-April, 1993, special issue, p . 3.
19. Shirin Akiner, *Islamic Peoples of the Soviet Union*, Kegan Paul International, 1983, p. 302.
20. *Ibid.*, pp. 338-82.
21. *Ibid.*, p. 17.
22. *Ibid.*, p. 20.
23. *Ibid.*, p. 33.
24. Ahmed Rashid, *The Resurgence of Central Asia, Islam or Nationalism*? Oxford University press (Karachi), 1994, p. 38.
25. V. Tishkov, *op. cit.*, p. 33.
26. Gerhard Simon, *op. cit.*, p. 279.

27. *Ibid.*, p. 278.
28. L.M. Drobizheva, *Role of Education and Cultural Perspective in Interpersonal Relations Among Nationalities*, L.M. Drobizheva, (Dukhovnaia obshchnost' narodov SSSR (Moscow, 1981), pp. 172-183, *Russian text 1981*, by 'Mysl' Publishers in M.B. Olcott, *op. cit.*, p. 191.
29. *Ibid.*, p. 191.
30. *Ibid.*, p. 194.
31. *Ibid.*, p. 195.
32. L.M. Drobizheva, National Self-Awareness, The Basis on Which it is Formed and the Sociocultural Factors Stimulating its Development, L.M. Drobizheva, Sovetskaia Etnografia, 1985, no. 5, *Russian text* by 'Nauka' Publishers M.B. Olcott, *ibid.*, p. 202.
33. *Ibid.*, p. 208.
34. *Ibid.*, p. 209.
35. *Ibid.*, p. 211.
36. Yu. V. Bromiei, V.I. Kozlov, To the Study of Present Ethnic Processes in the Sphere of the Spiritural Culture of the People of USSR, Sovetskaia Etnografia, 1975, vol. 1, Jan.-Feb.
37. *Ibid.*, p. 5.
38. *Ibid.*, p. 6.
39. *Ibid.*, p. 9.
40. *Ibid.*, p. 9.
41. *Ibid.*, p. 9.
42. *Ibid.*, pp. 9-10.
43. *Ibid.*, p. 10.
44. *Ibid.*, p. 16.
45. Drobizhera, *op. cit.*, p. 212.
46. *Ibid.*, p. 212.
47. *Ibid.*, p. 213.
48. G.P. Vasileva, *Sovetskaia Etnografia*, 1979, vol. 3, pp . 18-29.
49. *Ibid.*, p. 18.
50. *Ibid.*, p. 20.
51. *Ibid.*, p. 20.
52. *Ibid.*, p. 20.
53. *Ibid.*, p. 22.
54. *Ibid.*, p. 23.
55. *Ibid.*, p. 25.
56. *Ibid.*, p. 25.
57. *Ibid.*, p. 27.
58. *Ibid.*, p. 26.
59. *Ibid.*, p. 27.
60. *Ibid.*, p. 29.
61. *Ibid.*, p. 30.
62. A. Dashdamirov, Soviet Patriotism, *Pravda*, 29 December, 1982, p. 2. *Russian text 1982* by 'Pravda' in M.B. Olcott, *op. cit.*, p. 451.

63. *Ibid.*, p. 446.
64. *Ibid.*, p. 446.
65. *Ibid.*, p. 447.
66. Ajay Patnaik, *Central Asia: Between Modernity and Tradition*, Konark Publishers Ltd., 1996, p. 100.
67. *Ibid.*, p. 100.
68. Shams Ud Din, *op. cit.*, p. 96.
69. L.F. Monogarova, Structures of Modern Urban Family of the Tajiks (on the basis of the Cities of Ura-Tyube and Isfara), *Sovetskaya Etnografia*, 1980, No. 3, ISSN 0038-5050.
70. *Ibid.*, p. 22.
71. *Ibid.*, pp. 22-24.
72. *Ibid.*, p. 24.
73. Ajay Patnaik, *op. cit.*, p. 101.
74. L.V. Ostapenko and A.A. Suskolov. The Interregional Mixing and National Composition of Labour Resources (*Sto natsi i narodnostei: etnodemograficheskoe razvitie SSSR*, Moscow, 1985, pp. 40-56, *Russian text 1985*, by "Mysl" Publishers) Martha Brill Olcott, *op. cit.*, p 217.
75. *Ibid.*, pp. 219-20.
76. Ajay Patnaik, *op. cit.*, p. 102.
77. Shirin Akiner, *op. cit.*, pp. 278, 320, 333, 308, 295, 308.
78. Monogarova, *op. cit.*, p. 21.
79. R. Karklins, *op. cit.*, p. 120.
80. *Ibid.*, p. 160.
81. *Ibid.*, pp. 164-65.
82. *Ibid.*, pp. 169-70.
83. *Ibid.*, p. 177.
84. Ajay Patnaik, *op. cit.*, p. 104.
85. Monogarova, *op. cit.*, p. 21.
86. Seweryn Bialer, *Stalin's Successors: Leadership, Stability and Change in the Soviet Union*, Cambridge University Press, Cambridge, London, etc., 1989, p. 211.
87. L. Drobizheva, *More Democracy, Politicheskoe Obrazovanie*, 1988, No. 3. pp. 49-51, *Russian text 1988* by "Pravda" Publishers, M.B. Olcott,. *op. cit.*, p . 229.
88. *Ibid.*, p. 231.
89. *Ibid.*, p. 231.
90. *Ibid.*, p. 231.
91. *Ibid.*, p. 232.
92. *Ibid.*, p. 232.
93. V. Tishkov, *op. cit.*, p. 42.
94. *Ibid.*, p. 42.
95. S. Bialer, p. 213.
96. M. Haghayeghi, *op. cit.*, pp. 187 and 192.
97. *Ibid.*, p. 193.

98. T.R. Harmstone, *op. cit.*, pp. 76-82.
99. T.A. Sdanko, Natsionalno—Gasudarstvennoe Narodov Sriyedi Azii, *Sovetskaya Etnografia*, 1972, vol. VI, Sep.-Oct., p. 27.
100. B.R. pubin, "Fragmentation of Tajikistan", *Survival*, (34-4); *Winter*, 1993-94. p. 74.
101. S. Akiner, *op. cit.*, p. 277 and 307.
102. V. Tishkov, p. 20.
103. *Ibid.*, p. 20.
104. Oleg Glebov and John Crowfoot, ed. and Translated, *The Soviet Empire: Its Nations Speak out*, The First Congress of Peoples Deputies, Moscow, 25 May to 10 June, 1989, Harwood Academic Publishers, Apchur, London, Paris, New York, Melbourne, 1999, p. 141.
105. P.L. Dash, Ethno-Nationalism in Uzbekistan, in K. Warikoo ed. Central asia, Emerging New Order, Har Anand Publications, 1995, pp. 106-07.
106. V. Tishkov, *op. cit.*, p. 47.
107. A. Patnaik, *op. cit.*, p. 171.
108. Barnet, R. Rubin, *op. cit.*, p. 76.
109. Rakesh Gupta, Tajikistan: Locked Harms for Power, *Strategic Analysis*, 15(5); Sept., 1992, p. 523.
110. Aziz Nijazi, Tajikistan I: The Regional Dimension of Conflict, in Michael Waller, Bruno Coppieters and Alexei Malashenko ed., *Conflicting Loyalties and the State in Post—Soviet Russia and Eurasia*, Frank Cass, London, Poartland or, 1998. p. 153.
111. *Ibid.* pp. 145-146.
112. *Ibid.* p. 156.
113. *Ibid.* p. 155.
114. *Ibid.* p. 157.
115. B.R. Rubin, *op. cit.*, p. 77.
116. *Ibid.* p. 77.
117. Aziz Niyazi, p. 158.
118. *Ibid.*, p. 155.
119. B.R. Rubin, *op. cit.*, p. 78.
120. Abha Dixit, Tajikistan: Engulfed by Flames of Afgahan Civil War, *Shartegic Analysis* 15(9); December, 1992, p. 875.
121. K. Warikoo, Cockpit of Central Asia: Afhanistan Factor in Tajikistan's Crisis, in K. Warikoo, ed., *Central Asia, Emerging New Order*, Har Anand Publications, 1995, p. ?.
122. Muriel Atkin, Tajikistan's Relations With Iran and Afghanistan, in Ali Banauzizi and Myron Weiner ed., *The New Geopolitics of Central Asia and Its Borderlands*, I.B. Tauris, London, New York, 1994, pp. 105-06.
123. *Ibid.*, p. 112.
124. Said Akhmedov, *Tajikistan* II*: The Regional Conflict in Confessional and International Context*, Michael Waller Bruno Coppieters and Alexei Malashenko ed., op. cit., pp. 184-85.
125. Aziz Niyazi, *op. cit.*, p. 146.

126. Nezavisimaya Gazeta, 30 Sept., 1992.
127. Eden Naby, Ethnicity and Islam in Central Asia, *Central Asian Survey*, vol. 12, 1993, p. 164.

7. Perestroika, Glasno st and the Change in Central Asia

1. Carol Barner-Barry, Cynthia A. Hody, The Politics of Change, *The Transformation of the Former Soviet Union*, St. Martin's Press, New York, 1995, pp. 76-77.
2. M.S. Gorbachev, *Perestroika, Speeches and Writings*, Oxford: Pergamon, 1986, p. 17.
3. *Ibid.*, p. 50.
4. Dmitri Volkogonov, The Rise and Fall of the Soviet Empire, *Political Leaders from Lenin to Gorbachev*, Harper Collins Publishers, p. 434.
5. Perestroika, M.S. Gorbachev, *op. cit.*, p. 51.
6. *Ibid.*, p. 51.
7. *Ibid.*, p. 51.
8. *Pravda*, December 12, 1984.
9. Graham Smith, ed. *The Nationalities Question in the Soviet Union*, Longman, London and New York, 1990, p. 13.
10. John Anderson, *The International Politics of Central Asia*, Manchester University Press, Manchester and New York, 1997, p. 60.
11. Boris, Z. Rumer, *Central Asia: A Tragic Experiment*, Boston, 1989, p. 181.
12. John Anderson, *op. cit.*, p. 60.
13. B. Rumer, *op. cit.*, p. 181.
14. John Anderson, *op. cit.*, p. 61.
15. Shams Ud Din, ed. *Perestroika and the Nationalities Question in the USSR*, New Delhi: Vikas, 1990, p. 29.
16. Gorbachev, *Perestroika*, *op. cit.*, p. 120.
17. *Pravda*, 29 June, 1988.
18. Gorbachev, Perestroika, *op. cit.*, p. 121.
19. *Soviet News*, 5 July, 1989, p. 218.
20. Graham Smith, *op. cit.*, p. 16.
21. Tatyana Zaslavskaya, *The Second Socialist Revolution, An Alternative Soviet Strategy*, I.B. Tauris and Co. Ltd. London, 1990, p. 199.
22. *Literaturnaya Gazeta*, August, 1989, No. 32 (554) p. 11.
23. *Literaturnaya Gazeta*, Sept. 6th, 1989, (No. 36) 5288, p. 3.
24. *Ibid.* pp. 3-4.
25. *Literaturnaya Gazeta*, Sept. 6th, 1989, *op. cit.*, p. 11.
26. Abasmat Masiliev, 1st Secretary of the Central Committee of the Kirgiz Communist Party (territorial deputy, Kirgizia) 153, in *The Russian Empire: Its Nationalities Speak Out*, The First Congress of People's Deputies, Moscow, 25 May to 10 June, 1989, Edited and Translated by Oleg Glebov and John Crowfoot, Moscow, Harwood Academic Publishers, Apchur, London, Paris, New York, Melbourne, 1999, p. 139.

27. Kakhar Makhkamov, 1st Secretary of Tajik Communist Party Central Committee (territorial district, Dushambe, Tajikistan) 153, in *Oleg Glebov*, ed. *ibid.*, pp. 140-41.
28. Sapurmurad Niyazov, *ibid.*, pp. 141-43.
29. Mukhtar Umarkhodyzaev, Rector, Andhizhan Languages Teachers Training College, Andhizhan (national deputy, Uzbekistan) 155, *ibid.*, p. 143.
30. Pulatdzhan Akhunov, Assistant School Headmaster, Andhizhan Region, Uzbekistan (Young Communist League) 155, *ibid.*, p. 144.
31. Adyl Yakubov, 1st Secretary, Uzbek Writers Union, Tashkent (USSR writers Union) 162, *ibid.*, pp. 150-51.
32. Chingis Aitmatov, writer and chairman of Kirgiz SSR's writer's union. 155/4, *ibid.*, p. 147.
33. M.B. Olcott, Central Asia's Catapult to Independence, *Foreign Affairs*, 71(3), Summer 1992, p. 108.
34. Valery Tishkov, *Ethnicity, Nationalism and Conflict in and After the Soviet Union*, PRIO, UNRISD, Sage Publications, London, Thousand Oaks, New Delhi, 1997, p. 51.
35. Shirin Akiner, Post-Soviet Central Asia: Past is Prologue, in Peter Ferdinand, *Post-Soviet Central Asia*, Pinter Publishers, London, 1994, p. 15. M.B. Olcott, *op. cit.*, p. 108.
36. Bess Brown, Central Asia: The First Year of Unexpected Statehood, *RFE/RL Report*, Vol. 2, No. 1, 1 January, 1993.
37. Ahmed Rashid, *The Resurgence of Central Asia: Islam or Nationalism*? Oxford University Press, Karachi, 1994.
38. Dilip Hiro, *Between Marx and Muhammad: The Changing Face of Central Asia*, Harper Collins Publishers, London, 1994.
39. Ahmed Rashid, *op. cit.*, p. 159.
40. Uwe Halbach, World Politics and Indigenous Development in Central Asia, *Aussen Politik*, 43(4), 1992.
41. Muriel Atkin, The Survival of Islam in Soviet Tajikistan, *Middle East Journal*, Vol. 43, no. 4, Autumn, 1989.
42. John Obert Voll, Soviet Central Asia and China, integration or isolation of Muslim Societies, in John L. Esposito ed. *Islam in Asia: Religion, Politics and Society*, Oxford University Press, 1987.
43. Abha Dixit, Tajikistan: Engulfed by Flames of Afghan Civil War, *Strategic Analysis* 15(9); December 1992.
44. Barnett R. Rubin, The Fragmentation of Tajikistan, *Survival* (134-4), Winter 1993-94.
45. Eden Naby, Ethnicity and Islam in Central Asia, *Central Asian Survey*, 12(2), 1993.
46. Uwe Halbach, *op. cit.*, p. 391.
47. *Ibid.*, p. 383.
48. Pinar Akcali, Islam as a 'Common bond' in Central Asia: Islamic Renaissance Party and the Afghan Mujahidin", *Central Asian Survey*, 1998, 17(2), p. 271.

49. K. Warikoo, Emerging Order in Central Asia, *World Focus*, 14(3-4), March-April, 1993, *Special issue*, p. 9.
50. *Ibid*., p. 11.
51. Bess Brown, *op. cit*., p. 35.
52. *Ibid*., pp. 35-36.
53. Ajay Patnaik, *Central Asia, Between Modernity and Tradition*, Konark Publishers, 1996. pp. 200-04.
54. A. Rashid, *op. cit*., p. 159.
55. Allen Hetmenek, Islamic Revolution and Jihad Came to the Former Soviet Central Asia: The Case of Tajikistan, *Central Asian Survey* (1993), 12(3), pp. 365-66.
56. *Ibid*., p. 367.
57. *Ibid*., p. 371.
58. *Ibid*., p. 371.
59. A. Patnaik, *op. cit*., p. 202.
60. *Izvestia*, 2nd April, 1992.
61. Ahmed Rashid, *op. cit*., p. 160.
62. B.R. Rubin, *op. cit*., pp. 72-73.
63. Abha Dixit, *op. cit*., p. 873.
64. Rakesh Gupta, Tajikistan: Locked Horns for Powers, *Strategic Analysis* 15(6); September, 1992, p. 535.
65. K. Warikoo, Cockpit of Central Asia: Afghanistan Factor in Tajikistan's Crisis, in K. Warikoo ed., *Central Asia, Emerging New Order*, Har Anand Publciations, 1995, p. 199.

Socio-political movements 206, 235
Soloukhin, Vladimir 148
Soviet
-Afghan war 241
-multi-national experiment 2
nationalities policy 5
patriotism 139, 184–85
socialist regime 77
Socialist Republic 86, 128
Stalin, Joseph 30, 33
Stalinism 2, 227
Structural distortion 95
Suslov, Mikhail 59
Susokolov, A.A. 188
Swindling 51

Table oligarchy 74
Tajik civil war 237
Tajik Communist Party Central Committee 110, 202
Tajikistan Academy of Sciences 110, 115
Tajikistan, Ethnic Couldrion in 204
Tashkent 88
Theory of revolution 22
Third World countries 120, 249
Topornin, Boris 86
Trouble-torn multi-ethnic state 196
Tsarist 22
expansionism 103
period 4

Uzbek
nationalities 165
-Tajik conflicts 200

Warikoo, K. 236, 237, 242
Water diversion scheme 222
White-collar employees 188
World Religious Conference 118
World War II 106, 134

Yakubov, Adyl 230
Young Communist movement 126

Zaslavskaya, Tatyana 226
Zeravshan river basin 205
Ziautdin, Mufti Muhammad 246

Niyazi, Aziz 206
Nomanklatura 242
Non-black-earth zone 189
Non-participation of women outside home 115
Non-Russian
  lands 245
  nationalities 59, 142, 156, 166
  republics 102
Non-Slav republics 68
Non-Slavic people 155

October revolution 30, 34, 84
Olcott, Martha Brill 63, 233, 236
Oppression, abolition of 37
Ostapenko, L.V. 188
Over-centralisation 149
Over-simplification, tendency of 46

Palat, M.K. 6, 7
Pamiris 205
Pan-Islamic movement 130
Pan-Islamism 38–39, 129, 199, 234
Pan-Slavist Southern Slavs 19
Pan-Turkism 38–39, 199
Parasitism 51
Parochial tendencies 56
Party-state bureaucracy 228
Patnaik, Ajay x, 93, 94, 186, 189, 236, 240
Perestroika 197
  initiation of 216, 246
  revolutionary developments of 220
Petkel, V.V. 212
Post-communis' party 206
Post-perestroika 12, 156, 199, 234
Post-World War II stage 94
Pre-revolution Russian empire 28
Primakov, E. 125
Process of sblizheniye 75
Progressive reforms 124
Propagandists approach 111
Pro- and anti-Soviet categories 186

Qurgan-Tyube region 100, 206

Rashid, Ahmed 171
Rasulov, Jabar 81
Reassessing aethism 117
Red banner of labour 65
Revolutionary hegemony 104
Rosa Luxemburg 23, 25
Rowdyism 51
Rubin, Barnett R. 209, 211
Rumer, Boris Z. 90
Russian
  big-brotherhood 9
  chauvinism 39, 49, 70
  Christian believers 112
  esperanto 149
  invasion 168
  nationalism, growth of 129
Russification
  of the borderland 148
  accusation of 4
Rywikin, Michael 150

Secular Marxist rituals 107
Semi-nomadic Turkmens 183
Shams Ud Din 146, 155, 167
Silver, Brian D. 137, 141
Simon, Gerhard 166
Sjoberg, Andree F. 146
Smith, Graham 220
Socialism, economic legacy of 95
Socialist
  internationalism 185
  revolution 178
Social-production 114
Socio-anthropolgical phenomenon 159
Socio-economic
  developments 179
  indices 196

Internationalism, notion of 176
Inter-nationality
contacts 179
interactions 174
relations 173
Inter-republic redistribution of national income 91
Intra-community affairs 191
Intra-ethnic polarity 194
Islam 12, 15, 100, 103, 232
localised practices of 115
revival of 243
Islamic
fundamentalism 242
party 238
renainance party 14, 200, 206
revival party 240
revivalism 240
rituals and practices 103
survivals 112
Ismailis 205

Jewish nationalism 31

Karklins, Rasma 161
Keep, J. 90
KGB 76, 212
Khoda-Syzlar 105
Khojent-Quliab 99, 208
Khomenee 122
Khrushchev, removal of 107
Kirgiz Communist party 228
Kirkwood, Michael 144, 149
Kolakowsky, L. 29
Kolbin 220
Kommunist Tajikistana 89
Kozlov, V.I. 164
Kunaev, D. 220
Kurgan-Tyube zone 206

'labour surplus' zone 189
Lal-i-Badakhshani 207, 209
Law on religious associations 108
Lenin, V.I. 21, 133
Leninabadi group 247
Leninist principles of the nationalities policy 63
Liberation movements 51
Linguistic distinctiveness 132

Marxist socialism 121
Marxist-Leninist
nationalities 132
principles 2
purists 61
revolutionary regime 124
Mathews, Mervyn 79
Middle east crisis 118
Miller, John H. 78, 80
Mirror theory 123
Mixed marriages 190
Model programme of Russian language 140
Money-grabbing 51
Monogarova, L.F. 187
Moses, Joel C. 82
Motyl, Alexander I. 10, 163
Mujahidins 241
Multi-cultural zone 215, 247
Multi-ethnic zone 193, 200, 215
Multinational conglomeration 160
Muslim religious board for Central Asia and Kazakh 118

Nationaity question 224
National chauvinism 196
National question in Russia 36
National self-determination 23
Nationalism 18–19, 44
Soviet policy on 52
Nationalist movements, utilisation of the 27
National-territorial delimitation 171
'nauroz' festival 196

Cross-border terrorism 212
Cultural-linguistic minorities 156
Cyrillic scripts 135, 140

Dadabeva, S. 114
Dashdamirov, A. 185
Davlat Khudanzarov 207
'defence of father land' concept 27
Democratic Party of Tajikistan 209, 238
Dispensers of amulets 115
Dixit, Abha 212, 241
Drobizheva, L.M. 173
Dunlop, J.B. 61, 62, 130, 141, 148
Dwarf-workshopism 98

Egalitarian doctrines 72
Ethnic faultlines 196
Ethnic intermarriage, notion of 193
Ethnic self-awareness 175
Ethnic-cultural gap 163
Ethnic-national style 182
Ethno-cultural
  contiguity 242
  environment 163
  nature 212
Ethno-demographic
  equation 164
  trend 186
Ethno-linguistic identities 215
Ethno-national
  behaviour 186
  identities 11, 166
  people 146
  self-awareness 174
  traits 184
Ethno-political group identities 171
Ethno-regional
  character 204
  politics 214
  relations 211
European Slavs 166

Faith-healers 115
February revolution 35
Federalism, scope of 226
Ferghana
  canal 57
  riot 198

Galiev, Sultan 43
German civilisation 20
Gigantomania 95
Gorbachev, Mikhail 66, 217, 221, 228
  reforms, aspect of 226
Gorno-Badakhshan autonomous oblast 207
Great Russian Chauvinism 34, 37, 41, 44, 47, 51, 55, 60, 62
Guboglu, M.N. 152

Haberkern, E. 20
Haghyeghi, M. 106
Harmstone, T.R. 101, 140
Homo-Islamicus 13
Homo-Sovieticus 13

Ideological
  commitments 204
  struggle 61
  teaching 77
Imperialism, oppression of 45
Industrial development 91
Inner-party democracy 50
Intellectual bi-product of the cold war 120
Inter-ethnic
  communication 154
  international integration 178
  material cultures 183
  relations 200
  tensions 195
International preparatory committee 118

Index

Afghan
mujahidins 211, 241
tiger 185
Aitmatov, Kirgiz Chingiz 150
Akiner, Shirin 169, 190, 233
Alma-Ata 88
Anderson, John 223
Andhizan Language Teachers' Training College 229
Andropov's interregnum 96
Anti-American Islamic revolution 118
Anti-establishment struggle 242
Anti-imperialist revolution 122, 209
Anti-Islamic campaign 105
Anti-regime movement, 239
Anti-religious education 111
Anti-socialist phenomenon 69
Atheistic propaganda 116
Austro-Marxists 30–31, 33, 36
Autonomous Government 35

Babakhan, Ishan 246
Bagramov, E. 152
'Basmachi' 105
Bi-lingnalism 141, 152
practice of 132
Bipolar world 75
Bolshevik
party 17
policy 49
revolution 129
Bourgeois
democratic aspiration 17
leadership 19
Brezhnev, L.I. 79, 84, 176
Bruno Coppieters 7
Bukhari, Imam Ali 118

Caucasian social-democrats 31
Central Asia, ethnic diversity in 168
Chernenko regime 64–65
Chernenko, K.U. 64
Christian nation 129
Civil war 127
Class-struggle 24
Cold war 3, 10, 12, 15, 108, 127
state 247
Collapse of the Soviet system 232
Colonial struggles 18
Commonwealth of Independent States (CIS) 3, 13
Communism, phases of 104
Communist
manifesto 21
parties 7, 72, 225
upbringing 112
Communist Youth League 105
Communist Party of the Soviet Union (CPSU) 50
Comparatively fortunate zones 99
Constitutional reforms of 1977, 83
Cosmopolitan, urbanisation of a 94
Criminal Code 107–08